Menace to Empire

AMERICAN CROSSROADS

Edited by Earl Lewis, George Lipsitz, George Sánchez, Dana Takagi, Laura Briggs, and Nikhil Pal Singh

Menace to Empire

*Anticolonial Solidarities and
the Transpacific Origins of the
US Security State*

Moon-Ho Jung

UNIVERSITY OF CALIFORNIA PRESS

The publisher and the University of California Press
Foundation gratefully acknowledge the generous support
of the Peter Booth Wiley Endowment Fund in History.

University of California Press
Oakland, California

© 2022 by Moon-Ho Jung
First paperback printing 2023
Library of Congress Cataloging-in-Publication Data

Names: Jung, Moon-Ho, 1969– author.
Title: Menace to empire : anticolonial solidarities and the
    transpacific origins of the US security state / Moon-
    Ho Jung.
Other titles: American crossroads ; 63.
Description: Oakland, California : University of
    California Press, [2022] | Series: American crossroads ;
    63 | Includes bibliographical references and index.
Identifiers: LCCN 2021021860 | ISBN 978052097873
    (pbk) | ISBN 9780520387768 (ebook)
Subjects: LCSH: Anti-imperialist movements—Pacific
    Area—History—20th century. | Anti-racism—Pacific
    Area—History—20th century. | Asians—Social
    conditions—20th century. | Political violence—Pacific
    Area—History—20th century. | United States—
    Territories and possessions—History—20th century.
Classification: LCC F965 .J86 2022 |
    DDC 325/.320918230904—dc23
LC record available at https://lccn.loc.gov/2021021860

Manufactured in the United States of America

30 29 28 27 26 25 24 23
10 9 8 7 6 5 4 3 2 1

To Mina and Seri

Contents

Illustrations

Acknowledgments

I conceived of *Menace to Empire* a long time ago, at Oberlin College, where I taught for two years. As I prepared for a variety of courses in US history, I could not explain readily why US immigration laws fixated on Asians *and* radicals in the first three decades of the twentieth century. I sensed that there had to be a historical connection between those two targets, who fell mostly into disconnected fields of study. That inkling of an idea germinated in the back of my mind. In the meantime, I worked on my first book and witnessed the unrelenting violence of the US empire at the dawn of the twenty-first century. I was lucky to have David Kamitsuka and Pablo Mitchell as colleagues and friends at the beginning of my academic career.

I began to pursue the project in earnest at the University of Washington, my intellectual home for the last two decades. I am grateful to the Department of History (especially the Keller Endowed Fund, the Walker Family Endowed Professorship, and the Dio Richardson Professorship), the Simpson Center for the Humanities, the Royalty Research Fund, the Harry Bridges Center for Labor Studies, and the Center for the Study of the Pacific Northwest (particularly Kim McKaig) for their invaluable support over the years. In their turns as my research assistant, Seema Sohi, Chris Holmes, Joe Bernardo, and Frances O'Shaughnessy tracked down sources creatively and efficiently. My collaborative projects on racial capitalism with Chandan Reddy, Stephanie Smallwood, and Alys Weinbaum and then with Megan Ming Francis, Michael McCann,

Vicente Rafael, and Chip Turner granted me time and space to read and learn.

I could not have conducted my research without the work of archivists and librarians across the vast US empire, which, like other empires of today and yesterday, has been so prodigious at generating an endless sea of documents. I am in debt to the following repositories for keeping the past alive and accessible: National Archives in Washington, DC, College Park, Maryland, and San Bruno, California; Bentley Historical Library, University of Michigan; Bancroft Library, University of California, Berkeley; University of Hawai'i at Mānoa Library; Charles E. Young Research Library, University of California, Los Angeles; Tamiment Library and Robert F. Wagner Archives, New York University; National Library of the Philippines; American Historical Collection, Rizal Library, Ateneo de Manila University; University of Washington Libraries. I thank Mario Feir, Ben Weber, Ani Mukherji, Junaid Rana, and especially Trevor Griffey for generously sharing sources. Kiko Benitez's warm welcome enriched my stay in Manila. At several points, Vince Rafael shared encouraging words and key references.

I presented my ideas in progress at various gatherings over the years. I thank the following individuals and institutions for organizing and hosting my visits: Rosemary Feurer and Northern Illinois University; Henry Yu and the University of British Columbia; Elda Tsou, Susie Pak, and St. John's University; Tani Barlow and Rice University; Thavolia Glymph, Nayoung Aimee Kwon, and Duke University; Ethan Blue and the University of Western Australia; Jennifer Morgan and New York University; Jeff Sklansky and Oregon State University; Jean Kim and Dartmouth College; Tak Fujitani, Lisa Yoneyama, Dan Bender, and the University of Toronto; Mia Bay and Rutgers University; Christina Heatherton and the CUNY Graduate Center; Walter Johnson and Harvard University; Rebecca McKenna and the University of Notre Dame; John S. W. Park and the University of California, Santa Barbara; Sophie Loy-Wilson and the University of Sydney; Lisa Lowe and Tufts University; Kristin Hoganson and Oxford University; Beth Lew-Williams and Princeton University.

Discussions with students and scholar-activists remind me why we need to reckon with the past honestly and critically. I thank the thousands of students who have enrolled in my courses at the University of Washington. Their enthusiastic responses to my take on US history lift my spirits every time I step in the classroom. I have learned a great deal from my graduate students over the years—Seema Sohi, Caroline Yang,

Joe Bernardo, Allan Lumba, Jessie Kindig, Maria Quintana, Roneva Keel, Anna Nguyen, and Frances O'Shaughnessy. The guys incarcerated inside the Monroe Correctional Complex gave unfiltered and hilarious feedback on my various talks. Their humor and humility attest to the need to abolish the prison industrial complex. Soya Jung's expansive vision has been essential to radical Asian American politics in Seattle. Jack O'Dell and Jane Power inspired me to dig deeper and to think bigger whenever I saw them. Jack's legacy will shape the Black Radical Tradition for generations to come.

Niels Hooper recognized the potential of this project a long time ago. His patience and guidance made the book stronger and clearer. Niels recruited a remarkable lineup of reviewers when I finally submitted the manuscript. George Lipsitz, Matthew Frye Jacobson, Takashi Fujitani, and an anonymous reader provided exactly what I needed to clarify my argument. Frances O'Shaughnessy read the entire manuscript closely to point out critical lapses and careless phrasings. Moon-Kie Jung and Chandan Reddy read and reread various drafts of the introduction and conclusion. Mina Jung offered her sharp insights on the conclusion's first draft.

A community of principled colleagues and trusted friends has kept me grounded and motivated. I am where I am because of Gary Okihiro's mentorship over the decades. I am grateful to Gary and to Lisa Lowe for demonstrating what Asian American Studies could be. Rick Bonus is a model of ethical Ethnic Studies. Mary Lui has helped to keep work and life in perspective all these years. Mike Hochster has been a steady friend through life's many transitions and struggles. My conversations with Nikhil Singh invariably sparked new questions about race and empire. I have come to rely on Chandan Reddy, Ileana Rodríguez-Silva, and Stephanie Smallwood for everything that matters, big and small. Our camaraderie makes UW a very special place.

I thank my family for living with my rants against the US empire. My parents, Minja Ahn and Woo-Hyun Jung, and my grandmother, Soon-Ok Kwon, raised me to appreciate integrity and justice. My brother, Moon-Kie Jung, gets my worldview on a level no one else can. I wish he and Caroline Yang lived closer. The Lamsons still laugh at my jokes. My partnership with Tefi Lamson means everything. Over the span of researching and writing *Menace to Empire*, Tefi and I raised two wonderful people who brighten our world every single day. Although Mina could not yet read when I embarked on this project, she grew up to become its very first reader. Seri did not read the manuscript, but she got its essence when she dared to ask her fifth grade teacher during a unit celebrating "Colonial America": "Isn't colonialism bad?" Yes, it is. When Mina and Seri see the book's dedication, I hope they can feel how happy and hopeful they make me feel.

A small section of a very preliminary draft of chapter 1 appeared as "Seditious Subjects: Race, State Violence, and the U.S. Empire," *Journal of Asian American Studies* 14, no. 2 (June 2011): 221–47. Abbreviated versions of chapters 3 and 4 were published as: "Fighting John Bull and Uncle Sam: South Asian Revolutionaries Confront the Modern State," in *Crossing Empires: Taking U.S. History into Transimperial Terrain,* edited by Kristin L. Hoganson and Jay Sexton (Durham: Duke University Press, 2020), 261–80; "Revolutionary Currents: Interracial Solidarities, Imperial Japan, and the U.S. Empire," in *Making the Empire Work: Labor and United States Imperialism,* edited by Daniel E. Bender and Jana K. Lipman (New York: New York University Press, 2015), 59–84. I thank the editors for engaging my work.

Prologue

Worlds Empire Made

Hailing from northwestern Punjab in present-day Pakistan, Dada Amir Haider Khan learned to navigate the British empire from an early age, in South Asia and across the seas. British claims to sovereignty over the Punjab in the nineteenth century had included new laws on land taxes and land registration that disrupted familial roles and socioeconomic norms, driving more and more people, especially men, to seek life elsewhere, including in the British Indian Army. The outbreak of World War I in 1914 reverberated in Punjabi villages, where, Khan recalled, local officials rounded up "the humble and innocent peasants" to compel monetary contributions and military service toward the British war effort. Colonialism meant war; war meant colonialism. A young teenager at the time, with years of experience in running away from an abusive home environment, Khan attempted to enlist in the army, only to be turned away for being too young and too small. "I had no idea of the conditions in the army or its function during times of war," he recounted later. He soon ran away to Bombay (Mumbai), where he worked odd jobs on the docks until he joined a crew on a British army ship carrying soldiers and supplies. Khan grew up on the high seas, performing the dirty work below deck that made the British empire—and the US empire—possible. His trips crisscrossed the colonial world, from London and New York to the Suez Canal, the Panama Canal, Manila, and Singapore.[1]

In the context of Khan's growing disgust with the racial and colonial hierarchies that he witnessed and experienced aboard British ships and across the British empire, he imagined the United States to be a refuge. He jumped ship in New York in 1918 and immediately applied for naturalized citizenship to find work on US vessels. It was a pragmatic decision, but he made it readily because he "had never felt or declared any kind of allegiance to British India, the British Regime in India or the British Crown." Khan continued to sail to all corners of the world on US merchant marine ships, including to Trinidad, a British colony full of people of his background. "The sight of these Indian descendants opened my eyes to the treachery and criminality of the British ruling class against the people of our country in foreign lands," he wrote. Back in New York in 1920, his new home of sorts, he came across fellow South Asians and their allies engaged in a movement to overthrow the British empire in India. Khan's exposure to the Ghadar Party and the Friends of Freedom for India, including Agnes Smedley ("one of the foremost international fighters for the cause of freedom and progress of oppressed people"), introduced him to "various forms of anti-British politics and pro-Indian agitation." When discussing politics with Indian crews on British ships, he contrasted their suffering under British domination against "American social life, which appeared . . . quite salutary, full of happiness and hope for the future."[2]

As he set sail around the world again on a freighter ship, Khan's infatuation with the United States grew alongside his hatred of the British empire. Having agreed to smuggle revolutionary newspapers and pamphlets to South Asian compatriots he encountered en route, Khan felt "a higher form of duty—the duty to my native country." But he was wary of the British security state, which seemed to be everywhere, determined to suppress anticolonial activities. When Khan's ship landed in Hong Kong in the spring of 1921, "a swarm of uniformed and plain clothes police (all Europeans)" came aboard to search his belongings and to arrest him for sedition. "What do the police have to do with me?" he protested. "I am on board an American ship, which is flying the United States' flag." Fanning their American national pride, he convinced the ship's crew and captain to take up his cause. The captain turned to the US consulate in Hong Kong, who won his release from "the autocratic British authorities." In the meantime, his shipmates, joined on shore by sailors of the US Navy, sought national revenge by attacking "Britishers in every restaurant, café, bar and hotel." Freed from the British state, Khan proceeded to the ship's next stop, the US colony of the Philippines. There, he marveled at the schools, hospitals, roads, and other "imprints of America's technology and civilization," a stark contrast to the colony's "awfully backward" condition under Spanish rule and its later devastation under "Japanese invasion." Khan was falling in love with the US empire.[3]

In due course, Khan discovered that his mounting Americanism and maturing radicalism could not coexist. After returning to New York City in July 1921, he officially became a US citizen, a process expedited by his service in the US Merchant Marine. "I had become a full citizen of the country," he rejoiced, "and thereby became eligible to enjoy so much which I could not even dream of in the country of my birth." But observing mass unemployment after World War I, the "counterrevolutionary propaganda" of the American Legion and the Ku Klux Klan, the "racial arrogance" of white employers and white coworkers, the brutality of Jim Crow segregation down South, and the domination of "American finance capital" in Mexico shook his faith in America. He soon joined the Industrial Workers of the World (IWW), "the only body which stood for workers' solidarity and against the capitalist system." Khan then left his seafaring days behind to venture into America's industrial interior, finding work at a railway roundhouse in upstate New York and later at an automobile plant in Detroit. Because his stash of official documents, including his naturalization certificate, was stolen, Khan had to apply in 1923 for a duplicate certificate from the US federal government. As luck would have it, the US Supreme Court ruled months earlier that South Asians were racially "aliens ineligible to citizenship." When Khan learned that his reapplication had been denied, he decided not to appeal because he "had become sceptical of the political system."[4]

Khan's contact with political organizations in Detroit radicalized him. On his first day in the city in 1925, he attended an anti-British meeting organized by Chinese students and joined by South Asian residents. They were outraged by the news out of Shanghai, where British police forces had attacked students and workers, many of them affiliated with the Chinese Communist Party, who were protesting against imperialism. The May 30th Massacre had left thirteen Chinese protestors dead. At another political meeting, Khan heard a speech by "an American communist" that left a lasting impression. "It was the first time . . . I heard Marxian analysis of the national colonial problems," he recalled. "The interconnection and the interdependence of the national movement for emancipation of the colonial people with the working class struggle in the advanced capitalist countries, the role of the Communist International and the Soviet Union in the world revolutionary movement for ultimately emancipating humanity of a whole."

Khan stayed in Detroit to learn more. He became familiar with Black struggles for racial justice, including impassioned organizing around Ossian Sweet, a Black physician charged with murder for defending his home in a previously all-white neighborhood. Khan began to see the world differently, to see the intimate links between race, empire, and capitalism, but he wanted to gain a deeper understanding. When the Communist International (Third International), through local communist channels, offered him a chance to study in Moscow, Khan did not hesitate. After eight formative years in the heart of the US empire, he was ready to leave for a revolutionary education.[5]

A new political universe emerging in Moscow transformed Khan's worldview. After arriving in the Soviet Union's capital in March 1926, he became a student at the Communist University of Toilers of the East (KUTV), a school designed to train cadres of revolutionaries to advance national liberation and communist movements across and beyond Asia. In all his travels, Khan noted, he had never "met people of so many diverse races and nationalities, and been able to share a communal life with them, as in this university." He studied and lived with peoples from all over the Soviet Union and "the colonial and semi-colonial east, including Japan," in addition to "Turks, Greeks, Egyptians, Moroccans, Tunisians, and a few Negroes from the USA." He was among seven South Asian students, representing India but recruited from the United States. Khan made sense of the world through courses like "Finance Capital and its various forms, and Capitalistic Monopolies," "Historical Imperialism and Outlines of Dialectical Philosophy," and "Imperialism and the History of Colonial Expansion." Perhaps more than his formal courses, he felt a new kind of freedom in Moscow that had seemed impossible in the United States, where "a person is judged by his wealth and the colour of his skin." In contrast to the "individual motive" and "shameless hypocrisy" dominating "every aspect of American social life," he found in the Soviet Union an emphasis on "collective action or collective efforts for the survival of all." He felt at home.[6]

Although Khan would not set foot in the United States again, the US empire would continue to affect his life for decades to come. After two years of study at KUTV, he and other graduates were ready to be dispatched around the world. Khan had the choice between returning to the United States, as his "Negro comrades" urged, or to India. He chose the latter, since "India was the land of my birth and I owed my duty and allegiance to her." He was back in Bombay by September 1928, working underground to liberate India from British rule and to organize

FIGURE 1. Dada Amir Haider Khan.
Courtesy of Amarjit Chandan
Collection.

peasants and workers. Agents of the British security apparatus tracked his activities and, as part of a wider anticommunist dragnet in 1929, issued a warrant for his arrest. Khan hastily fled to the Portuguese colony of Goa and then on to Germany and the Soviet Union. He returned to India in 1931 and moved to Madras (Chennai), where he organized the Young Workers League and disseminated lessons on Marxist theory and revolutionary nationalism.[7] Beginning in 1932, Khan faced cycles of arrest and imprisonment for violating colonial laws on sedition and security. The founding of the nation-states of India and Pakistan in 1947 failed to ease his plight. Under pressure from the US government, which promised aid in exchange, Pakistan's government proclaimed the Communist Party of Pakistan illegal in 1954. Khan, the old anticolonial communist, landed back in jail, a casualty of being a citizen of Pakistan and a subject of the US empire.[8]

Liberal narratives of "immigration" and "assimilation"—and national "independence"—could not capture or contain Khan's personal story. Toward the end of his life, he tried in vain to understand the constancy of counterrevolutionary repression. He expected as much from the British Raj, against which Khan was an "irreconcilable enemy," but he continued to be criminalized as seditious. "Since the freedom of India and the creation of the 'Islamic Republic of Pakistan,' I have done nothing against the country, against the people or anyone's person or property that can be proved in a court of law," he noted ruefully. "Yet I have not been spared by the authorities." Khan could have laid the same protests against the United States, which had promised his inclusion through naturalization but ultimately rejected him for his racial background and radical politics. That was "national security" in the modern state, rooted in a colonial past that was always present. In the end, Khan was not a national hero, as Prime Minister Benazir Bhutto suggested upon his death in 1989, or a revolutionary prophet who had all of the answers. Like all human beings, he was full of contradictions, a reflection and a creation of the largely homosocial, masculinist settings of migrant labor and radical organizing.[9] Alongside fellow revolutionaries who crossed the oceans in the first half of the twentieth century, Khan embodied the colonial histories and revolutionary hopes of peoples who attempted to forge a world against and beyond white supremacy and empire. Their hopes, their struggles, are with us still.

Introduction

Reckoning with History and Empire

I believe in the Prince of Peace. I believe that War is Murder. I believe that armies and navies are at bottom the tinsel and braggadocio of oppression and wrong, and I believe that the wicked conquest of weaker and darker nations by nations whiter and stronger but foreshadows the death of that strength.

—W. E. B. Du Bois, *Darkwater: Voices from within the Veil* (1920)

We are Asians, and as such, identify ourselves with the baddest motherfuckers alive. We can no longer be a witness to the daily slaughter of our people in Asia nor to the oppression of the Asians here in America and be afraid of death or prison. We must fight because that's what Asians are all about.

—Alex Hing, "The Need for a United Asian-American Front" (1970)

Pedro B. Bunoan's rage against the United States mounted the longer he stayed in the seat of empire. He was among the thousands of young Filipino men who migrated across the Pacific in the 1910s and 1920s in response to, as he put it, America's "call of humanity, equality and honesty, so that in time we will supply our country with Filipino American graduates to cooperate with you to bring the seed of democracy even to the darkest corners of the world." Constantly shut out of better jobs, decent housing, and railroad cars in the incorporated United States, he soon realized the true state of affairs in the Philippines. "The American grafters that constitute the few have demo[n]strated themselves to take the place of the catholic priests and pastors in the past, who were engaged in mental lying, debouchery [*sic*] and corruptions," Bunoan wrote to the US Congress in 1927. He demanded Philippine independence from the US empire, as the only way for Filipinos, as enlightened men, to remain "loyal to the cause of America as we have shown and demo[n]strated during the World War." Any lingering hope for America dissolved by 1935, when Bunoan applied for repatriation to the Philippines, now a colony called a "commonwealth." "In conclusion, the American white insulting dogs has commit[t]ed the best lies to the world and the most interesting human law in . . . American history," Bunoan protested sarcastically, as he bid America farewell. "God may further your fin[e] government, your wonderful educational institution and the moral of the white insulting dogs."[1]

W. E. B. Du Bois, the incomparable Black scholar-activist, felt the same rage in the wake of World War I. In *Darkwater,* he railed against the state of the world, within which the United States pretended to be a leader. "It is curious to see America, the United States, looking on herself, first, as a sort of natural peacemaker, then as a moral protagonist in this terrible time," he noted wryly. "No nation is less fitted for this rôle." Du Bois wanted to unveil the vicious logic of race, war, and empire and "its awful cost." "The cause of war is preparation for war," he argued, "and of all that Europe has done in a century there is nothing that has equaled in energy, thought, and time [more than] her preparation for wholesale murder." And the US empire, he contended, stood "shoulder to shoulder with Europe in Europe's worst sin against civilization." But there was hope. Du Bois found hope among the colonized and racialized "dark world." He prophesied a day of reckoning, more "wild and awful" than World War I, when "*that fight for freedom which black and brown and yellow men must and will make unless their oppression and humiliation and insult at the hands of the White World cease.*" Du Bois issued a warning, a manifesto. "*The Dark World is going to submit to its present treatment just as long as it must and not one moment longer,*" he declared emphatically.[2]

Menace to Empire traces both the colonial violence and the anticolonial rage percolating across the Pacific between the Philippine-American War and World War II. It is a history that can bring to light the ongoing racial and colonial order that has constituted the United States of America and the revolutionary dreams that its pretensions and machinations tried to smother and kill. To tell that history, I have to underscore some premises that will guide my interpretation. The United States was and is an empire. White supremacy has fueled and justified that empire, even as liberal claims to universal citizenship have obscured that history of violence. The tensions and contradictions of race, nation, and empire generated revolutionary movements that exposed, confronted, and challenged the US empire. In response, the US state has sought to monitor, criminalize, and suppress those movements, in part by racializing and sexualizing particular politics and distinct communities as seditious to rationalize violence on those ideas and communities. That is, the US state emerged and expanded largely to secure empire, within and beyond the territorial borders it has claimed. That entangled history of colonial conquest, white supremacy, and anticolonial struggle is what I strive to uncover and understand. Radicalized by their opposition to the US empire, different peoples in and from Asia articulated and organized a revolutionary politics that, I argue, racialized Asians as seditious threats to US security and gave rise to what would become the US national security state, the heart and soul of the US empire ever since.

EMPIRE, HISTORY, SECURITY

To propose that the United States was and is the US empire poses a challenge to a teleology that posits nation against empire. Like the thirteen British colonies in North America, modern nations seemingly liberate themselves from tyrannical empires, across time and space. Although terms like Thomas Jefferson's "empire of liberty" muddied that notion, the idea of individual, liberal subjects forming a nation can appear incompatible with colonial subjects suffering under imperial rule. But the birth of the US state simultaneously marked its genesis as an empire. "The paradox . . . is one of a nation being born in the fires of an anticolonial revolution while at the same time consolidating its state power and sovereignty on the basis of preserving the slavery variety of colonialism," Jack O'Dell, a major intellectual and organizer of the Black freedom movement, argued in *Freedomways*. Building a nation was not inconsistent with building an empire. Quite the opposite, they operated hand in hand, an ongoing process that has shaped and defined the United States. The abolition of slavery and the beginning and end of Reconstruction, O'Dell continued, took place in the context of Europe's partition and colonization of the African continent, unleashing a renewed era of imperial aggression and white supremacy around the world. From that perspective, it was possible and necessary to see that the US subjugation of Black and Indigenous peoples was "consistent with, and part of, the Western capitalist world strategy of continued domination over the people of Africa, Asia and Latin America."[3]

Empire, however, can often appear as exceptional in US history. The term *empire* usually conjures images of a distant past, a relic of yesteryear, as implied by the lead definition in the *Oxford English Dictionary*: "Anything considered as or likened to a realm or domain having an absolute ruler, such as heaven, hell, the oceans, etc." Medieval Europe comes to mind, with lavish palaces, fancy crowns, and royal battles. In his influential treatise *Imperialism*, originally published in 1917, V.I. Lenin radically renovated the concept for the twentieth century, arguing that imperialism represented "the monopoly stage of capitalism" dominated by "finance capital" and "the territorial division of the whole world among the greatest capitalist powers." From a different vantage point, the economic motive behind imperial expansion likewise shaped the influential Wisconsin School of US diplomatic history. Writing critically of the US empire in the 1950s and 1960s, when anticommunism—aligned with white supremacy and heteropatriarchy—haunted academia, William Appleman Williams, Walter LaFeber, Thomas J. McCormick, and others stressed US diplomatic efforts to expand capitalist markets, an interpretive framework that emphasized the "informal" essence of the US empire. The United States was accordingly an empire, but seemingly an exceptional empire, supposedly in search of markets, not territorial conquest. The insistence on the "informal," presumably in opposition to "formal" empires, produced confusing geographies and chronologies that cumulatively, if unintentionally, naturalized "continental" expansion, cleansed generations of genocidal violence, and obsessed over singular "overseas" moments like the Spanish-American War.[4]

Reckoning with empire necessitates thinking against the nation, beyond the national myths of America. In her critique of modern liberalism, Lisa Lowe reminds us of the colonial world in which national histories of progress materialized. The simplification and the parochialization of the past, she argues, rendered invisible the subordination and exploitation of colonized and dispossessed peoples, whose labor and other resources had produced the conditions of possibility for conceptions of the universal human with liberties and rights but whose own freedoms were denied and exempted by liberal philosophy. Race and gender enabled and nurtured those processes. Demands for political liberty in Europe and North America, Lowe observes astutely, translated into new forms of imperial sovereignty and security apparatuses in the colonies, all under the banner of advancing freedom. Empire, slavery, and race were not exceptions to the central tenets of liberal freedom: political emancipation through citizenship in a nation-state and economic independence through free labor and free trade. They set the stage for individual rights, declared universally but conceived and practiced provincially. Imperial sovereignty, chattel slavery, and white supremacy made liberal democracy imaginable, even as more recent celebrations of diversity have whitewashed that history into the "multicultural" nation. US nationalist historical narratives, where the colonial era evokes nostalgia for the thirteen British colonies and where all Americans or their forebears appear as "immigrants," are not merely inaccurate representations of the past. They are acts of violence that coerce historical amnesia and national assimilation.[5]

In recent years, when the scale of imperial claims and state violence has reached unprecedented heights, the term *empire* has made a comeback. Some right-wing scholars continue to extol empire to glorify colonial misdeeds of the past and the present, unabashedly and unironically equating the US empire with "democracy, capitalism, and freedom."[6] More common, at least among US historians, have been efforts to disavow empire, to suggest its inapplicability to most periods of US history, more often than not by recycling the notion of informal domination without territorial rule. It then somehow becomes possible to interpret history without making "a judgment about the malign or benign consequences of empire" or to claim the "territories" on behalf of American "mainlanders" (yet again).[7] Those subjected to the US empire's brutal violence could not afford the luxury of weighing its benevolence and malevolence. "While bombs rain down on us and cruise missiles skid across the skies," Arundhati Roy noted in 2003, "we know that contracts are being signed, patents are being registered, oil pipelines are being laid, natural resources are being plundered, water is being privatized, and George Bush is planning to go to war against Iraq." That was empire, she said, "this obscene accumulation of power, this greatly increased distance between those who make the decisions and those who have to suffer them." In my search for a concise definition of empire that could encompass different historical moments, I could find none more precise and expansive than Roy's piercing words.[8]

Beyond definitions, reckoning with empire is fundamentally a historical project, a search for radical, alternative pasts. To commemorate the United States as a "nation of immigrants"—so habitual, so toxic—is to be complicit in its racial and imperial project, to discount Indigenous peoples' and Black people's struggles against empire and slavery and to justify the mass violence of the US empire. History should be about disrupting and defamiliarizing what we thought we knew about the past, to open up new possibilities in our collective knowledge and in our collective politics. To contest teleological and nationalist understandings of history, Lowe calls for "a *past conditional temporality*," arguing that "it is possible to conceive the past, not as fixed or settled, not as inaugurating the temporality into which our present falls, but as a configuration of multiple contingent possibilities, all present, yet not inevitable." That project, she continues, can drive us to see "other conditions of possibility that were vanquished by liberal political reason and its promises of freedom" and "to open those conditions to pursue what might have been." Roy likewise urges us to use our radical imagination. "Our strategy should be not only to confront Empire but to lay siege to it," she proposed. "To deprive it of oxygen. To shame it. To mock it. With our art, our music, our literature, our stubbornness, our joy, our brilliance, our sheer relentlessness—and our ability to tell our own stories. Stories that are different from the ones we're being brainwashed to believe."[9]

Menace to Empire is my attempt to tell a different story, a history that presents peoples in and from Asia as racialized and radicalized subjects of the US empire, not as immigrants aspiring to become Americans. That history was part of an ongoing process of claiming and contesting imperial sovereignty that has made the modern world. Although I refer to the US empire over and over, I do not mean to reify a political authority that it has claimed over and over. Absolute sovereignty has never existed; it has always been claimed and contested. In that respect, I am invoking an obsolete use of *empire,* an intransitive verb until the nineteenth century. (The US military empired over us.) To read the verb behind the noun is to recognize an empire's instability, incoherence, and constructedness.[10] At the same time, we need to identify the United States for what it is and what it has always been, because it is the recognition of that thing—the US empire, a modified noun, so real, so violent—that can make us feel awakened, enraged, and politicized. In studying how colonized subjects based in and moving to or through the Philippines, Hawai'i, and the Pacific Coast of North America engaged the US empire, I mean to illustrate how they pursued a politics, a world, against and beyond empire. It is a story of how they mocked and shamed the US empire, all the while suffering under its wrath.

If reckoning with empire compels us to think radically and historically, securing empire rests on butchering history with abandon to conceal its colonial traces. Rallying around euphemistic terms to rationalize state violence speciously freed the US empire from the bounds of history. The United States was not killing people to subject them to colonial rule; it was engaging in acts of "pacification" to liberate them toward democracy. In US military parlance, pacification came to be increasingly rooted in counterinsurgency, a mode of warfare supposedly different from conventional conflicts. As the US empire rebranded itself as the last superpower, counterinsurgency seemingly took on greater urgency. More than ever, US military personnel required training as "nation builders" and ruthless "warriors," as a field manual instructed in 2006, always "ready to be greeted with either a handshake or a hand grenade." An enemy could be an ally; an ally could be an enemy. Counterinsurgency had to deal with both scenarios to fight "insurgents" who resorted to "all available tools—political (including diplomatic), informational (including appeals to religious, ethnic, or ideological beliefs), military, and economic—to overthrow the existing authority." Counterinsurgents had to respond in kind, except toward an opposite end, to "use all instruments of national power to sustain the established or emerging government and reduce the likelihood of another crisis emerging." Collapsing and delegitimizing insurgents across time and space, the field manual was inherently antihistorical, but it was littered with historical references that erased and glorified the US empire, beginning with the pacification of "the Philippine Insurrection."[11]

While US military leaders might have seen their mission, however chimerically, in a wider historical landscape of colonial rule and anticolonial struggles, academic scholars of national security have tended to preclude histories of empire altogether. National security—the signature emblem of the atomic age that was at once a discourse, an ideology, a policy, and an institution—ostensibly arose from the ashes of World War II. Writing in 1966 when the study of national security appeared to be cohering into an academic field, P. G. Bock and Morton Berkowitz attributed the formation to "two major changes in the international environment," namely "the atmosphere of urgency generated by the unremitting stress of the cold war and the emergence of a fabulous new technology of violence." Not unlike counterinsurgency, that context made outright war "a self-defeating policy alternative," forcing military officials and "civilian experts" to look for "methods of conflict containment and conflict resolution." Bock and Berkowitz proposed a definition of national security that has endured: *the ability of a nation to protect its internal values from external threats.*" Consumed by US relations with western Europe to contain "Soviet aggression," those studying US national security accordingly sought to identify "national interests," "domestic core values," and "foreign threats." The preoccupation with transatlantic alliances naturalized nation-states and the "international" system that elided and supplanted histories of colonialism.[12] By tracing the colonial origins of the US national security state across the Pacific before World War II, *Menace to Empire* suggests the need to deconstruct the entire artifice of national security.

TRANSPACIFIC TRACES

When Alex Hing claimed a revolutionary pan-Asian identity in 1970, he was part of a movement that aspired to forge a collective identity beyond the nation that gave birth to Ethnic Studies and Asian American Studies. In most articulations, the Asian American movement was an unapologetically radical project, committed to democratizing higher education, to producing new forms of knowledge, and to critiquing the US empire, particularly its war in Southeast Asia. As Filipino students at San Francisco State College stated, "We seek . . . simply to function as human beings, to control our own lives. . . . So we have decided to fuse ourselves with the masses of Third World people, which are the majority of the world's peoples, to create, through struggle, a new humanity, a new humanism, a New World Consciousness, and within that context collectively control our own destinies."[13] While Asian American activists looked to a revolutionary future across the Pacific and the world, the field of Asian American Studies had to wrestle with a longer intellectual pedigree that had cast anti-Asian racism, the "Oriental Problem," within an entrenched, nationalist foundation. In the first half of the twentieth century, a legion of social scientists located anti-Asian racism in the minds and votes of white workers, whose socioeconomic insecurities, foreign sensibilities, and southern origins had led them to demand racial exclusion. For those academics, the Chinese and the Japanese after them were misunderstood, misrepresented, and betrayed by the "nation of immigrants," whose core value was presumably its immanent capacity for inclusion.[14]

In *Menace to Empire*, I look for a revolutionary past across the Pacific, a past hardly visible in a sea of historical narratives promoting national inclusion and renouncing racial exclusion. Over the past half century, Asian Americanists and US historians have tended to retain and reinforce the fundamental assumptions of their liberal progenitors, reclaiming and proclaiming our American roots, as if the exclusion of Asian workers and the incarceration of Japanese Americans were

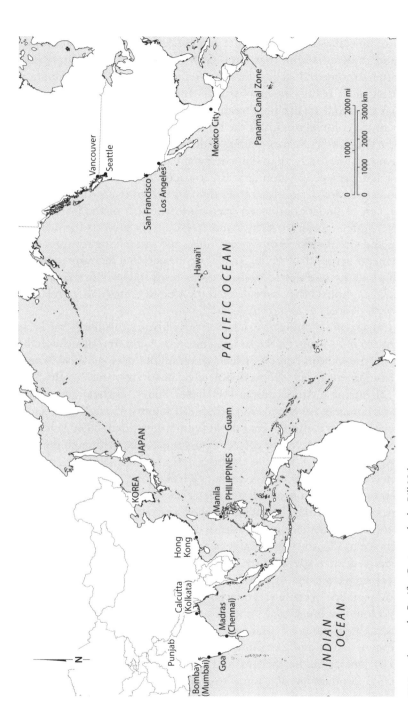

MAP 1. Across the Pacific. Cartography by Bill Nelson.

aberrant mistakes that the US state and the American nation could remedy and resolve. Within that nationalist framework, white supremacy has often become reduced to racial prejudice and racial discrimination, manifest most readily in nativist calls for US federal laws to restrict immigration and to prohibit naturalized citizenship.[15] By shifting our focus to the colonial origins of the US national security state, *Menace to Empire* situates US history within wider histories of empire and white supremacy, the forces that shaped racial capitalism across the world. From that perspective, immigration restrictions based on racial backgrounds and radical politics, rather than an affront to an American core value, can be understood as an ongoing instrument of the US national security state, a means to silence and arrest unruly subjects from articulating and circulating revolutionary ideas and organizing revolutionary movements across the Pacific. Appealing for national inclusion and citizenship rights could not address, let alone resist, those underlying logics of racial capitalism that have defined the United States and its relationship with peoples in and from Asia.[16]

A transpacific framing of Asian American history can clarify the limits and effects of insisting on the Americanness of Asian Americans. Reeling from the mass incarceration of their communities during World War II, Japanese American lay leaders, followed by historians, affirmed the "loyalty" of Japanese Americans to the United States. Postwar representations of Japanese Americans as the "model minority" and Japan as the "model minority nation," Takashi Fujitani argues, demanded a historical reckoning with race and empire across the Pacific. Although the total war regimes of Japan and the United States practiced violence on racial grounds, they both began disavowing racism during the war, a shift that hinged on the creation of self-conscious liberal, national subjects. The Japanese state and the US state compelled Koreans and Japanese Americans to decide whether or not to serve the benevolent nation. That putative choice to join the nation came at a great price—the sacrifice of loyal subjects as drafted soldiers, coerced workers, and comfort women while disloyal subjects came to be renewed targets of state violence. Liberal governmentality likewise reproduced the global order. Rather than outright colonial subjugation, Fujitani suggests, imperial authority rested increasingly on nominally self-governing nation-states allied to serve the interests of Japan and the United States, an "international" order heralded by Japan's call for the Greater East Asia Co-Prosperity Sphere. The continual production of "loyal" Asian Americans and the military deployment of "good" Asians across the Asia-Pacific in subsequent decades, Simeon Man argues, regenerated the US empire under the banner of decolonization.[17]

Concentrating on the politics of revolution and empire in the first four decades of the twentieth century, *Menace to Empire* traces the transpacific formation of "bad" Asians—revolutionaries who challenged the US empire—long before the Asian American movement. To praise the "good," "loyal," and "American" rested on the concurrent production of the "bad," "disloyal," and "un-American." The vilification of Asia and Asians as the "yellow peril" has long been a staple of "Western civilization," but it took on a distinctly revolutionary (and counterrevolutionary) character during and after the Philippine-American War (officially 1899–1902).[18] The Spanish-American War (1898) and its aftermath extended US colonial claims across the vast Pacific, generating new strains and fictions on what it meant to be "incorporated" and "foreign" within the lands and spaces under US sovereignty. As Philippine peoples struggled against the US empire, the critical pieces of the US security state, already in place but nothing in scope to what it would become, began to propagate and proliferate across the Pacific.[19] Agencies focusing on intelligence and surveillance and laws criminalizing sedition and immigration attempted to make US claims to sovereignty real, guarding against foes and threats, within and without. A barrage of laws on sedition, immigration, and naturalization targeting Asians and revolutionaries ensued, a convergence of racial proscriptions and political prohibitions epitomized by revolutionary Asians contesting the US empire. The overlapping regulation of race and politics eventually drove the US state to obsess over the transpacific movements of revolutionary peoples, a heterogeneous mix of humanity homogenized over time as seditious and pan-Asian.

Particularly after the Philippine-American War, growing numbers of peoples came face to face with the US state across the Pacific, through its agents and agencies dispatched to secure empire under widening and tightening claims of national defense. The US state's expansion highlighted a historical moment when the idea of the nation-state as a fundamental means to political freedom came to be entrenched and embraced on a global scale. With imperial states and colonial subjects increasingly adopting the nation-state form, empires became "big nations" and colonies "little nations," as US President Theodore Roosevelt put it in 1905, all abstractly equal but patently unequal. In that world of nations, the US state criminalized revolutionary ideas and anticolonial movements that challenged the emerging world order as seditious. Laws restricting and prohibiting immigration and naturalization and facilitating deportation and repatriation inscribed the same logic. Those with seditious ideas and plots had to be kept out of the nation. Laws on sedition and immigration naturalized the US empire by classifying those resisting empire as seditious, criminal, and alien. Filipinos like Pedro Bunoan lived through those shifting categories. Born in an unincorporated US colony, the Philippines, Bunoan entered the incorporated regions of the US empire as a US national, but he exited in 1935 as a repatriated citizen of the Philippine Commonwealth, which remained subject to the US empire, and an "alien ineligible to citizenship" in the US nation.[20]

The criminalization of those who contested the US empire as seditious, so blatant in the war-torn Philippines, reflected a reaction not only to guerrilla forces waging war against US troops but also to the popularization of revolutionary ideas and the organization of revolutionary movements around the world. Through surveillance reports, criminal prosecution, and overt violence, agents of the US security state had ensnared and incarcerated enlarging circles of intractable subjects who dared to challenge white supremacy and empire.[21] At the dawn of the twentieth century, officials within the US state's military ranks, intelligence network, and immigration system began targeting anticolonial revolutionaries across the Pacific in particular because of their suspected affiliations with radical movements radiating from Europe, most notably anarchism and communism, *and* their presumed associations with imperial Japan. Between the Philippine-American War and World War II, Japan came to represent contradictory possibilities, at once a menace to white supremacy and an exemplar of a rising empire. If the former could inspire visions of racial justice, that dual image—a racial enemy and an imperial rival—galvanized transimperial campaigns to vilify Japan and anyone who might support and otherwise ally with its nefarious schemes to lead a pan-Asian struggle against worldwide white supremacy. In 1920, Du Bois, who, like many Black activists, was smitten by Japan's potential to disrupt the racial order, noted the disproportionate reaction when "the white world immediately sensed the peril of such 'yellow' presumption!" Potential affiliation with imperial Japan marked different peoples racially and politically as revolutionary and seditious.[22]

Across the US empire, from the Philippines to Hawai'i to California and beyond, the US state melded the yellow peril and the red scare to contain waves of seditious subjects who seemingly incited and warranted state violence. That was race at work. Through and alongside gender, nation, and empire, race was an unstable and incoherent construction that rested on repetition and reproduction. Racial ideas, racial representations, and racial practices have always been in historical formation, even as racial concepts have presented and represented racial divides and racial categories as natural, biological, and cultural, outside of time and space. "This theory of human culture and its aims has worked itself through warp and woof of our daily thought with a thoroughness that few realize," Du Bois contended. "Everything great, good, efficient, fair, and honorable is 'white'; everything mean, bad, blundering, cheating, and dishonorable is 'yellow'; a bad taste is 'brown'; and the devil is 'black.'" Those laughable and gendering notions of racial security and racial menace had dramatic consequences. Using Ruth Wilson Gilmore's definition of racism as "the state-sanctioned or extralegal production and exploitation of group-differentiated vulnerability to premature death," *Menace to Empire* tells a history of the mobilization of "yellow" and "brown" peoples against empire, revolutionary acts that rendered them vulnerable to premature death by the massive political and military arsenal that secured the US empire on behalf of the honorable "white" people. To reckon with empire is to grapple with the expanding scale of racial violence sanctioned and organized by the modern state.[23]

Framed around colonial claims, anticolonial struggles, and state violence, *Menace to Empire* reveals racial formations across the Pacific that challenged and bolstered the US empire. The Philippine-American War did not signal the birth of the US empire or the reorientation of its state toward claiming empire. The US Constitution's provisions on slavery, militias, and "Indians" had established much earlier a political blueprint and a legal system that colonized, racialized, and thereby naturalized the lands and peoples of the United States.[24] Like Indigenous and Black subjects before them, anticolonial revolutionaries in and from Asia became "monsters," a "many-headed hydra" critical to what Michael Paul Rogin called a "countersubversive tradition at the center of American politics." For centuries, that insidious tradition preceding and exceeding the United States had divided the world into races, empires, and nations and gave rise to the liberal nation-state, a testament to the power of revolutionary movements and to the fragility of imperial rule. To protect democracy from the unruly masses, the liberal state monitored, repressed, and exaggerated anticolonial insurgencies, rendering them criminal and illegitimate and, in the process, producing the conditions and rationales for its existence and expansion. That was empire. Fears of a collective pan-Asian identity—an incipient and oftentimes fleeting aspiration for anticolonial solidarities as much as a racial figment animating and motivating the US empire and later the Japanese empire—prompted the US state to justify and fortify the racial and colonial order that was the United States.[25]

Even as liberal narratives of US history and Asian American history promote diversity and equality as hallmarks of the American nation, the overflowing archive of the US state betrays a history of white masculine domination that exposes, occludes, and advances its colonial mission. The colonial archive, Ann Laura Stoler argues, beholds "records of uncertainty and doubt in how people imagined they could and might make the rubrics of rule correspond to a changing imperial world."[26] Colonial authorities claimed unilateral sovereignty, all the while aware of the limits of their claims. The archival records of a budding transpacific security apparatus—including the Philippine Constabulary, the Military Information Division, the Office of Naval Intelligence, the Bureau of Investigation, the Bureau of Immigration—documented in detail US officials' claims to state authority over peoples who unnervingly resisted that authority. As those officials sought endlessly for security, they glimpsed radical movements and interracial solidarities that could not but produce greater insecurity. That was the circular logic of national security, a nebulous and ridiculous conceit that signified racial anxieties and imperial insecurities. In that light, the search for US national security began long before the Cold War, articulated through and around legal regimes, state surveillance, and racial violence. That was the work of the US state, which has since become an unparalleled behemoth subjecting racialized and radicalized peoples around the world—demonized and criminalized over the last century as anarchists, communists, gooks, terrorists—to unrelenting violence, all in the name of national security. That is the United States, the US empire, then and now.

By highlighting transpacific traces of the US empire and its national security state, I do not mean to suggest that a pan-Asian racial formation eclipsed or replaced transatlantic and transcontinental processes of racialized settler colonialism. Those are enduring processes that extend far beyond the Atlantic Ocean and North America, based on pernicious logics that make places like California and Hawai'i appear as fully incorporated in the American nation, where Indigenous peoples appear, or disappear, as "ethnic minorities" in a multicultural democracy. That is why race cannot be reduced to a domestic matter of national exclusion or national inclusion—as in the search for the Americanness of Asian Americans—and why racialization cannot be conflated with colonization. By framing different peoples in and from Asia as racialized subjects of the US empire,

I am not asserting their indigeneity or denying their capacity to champion settler colonialism.[27] Ideas about and representations of Indigenous peoples of the Americas, "Indianness," Chickasaw scholar Jodi A. Byrd argues, constituted a transit, "a site through which US empire orients and replicates itself by transforming those to be colonized into 'Indians' through continual reiterations of pioneer logics, whether in the Pacific, the Caribbean, or the Middle East." *Menace to Empire,* in that sense, is not an originary tale or a comprehensive history. It is a particular history of a variant of a deeper colonizing and racializing discourse that can be traced to the origination of the United States. It is a humble offering in our larger project to imagine and pursue a world beyond the terms of what Byrd calls "liberal multicultural settler colonialism."[28]

MENACE TO EMPIRE

The particular history I construct here begins at the turn of the twentieth century when the US state waged two seemingly unrelated wars, a bloody war against Filipino *insurrectos* and a global war against anarchism. The two wars, chapter 1 argues, came together in the Philippines, where US officials repeatedly conjured images of a backward colony about to descend further into anarchy without US intervention. Anarchy, or anarchism, was more than a racial metaphor. It was a radical philosophy and a revolutionary movement unsettling politics around the world, including in the Philippines. Incarcerated in a Barcelona prison for crimes against the Spanish empire, anticolonial critics like Isabelo de los Reyes embraced anarchism to demand an end to colonialism. Once back in the Philippines, he helped to mobilize Filipino workers against their employers and the US state, which, like the Spanish state before it, responded with agencies and laws to pacify— that is, to colonize—the peoples and lands of the Philippines. Through the Philippine Constabulary, an heir to the Spanish Guardia Civil, and the Sedition Act (1901), the US state proclaimed sovereignty over the Philippines, criminalizing ideas, organizations, and persons who contested that colonial claim. In the meantime, on the other side of the Pacific, the US federal government passed a new immigration law targeting anarchists after a self-identified anarchist assassinated President William McKinley in 1901. Through and during the Philippine-American War, the US state racialized Filipino *insurrectos,* potential anarchists, and Asian workers in general as politically and sexually deviant subjects who deserved exclusion, deportation, incarceration, and death.

The end of the Philippine-American War, as decreed by President Theodore Roosevelt on July 4, 1902, scarcely eliminated the specter of sedition and revolution in the Philippines. Particularly after the Russo-Japanese War (1904–5), chapter 2 suggests, US colonial officials and anticolonial Filipinos increasingly cast their gaze toward Japan, out of fear and hope. Even as diplomatic agreements between the United States and Japan sanctified empire by recognizing each other's colonial claims in East Asia and Southeast Asia, US officials grew alarmed by Japan's imperial ambitions, which they interpreted as a grave threat to the colonial order rooted in white supremacy. Rumors and reports of an impending racial war between Japan and the United States began to circulate widely in the wake of Japan's military triumph against Russia, including in intelligence reports from the Philippines. Because many anticolonial revolutionaries saw in Japan a potential ally, a kindred people waging war against white supremacy, agents of the Philippine Constabulary came to fixate on Japan's presumed support of a revolution in the Philippines. Those reports not only deflected and delegitimized Filipino grievances against the US empire, they gave rise to a racial narrative of US national security where repressing Filipino struggles became part of a national project of defending the United States against an international rival, Japan. The racial conflation of Filipino anticolonial struggles and Japanese imperial ambitions exacerbated US imperial insecurities and ironically framed Japan and the United States as anticolonial empires, with both claiming to stand against the other's imperial designs to justify counterrevolutionary violence across the Pacific.

Shifting the focus to South Asian revolutionaries along the Pacific Coast of North America, chapter 3 explores how organizing against the British empire came to be racialized as a seditious threat to US national security before and during World War I. Across the British empire, contrary to promises of equal imperial citizenship, South Asians confronted racist and misogynist laws to regulate and prohibit their migration. When US immigration authorities targeted them for exclusion, South Asian communities in North America forged an anticolonial politics that condemned and challenged racial hierarchies. That political movement, articulated forcefully by the newspaper *Ghadar* and the Ghadar Party beginning in 1913, motivated British authorities to monitor South Asian migrants' anticolonial activities around the world, criminalized by the British imperial state as sedition, and to lobby the US government for assistance. Already incensed by their treatment at the hands of US immigration officials, South Asian communities likewise mobilized against the US state, evading and defying British and US state surveillance in the Philippines, Canada, India, California, Panama, and beyond. Restrictions on immigration and sedition tightened in the British empire and in the US empire during World War I, when many Ghadar Party members attempted to foment an anticolonial revolution in South Asia. In alliance with the British empire, the US state expanded its authority to monitor, exclude, and deport anticolonial activists as anarchists. The end result was a new world order, under the banner of an international alliance defending democracy, determined to secure the old world order of white supremacy and empire.

The emerging US security state, chapter 4 argues, also took root in Hawai'i, a US colony in the throes of labor struggles that brought Japanese and Filipino workers together. For a decade before World War I, while US officials in the Philippines dispatched countless reports on an impending revolution aided and abetted by imperial Japan, Hawai'i's sugar barons had recruited plantation workers from the Philippines to undercut and undermine local Japanese workers' organizing efforts. When Filipino workers and Japanese workers went on strike in 1920, agents of the US state interpreted the walkout as an expression of pan-Asian solidarity, part of a vast conspiracy coordinated by imperial Japan. Calls for pan-Asian solidarity, as heard among Filipino and South Asian radical circuits, belied racial tensions on the ground in Hawai'i, but US military officials and sugar planters promoted and pursued the racial fantasy of a Japanese conspiracy to cast labor struggles as seditious acts against the United States. The racial projection of Japanese workers as subversive, revolutionary agents of the Japanese empire, in turn, led various agencies of the US government to interpret interracial solidarities against white supremacy, anywhere and everywhere, as evidence of the Japanese empire at work, an interpretation that effectively dismissed Filipino, Black, and other struggles for racial justice. Conjuring images of Japanese "invasion" and "infiltration" in the Philippines, Hawai'i, Harlem, and elsewhere fed an insatiable, imperial process of assigning more and more agents of the US security state across the "domestic" and "foreign" spaces of the US empire.

Interimperial alliances that positioned the United States, Great Britain, Japan, and Russia on the same side during World War I, chapter 5 contends, camouflaged a panoply of racial tensions and political divisions that would shape racial politics and revolutionary movements. The Bolshevik Revolution (1917), in particular, launched new political formations that reanimated and recalibrated racial fears of sedition and revolution. Inspired by the Third International's unequivocal critique of empire, throngs of anticolonial revolutionaries gravitated to the communist movement in the 1920s. In Moscow and in communist nodes around the world, notably Mexico City during the Mexican Revolution (roughly 1910–20), many colonized subjects came together to theorize and pursue interracial solidarities, revolutionary nationalism, and communist internationalism. Those intellectual discussions and personal encounters helped to radicalize the New Negro movement and to foster anticolonial struggles across Asia for generations. Communist internationalism's juxtaposition and integration of Black struggles against white supremacy in the United States and anticolonial struggles in Asia sustained ironic figurations of Japan. Regardless of the Japanese state's violent repudiation of communism and radicalism of any kind, agents of the US security state continued to see Japan and its acolytes everywhere, seemingly prepared to ally with communists, Mexicans, African Americans, South Asians, and anyone else to undermine US sovereignty. As the conviction of Ghadar Party members and its aftermath portended, the main transimperial alignment that withstood the end of World War I and the rise of communism was the Anglo-American alliance, a racial and colonial pact standing fast for white supremacy and empire.

The interimperial rivalries and political ideologies nominally delineating allies and enemies before and during World War II, chapter 6 argues, produced a cacophony of ironic discourses and anticolonial movements that critiqued and promoted the US empire. Across the US empire, incipient efforts at pan-Asian solidarity through anticolonial communism encountered a wave of racial violence and state repression. In the Philippines, alongside the criminalization of communism, the US state increasingly endorsed the "Filipinization" of colonial governance, or Filipino collaboration, under the promise of eventual independence. As tensions between Japan and the United States, two empires that stood equivalently against communism, intensified in the 1930s, the Sakdalista movement, and its invocation of Japan's support, captured the imagination of many Filipinos yearning for liberation and stoked the fears of US authorities determined to preserve the racial and colonial order. The brutal suppression of the Sakdalista uprising and the simultaneous establishment of the Philippine Commonwealth in 1935 hardly alleviated longstanding fears of sedition and revolution. By blaming a constellation of forces within and outside of the Philippines—reckless leaders, gullible followers, communist internationalism, imperial Japan—for the armed insurrection *and* the state massacre, US officials obfuscated a long history of anticolonial struggles and counterrevolutionary violence that constituted the US empire. Fighting communism and fascism remade the Philippines and the United States into allies for "democracy," a farce and a fiction that refashioned conquest into liberation. The US empire, guided by the tropes of US national security, stretched across the Pacific, ready to lead the "free world" into violent submission and collaborative colonialism.

The stories of individuals and movements that I weave together in the chapters that follow ultimately cultivated a historical consciousness, an acute awareness of histories of empire and white supremacy and of histories of collective struggles against those overwhelming forces. Their strivings to create other possibilities—to reject racial capitalism's norms, to exploit and critique the nation-state, to forge social relations of common struggle—marked them as revolutionary and pan-Asian and, especially to agents of the US security state, seditious. My aim is not to idealize their ideologies, to dwell on their lapses, or to overlook their contradictions and hypocrisies. It is instead to excavate persistent struggles against and beyond white supremacy and empire, to inform (and hopefully transform) our own historical consciousness, our own politics. Tracing those struggles mostly through the archives of the US state makes it abundantly clear that the US security state, as omnipresent as it is, is ultimately founded on imperial insecurities. It is not possible to eradicate those insecurities because they produce the subversion they purport to quell, as racialized subjects of the US empire have always imagined and pursued radical alternatives to colonial authority, racial capitalism, and state violence. The book's title points to those historical dynamics that Carlos Bulosan, whose revolutionary dreams I discuss in the conclusion, recognized decades ago. To empire is a menace to justice and democracy. But in the struggle for justice and democracy, we cannot but be a menace to empire.

Suppressing Anarchy and Sedition

I've chased the wild Apache through his God-forsaken land,
I've tracked the daring horsethief where his footprints
   marked the sand,
I've summered with the robbers down at Coney by the sea,
But the gentle Filipino! Say, he beats them all for me.
He beats them all for me, son, the whole immortal lot,
In his lushy, mushy country, where the climate's good and hot.
I've tracked the red and yellow, and I've tracked the wild and
   tame,
But the gentle Filipino is high, low, jack, and game.

With his timid little manners and his sweet and loving smile,
And his easy way of swearing that he loves you all the while;
With a white flag on his shanty, hanging there to catch
   your eye,
And his little rifle ready to plunk you by and by.
For to plunk you by and by, boy, to shoot you in the back,
And to slip away as swiftly as a sprinter down the track,
To come 'round when they plant you just to drop a little tear,
For the gentle Filipino is a tender-hearted dear.

He's as playful as a kitten, and his pastime as a rule
Is shoot the flag of truce man as sort of April fool;
And if he can find a tree top and get up there with his gun
And pick off the lads all wounded, then he knows he's
   having fun.
He knows he's having fun, boys, a grand good time all
   'round,
They look so awkward tumbling from the stretchers to the
   ground.
It was such fun to shoot them and kill them where they lay,
For the gentle Filipino loves his sweet and childish play.

But I know that he's an angel, pure and white as ocean foam,
'Cause I read it in the papers that they sent me from home;

And I know I am a butcher, 'cause the pamphlet says I am,
But I think I'll keep a-fighting just the same, for Uncle Sam.
Just the same for Uncle Sam, boys, and just bear this in mind,
That the watchdog is much better than the cur that sneaks
    behind.
And I'll try to bear up somehow under this, my murderous
    taint,
For the gentle Filipino is a damned queer kind of saint.

—Jack Daly, Eighth US Infantry, "The Gentle Filipinos," August 1902

A month before President Theodore Roosevelt proclaimed the formal
end to the Philippine-American War on July 4, 1902, a massive wave of
labor strikes rocked the Philippines, involving printers, lumbermen,
sawyers, tailors, butchers, stevedores, and tobacco workers. Although
the strikes were largely uncoordinated walkouts by aggrieved workers
in particular industries and locales, there was no question that the formation of the first Filipino labor federation in February 1902 had
ignited the spark. Building on a tradition of mutual-aid labor associations under Spanish rule and a history of organized labor strikes dating
back to at least 1872, the Unión Democrática de Litógrafos, Impre-
sores, Encuadernadores y Otros Obreros (Democratic Union of Lithog-
raphers, Printers, Bookbinders and Other Workers) immediately
attracted throngs of "other workers" by the summer of 1902. Within
six months, the Unión Obrera Democrática (UOD), as it came to be
known popularly, had branches composed of barbers, carpenters and
sawyers, cigar makers, office workers, draftsmen and painters, dress-
makers and seamstresses, sailors and shipyard workers, tobacco workers, and farmers. UOD's mass appeal, a Manila newspaper editorialized, represented a "new revolution . . . rapidly approaching, more
formidable than the one [Emilio] Aguinaldo headed."[1]

Isabelo de los Reyes, UOD's founding president and a major figure of
the Philippine left, conceived the idea of organizing "other workers."
He had been a respected newspaper writer and owner in 1897, when
his criticisms of the Spanish empire led to his summary arrest and

deportation to Spain. De los Reyes's incarceration in Montjuich, a prison notorious for its torture chambers, radicalized him, as fellow political prisoners introduced him to anarchism. "I repeat, on my word of honor, that the so-called anarchists, Nihilists or, as they say nowadays, Bolsheviks, are the true saviours and disinterested defenders of justice and universal brotherhood," he would state later. "When the prejudices of these days of moribund imperialism have disappeared, they will rightfully occupy our altars." After his release in 1898, de los Reyes immersed himself in the world of Spanish radicalism, savoring the relative freedom of political expression in the metropole. He began publishing *Filipinas ante Europa* during the Philippine-American War—with the motto, "Contra Norte-America, no; contra imperialismo, sí, hasta la muerte"—before deciding to return to the Philippines in October 1901. When asked to head the UOD a few months later, de los Reyes leaped at the chance. It was an opportunity, he recalled later, "to put into practice the good ideas I had learned from the anarchists of Barcelona who were imprisoned with me in the infamous Castle of Montjuich."[2]

US officials struck back, unconstrained by the US Constitution in the revolutionary Philippines. From the moment de los Reyes returned to the Philippines, they had tried to stifle his activities, forbidding him to publish a newspaper, which was to be titled *El Defensor de Filipinas*, and to form an independent political party. Having already branded him a "radical" and an "agitator and anarchist" before the strikes, American-owned newspapers in Manila printed fiery attacks on de los Reyes that linked his labor organizing to the ongoing uprising against the US empire. De los Reyes was arrested immediately and sentenced to four months in prison for violating a Spanish law against affecting "the price of labor" or regulating "its condition abusively," a law that the US Supreme Court had recently ruled unconstitutional in relation to a Puerto Rican labor organizer. De los Reyes's appeals went nowhere until William H. Taft, the governor-general of the Philippines, pardoned him in January 1903. Taft used the occasion to defame de los Reyes further, calling him "a born agitator, entirely irresponsible, fecund in writing and in speech, who has at times earnestly and vigorously, in Spain and elsewhere, striven to subvert this Government." The *Manila American* lamented that de los Reyes should have been deported to the US mainland, where "he would have at least supplied the roast beef for a tree hanging."[3]

The UOD briefly, if dramatically, survived de los Reyes's resignation in September 1902. Reorganized into a political party by the succeeding

FIGURE 2. Isabelo de los Reyes.
Courtesy of Filipinas Heritage Library.

president, its membership multiplied exponentially through bold labor confrontations and subversive theatrical productions. Those nationalist melodramas, in particular, proved infectiously popular in the early years of US invasion and occupation, playing before packed houses of working-class audiences. With characters not so discreetly representing foreign intruders, local collaborators, and Filipino patriots engaged in a moral struggle for the motherland, historian Vicente L. Rafael argues, they projected "profoundly felt and widely shared social experiences of revolution, colonial occupation, war, and intense longing for freedom (kalayaan)." And the vernacular plays made US officials very nervous. Without notice, productions could include improvised verses for Philippine independence, defiant trampling of the Stars and Stripes, and momentary displays of the banned Philippine flag through actors' costumes and movements. Arm in arm with American soldiers destroying stage equipment, US officials harassed and arrested playwrights, casts, and crews for "sedition," the same charge that dogged the UOD. Taft accused UOD's new president of inciting "the ignorant classes of people to disorder by means of deftly worded and staged seditious and treasonable dramas and in many other ways," an accusation that translated into formal charges of sedition and embezzlement. In quick order, the first Filipino labor federation and the "seditious plays" were driven underground, where Filipino demands for *kalayaan* took root for another time.[4]

The US state's draconian responses in the Philippines emerged out of local and global contexts that conjured multiple and convergent threats to US security, insecurities that appeared to beckon and rationalize a state fortified with new laws, agencies, and powers. Particularly as US officials confronted anticolonial movements heralded by de los Reyes, an anticolonial revolutionary versed in a wider world of anarchism, they began to imagine a racial and radical enemy who confused and collapsed the bounds of race, gender, and politics. That was the "gentle Filipino" that Jack Daly's poem mocked and feared. "In his lushy, mushy country," the new enemy recalled "the wild Apache" but combined "the wild and tame" to become "high, low, jack, and game." Gendered male, yet exhibiting "his timid little manners and his sweet and loving smile" that seduced and diverted US troops to their death, Filipinos represented duplicity—the inscrutable, passive "Oriental," incarnated as a guerrilla soldier, biding his time up "a tree top." Conceding the US soldier's portrayal as "a butcher," the poem's protagonist ultimately defended his racial and masculine violence on behalf of "Uncle Sam," against "a damned queer kind of saint."[5] In the end, Filipinos represented new racial and radical possibilities, embodying histories of colonialism and anticolonialism that the US state recognized and disavowed. To contain those possibilities, the US state criminalized and racialized anticolonial Filipinos firmly alongside Asian workers and revolutionary anarchists as seditious and "foreign" subjects requiring national exclusion and political death.

RACE WAR AGAINST ANARCHY IN THE PHILIPPINES

Defeating the vestiges of the Spanish empire in the spring and summer of 1898 produced tensions and contradictions that US officials had not planned for. The US empire faced revolutions on the ground. Spain had been trying for three years to suppress anticolonial insurgencies in the Philippines and Cuba, campaigns that had left its forces depleted and besieged even before the US troops arrived. As Commodore George Dewey awaited reinforcements to wage war on land, Emilio Aguinaldo, the Filipino revolutionary leader exiled in Hong Kong, returned aboard a US cruiser and promptly declared the Philippines independent on June 12, 1898. The US government never recognized Aguinaldo's declaration and, with the arrival of the US Army, saw Filipino revolutionaries no longer as necessary allies but as troublesome obstacles to the US mission. When US commanders prepared their final offensive on Manila, they had already agreed with their Spanish counterparts to keep Aguinaldo's troops out of the city, a plan that resulted in tense encounters and armed skirmishes between putative allies. The raising of the US flag over Manila in August 1898 hardly restored peace to what a US Army officer called "this revolutionary and insurrectionary city of . . . 250,000 inhabitants of the most diverse nationality."[6] With the Spanish surrender materialized a greater enemy, a racial, revolutionary enemy.

The ensuing Philippine-American War was a race war, historian Paul A. Kramer argues, in that US forces engaged in a mutually reinforcing process of casting Filipinos and themselves as racially unequal and justifying colonial violence in racial terms. While Aguinaldo attempted to gain US recognition of his "Revolutionary Government" in the months leading up to the signing of the Treaty of Paris between Spain and the United States in December 1898, President William McKinley revealed his intent to claim sovereignty over the entire archipelago. The United States agreed to pay Spain $20 million for the Philippines. McKinley, in turn, vowed that his nation came "not as invaders or conquerors, but as friends," and would strive to "win the confidence, respect, and affection of the inhabitants of the Philippines by assuring them in every possible way that full measure of individual rights and liberties which is the heritage of free peoples, and by proving to them that the mission of the United States is one of benevolent assimilation, substituting the mild sway of justice and right for arbitrary rule." His racializing language of uplift—and attendant feminizing demand of submission—found a receptive hearing on the domestic front but not on the front lines, where a standoff between US troops and Filipino forces erupted in gunfire on February 4, 1899. A protracted war of US colonial conquest had begun.[7]

US military personnel and politicians predictably turned to entrenched, gendered racial idioms to make sense of an armed enemy in a distant land. An African American sergeant wrote, "I feel sorry for these people and all that have come under the control of the United States. . . . The first thing in the morning is the 'Nigger' and the last thing at night is the 'Nigger.'" White troops, another Black soldier related, "talked with impunity of 'niggers' to our soldiers, never once thinking that they were talking to home 'niggers' and should they be brought to remember that at home this is the same vile epithet they hurl at us, they beg pardon and make some effiminate [*sic*] excuse about what the Filipino is called." Theodore Roosevelt, for his part, liked to draw a different racial analogy. "We have no more right to leave the Filipinos to butcher one another and sink slowly back into savagery," he preached before American audiences, "than we would have the right, in an excess of sentimentality, to declare the Sioux and Apaches free to expel all white settlers from the lands they once held." The US forces, he vowed, were fighting for "the greatness of the Nation—the greatness of the race."[8]

The new context, across the Pacific, and the new enemy, of "Asiatic" and mixed origins, also produced a new race vernacular conducive to perpetrating violence on Filipinos more specifically. The Philippine Islands presented new challenges since they were populated by, in Roosevelt's worldview, "half-caste and native Christians, warlike Moslems, with wild pagans." The heterogeneity and indefinability of Filipinos came to define the Philippines, a racial projection critical to the delegitimation of the "insurrection" and "insurrectos." "The Filipinos are not a nation, but a variegated assemblage of different tribes and peoples, and their loyalty is still of the tribal type," concluded the Philippine Commission, a body delegated to investigate conditions on the islands in 1899. Self-government was out of the question for "the multiplicity of tribes . . . and the multifarious phases of civilization—ranging all the way from the highest to the lowest—exhibited by the natives of the several provinces and islands." US troops on the ground had little use for ethnological distinctions, preferring to call all Filipinos "niggers" or, increasingly, "gugus" or "goo-goos." Derived from a Tagalog word for a slippery shampoo made of coconut oil or US soldiers' misogynist taunts of Filipinas making "goo-goo eyes," the word gained wide usage and eventually evolved to "gook," soon to become a staple of US military occupation in Asia, Latin America, and the Caribbean.[9]

"Gu-gus" turned more slippery in November 1899, when US generals first declared their mission accomplished and Aguinaldo adopted a new strategy of guerrilla warfare. Blending into the rural populace, which provided crucial networks of financial and material support, Filipino forces wreaked havoc on US designs, as the Philippine Commission put it, to prosecute "the war until the insurgents are reduced to submission." "The enemy existed unseen in the dripping jungle, in the moldering towns and in the smoky clearings on the hillsides, and since a natural prudence bade him not risk any open encounter, the enemy was not to be found," a US veteran recalled. "But they existed nonetheless." Filipinos had "that particular faculty of all Orientals to say one thing" and mean something else, another veteran stated. They "professed to be 'mucho amigo' (good friends) to our faces, while secretly aiding the insurrection with all the means at their command." Organizing into

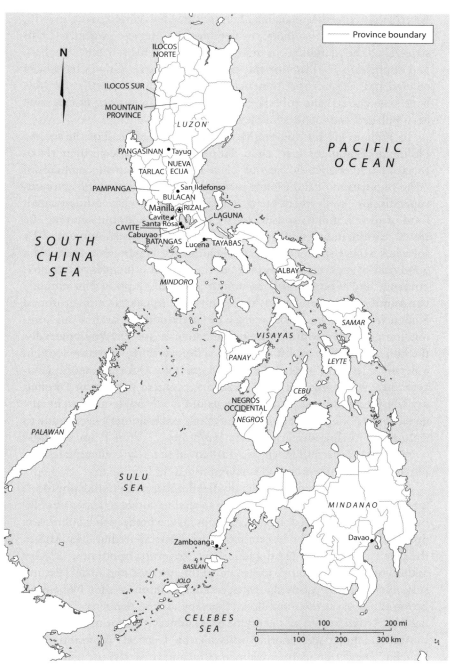

Legend:
———— Province boundary

N

PACIFIC
OCEAN

ILOCOS
NORTE

ILOCOS SUR

MOUNTAIN
PROVINCE

LUZON

PANGASINAN •Tayug

NUEVA
TARLAC ECIJA

PAMPANGA

San Ildefonso
BULACAN

Manila ⊛ RIZAL
Cavite
Santa Rosa LAGUNA
CAVITE
Cabuyao
BATANGAS Lucena TAYABAS

ALBAY

MINDORO

SOUTH
CHINA
SEA

VISAYAS

SAMAR

PANAY

LEYTE

CEBU

NEGROS
OCCIDENTAL

NEGROS

PALAWAN

SULU
SEA

MINDANAO

Davao

Zamboanga

BASILAN

JOLO

CELEBES
SEA

0   100   200 mi
0   100   200   300 km

MAP 2. The Philippines. Cartography by Bill Nelson.

guerrilla units further racialized Filipinos as "uncivilized" and, in turn, seemed to justify US soldiers' own embrace of "savage" warfare. "This struggle on the islands has been naught but a gigantic scheme of robbery and oppression," a Black private observed in 1901. "Graves have been entered and searches have been made for riches; churches and cathedrals have been entered and robbed of their precious ornaments; homes have been pillaged and moneys and jewelry stolen."[10]

To William H. Taft, whom McKinley appointed head of the second Philippine Commission in 1900, Filipinos embodied a peculiar set of racial characteristics borne out of centuries of Spanish colonialism. "The population of the Islands is made up of a vast mass of ignorant, superstitious, well intentioned, temperate, somewhat domesticated, fond of their families, and deeply wedded to the Catholic church," he stated within months of his arrival. "They are easily influenced by speeches from a small class of educated Mestizos who have collected a good deal of superficial knowledge of the general principles of free government, and who are able to mouth sentences supposed to embody constitutional law, and who like to give the appearance of profound analytical knowledge of the science of Government." Even as his commission gestured toward an eventual transition to "the Philippines for the Filipinos," Taft saw little hope for self-government anytime soon. In a personal letter he alleged, "They are generally lacking in moral character; are, with some notable exceptions, prone to yield to any pecuniary consideration; and difficult persons out of whom to make an honest government. . . . They are born politicians, as ambitious as Satan and as jealous as possible of each other's preferment." Until Filipinos could overcome such racial tendencies, Taft could scarcely contemplate anything but US domination and tutelage.[11]

As the war dragged on, officially until 1902 and unofficially for at least another decade, the US military turned to ruthless tactics of colonial warfare that treated the general populace, whether armed or not, as potential insurgents. In December 1900, General Arthur MacArthur, the commanding US general and military governor, announced a "new and more stringent policy" toward breaking up the "organized system" sustaining Filipino guerrilla units, stating ominously that "whenever action is necessary the more drastic the application the better." Following MacArthur's orders, US commanders in many hostile areas adopted a strategy made notorious worldwide by General Valeriano "The Butcher" Weyler of Spain in Cuba in 1896 and revived more recently by British troops against the Boers in South Africa. With the largest military force dispatched across the Atlantic, Weyler had systematically forced the Cuban population into concentration camps to isolate anti-colonial revolutionaries, a campaign that President McKinley had denounced as tantamount to "extermination." US orders to Filipino peasants to relocate to "protected zones" differed little in form. Outside of designated "reconcentration camps," US troops torched crops and residences, to cut off the guerrillas' food supply and to punish their supporters, and fired on anyone they came across.[12] Even if in disavowal, the United States was undeniably an empire fighting a war of conquest.

While US military officers ordered their men to make the Philippines into "a howling wilderness," as one described their objective, they and their supporters claimed over and over that the withdrawal of US forces would lead to anarchy in the Philippines. They came as an army of liberation, not of enslavement. "Should our power by any fatality be withdrawn . . . the government of the Philippines would speedily lapse into anarchy, which would excuse, if it did not necessitate, the intervention of other powers, and the eventual division of the islands among them," the Philippine Commission stated. "Only through American occupation, therefore, is the idea of a free, self-governing, and unified Philippine commonwealth at all conceivable." Whiteness and manhood obliged colonial rule. "If England were to abandon all claim to influence the internal affairs of the Transvaal and give up the title to suzerainty . . . the State would remain an organized community . . . likely to work out its problems after the general fashion of modern society," the *New York Times* waxed benevolent. "If the United States should abandon the Philippines . . . there is no reason . . . to infer that anarchy, and the worst form of it, would not ensue." Unlike the Dutch descendants of South Africa, Filipinos seemed incapable of cultivating a "modern society" on their own.[13]

Although those utterances counterposed modernity and anarchy, by which they meant disorder and backwardness, anarchism as a radical critique and a political movement emerged in the "modern" world of Europe in the nineteenth century. What anarchists sought was not disorder but a new order to replace the mass disorder created by state authority and private property. "*Anarchy,* that is the absence of a ruler or a sovereign," Pierre-Joseph Proudhon famously stated in his seminal text *What Is Property?* (1840). "That is the form of government we are moving closer to every day." Alongside and often against their contemporaries Karl Marx and Friedrich Engels, Proudhon, Mikhail Bakunin, and other increasingly self-conscious anarchists deeply influenced how generations of radical thinkers and working-class movements interpreted capitalism, socialism, and the proletariat. At the Basel Congress of the International Working Men's Association (IWMA, commonly called the First International) in 1869, a growing rift between Marx's adherents and Bakunin's supporters boiled over when debates on the role of the state in the collective ownership of property split the International into two factions. Although inconsistencies and contradictions characterized Bakunin's political philosophy, his persistent condemnation of state power helped to define anarchism, in contrast to Marx's notion of a dictatorship of the proletariat. "If there is a State, there must be domination of one class by another and, as a result, slavery," Bakunin argued. "The State without slavery is unthinkable—and this is why we are enemies of the State."[14]

Bakunin's ideas, including his emphasis on the revolutionary potential of the peasantry and embrace of revolutionary violence, resonated particularly with rural and industrial workers of Spain. Before his expulsion from the First International in 1872, Bakunin sent trusted colleagues to organize workers already invigorated by the dethroning of Queen Isabella II in 1868. They soon helped to establish IWMA branches in Madrid and Barcelona and then a labor federation across Spain. The Bourbon Restoration, engineered by Antonio Cánovas del Castillo in 1874, drove the labor movement deeper underground for many years and reinforced its antistatist and anarchist trajectory. By the 1880s and 1890s, when economic crises, antiradical repression, and anarchist conceptions of "propaganda by the deed" reverberated across Europe, some anarchists carried out acts of spectacular violence that shook Spain's political landscape. After the mass uprising in Jerez, Andalusia, in 1892 and a series of bombings in Barcelona in 1893 and 1896, Spanish authorities, led by the Guardia Civil, cracked down with brute force, imprisoning and torturing anarchists and workers en masse, most notably in the dungeons of Montjuich. The Barcelona prison quickly became the symbol of state authority in its worst form, as anarchists and their allies publicized the crimes that the Spanish regime committed there. In 1897, Michele Angiolillo, an anarchist originally from Italy, assassinated Prime Minister Cánovas with three point-blank shots. "I have done my duty and I am at peace," he explained. "I have avenged my brothers of Montjuich."[15]

Although leading anarchist intellectuals focused largely on theorizing and organizing European workers—at times, as Proudhon exemplified, in overtly patriarchal and racist terms—the anarchist movement's struggles with the Spanish state exposed the colonial roots of state violence. In response to the Barcelona bombings in 1893, Cánovas had appointed Valeriano Weyler the captain general of Catalonia to oversee the repression of anarchists, Catalán separatists, and other radicals. Weyler's long journey to becoming "The Butcher" had carried him across the Spanish empire, beginning with military expeditions to quell anticolonial rebellions in the Dominican Republic and Cuba in the 1860s. He was recalled to the Iberian Peninsula in the 1870s to secure the reconstituted Spanish state in Valencia and Catalonia, where his attacks on civilians briefly garnered widespread rebuke. But the Spanish empire needed a man like Weyler on the front lines. Between 1888 and 1891, he served as the captain general of the Philippines, applying and refining his approach to counterinsurgency. When an anticolonial rebellion erupted on the island of Mindanao in 1891, Weyler forced the local civilian population into fortified areas supposedly to protect them from "pirates." When revolutionaries in Cuba took up arms for independence in 1895, Cánovas vowed to bring the colony back into the Spanish fold and dispatched Weyler to carry out the task. Before leaving for Havana, Weyler told a colleague, "what we became in the Philippines will serve us well" in Cuba. In the Caribbean, he soon earned the title of "The Butcher" for good.[16]

Traveling on the same imperial routes as Weyler, colonial subjects and budding anticolonial nationalists developed worldly visions and global connections that exceeded and challenged the bounds of empire. In June 1897, when the Spanish were contending with rebellions in Barcelona, Cuba, and the Philippines, the colonial regime in the Philippines had Isabelo de los Reyes arrested for daring to question Spanish policies. De los Reyes landed in Manila's Bilibid prison, before being deported to Catalonia. In Barcelona's municipal jail, he encountered a Catalán anarchist imprisoned for opposing Weyler's campaign in Cuba. When de los Reyes was transferred to Montjuich, he joined other Filipinos deported for rising up against Spain. Montjuich opened de los Reyes's eyes to radical possibilities. It was there that Federico Urales, another Catalán anarchist, witnessed the horror of recent Filipino deportees, dressed in their lightweight "native attire," trying to keep warm in Montjuich's courtyard. But that dreadful scene allowed for new political awakenings and collective solidarities. "It was a noble, beautiful sight to see the prison inmates throwing down into the courtyard shoes, rope-sandals, trousers, vests, jackets, caps, and socks to warm the poor Filipino deportees," Urales observed. And that kind of camaraderie was what anarchism seemed to be about, de los Reyes learned. It was about "the abolition of boundaries . . . with all of us associating together without any need of fraudulent laws or ordinances which trap the unfortunate but leave the real criminals untouched."[17]

In October 1901, de los Reyes returned home to put into practice in the war-torn Philippines what he had learned in Europe, but he encountered an incipient colonial state becoming as repressive as the old Spanish regime. Within weeks of his arrival, de los Reyes appeared before the Philippine Commission to voice his opposition to a contemplated law on sedition. The commission disregarded his opinion and decreed the Sedition Act on November 4, 1901. The law prohibited all residents of the Philippines from waging war or inciting, organizing, or assisting "any rebellion or insurrection against the authority of the United States or of the Government of the Philippine Islands, or the laws thereof." The sections on sedition outlawed persons from preventing "the promulgation or execution of any law or the free holding of any popular election" and impeding public officials from carrying out their duties. To "inflict any act of hate or revenge" or to "despoil, with a political or social object, any class of persons, natural or artificial, a Municipality, a Province, or the Insular Government or the Government of the United States, or any part of its property" also fell into the legal category of sedition. Finally, until the official end of "a state of war or insurrection against the authority or sovereignty of the United States," it was "unlawful for any person to advocate orally or by writing or printing or like methods, the independence of the Philippine Islands or their separation from the United States whether by peaceable or forcible means."[18]

About a century after fears of revolutionary ideas and revolutionary peoples from France and Saint-Domingue (Haiti) led to the passage of the Alien and Sedition Acts in 1798, the US state again criminalized political beliefs and political expressions, this time in an archipelago across the vast Pacific. Virtually any political, social, and even personal utterance disparaging of the US government, its agents, or its supporters could be legal grounds for imprisonment and fine. With the Philippine Islands full of active and potential revolutionaries, by definition subjects intending to commit treason or sedition, the US state possessed an investment in identifying and criminalizing anyone who might fit that description. Alongside US soldiers inflicting violence on Filipino peoples and their homes, the act of claiming legal authority over the Philippines, and simultaneously prohibiting political views critical of that authority, constituted the expanding US empire. Theodore Roosevelt, who would soon ascend to the White House, understood that imperial logic of national security. In 1899 he remarked, "Those who would encourage

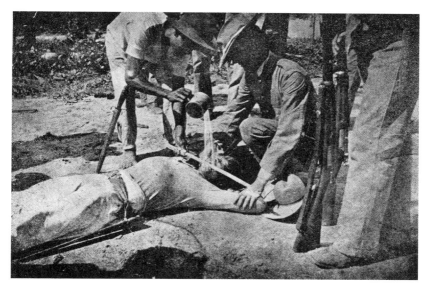

FIGURE 3. A US soldier explained the "water cure" in 1900: "Lay them on their backs, a man standing on each hand and each foot, then put a round stick in the mouth and pour a pail of water in the mouth and nose, and if they don't give up pour in another pail. They swell up like toads. I'll tell you it is a terrible torture." Quote from Paul Kramer, "The Water Cure," *New Yorker*, February 25, 2008. Photograph by Corporal George J. Vennage. Courtesy of Rare Books and Manuscripts Library of The Ohio State University Libraries.

anarchy at home most naturally strike hands with the enemies of our country abroad. . . . Fundamentally the causes which they champion are the same. The step encouraging the assassination of the guardians of the law at home, to the aiding and abetting of the shooting down of our soldiers abroad is but a short one."[19] Empire was fundamentally about claiming and defending sovereignty, at once recognizing, realigning, and denying what was foreign and domestic.

To thwart such threats, the US state constructed an extensive infrastructure of intelligence and surveillance across the Pacific. In February 1901, the War Department dispatched an officer from the Military Information Division (MID) to Manila, who, within a few months, hired undercover agents to report on the civilian population and systematized intelligence reports on opposition to US rule. On the eve of the US declaration of victory in 1902, the War Department further centralized its intelligence network, making Manila home to its first MID field office, which was ordered to report directly to MID headquarters in Washington, DC. That was a stark contrast from the beginning of the Spanish-American War, when the MID had so little information on the Philippines that its officers hastily copied "confidential" excerpts from the *Encyclopaedia Britannica*. Within five years, the US Signal Corps laid 5,355 miles of cable on land and another 1,615 miles undersea across the Philippines, connecting nearly three hundred telegraph and telephone stations. In 1903 alone, that network carried 3.1 million messages of one hundred million words. A war against anarchy was a war for information. And US soldiers admittedly committed torture in the Philippines, most infamously through the "water cure," as Governor-General Taft put it, "to extract information." Institutionalizing a tradition of unilateral military intervention in Asia, the Philippine-American War produced a transpacific security state fixated on weeding out sedition and revolution against the US empire.[20]

RECONCENTRATING SECURITY

Central to the emergent security apparatus was the Philippine Constabulary, a civilian police force established by the Philippine Commission in 1901. The Constabulary's mission, in the words of the assistant director, was "to be the friend and protector of the Filipino, accomplishing its ends by sympathetic supervision rather than force, suppressing brigandage and turning the people toward habits of peace." Led by US Army officers and staffed on the ground by Filipino recruits, the Constabulary assumed the lead in the "pacification" of the Philippines in 1902. Often working side by side with Philippine Scouts, "native" military regiments within the US Army's chain of command, Constabulary forces crossed the divide between civilian authority and military authority, a defining feature of the US colonial security state materializing in the Philippines. At the same time, US officials constructed a firm racial divide within the ranks to guard against sedition and revolution. As Filipinos in the Constabulary and the Scouts replaced American troops, whose numbers had been reduced to 15,500 by July 1902, white officers continued to instruct brown men on the ways of law and order. Fearful of arming Filipinos who might switch allegiances down the road, the US Army assigned antiquated weaponry to Constabulary units, a racial division of arms that attested to the precariousness of US declarations of the end of the "Philippine Insurrection."[21]

The insurrection, along with counterinsurgency tactics to suppress it, persisted. When Harry Hill Bandholtz took charge of Tayabas (Quezon) province in March 1902, four months before President Roosevelt declared the war's end, he discovered that "a state of insurrection existed and always had existed throughout the province since the first American occupation." There had been, in effect, two states claiming sovereignty in Tayabas, with the *insurrecto* government receiving a larger share of the taxes, until the US Army's "thorough military reconcentration" of towns. In the summer of 1902, as Filipino recruits succeeded US troops in Tayabas, Ruperto Rios, a former *insurrecto* who had surrendered to US forces but then renounced his allegiance to the United States, initiated a messianic movement for Philippine independence. "Rios frequently concealed himself at night and would appear in the morning announcing to his followers that he had spent the evening in conversation with the Emperors of Russia and Germany, and the President of France," reported Bandholtz, "and that these potentates would soon send over large fleets which would distribute 10,000 arms with necessary ammunition on the shores of Tayabas Province." With Constabulary and Scout forces under his command and the cooperation of "the higher class of natives," Bandholtz stated proudly, "this pernicious organization has been completely destroyed, and a large majority of its members captured or killed." He was especially pleased that the Constabulary had "practically committed no abuses."[22]

But the Constabulary, like the US Army before it, gained a reputation for committing abuses. Since returning residents to their barrios, the governor of Albay province reported in January 1903, "there has been apparently wanton and wholesale destruction of property; houses have been burnt throughout the mountains and, in some cases, entire pueblos have been entirely wiped out." The destructive violence against Filipino homes and communities undermined efforts to secure US sovereignty, unleashing new rounds of collective resistance. "It is such acts as these that turn the people against the Constabulary and makes it so difficult for them to receive information from the people," the governor observed. "If the reports that reach this office prove to be true, the destruction of property by the Constabulary is far in excess of anything attempted by the ladrones [bandits]." Over the following five months, the growing resentment in the countryside drove about a thousand peasants to rally around Simeon Ola, a former revolutionary major trying to mount what US officials referred to as the "Albay Insurrection." Armed with two hundred guns and eight hundred bolos (knives), Ola's movement threatened to attract wider support. In June 1903, Bandholtz, in charge of nearly a thousand men in the Constabulary and the Philippine Scouts, was assigned the task of quelling the Albay insurrection.[23]

FIGURE 4. Harry Hill Bandholtz. Courtesy of Filipinas Heritage Library.

At once recalling and distancing his actions from wartime atrocities, Bandholtz immediately ordered that all towns be "reconcentrated." The reconcentration of Albay, he explained, "was such only in name, without any pitiless shooting down of defenseless women and children and such other attendant horrors as are generally associated with the word reconcentration." In his mind, he had no other option, since the surrounding civilian population far outnumbered his troops. "The object of the reconcentration was not to punish the people indiscriminately," Bandholtz stated, echoing his predecessors, "but to deprive the ladrones of the means of subsistence in the interior, and to enable the troops to operate freely without fear of injuring innocent people." Over four months in 1903, the counterinsurgency campaign in Albay killed 250 "ladrones" and captured a thousand others, including Ola. Bandholtz's work in pacification earned him appointments as assistant chief of the Constabulary that year and chief four years later, deepening his resolve to secure the Philippines for the United States. Filipinos "have many grave defects which are to be expected when we consider the treatment they have received for over 300 years from the Spaniards," he reasoned. "I find in my experiences that they need a firm hand and seldom resent severe punishment if they feel it is just."[24]

The specter of sedition and revolution refused to fade away. In January 1903, the Constabulary forwarded to Governor-General Taft the transcript of an interview with Cenon Nigdao, who admitted to being a leading officer in a revived Katipunan, the name of the organization that had led the Philippine Revolution against Spain. "We wish to defend our country and our rights," Nigdao stated. "By any possible means." He personally surrendered to US authorities because he was "tired," but Nigdao implied that there was a larger movement afoot headed by Macario Sakay, president of the new Katipunan. Taft forwarded the transcript to the US secretary of war "as an illustration of little Katipunan mushroom organizations springing up and dying out, organized for the purpose of aiding ladrone operations of larger men." In September 1903, the director of posts in Manila discovered a widespread plot "to mail private postal cards bearing pictures on the back of Rizal and Aguinaldo (the latter in insurgent uniform), with insurgent flags between them, in the mails of the Philippine Islands." He ordered that all such postcards be confiscated and destroyed immediately. "Postmasters are informed that these postal cards, as well as all others bearing pictures of leaders of the Insurrection, are considered by the Civil Governor to be attempts to revive the memories of the Insurrection and to encourage the hope of another, and are therefore unmailable."[25]

If the resuscitation of revolutionary organizations and insurgent icons unnerved US officials, the radical ideology and practical effects of the Unión Obrera Democrática registered a deeper fear. In September 1902, Dominador Gomez, a physician who had befriended and worked with de los Reyes in Spain, took over as UOD's president and conveyed to US officials his plans to steer the union in a more moderate direction. Renaming it Unión Obrera Democrática de Filipinas, Gomez set out to build a political party out of the labor union—with a distinctly antidemocratic constitution—but the working peoples of the Philippines voiced their own priorities. Fed up with poor economic conditions and fired by dreams of national independence, workers joined UOD's ranks by the thousands. When the Tondo branch opened in Manila in April 1903, its vice president brazenly unfurled the Philippine flag and exclaimed: "Whoever does not desire to unite with us, let him rise that we may know him; let him throw mud on the sun of our flag; let him break this emblem of revolution; let him trample upon the flag of the union of all the workers who are the real sons of the Filipino people." In Cavite, the heart of revolutionary Philippines, workers formally organized a UOD branch on Rizal Day in 1902 and promptly initiated a strike in the shipyards, supported and galvanized by anticolonial (or "seditious") theatrical productions.[26]

Agents of the US colonial security state decided to take action. "I can predict only misfortune for the organization of the Union Obrera," a Constabulary officer stated. "The people are not prepared for an organization of this kind, and I feel considerable misgiving as to the results if it is allowed to continue and spread." The "welfare of the people" was at stake, requiring the radical union's "suppression." "The far reaching effects of such an organization upon the masses of an ignorant people whose country is just recovering from the effects of war, many of whom are idle and easily influenced by designing and unprincipled leaders, needs no comment or argument," he explained. On May 29, 1903, Gomez was arrested and charged with sedition, brigandage, and embezzlement, on the same day that the UOD was declared bankrupt. With Gomez in jail, a special commissioner from the American Federation of Labor (AFL), originally dispatched to gather evidence to bolster AFL's opposition to Chinese immigration, offered to help reorganize Filipino workers, an effort US authorities supported as long as "agitators" like Gomez and de los Reyes were not involved. In October 1903, the Philippine Commission approved the Unión del Trabajo de Filipinas, a new labor federation far removed from de los Reyes's anarchistic inspiration and the UOD's bold confrontations of the previous year.[27]

The Unión Obrera Democrática and its first presidents did not represent radical yearnings without compromise or contradictions. For all of his radical pronouncements on anarchism and socialism, de los Reyes also tended to emphasize individual self-improvement and cooperation between capital and labor. In matters concerning the role of the Chinese in the Philippines, he and Gomez voiced anti-Chinese opinions not too different from AFL's longstanding opposition to Chinese workers in the United States. Gomez went so far as to try to reconcile US imperialism and Philippine nationalism, at times to a farcical degree. On May Day 1903, shortly before his arrest, Gomez proudly proclaimed UOD's loyalty to the Stars and Stripes. "At the foot of this banner, we promise fealty, nobility and loyalty," he exhorted. "Around it, spirited and honest workers of both sexes salute, give acclaim, and form its honor guard—a people jubilant with enthusiasm and numerous musical bands that raise the brave chords of the American Hymn and the brisk notes of the *Marcha Filipina* to the skies." The proceedings were "most solemn, moving and indescribable because we realize with deep emotion and joy that from the cadaver of an oppressed people," Gomez concluded, "the United States with its powerful support is founding a new nation—young, strong and forever free."[28]

Amid a raging pacification campaign, such florid oratory only intensified the US colonial security state's determination to monitor and contain de los Reyes, Gomez, and other potential revolutionaries. When Bandholtz was reassigned to Manila in 1905, he made a point of meeting with Gomez and "other celebrities" right away to cultivate a personal relationship in what he called "this cosmopolitan center of superficial civilization." Bandholtz had a lot on his mind. In the mountains south of Manila, Macario Sakay, a former revolutionary officer leading guerrilla units against Constabulary and Scout forces, was engineering bold attacks that drove US officials to fortify their arsenal of military and political weapons. With the suspension of habeas corpus and the reconcentration of large swathes of Cavite and Batangas, Constabulary and Scout units waged a ferocious operation that harkened back to the bloodiest days of the Philippine-American War. Bandholtz entered the fray in late 1905, assured by the governor-general of all "secret service funds" and full government support, but his first days in the new district went horribly wrong. His own men in the Constabulary, in their "over-zeal and excitement" to capture Sakay, accidentally shot and killed an informant and the chief operator of the Information Division. More bad news arrived when he heard that "a damn fool Constabulary sergeant up in Pampanga had to arrest a whole Methodist congregation and, incidentally, beat up the preacher."[29]

Bandholtz enlisted Gomez to help apprehend Sakay. "I experienced considerable difficulty in handling Dominador but managed to win out, I suppose, by pure luck," he wrote. As Gomez negotiated with Sakay, Bandholtz endorsed a plan of "playing upon the emotional and sentimental part of the Filipino character." "We laid great stress upon the fact that unless Bandolerismo [banditry] was extinct in Cavite and Batangas, these provinces would undoubtedly be cut off from representation in the assembly and the assembly jeopardized," he explained. It was a bogus threat, a false promise of self-government. Shortly afterward, in the summer of 1906, an American newspaperman announced before five thousand UOD members that Gomez was apparently no longer their "cacique." Gomez, who was at the meeting, responded "in mellifluous and correct

FIGURE 5. Dominador Gomez. Courtesy of Filipinas Heritage Library.

castellano" and concluded his remarks by spitting in the American's face. While Gomez was able to salvage his radical credentials and Filipino manhood through his rhetorical outburst, Sakay and his comrades could not escape the colonial security state's wrath. Based on the testimony of witnesses gathered by the Constabulary's Information Division, they were charged with brigandage and sentenced to death. Just before his execution in 1907, Sakay declared his abiding commitment to revolution. "Death comes to all of us sooner or later. . . . But I want to tell you that we are not bandits and robbers, as the Americans have accused us, but members of the revolutionary force that defended our mother country, the Philippines! Farewell! . . . Long live the Philippines!"[30]

If revolutionary and, by definition and extension, seditious subjects like Sakay appeared as self-evident targets of the colonial security apparatus, Gomez and the Philippines in general proved impossible to pin down politically. Sending in "the army after ladrones" was "like a locomotive in a ten acre field chasing a flea," Bandholtz admitted. "You cannot do anything with little bands of that kind unless you have the people with you." But the Constabulary continued to reconcentrate civilians for years, a practice that did little to persuade Filipinos to consent to US sovereignty. "I understand that in many provinces they were still doing the fire and sword act," Bandholtz wrote in April 1907. "Whenever they saw a group of remontados at anything within a thousand yards, they would give them a volley and burn their houses." Although he objected to such habits that disregarded "our general policy," the Constabulary chief believed that the proper way to handle Filipinos was "spanking them whenever they were recalcitrant." Bandholtz detested relying on Gomez, who was but a synecdoche for the Philippines. "Working with Dominador Gomez is like playing with a two-edged tool or with fire," he stated. "I consider that he is the most influential native in the Islands today and I am inclined to believe that, if he really so desired, he could at any time start a serious up-rising or, if one were started, that he himself could put an end to it."[31]

When a new wave of labor strikes commenced in 1909, Bandholtz saw the beginnings of a race war, even as he found Filipinos impossible to define racially. The strike by Manila's streetcar workers was "purely racial," he believed, with "all of the soul-stirring appeals of newspapers and unions . . . made to 'the Filipino people.'" The turn of events, Bandholtz warned, "may sometime fan the spark of racial hatred into the flame of insurrection." He blamed Gomez for everything. "All of the 'obreros' are now controlled by Dominador Gomez and it is not a good control," he fumed. Gomez's mestizo background and contradictory politics confused the colonial order that the US state was trying to establish. Instead of expressing their discontent through the Philippine Assembly, which the US authorities inaugurated in 1907, Filipinos seemed to take matters into their own hands. Bandholtz saw an anarchistic scene. "The Philippine Assembly has decided that Gomez is not a Philippine citizen," Bandholtz noted. "The Spanish consul declares he is not a Spanish citizen, and Gomez himself denies his Chinese blood. He is therefore a man without a country but with a tremendous following. He should either be bought or summarily disposed of." Efforts to prosecute Gomez, however, were making him into "a second Rizal."[32] Mobilizing workers, fomenting sedition, and proclaiming loyalty to the United States, Gomez was, like all Filipinos, a colonial subject without a country. As long as that remained the case, fighting anarchy and sedition in the Philippines would prove an endless war.

A GLOBAL WAR ON ANARCHISM

Almost a year after his reelection, which had served as a referendum on his policies in the Philippines, Cuba, and Puerto Rico, President William

FIGURE 6. "A Thing Well Begun Is Half Done," *The Judge* 37, no. 938 (October 7, 1899). Courtesy of Prints and Photographs Division, Library of Congress.

McKinley was still basking in the imperial moment. On September 4, 1901, a huge crowd and a twenty-one gun salute greeted his train's arrival on the grounds of the Pan-American Exposition in Buffalo, New York. McKinley delivered a major address the following day, designated the President's Day at the fair. "The Pan-American Exposition has done its work thoroughly," he stated, "presenting in its exhibits evidences of the highest skill and illustrating the progress of the human family in the Western Hemisphere . . . [which] invites the friendly rivalry of all the powers in the peaceful pursuits of trade and commerce, and will co-operate with all in advancing the highest and best interests of humanity." After marveling at recent technological advances, especially the telegraph, McKinley announced that "God and man have linked the nations together." And he had greater ambitions for man, particularly the American variety. "We must build the Isthmian Canal, which will unite the two oceans and give a straight line of water communication with the western coasts of Central and South America and Mexico," he declared. "The construction of a Pacific cable cannot be longer postponed." As he mapped the future course of the US empire, McKinley cautioned that "our interest is in concord, not conflict, and that our real eminence rests in the victories of peace, not those of war."[33]

Race and violence ruled the day, though. On September 6, McKinley visited Niagara Falls and returned to the exposition in the late afternoon, in time to receive a long line of fairgoers hoping to shake his hand. Race, in one sense, killed the president. When Leon F. Czolgosz, with his hand heavily wrapped in bandage, reached the head of the line, a Secret Service agent standing next to McKinley noticed nothing out of the ordinary and focused his suspicious gaze on a Black man nearby. In that instant, Czolgosz unveiled his pistol and pulled the trigger twice. Minutes after his transfer to the Buffalo Police Headquarters, it was reported, "the crowd had grown from tens to hundreds, and these in turn quickly swelled to thousands, until the street was completely blocked by a surging mass of eager humanity." Cries of "Lynch the anarchist!" echoed through the streets of Buffalo. Only a show of force by the police prevented the mass spectacle gaining popularity in the United States, especially but not solely in the South. By the end of the day, Czolgosz professed to being an anarchist and signed a confession that read: "I killed President McKinley because I done my duty. I don't believe in one man having so much service and another man having none." In a week's time, McKinley was dead.[34]

If the pale, clean-shaven Czolgosz could pass as an ordinary white workingman in Buffalo, his embrace of anarchism, combined with his Polish family background, placed him at the very outer limits of whiteness and, for many, pushed him beyond it. According to Theodore Roosevelt, McKinley's successor, Czolgosz was "an utterly depraved criminal belonging to that body of criminals who object to all Governments, good and bad alike." In his first presidential message to the US Congress in December 1901, Roosevelt vowed to wage a global war on anarchism. "Anarchy is a crime against the whole human race, and all mankind should band against the Anarchist," he intoned. "His crime should be made an offense against the law of nations, like piracy and that form of man-stealing known as the slave trade; for it is of far blacker infamy than either." The United States, Roosevelt intimated, would stop at nothing to suppress anarchism. "This great country will not fall into anarchy, and if Anarchists should ever become a serious menace to its institutions," he said, "they would not merely be stamped out, but would involve in their own ruin every active or passive sympathizer with their doctrines." There was no room for revolution or sedition in the United States.[35]

For Czolgosz, anarchism helped to explain the world around him. Born to Polish immigrants in Michigan soon after their arrival in the

United States, Czolgosz grew up in the industrial Midwest, where a booming economy turned to bust after the financial collapse of 1893. Fired and blacklisted for joining a labor strike that year, he began frequenting socialist and anarchist meetings around Cleveland, Ohio. President McKinley's imperial policies also disillusioned Czolgosz, whose brother's return from military service in the Philippines coincided with his radicalizing politics. Shortly before departing for Buffalo in 1901, Czolgosz complained to a veteran anarchist in Chicago about the "outrages committed by the American government in the Philippine islands." He claimed to have been inspired by Emma Goldman, the most prominent anarchist in the United States. As most anarchists distanced themselves and their political philosophy from Czolgosz, Goldman defiantly defended the presidential assassin. But she could not help but wonder why he had shot McKinley instead of a capitalist. "Was it because he saw in McKinley the willing tool of Wall Street and of the new American imperialism that flowered under his administration?" she conjectured. "One of its first steps had been the annexation of the Philippines, an act of treachery to the people whom America had pledged to set free during the Spanish War."[36] McKinley's chickens had come home to roost.

As Roosevelt sought to eliminate anarchism in the wake of the presidential assassination, he saw similar, if not graver, threats to US sovereignty and security across the Pacific. Roosevelt, who appreciated history's social and political significance, understood in his own way that US history was fundamentally about empire and that empire was fundamentally about security. "Encouragement, direct or indirect, to these insurrectos stands on the same footing as encouragement of hostile Indians in the days when we still had Indian wars," he argued. "While we will do everything in our power for the Filipino who is peaceful, we will take the sternest measures with the Filipino who follows the path of the insurrecto and the ladrone." In contrast to Puerto Rico, Cuba, and Hawaiʻi, where Roosevelt saw promise and hope, he could not ignore the "problems" plaguing the Philippines. But he was secure in his faith that those problems would soon pass into the annals of history. "History may safely be challenged to show a single instance in which a masterful race such as ours, having been forced by the exigencies of war to take possession of an alien land, has behaved to its inhabitants with the disinterested zeal for their progress that our people have shown in the Philippines," he stated. "To leave the islands at this time would mean that they would fall into a welter of murderous anarchy. Such desertion of duty on our part would be a crime against humanity."[37]

If the specter of anarchism and sedition haunted the United States and the Philippines in 1901, the two locales appeared to require different, though related, tools of state violence. Race marked the difference. The Philippines necessitated a strong military, which Roosevelt requested from Congress, since wars "with barbarous or semi-barbarous peoples . . . [were] merely a most regrettable but necessary international police duty which must be performed for the sake of the welfare of mankind." To deal with anarchists closer to home, Roosevelt asked for a new immigration law, implying that the problem lay fundamentally beyond the American nation. Czolgosz's birthplace, Michigan, was only an inconvenient fact. Anarchists, Roosevelt believed, "should be kept out of this country, and if found here they should be promptly deported to the country whence they came, and far-reaching provision should be made for the punishment of those who stay." Anarchists, in his eyes, deserved the same legal standing as Chinese laborers, whose exclusion Roosevelt hoped Congress would also "re-enact immediately" on behalf of American workingmen. The new president, moreover, wished for a new comprehensive immigration law to add a host of other excludables: "all persons . . . of a low moral tendency or of unsavory reputation"; uneducated individuals, whose ignorance made them more liable to imbibe "Anarchistic sentiment"; and persons falling "below a certain standard of economic fitness," who would increase "the pestilential social conditions in our great cities, where Anarchistic organizations have their greatest possibility of growth."[38]

As the US Congress took up Roosevelt's request in 1902, the imperative for some kind of legislative remedy to preserve the political order seemed self-evident. The Senate Committee on Immigration felt no need to "offer any justification" for adding epileptics, insane persons, prostitutes, and anarchists to "the excluded classes, since they either become public charges within a short time, constitute a menace to our social and political order, or conduce to the moral and physical degradation of the American people." Those arriving from Europe appeared particularly insidious, perhaps even more than the dreaded Chinese, since they bore "the risks of altering completely the complexion of our population, by admixture with another, which, be it remembered, with but slight and formal restrictions, under our naturalization laws, can be, and usually is, in a few short years clothed with all the rights, privileges, and immunities of American citizenship." Armed with citizenship rights, anarchists apparently possessed formidable traits that would infect the US body politic. "Who can feel assured that in a brief generation or two those traits of personal character—the love of constitutional freedom, the willing obedience to constituted law and authority . . . —upon which the stability of our existence as a free people depends," the committee asked, "may not become so adulterated that those other traits, borne of ages of oppression and social and political heresy, may not become predominant?" Political stability seemingly demanded racial and sexual segregation, administered through immigration restrictions.[39]

Even as access to naturalization rights placed Europeans in a racial category apart from Asians—the former generally qualified as "a free white person"—those who testified on behalf of a stricter immigration law called for new racial understandings. In matters of crime and education, Prescott F. Hall of the Immigration Restriction League argued, "the distinction between western Europe and eastern Europe holds true, and there is a progression between criminal tendencies and illiteracy." He advocated for an educational provision because "it so happens that the people who are undesirable for other reasons will be those, in fact, who will be shut out by an educational test." When a senator asked Hall to specify which nations would be affected, he responded immediately, "the immigration from southern and eastern countries of Europe and from Asia." Labor economist John R. Commons reinforced Hall's points, noting that "the farmers who would employ these immigrants do not want the eastern European class of immigrants." But recent immigration patterns demonstrated a rapid increase from "southern and eastern Europe and Asiatic Turkey" relative to "northwestern Europe," a shift "farther and farther to the east" that alarmed Commons. Radicalism posed another reason to restrict immigration. Aside from a group in Boston with a "broad humanitarian view," Commons added, the only "class of labor people" opposed to an educational restriction were socialists committed to fomenting "a final revolution." That opposition, he said, "is to my mind the strongest argument in favor of it."[40]

Although the congressional hearings emanated from McKinley's assassination and Roosevelt's war against anarchism, debates over immigration could not but harken back to their anti-Asian roots. Attempting to associate immigrants from southern and eastern Europe with those arriving from Asia, Hall alerted the committee to "the great increase in Asiatic immigration coming through the ports of Europe." Representing Hawai'i's sugar interests, William Haywood offered a contrasting argument against tighter restrictions. "We are struggling now under the laws of the United States, which are all right for the mainland," he said, "but they are not adapted to the Tropics, and when you come to extend them to Porto Rico and to the Philippines you will know that what I say is true." He appealed for an exemption from Chinese exclusion to offset the sugar planters' dependence on Japanese labor. They tried to recruit white workers, even from Galicia, whose "social condition . . . is about as low as you will find anywhere that white people live," Haywood argued, but they all "deserted and went to the mainland the first chance they got." The number of white people in Hawai'i—grossly overcounted in the 1900 census by including the Portuguese, whom, Haywood reported, "we do not always class . . . as whites"—could never fill Hawai'i's labor needs. "I think we are forced to admit that the only persons who can work in the cane fields of Hawaii are Asiatics," he insisted.[41]

Meanwhile, proponents of a stricter immigration bill called attention to the influx of Asians along the Pacific Coast as a warning against racial and sexual deviancy. After Hawai'i became a US territory in 1900, reported the US commissioner of immigration stationed in Vancouver, Canada, a wave of "Japanese cooly labor" made their way from the islands to the Pacific Northwest. The US federal government dispatched a vigilant immigration inspector to stem the tide, he noted happily, deporting the Japanese wholesale for "suffering from peculiarly loathsome and contagious diseases—largely syphilis, trachoma, and scurvy—physical deformity, and idiotic persons." But greater dangers loomed ahead. The Japanese "have a greater population than Italy, a greater population than Austria-Hungary, and when they see from the report that 170,000 came from Austria-Hungary and 180,000 from Italy," the commissioner asked, "what can be more logical or natural for the Japanese Government than to say, 'We will accord to our people the same privileges that are obtained by the people of all other nations.'" He demanded greater restrictions and enforcement powers to address Japanese immigration and the unlawful smuggling of Chinese contract workers and "Chinese and Japanese women of ill fame." Along similar lines, the AFL secretary condemned railroad barons and Hawai'i's sugar planters for trying to import "Chinese coolies" and other unfit workers and pleaded for immigration restrictions on behalf of "millions of American workingmen." By the end of the hearings, tightening immigration restrictions became tantamount to taking a firm stand against Asian workers, rejected once again as "coolies" and prostitutes.[42]

President Roosevelt signed into law a new immigration bill in 1903. Encompassing and expanding the list of "excluded classes" compiled over the previous quarter century, the new law prohibited the entry of:

"All idiots, insane persons, epileptics, . . . paupers; persons likely to become a public charge; professional beggars; persons afflicted with a loathsome or with a dangerous contagious disease; persons who have been convicted of a felony or other crime or misdemeanor involving moral turpitude; polygamists, anarchists, or persons who believe in or advocate the overthrow by force or violence of the Government of the United States or of all government or of all forms of law, or the assassination of public officials; prostitutes, and persons who procure or attempt to bring in prostitutes or women for the purpose of prostitution; those who have been, within one year from the date of the application for admission to the United States, deported as being under offers, solicitations, promises or agreements to perform labor or service of some kind therein." Reinforcing late nineteenth-century representations of prostitutes and contract laborers as embodiments of enslavement after slavery—and thereby threats to a "free" United States—the 1903 law continued to dwell on those historically proscribed "classes." The Chinese, whose exclusion inaugurated and enlarged the federal surveillance of migrants and borders beginning in 1882, were not included in the latest list, since "this Act shall not be construed to repeal, alter, or amend existing laws relating to the immigration, or exclusion of, Chinese persons or persons of Chinese descent."[43]

The law's most significant addition was anarchists, whom Roosevelt denounced as "essentially seditious and treasonable." The provisions specifically targeting anarchists prohibited the immigration and naturalization of anyone "who disbelieves in or who is opposed to all organized government, or who is a member of or affiliated with any organization entertaining and teaching such disbelief in or opposition to all organized government, or who advocates or teaches the duty, necessity, or propriety of the unlawful assaulting or killing of any officer or officers, either of specific individuals or of officers generally, of the Government of the United States or of any other organized government, because of his or their official character." An unmistakable response to McKinley's assassination, the law's definition of anarchism established a vast and loose definition of what constituted criminal political beliefs and political affiliations, in a way that went farther than even the 1901 Sedition Act in the Philippines. Opposing imperial governance, colonial officials, and their underlings anywhere in the world—not only in the US-occupied Philippines—could be grounds for exclusion and expulsion. And the new law applied to the Philippines as much as to Michigan, since it explicitly defined the "United States" as "the United States and any waters, territory or other place now subject to the jurisdiction thereof."[44] Claims to sovereignty, or "jurisdiction," naturalized the bounds of the US empire.

To carry out the exclusion of anarchists and others, the 1903 immigration statute allocated immense administrative and discretionary powers to US federal officials. In particular, the bureaucrats who oversaw the admission and exclusion of aliens—the commissioner-general of immigration and the immigration commissioners, officers, clerks, and other employees at individual ports of entry—held the power to exclude and expel aliens, subject to no judicial oversight whatsoever. All aliens not "clearly and beyond a doubt entitled to land" were to receive a hearing before a "board of special inquiry" of three immigration officers appointed by the immigration commissioners. The hearings were to be "separate and apart from the public," with the board's majority vote to be "final." Discontent aliens or dissenting board members, however, could appeal the board's ruling through the immigration commissioners and the commissioner-general of immigration to the secretary of treasury (changed later to the secretary of commerce and labor), "whose decision shall then be final." Such procedures and decisions concerned cases not only of exclusion but also of deportation. Any alien found to have entered the United States unlawfully within three years of landing was "to be taken into custody and returned to the country whence he came."[45] A global war against anarchism, in the end, classified together anarchists and Asians, both subject to an expanding legal regime committed to, like the Philippine Constabulary on the other side of the Pacific, weeding out sedition and revolution against the US empire.

RACE, EMPIRE, AND NATIONAL SECURITY

Although US officials did not yet utter the words *national security* to defend their emerging transpacific security state, the racializing and colonizing discourse of national security was taking shape. Laws and legal cases on Chinese exclusion had endowed the US federal government with unilateral and exclusive power in matters related to immigration and deportation, all in the name of security. "To preserve its independence, and give security against foreign aggression and encroachment, is the highest duty of every nation . . . whether from the foreign nation acting in its national character or from vast hordes of its people crowding in upon us," the US Supreme Court ruled in *Chae Chan Ping v. United States* (1889). "The government, possessing the powers which are to be exercised for protection and security, is clothed with authority to determine the occasion on which the powers shall be called forth; and its determination, so far as the subjects affected are concerned, are [*sic*] necessarily conclusive upon all its departments and officers." If the US government categorized "foreigners of a different race" as "dangerous to its peace and security," the court reasoned, its designation and exclusion could not "be stayed because at the time there are no actual hostilities with the nation of which the foreigners are subjects." Four years later in *Fong Yue Ting v. United States* (1893), the Supreme Court strongly affirmed the state's power "to expel or deport foreigners . . . as absolute and unqualified as the right to prohibit and prevent their entrance into the country."[46]

Those legal decisions characterized and portended the circular, reinforcing logic of race, empire, and national security. Chinese workers, racialized as "dangerous" to the "peace and security" of the United States, became subjected to a state proclaiming the absolute authority to designate persons or groups as such. Once classified as "foreigners of a different race" who posed threats to US security, regardless of "actual hostilities," Chinese laborers and other excluded persons fell into a legal and political status not unlike Filipinos in the revolutionary Philippines. They were not future citizens of the American nation, but subjects of a state claiming unilateral jurisdiction over their physical movements and political beliefs. As a result, they were rendered vulnerable to interrogation, detention, and expulsion. It was through that process of identifying and repressing racialized and radicalized threats to US national security—an integral element in the modern state's always unfinished project of defending against "foreign aggression and encroachment"—that transformed claims of imperial sovereignty into acts of national defense.[47] Asian workers and revolutionary anarchists remained foreigners in the incorporated states of the US empire, otherwise known as the United States of America, while Filipinos struggling against the US empire, in effect, became seditious subjects in the US-occupied Philippines. The US state's claims to authority to fight whomever it identified as threats to its security, in turn, rationalized its expansion through military intelligence and immigration laws, linchpins of a security apparatus that elided, constituted, and advanced the US empire in North America and in the Philippines.

But those subjected to the US empire continued to create their own histories and identities that flummoxed and frustrated US officials. In the fall of 1901, within weeks of McKinley's assassination, President

Roosevelt received an unsolicited package from Manuel Xerez Burgos of Manila. Xerez Burgos praised the new president for having "fought bravely in Cuba for the overthrow of Spanish sovereignty" and for having "aided the American whom today we mourn in making these Philippine Islands a free nation and sister of the nation whose independence Washington won." Amid the US military campaign against "insurrectos," whom he hoped the "American nation" would "regard with leniency," Xerez Burgos undoubtedly realized that the Philippines was hardly a "free nation." But that did not stop him from making declarations that Roosevelt would have found outlandish. "The Philippine nation longs ardently for justice, and hopes the American Government will . . . never abandon us until it has conferred upon us the benefits of its Constitution and of American citizenship." His ingratiating tone and incongruous claims—asserting the "Philippine nation" and asking for "American citizenship"—hardly masked Xerez Burgos's underlying aspiration for Philippine independence. "Peace will soon reign throughout these Islands," he concluded, "and the rebel Filipinos will then learn what it is worth to be American citizens, and will unite with those who today are loyal in loving the flag that consecrates and sanctifies the liberties of all whom it covers." The divide between loyalty and sedition, Xerez Burgos suggested, would eventually pass into historical insignificance.[48]

Xerez Burgos addressed those themes in his play *With Cross and Sword*, the main item in his package to Roosevelt. First performed in Manila's Teatro Libertad in January 1900 and "inspired by the thoughts of the never to be forgotten, Doctor José Rizal," the nationalist melodrama is set in 1884, twelve years before the Philippine Revolution. In the opening scene, Martin, the patriarch of a prosperous farming family, takes pride in the accomplishments of his daughters Pia and Fausta and son Paco, but laments how "it will all end in smoke, on account of these brigands with their dishonorable schemes!" His wife Petrona tries to comfort Martin, but admits the injustice of having to "pay our dues religiously, besides all the extras that we have to give the priest, the chief of police, the sergeant, the governor, and the tax-collector." Friar Thomas, the local priest, and Gonzales, the lieutenant of police, enter the family compound and obsess over the two daughters. "What a happy man will be he who wins your heart!" Thomas tells Fausta. Pia and Fausta manage to escape the Spaniards' lewd advances, while Martin "lays his hand on his bolo, as if to draw to stab them." Thomas and Gonzales then demand the daughters in exchange for the family's protection. "With my influence I can get your husband deported, and your son as well,"

FIGURE 7. Manuel Xerez Burgos. Courtesy of Philippine Photographs Digital Archive, Special Collections Research Center, University of Michigan.

Thomas informs Petrona. "You Indians are obliged to respect, obey, and adore the Friars, to whom you owe eternal gratitude!"[49] Martin responds with fury, recognizing all the while that he was opening "the door to overwhelming calamities for myself and my family." "I am an Indian and therefore I am laughed at for all the protest I make in defense of my outraged honor and dignity!" he shouts back. "There is no justice for Indians in the Philippines." Although he has made every payment "to avoid suspicion of disloyalty," he could not have his "honor in the slightest degree stained." "I also have Spanish blood in my veins," he points out, but that mattered little to a Spanish regime set upon imprisoning any Filipino deemed "dangerous." He grabs his bolo and attacks Thomas and Gonzales, who finally leave but threaten, "Your fate is sealed!" Martin decides quickly that he and his family must seek refuge from their home in Imus, Cavite. As if speaking directly to Roosevelt, Xerez Burgos's protagonist disparages Spanish notions of racial hierarchy. "They consider us an inferior race without honor or dignity or shame, without any sort of feeling," Martin says. "Fools! Where is there another race like the Filipino, docile, submissive, long-suffering, obedient to the precepts of the Divine Redeemer? A people primitive, progressive, eager to blend with the ruling race and easy to make happy! If only our rulers would hear our wrongs!"[50] Anyone reading those words in 1901 could not but infer that "our rulers," the "fools," signified the Americans as much as the Spaniards.

Martin and his family make their way to Batangas, where they experience the promise of Filipino nationalism, albeit in heteropatriarchal terms that hardly prefigure a revolution in the social relations of production. They are taken in by Captain Memong, Martin's childhood friend. "Memong is a good Filipino, a true lover of his countrymen and his country, but not with the common kind of patriotism, for his sole desire is to see all the people in the Archipelago united as one man, with one sentiment and one hope," Martin explains. "His wish is to see all, with heads erect and bearing the seal of enlightenment, living in peace and enjoying all the benefits of modern liberty, won by reason and philosophy." Together, they lead a life of industry, frugality, and generosity, with Martin managing a sugar plantation for Memong. Two years after leaving Imus, Martin and his family see hope for the future. Pia and Fausta are engaged to marry industrious, "well-bred young men," while Paco is to resume his education with Memong's financial assistance. When Paco expresses his overriding hope to "arouse this people to wake out of its stupor," Martin commends his son's nationalist aspirations. "The longer we leave unchecked all these abuses, robberies, impositions and infamies, the worse they are bound to grow," he tells Paco. "There is no need for a call to arms yet. The best way to liberty and enlightenment is by educating and dignifying the race, and developing its thinking capacity by learning."[51]

Xerez Burgos's play, however, suggested that it might be time for Filipinos to take up arms against the Spaniards and implicitly the Americans. As soon as Martin and Paco leave for Loboo (Lobo) to collect a debt on behalf of Memong, a squad of the Guardia Civil, the Spanish precursor to the Philippine Constabulary, ambush the family home and kidnap Pia and Fausta. When Petrona tries to stop them, she is bayoneted and left behind to die. Thomas and Gonzales orchestrated the raid, exacting the revenge that they had promised. When they arrive on the scene and notice Petrona's dying body, Gonzales instinctively moves to "finish her and then there will be no witnesses." Thomas convinces his "brute" of an accomplice to leave Petrona alone, since she appeared only moments away from death and his "sacred calling" could not allow such a "criminal act." He is also overcome by sexual excitement. "Oh, Fausta, Fausta, you will soon be mine now, all mine and nobody else's," the priest exclaims. Gonzales agrees to leave with Thomas, confident of their racial and imperial authority. "Who would have the nerve to lay criminal charges against a Friar and an officer of the Civil Guardia," he asks, "and raise a row about niggers?"[52] Xerez Burgos's decision to refer to Filipinos as "niggers" in that instance—as opposed to "Indians," a translation of the Spanish term *indios*—further Americanized the racial landscape of the Philippines. Who did these "Indians" and "niggers" think they were up against? The almighty Spanish? The Yankees?

Xerez Burgos's play implied both. When Martin and Paco land in Loboo, they are taken to the Guardia Civil station to have their cedulas (mandatory government documents) inspected. When they are almost out the door, Gonzales enters the station and, recognizing his old nemesis, strikes Martin in the face. Paco tries to come to his father's defense, but the guards knock him unconscious. "My brothers, you are Indians like myself," Martin says to the guards, "your blood should boil within you at the sight of such an outrage on your own kith and kin before your very eyes." Gonzales orders his men to arrest and whip Martin, denouncing him as "one of the worst agitators in Cavite Province" who "has come to Batangas solely for the purpose of agitating and stirring up rebellion." When his guards hesitate, Gonzales lashes out. "Oh-O! It seems this enemy of Spain is a friend of yours, you blackguards, and you sympathize with him, do you?" he screams. "Tie him up, I tell you, you scoundrels as bad as he, you bandits, you carabaos, you swine, you reptiles, you black beasts, you monkeys." Martin advises the guards to do as they are told, adding that "the day of vengeance will come, and then it will be their turn to beg for mercy!"[53] That was the secret weapon, Xerez Burgos seemed to suggest, that all Filipinos carried with them and that their rulers recognized and tried to contain and suppress—an undying hope for *kalayaan*, freedom.

With Cross and Sword ultimately offered imperial authorities a means to redeem themselves, to acknowledge what they condemned as sedition was, in truth, loyalty to God and the Philippine nation. When Paco regains consciousness, he cannot contain his rage against the Spanish. "Oh, shame, shame, out upon this foul breed that calls itself a superior race!" he shouts. "Whose crimes put them on a level with savages and cannibals!" And he is determined to resist, reminding fellow Filipinos, "There can be no tyrants where there are no slaves." With the aid of two kind Spaniards, who represent the possibility of reconciliation between the metropole and the colony, Paco is able to see his father and mother immediately before their deaths, the former from a premeditated assassination and the latter from her stab wounds and unremitting grief. Paco promises his father not to seek revenge on his killers so that he could pursue a larger mission. "I purpose to avenge the infamies which have been done by such rascals," he proclaims. "I only wish that Spain would do us justice and that she would listen to the complaints of nine million human beings who suffer thousands and thousands of vexations. . . . I would not like the Philippines to be separated from her mother country; no, I only wish to uphold the fact that we are men equally as much as they, and that we the Filipinos have the same right which God gave to all rational beings."[54]

Given the historical trajectory of the Philippines after 1884—the outbreak of the Philippine Revolution, the Spanish-American War, and the ongoing "Philippine Insurrection"—that made the separation of the Philippines from Spain a fait accompli, Xerez Burgos was, in effect, addressing Roosevelt and US officials in the Philippines. Could they choose a different path from the Spanish? Xerez Burgos might have been sincere in his appeal for American benevolence, explicitly in his letter to Roosevelt and implicitly through Paco's plea in his play, but his personal history suggested that his invocations were, at least on one level, ironic. He was the nephew of José Burgos, the priest executed by the Spanish in response to the Cavite Mutiny of 1872. Xerez Burgos, a physician by training, served as a delegate to the Malolos Congress in 1898 and 1899, organized under Aguinaldo's leadership. By January 1899, he was also working for the Americans as a surgeon at Bilibid prison and, according to US authorities, simultaneously plotting with Aguinaldo and other insurgent leaders to incite a general uprising. Within days after the beginning of the Philippine-American War, Xerez Burgos turned into an informant for the United States, playing a pivotal role in exposing what US officials claimed was an insurgent plot to massacre all white people in Manila. But it was a decision rooted in expediency. "He wanted to stay out of prison, and he wanted to remain surgeon of Bilibid prison," noted a US military official.[55]

When Xerez Burgos appeared before the Philippine Commission in September 1899, he attested to Philippine yearnings for independence *and* for American tutelage. Spanish friars treated Filipinos, he said, "with a great deal of harshness; with blows, with threats, and with deportation when they did not obey them." In the early 1890s, the Katipunan Society unified everyone across "different provinces and different races," he continued, "to ask for the expulsion of the friars and so secure liberty for the Philip[p]ine people." As in his play, Xerez Burgos elaborated on the many crimes committed by the friars and the Spanish government, especially the Guardia Civil. "They injured women; abused the women of the country by making them prostitutes," he stated, "and many times they caused women to marry men, not to make them live with these men, but to make them mistresses of the priests." The friars, moreover, now opposed the Americans, "in order that they may preserve their power here, or that they may create a new power." Asked if he thought Filipinos were ready for self-government, Xerez Burgos replied that "it is too soon at present." "I think that the Filipinos will need the direction of the Americans for many years," he explained. "They are educated very much in the Spanish way, and it is necessary to get the Spanish ways eradicated little by little."[56] Perhaps these were the sincere views of a political opportunist, an elite patriarchal Filipino wary of too much democracy too soon.

At the same time, Xerez Burgos could also stand for the "gentle Filipino" that Jack Daly's poem warned against: he had an "easy way of swearing that he loves you all the while" he has "his little rifle ready to plunk you by and by." It was that refusal to abide by US rules of engagement that baffled, and thereby gave rise to, the US security state in the Philippines and across the US empire. When *With Sword and Cross* played before "packed audiences of people who realized its force and its truth" in 1900, it was reported, the play's anticolonial message did not go unnoticed. But US officials did not suppress its production. They, however, did not hesitate to shut down the staging of *For Love of Country,* which had audiences crying "Vive Filipinos!" and "Vive Aguinaldo!" by the final scene. That was too incendiary. Banning seditious plays, subduing armed *insurrectos,* and executing Czolgosz pointed to bigger dangers—of revolutionary ideas and revolutionary movements requiring greater surveillance and vigilance to detect and suppress. When the White House received Xerez Burgos's play, its staff passed along Roosevelt's "appreciation" to the author. If Roosevelt actually read the play, he might have recognized its potentially subversive message.[57] Regardless, Roosevelt appreciated the need for a state invested in identifying—and, in the process, racializing—revolutionary threats to US security. For that revelation, he could thank anticolonial *insurrectos* in the Philippines as much as an anarchist assassin from Michigan.

CHAPTER 2

Conflating Race and Revolution

The revolutionary struggle for Philippine independence defined Artemio Ricarte's life. On the eve of the Philippine Revolution, Ricarte was a school teacher in Cavite, instructing emergent Filipinos on the five *R*'s of his generation—reading, writing, arithmetic, religion, and revolution. Once night fell, he concentrated on revolution. As a leading member of the Katipunan, Ricarte was in charge of initiating new revolutionaries into the secret society. "Of every neophyte, who passed a test as to the firmness of his character, his daring and his patriotism," he recalled later, "was demanded an oath which he had to subscribe to in his blood drawn from one of his arms." After the Katipunan decided to wage attacks on Spanish garrisons in 1896, Ricarte led the fighting in Cavite against the despised Guardia Civil. By the time US forces landed in the Philippines in 1898, he was an experienced general better known by his nom de guerre, Vibora (Viper). He quickly grew wary of the Spanish-American War and US imperial designs. In August 1898, shortly before Spain surrendered Manila to the United States, Ricarte warned Emilio Aguinaldo "to be careful because it seems that the Americans want to fool us." Ricarte took up arms against the United States the following year. In the summer of 1900, he was captured by US authorities, who demanded that he pledge allegiance to the Stars and Stripes. He refused.[1]

For that decision, Ricarte faced years of imprisonment and exile. US officials deported him to Guam, another former Spanish colony now claimed by the United States, where they hoped he would reconsider his allegiances. In February 1903, they took him back to the Philippines, but, when Ricarte again refused to take an oath to the United States, they shipped him to Hong Kong. In the British colony, he and fellow Filipino exiles tried to organize a "Universal and Democratic Republic of the Philippines" to replace the US regime and denounced Manuel Xerez Burgos and other Filipino collaborators as "followers of Taft and criminals whose crimes cannot be pardoned." In December 1903, Ricarte concluded that an imminent war between Japan and Russia might produce political conditions favorable to a revolution in the Philippines. He secretly returned to the Philippines and brazenly announced his arrival in Manila's newspapers. "Where is the boasted right of assembly, the freedom of the press and the liberty of speech?" Ricarte asked. "There is no other way, beloved brothers, than *arms* and *patriotism.*" He ended his announcement with a series of taunts and appeals. "Come then, proud star-spangled eagles! Come to rend me and to satiate further your gluttonous hunger! Come then you traitorous natives, plot and make the sale of my body or my life that you may have more gold in your purses! Come then my beloved fellow citizens! To arms!!! To arms!!!"[2]

Over the next five months, Ricarte eluded US authorities and set out to foment a rebellion against the United States. He immediately held meetings with former revolutionaries, beginning with Aguinaldo. "I reproached Aguinaldo for having sworn allegiance to the American government and not having preferred death," Ricarte said, "and for having deceived the people and caused so many deaths." Aguinaldo declined to participate in a new revolution. Isabelo de los Reyes and Dominador Gomez likewise raised questions on the feasibility of an armed revolution, reasoning that "the people would not respond." Undaunted, Ricarte met and corresponded with former comrades, including those now in the Philippine Constabulary, who, along with likeminded Philippine Scouts, he hoped would incite "a general uprising." He also conferred with representatives of Macario Sakay, who was then leading an armed movement against the United States and who would ultimately be executed by US officials several years later. All across the Philippines, Constabulary officers kept an eye out for Ricarte and offered a monetary reward for his arrest. Ricarte, according to a Constabulary report, continued to "organize an insurrection" and, in late February 1904, "made statement to the effect that the Russians, French and Germans were going to help the Filipinos to gain their independence." By the spring of 1904, Ricarte had assumed the pseudonym José Garcia and was working as a clerk for a justice of the peace in Mariveles, Bataan.[3]

Although Ricarte had a difficult time convincing fellow Filipinos to join an armed insurrection, his name came to symbolize an undying commitment to Philippine independence. On May 29, 1904, Ricarte was arrested by the clerk of the court in Bataan—"by deceit," he claimed—and handed over to the Constabulary. Quickly charged and convicted of conspiring against the United States and illegally possessing firearms, Ricarte was sentenced to six years' imprisonment. Subjected to solitary confinement at Bilibid prison, his social contacts were largely limited to US authorities demanding his loyalty to the United States. When Ricarte was allowed to meet with a British journalist to write down his memories of the Katipunan, he did not hesitate to condemn the United States. "The Americans seeks [sic] to establish themselves more securely than the Czar of Russia or the most despotic ruler on the face of the Universe," Ricarte wrote, "and the Philippine Islands are now sheltered in all confidence from the tempestuous storms of time, known as the Time of Light." Three years into his prison sentence, the Constabulary reported that "Ricarte was making 'blood pacts' (*pactos de sangre*) and was organizing a political society." Upon winning his release in June 1910 after a habeas corpus hearing, Ricarte was transported to the Manila customhouse, where US officials ordered him to pledge his allegiance to the United States. When he refused, Ricarte was again placed on a ship bound for Hong Kong.[4]

Though cast out of the Philippines for decades, Ricarte continued to haunt the US empire, especially as the specter of his alliance with imperial Japan seemed to represent a wider network of revolutionary threats to the United States. "As soon as Ricarte reaches Hongkong," a Constabulary agent reported the day after Ricarte's release and expulsion, "he will go to Japan to join Isabelo de los Reyes." Although that report proved false, the expanding US security apparatus continually collected information on an insurrectionary plot involving Ricarte and Japan. Ricarte himself expected and exploited the attention. In August 1910, from Hong Kong, Ricarte penned a widely circulated letter to a Filipino compatriot in Saigon that alarmed the Constabulary. Regretfully turning down the offer of "good employment in that French colony," Ricarte wrote, "I have to make a trip to Japan in order to restore my broken health, after six years of inquisitorial martyrdom which I unjustly suffered in Bilibid." He reminded Filipinos everywhere that they "should never hope for their redemption from the Capitol at Washington" and that their redemption would result instead from "a war of separation" or "a conflict between Japan and the United States." There was only

FIGURE 8. Artemio Ricarte in Tokyo, 1944. Courtesy of
Wikimedia Commons.

one path forward, he exclaimed, *"the road of revolution with all its
consequences!"* He was convinced that the course of colonial oppression would prepare the Philippines "for the future events for which the
Far East will undoubtedly be the theatre."[5]

Long after the official end of the Philippine-American War, Filipinos
continued to represent new racial and radical possibilities, refusing to be
pacified and imagining a potential alliance with Japan, defiant acts that
mocked and motivated the emerging US security state. In the wake of
Japan's triumph in the Russo-Japanese War (1904–5), anticolonial nationalists across colonized Asia looked to Japan as a source of inspiration. US
officials, in turn, increasingly perceived Japan as the greatest threat to US
claims to sovereignty over the Philippines, Hawai'i, California, and

beyond. In particular, wherever the Japanese and Filipinos converged—physically, ideologically, symbolically, and otherwise—agents of the US state came to see a revolutionary conspiracy to undermine and overthrow the US empire. In the summer of 1910, when Ricarte was in Hong Kong, a Constabulary agent reported on the incendiary climate in Cavite. "Snatch phrases, reticence, similes, and, in a word, in all conversations, there is something of hostility towards Americans and a desire to compel them to leave this country," he stated. "There is blind confidence among all of them in the aid which it is said Japan has secretly offered."[6] Such intelligence reports confused Filipino struggles for freedom and Japan's imperial ambitions, a racial conflation that seemed to materialize in the form of a pan-Asian menace to the US empire. US officials' preoccupation with Japan's "Oriental" deceits and revolutionary conspiracies cumulatively justified and transfigured their own colonial mission as a masculine search for national security against an inscrutable plot masterminded by a racial and imperial rival across the Pacific.

JAPAN RISING

Defending the US empire has always been, in part, a historical project. As tension mounted between the United States and Japan in 1940, the US War Department discovered a document that appeared to prove what they feared. Signed by José Rizal and Andrés Bonifacio, central figures in the history of Philippine nationalism, and Togo Geisyu and dated July 7, 1892, the agreement promised Japan's support of Philippine independence from Spain. "In view thereof, the possession of this sacred document by any Filipino effectively recommends him and gives him full liberty to request assistance of his brother, the Japanese people," it read, "so that he may be helped by every means to free himself from slavery." A "Japanese expert" in the US State Department questioned "the authenticity of the signature of the Japanese 'Admiral,'" but that evidently did not invalidate a historical truth. "Unquestionably, as history records," a US official concluded, "the Japanese long ago evinced a keen interest in the Philippines and at one time during the Spanish regime actually made preparations to invade the Islands." That Japan had not attacked the Philippines—while the United States had, in 1898—did not factor into the historical equation. On the eve of US entry into World War II, the US state apparently unearthed a revolutionary (and seditious) plot involving Rizal, Bonifacio, and the Japanese military that now seemed to threaten the US empire. A historical truth came alive as a present-day threat.[7]

The US historical project to uncover links between Filipino revolutionaries and the Japanese state began long before 1940. It began in earnest in 1907, when the Information Division of the Philippine Constabulary commenced compiling papers on "Japanese Propagandism." In August 1907, Rafael Crame, head of the division, declared unequivocally that "since 1896 Filipino revolutionists have been intriguing with Japan and the Japanese officials with a view to bringing about the independence of the Philippines, and, on account of race, color and ethnological affinities, have looked to that country and those officials for help and sympathy in the attaining of their object." He had "no evidence" of "covert assistance or open countenance from Japan" after 1899, Crame noted, but he had no doubt that "considerable encouragement and sympathy have been extended to these revolutionists by high Japanese officials, if not in their official capacity at least as individuals." To Filipinos struggling for independence from the United States, he admitted, "the intervention of Japan is the story of American intervention as between Spain and the Filipinos [all] over again, namely: there was then, and is now, no love for an intervening nation, no matter what nation that may be, nor a desire for its presence in the archipelago beyond the establishment by its assistance of the independence of the Philippines." There was no reservation on the part of Japan, though, whose "ultimate object" was "to annex the Philippine Islands to that empire, regardless of the means she may employ in so doing."[8]

US officials identified two sources behind Japan's object in the Philippines—empire and race—that they eventually came to fixate on to explain Filipino resistance to US rule. Japan held imperial ambitions in the Philippines as early as 1609, according to the Constabulary's compilation, when a Spanish friar filed a report on Japan's designs. "This king (of Japan) has had his desire whetted by that which was robbed from the 'San Felipe,'" the friar warned, "and they say that in the coming year he intends to go to Luzon; being occupied at present with the Coreans, he will not go this year." Three centuries later, a series of correspondence and meetings between Filipino *insurrectos* and Japanese officials appeared to provide clear evidence of Japan's support of Philippine independence. Acting like the French during the American Revolutionary War, according to a recovered letter from 1900, Japanese officials offered arms and other assistance to Filipinos because they saw it as a matter of "race, and for this reason the Japanese want the Asiatics to unite because the white people want to control the Asiatics." At a meeting of insurgent leaders and the Japanese consulate in Cavite, reported another captured letter, a Filipino military officer stated that "the Filipinos might be forced to accept an American protectorate, but that they would prefer to grant such concessions to Japan, as they were connected by ties of race and blood with that country."[9] Racial ties and fraternal bonds seemingly fed an imperial conspiracy and a revolutionary insurrection.

If Japan's support of Philippine independence appeared patently clear to US officials in 1907, that had not been the case years earlier. Following the Meiji Restoration in 1868, Japanese officials looked across the seas to consolidate their new state at home and to bolster their standing around the world. In a series of armed conflicts with China, Japan claimed sovereignty over the Ryukyu Islands, including Okinawa, in 1879 and the island of Formosa (Taiwan) in 1895. Although Japan's march southward signaled its rising imperial status, there was no question that European powers directed the world stage, including in East Asia. Russia, Germany, and France dictated the terms that ended the Sino-Japanese War (1894–95), forcing victorious Japan to retreat from Manchuria and Korea. If for no other reason than to fortify its annexation of Formosa, Japan had no reason to antagonize the United States. During the Spanish-American War, Japan declared neutrality. With the war's end, the Japanese delegation in Washington, DC, intimated that the "extension of the sovereignty of the United States over those [Spanish] Possessions would furnish a complete solution of the question which would be entirely satisfactory to Japan." If the United States declined, Japan was willing to help the United States oversee the organization of "a suitable government," since neither Spain nor the Filipino people were suited to the task. A "purely native Government" would lead only to "intrigue and disorder," with the Philippines becoming "an easy prey to the aggressive tendencies of other powers."[10] Racial affinities evidently had their limits.

As violence erupted in northeast Asia, relations between Japan and the United States remained amicable and even cooperative. When the Boxer Rebellion threatened to drive foreigners out of China in 1899 and 1900, US Secretary of State John Hay proposed an "open-door" policy in China, whereby the world's great powers would guarantee one another equal treatment in commerce and industry while honoring China's territorial integrity. Tokyo was the first party to sign on. Both Japan and the United States also dispatched troops to quell the Boxer Rebellion, the former outpacing all other "allied" forces. "What extraordinary soldiers those little Japs are!" exclaimed Theodore Roosevelt in scornful admiration. And Japan demanded a seat among the world's imperial powers as a racial and martial equal. "One says that the Japanese and Chinese are of another race and that the yellow race will always have a tendency to draw together and unite against the white race," the Japanese prime minister stated. "Nothing is farther from the truth or more absurd." The global alliance in China proved fleeting, though, as Russia's growing presence in Manchuria appeared to endanger the balance of power. Alarmed by Russia's military and financial advances in the region, Japan signed a treaty of alliance with Great Britain in 1902. Two years later, with the tacit support of the United States—which, like Britain and Japan, hoped to contain Russia's sphere of influence—Japan launched a military attack on the Russian fleet in Port Arthur (in Manchuria) and landed ground troops in Korea.[11]

Resolving the "Korea problem"—as Japanese officials conceived their neighbor's military vulnerability, independent diplomacy, and general backwardness—lay at the heart of the Russo-Japanese War. In February 1904, even before the official declaration of war, Japanese forces quickly occupied the port city of Incheon and made their way to Seoul. King Kojong, who had insisted on Korea's neutrality in case of war between Japan and Russia, was compelled to sign a protocol permitting Japanese military operations in Korea that ostensibly also guaranteed "the independence and territorial integrity of the Korean Empire." As word of the protocol spread to the streets of Seoul, so did popular resentment against Japan. Public rallies called for the abrogation of the agreement and the dismissal of Korean officials who had acceded to Japan's demands. Particularly as Koreans engaged in violent acts of resistance—throwing dynamite at the Korean foreign minister's house and sabotaging telegraph lines, roads, and railways—Japanese military authorities usurped the authority of local Korean governments. With the Japanese security state in place, Japan's leaders moved to formalize their control of Korea through a protectorate treaty. Using heavy-handed pressure on King Kojong and his cabinet, Japan exacted the treaty in November 1905 that ceded to Japan complete control over Korea's foreign affairs and a supervisory role in internal matters. Popular outcry against the treaty was immediate and widespread in Korea, creating a new "problem" for the expanding Japanese security state.[12]

As Japan used the Russo-Japanese War to claim sovereignty over Korea, the weakening Korean state desperately sought assistance from the United States. The US-Korea treaty from 1882 afforded a glimmer of hope. The first article stated, "If other Powers deal unjustly or oppressively with either Government, the other will exert their good offices, on being informed of the case, to bring about an amicable arrangement, thus showing their friendly feelings." King Kojong "falls back in his extremity upon his old friendship with America," reported Horace N. Allen, the US minister to Korea. "He is inclined to give a very free and favorable translation to Article I of our treaty of Jenchuan of 1882." The State Department was not so inclined, ordering Allen to "observe absolute neutrality." Allen did not need to be convinced, for he did not see Japan's takeover of Korea as inimical to Korea's interests or America's ambitions. "We will make a real mistake if we allow sentimental reasons to induce us to attempt to bolster up this 'Empire' in its independence," he counseled before the Russo-Japanese War. "These people can not govern themselves. I am no pro-Japanese enthusiast . . . but neither am I opposed to any civilized race taking over the management of these kindly Asiatics for the good of the people and the suppression of oppressive officials, the establishment of order and the development of commerce." Once Japan's protectorate treaty over Korea became official, the United States was the first foreign delegation to withdraw from Seoul.[13]

The Philippines, islands full of active and potential revolutionaries, were not forgotten in the diplomatic negotiations over Korea. As the United States played host to the peace talks in Portsmouth, New Hampshire, to end the Russo-Japanese War in the summer of 1905, US Secretary of War William Howard Taft crossed the Pacific to inspect the Philippines, his old stomping grounds. He stopped over in Tokyo, where he met with Prime Minister Taro Katsura. The resulting Taft-Katsura agreement, endorsed by President Roosevelt and submerged in secrecy for two decades, spelled out the two empires' shared views on "the questions of the Philippine Islands, of Korea, and of the maintenance of general peace in the Far East." Taft began by stating that "Japan's only interest in the Philippines would be, in his opinion, to have these Islands governed by a strong and friendly nation like the United States, and not to have them placed either under the misrule of the natives, yet unfit for self-government, or in the hands of some unfriendly European power." Race always seemed to trump democracy, a view consistent with Japan's previous statements on the Philippines. Katsura, in turn, "confirmed in the strongest terms the correctness of his [Taft's] views . . . and positively stated that Japan does not harbor any aggressive designs whatever on the Philippines; adding that all the insinuations of the yellow peril type are nothing more or less than malicious and clumsy slanders calculated to do mischief to Japan."[14]

With US claims over the Philippines conceded and secured, Taft and Katsura turned their attention to Korea. Katsura noted that "Korea being the direct cause of our war with Russia it is a matter of absolute importance to Japan that a complete solution of the peninsula question should be made as the logical consequence of the war." Like Filipinos, Koreans could not be trusted to govern themselves, lest Korea "draw back to her habit of improvidently resuscitating the same international complications as existed before the war." Japan's mission in Korea, like America's in the Philippines, was avowedly about peace and security. "In view of the foregoing circumstances Japan feels absolutely constrained to take some definite step with a view to precluding the possibility of Korea falling back into her former condition and of placing us again under the necessity of entering upon another foreign war," Katsura argued. Taft sympathized, agreeing that, "in his personal opinion, the establishment by Japanese troops of a suzerainty over Korea to the extent of requiring that Korea enter into no foreign treaties without the consent of Japan was the logical result of the present war and would directly contribute to permanent peace in the East."[15] Essentially disregarding the 1882 treaty with Korea, Taft secured the US empire through imperial Japan. Japan likewise viewed the United States as a critical ally in realizing its imperial ambitions in East Asia. On the Philippines and Korea, US and Japanese officials were in perfect agreement.

High-level diplomacy gradually proved fundamental to securing empire, in part by transforming warmongers into peacemakers and empires into nations. Scarcely seven years after leading the United States to war across the Pacific, Theodore Roosevelt played a prominent role in ending the Russo-Japanese War, a role that earned him the Nobel Peace Prize. In his address to Congress in 1905, President Roosevelt felt arrogant enough to pontificate on peace. "Peace is normally the handmaiden of righteousness," he said, "but when peace and righteousness conflict then a great and upright people can never for a moment hesitate to follow the path which leads toward righteousness, even though that path also leads to war." War was peace, in so many words. Roosevelt called for a second "Conference of Nations," to follow the first held in The Hague in 1899, "in the cause of international peace, justice and good will." It was the "clear duty" of the United States, Roosevelt continued, "to bring nearer the time when the sword shall not be the arbiter among nations" and "to offer, at least to all civilized powers, some substitute for war which will be available in at least a considerable number of instances." His was a vision for the future, when "enlightened statesmanship" might lead to "the protection of the little nations" and "the prevention of war between the big nations." In the emerging hegemonic world order, empires became "civilized powers" and "big nations" while colonies were rendered "protectorates" and "little nations."[16]

As the Russo-Japanese War drew to a close, Korea suffered the fate reserved for "little nations." On August 3, 1905, Roosevelt and his staff were at his home on Long Island, busy preparing for a reception to welcome Japanese and Russian diplomats to the United States, when, according to the *New York Times,* "two diminutive, unassuming Koreans, bent on one of the oddest diplomatic missions in history, appeared, unannounced, in Oyster Bay." They were P. K. Yoon, a Christian pastor from Honolulu, and Syngman Rhee, an undergraduate at George Washington University. "We are not the accredited representatives of the Korean Government," Yoon explained. "We represent the common people of Korea. . . . Among the 'true-seeking hearts' of my country the present crisis has brought about an awakening, and the same is true about the 8,000 Koreans who reside in Hawaii." When asked if Koreans would prefer Russian rule, Rhee responded vehemently. "Russia is looked upon by us as the avowed enemy of all the ancient races in the Far East," he said. "If it came to resisting Russian sovereignty the so-called yellow peoples of Asia would stand together as a unit." Yoon and Rhee hoped that Roosevelt, as the leader of Korea's "oldest friend," would support Korean independence. Roosevelt agreed to a meeting, at which he told them to transmit their memorial through official diplomatic channels. Righteousness and official diplomacy apparently never came into conflict. Without delay, Great Britain and then Russia, through the Portsmouth Treaty, recognized Japan's authority over Korea.[17]

For Roosevelt, whiteness and manhood resolved his virile notions of wielding the "big stick" and manly aspirations of promoting civilized diplomacy, a combination of traits that "Orientals" seemed to contravene. When he received Yoon and Rhee, he was dressed in his "Rough Rider" outfit, evidently reliving his glory days on San Juan Hill. For years, Roosevelt had relished what he considered the regenerating quality of wars, pointing to China as a cautionary tale, for he did not want the United States to "go down before other nations which have not lost the manly and adventurous qualities." In that respect, Roosevelt appreciated and even admired Japan's martial disposition, but he sensed a deeper racial conflict on the horizon. Japan was "a great civilized power of a formidable type," he believed, but "with motives and ways of thought which are not quite those of the powers of our race." During the Russo-Japanese War, Roosevelt pondered Japan's racial motivations. "I am not at all sure that the Japanese people draw any distinctions between the Russians and other foreigners, including ourselves," he wrote privately. "I have no doubt that they include all white men as being people who, as a whole, they dislike, and whose past arrogance they resent; and doubtless they believe their own yellow civilization to be better . . . Japan is an oriental nation, and the individual standard of truthfulness in Japan is low." To Roosevelt, Japan loomed large as a "civilized" threat to white supremacy.[18]

And the Russo-Japanese War quickly took on a racial significance well beyond the realm of high diplomacy. The march of the "nimble, shrewd and enterprising people" over Russia into Korea and the rest of East Asia appeared to signal a threatening pan-Asian formation, according to the *Los Angeles Times*. "The yellow races will be cemented into as homogeneous a sentiment as can be in the least time possible," an editorial surmised in November 1905. Japan deserved "our unstinted admiration" and "our money" in its modernization campaign, including the renovation of its naval fleet, but the newspaper feared an impending race war. "But should this fleet appear some day off the Farallones and shell San Francisco, or in Santa Monica Bay and open fire on Los Angeles," the editorial concluded, "there might be cause to regret."[19] Many African American intellectuals critical of white supremacy and empire were ecstatic. "Triumphant Japan in a class by itself," W. E. B. Du Bois commented. The war, he believed, would break the "foolish modern magic of the word 'white'" and strengthen the possibility of a "colored revolt against white exploitation." The Japanese, classics scholar W. S. Scarborough argued, "have not stopped to argue with the world as to whether they were yellow or white, red or black; they have simply forged ahead in this battle for their rights in spite of the prejudice against them." To white supremacist Lothrop Stoddard, the Russo-Japanese War's greatest casualty was that "the legend of white invincibility lay, a fallen idol, in the dust."[20]

In Japan and across colonized Asia, extending westward to the Ottoman empire, dreams of Japan leading a pan-Asian movement against the West and its colonial order began to take root after the Russo-Japanese War. As colonial exiles and anticolonial students from China, India, Vietnam, the Philippines, and elsewhere gravitated to Tokyo in the opening decade of the twentieth century, they forged links with ultranationalist

Japanese intellectuals envisaging a mighty Japan at the helm of a decolonizing movement toward "Asia for Asians." Organized in 1909, Ajia Gi Kai (Association for the Defense of Asia) looked to a past when "Asia was incomparably the richest continent in terms of nature, population, and agricultural products" that "gave birth to various civilizations and sages." That past gave way to "internal discord, jealousy, and hate" that allowed "Western expansion" to take over. But there was hope for the future in a common past. "Because we Asians have common customs and manners, common spirit and character," Ajia Gi Kai stated, "we must make a hard struggle ourselves for the betterment and development of Asia." An intellectual and political vision borne out of the Russo-Japanese War, pan-Asian solidarity, including a pan-Islamic variant, represented one of the earliest articulations of a global movement against white supremacy and empire. Although the Japanese state continued to focus on cultivating alliances with other imperial powers—to join the West, not to fight it—budding nationalists across Asia interpreted the war as a moment of "awakening" and Japan as a model of inspiration and imitation.[21]

In that context, race threatened to place the United States and Japan on opposing sides of a belligerent line across the Pacific. In the wake of a destructive earthquake in 1906, the San Francisco school board assigned all Chinese, Japanese, and Korean children to a segregated "Oriental" school, an order that rankled Japanese officials and lay persons in Japan and in the United States. Kazan Kayahara, a prominent journalist who wrote for newspapers in Japan and California, expressed the mounting frustration of Japanese migrants in the United States. "Struggle. Struggle like men. . . . Japan is not China. Behind you stand the navy of five hundred thousand tons and the army of one million men. Above all you have the support of forty-five million countrymen. Struggle, endeavor, and overwhelm the white race." The school controversy reached the highest level of government, with Roosevelt trying to cast blame on "only a very small body of our citizens that act badly." "The overwhelming mass of our people cherish a lively regard and respect for the people of Japan," he explained, "and in almost every quarter of the Union the stranger from Japan . . . is treated as the stranger from any part of civilized Europe is and deserves to be treated." Roosevelt went so far as to recommend the extension of naturalization rights to "Japanese who come here intending to become American citizens." His administration never pursued that recommendation.[22]

A diplomatic resolution to the school segregation crisis—through a "Gentlemen's Agreement" in 1907 and 1908 where Japan's government

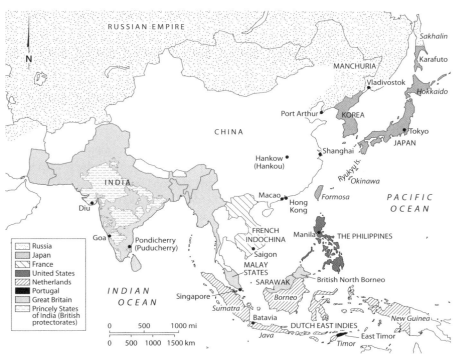

MAP 3. Colonized Asia, ca. 1910. Cartography by Bill Nelson.

promised to curb the emigration of laborers to the United States—
hardly reconciled the two empires' differences. While Japanese officials
saw no contradiction between imperial expansion and international
peace and between loyal Japanese subjects and assimilable American
citizens, US officials increasingly viewed the migration of Japanese subjects as a racial act of war against the United States. Roosevelt had to
pay attention to "the great fact of difference of race," he wrote privately
in 1906, since the mass influx of Japanese "would be a very, very bad
thing indeed, and it would then be too late to have a peaceful, or at least
a non-irritating solution." As American newspapers carried headlines
forecasting an imminent war between Japan and the United States in
1906 and 1907, Roosevelt and his administration prepared the first war
plan on how US forces would fight Japan in particular. To flaunt US
military prowess, Roosevelt decided to send the "Great White Fleet" of
naval cruisers around the world, including a stop in Japan. In October
1908, hundreds of thousands of Japanese welcomed the US fleet to

Tokyo, waving American flags and singing "The Star-Spangled Banner." The overwrought reception, combined with another diplomatic agreement a month later affirming the transpacific status quo, testified to, above all else, existing and escalating tensions between the United States and Japan.[23]

NARRATING REVOLUTION AND SECURITY

Even as official wars, peace treaties, and diplomatic agreements solidified geopolitical boundaries and sanctified imperial states, in part by recasting them as civilized nations, they could not contain subterranean fissures encircling the Pacific. Unruly subjects refused to abide by the dictates of empires and states. In 1874, Nicholas Russel, born Nikolai Sudzilovskii, fled Russia to evade the czarist police trying to arrest him for engaging in revolutionary propaganda and political agitation. After a brief stay in London, where he once spoke at a rally with Karl Marx and Friedrich Engels, Russel earned a medical degree in Bucharest and then moved around Europe, spreading socialist propaganda wherever he could. In 1887, he arrived in San Francisco and became a naturalized US citizen, but Russel had no illusions about what America stood for. "All our democracy is superfluous, about a millimeter deep," he noted. "America is a purely Anglo-Saxon mixture of unsatiated greed, brutal cruelty, and hypocritical bigotry." After the Russian government rejected his petition for permission to return home, Russel set sail for the Kingdom of Hawai'i in 1892, one year before the *haole* (white foreigner) elite staged a coup d'état with the support of the US military. While working as a physician on a sugar plantation, he expressed opposition to the coup. "The rapacious state with white capitalists at its head would to the utmost and unnecessarily restrain the independent Kanaka," he stated. It "would subject him to the iron law of the economic minimum, and would make him adapt to a very intensive economy."[24]

Russel immersed himself in Hawaiian society and politics. By the time the United States annexed Hawai'i in 1898, Russel had established himself as a coffee planter and a vocal critic of *haole* domination. Riding a wave of indigenous political mobilization before the territorial elections of 1900, Russel and the Independent Home Rule Party won a plurality of seats in Hawai'i's senate. "The end of eight years of missionary-sugar planter oligarchy," he predicted after the election. "In order to arouse the natives, we responded with incendiary speeches against the existing government of sugar planters, missionaries, and other white enemies of the Hawaiian Islands. The results of the campaign exceeded our expectations. . . . We are confronted with the prospect of committing a genuine revolution in all Hawaiian legislation from top to bottom." Perhaps buoyed by those results and prospects, Russel was less than modest, racially and otherwise. "Since I am almost the sole white person in both chambers who knows anything about the techniques of the legislative machinery in [a] civilized country," he related in a personal letter, "probably the main part of the burden for the compilation of draft laws, and for the same reason, of literary and scientific documents, will lie with me." Russel's legislative career, however, came to be mired in frustration. Unable to pass even modest reform bills, Russel's brief career in electoral politics hardly effected a legislative revolution. He declined to run again in 1902.[25]

Russel looked farther west to resume his revolutionary activities, which promptly marked him as an enemy of the state in Russia and the United States. After a brief sojourn in China, he agreed in 1905 to represent the Society of Friends of Russian Freedom in Japan. "According to the members of the local society he had succeeded beyond all expectation," the *New York Times* stated, "as is shown by the fact that he has organized under the banner of Socialism nearly all of the Russian soldiers taken prisoners by the Japanese, who are now in detention camps in Japan awaiting transportation to their homes." Upward of thirty thousand Russian soldiers reportedly converted to socialism while imprisoned in Japan, evidently with the blessing of Japanese authorities who were content to undermine the Russian state. Russian officials, in turn, planned to transport most of the radicalized soldiers to Siberia to thwart a revolution at home and pressed the US government to restrict Russel's movements. The US state revoked his passport and citizenship. Russel relocated to Japan, where he published revolutionary literature for Russian exiles and met with aspiring revolutionaries like Sun Yat-sen. Russel moved again in 1907, this time to the Philippines. Although it is not clear why he chose to practice medicine in the US colony, there is no question that he picked a moment ripe with revolutionary possibilities. As rumors of war between the United States and Japan spread, growing numbers of Filipinos, like Russel, looked to Japan to foment a revolution.[26]

News of an impending war between Japan and the United States took on a revolutionary character in and through the Philippines. Almost immediately upon the conclusion of the Russo-Japanese War, Filipinos struggling for independence began sharing stories of a wider conflict in East Asia that might provide an opening to attack the United

States. "There are secret rumors circulating among the inhabitants of the district to the effect that very shortly hostilities will break out between the United States, China and Japan," reported an agent for the Philippine Constabulary in 1906. "It will be the opportunity for the troops in the field to fight against the United States Army, and that the independence to which they aspire will be easily obtained." Intelligence reports indicated that Filipinos kept apprised of the school segregation controversy in San Francisco and other sources of tension between Japan and the United States to determine when war—and their chance to strike for liberation—would commence. By the beginning of 1907, the growing resentment against US colonial rule and rising faith in Japan's assistance had become inextricable, at least in the minds of US officials. "Superficially, everything in Luzon is in a fairly quiet condition, but there is a very strong and nasty undercurrent," related a Constabulary official to the US ambassador to Japan. "The people all over are convinced that there will soon be war with Japan and wild-eyed rumors of all kinds are flying about as to its effect upon the country."[27]

The Constabulary's Information Division initially attempted to attribute the rumors to a lone individual, José Anacleto Ramos, who had adopted the Japanese name Ishikawa. An active participant in movements for Philippine independence since 1880, according to the Constabulary, Ramos first traveled to Japan soon after the Sino-Japanese War, in part to try to secure the Japanese government's support of Philippine independence. While in Japan, he married a Japanese woman, became a naturalized subject of Japan, and received a government pension. Ramos reportedly maintained contact with Filipino *insurrectos* and, during and after the Philippine-American War, traveled back and forth to the Philippines. In December 1906, Rafael Crame of the Information Division interviewed Ramos and then composed Ramos's "memoir" for the US government. "The Japanese, more especially since the successful issue of the late war with Russia," the memoir began, "aim at, if not the absolute domination of Eastern Asia, at least at being the preponderating power in it, and, if not the complete expulsion of the Caucasian races, as represented by the European and American nations, from that quarter of the globe, the relegation of them to an unimportant position." Japan was preparing for war with the United States, Ramos related, to effect those ambitions, including military plans against Hawai'i and the Philippines. Filipinos, he predicted, would be either "indifferent" or "if they, as a people, took any part in a war it is safe to say it would be in the shape of an uprising in favor of the Japanese intervention."[28]

While Constabulary agents monitored Ramos's contacts and conversations, they began to fear a movement potentially much larger and more revolutionary than Ramos. By the second half of 1907, US officials were on high alert, fearing a general uprising involving Aguinaldo and other former revolutionary leaders. "As much in Cavite as in Tondo the Japanese propaganda spreads in such a manner that the opinion of the lower class will go in favor of the Japanese in the event of war with them," noted Justo Sagasa, a Constabulary informant. Ordinary working peoples of the Philippines were enraged by the state of affairs under US colonial rule. An actor who performed at Rizal Theatre, Sagasa related, told him what he heard regularly from the "workmen's gallery." "Perhaps when the Japanese govern the Islands our theatres will have more liberties, and then we will be able to criticise the government men without incurring responsibilities as now," they reportedly said. "For every word against these government men the sedition law is applied to us, . . . [but we will] get more liberties if Japan fulfills her word to allow the Filipino people self-government, although we must pay a peso poll tax for her protectorate." Witnessing political rallies displaying huge Katipunan flags and trampling of the Stars and Stripes, US officials felt the need to wage a propaganda campaign of their own. Harry H. Bandholtz, head of the Constabulary, recommended reminding Filipinos of cordial relations between the United States and Japan and of Japan's usurpation of Korea and Formosa.[29]

In the context of US insecurities over the Philippines, the Japanese state's historical record mattered less than what Japan came to symbolize: hope for Philippine liberation—*kalayaan*. In October 1907, Mariano Nicolas, a Constabulary agent, filed a report on his conversation with Angel Catsalian, an electrician who had received his vocational training in Japan. Catsalian came to the Constabulary's attention several months earlier when he and a group of friends, who had also studied in Japan, were caught making "some chemical experiments with dynamite." Dominador Gomez, the outspoken labor leader who was not above collaborating with the colonial regime, reported them to the US authorities as "a group of Anarchists." "We are continually receiving from our friends and countrymen in Japan formulae for dynamite of different strengths that have been experimented with in that place," Catsalian told Nicolas. "But . . . we know that if we do not have Anarchy in the Philippines we will never have liberty." Asked if anarchism was truly possible in the Philippines, he responded, "Yes Sir, sooner or later we will have it but not through those who represent us." When

Nicolas offered to join an anarchist society if one were started in the Philippines, Catsalian suggested that he go to Japan, where he said that such an association of Filipino and Japanese members already existed. Other intelligence reports on "extremely radical" Filipino political leaders "flirting with the Japs" and preaching "socialistic independence" increasingly melded Japan and radicalism in the Philippines, projecting onto Japan far more than Japan's official treaties and policies.[30]

Japan, henceforth deemed a grave threat to US security and sovereignty, acquired a central place in US narratives of revolution and sedition in the Philippines. Within months after being appointed the Constabulary chief, Bandholtz wrote a lengthy letter to Captain Ralph H. Van Deman, a US Army officer who had systematized military intelligence during the Philippine-American War. Van Deman was now back with the Military Information Division (MID) in Washington, DC. "It has often impressed me as strange that our government makes such little effort to protect our interests from spies of other countries," Bandholtz wrote. "Here in the Philippines today, we are simply slopping over with Japanese spies. . . . As a rule, they are undoubtedly engaged in making maps but, in some places, when they strike a receptive condition, they do what they can to stir up feeling against the American government." "At heart, all of the Filipinos desire their independence," he admitted, but Japan, in his mind, ultimately explained the upsurge in anti-American activities. "From present indications, I should say that their policy instead of armed intervention was to incite the Filipinos to frequent uprisings and disturbances in the hopes of creating such a disgust in America that our government would be willing to get rid of the Islands at any price," Bandholtz concluded. "And, as near as I can see, our government is not well equipped for stopping or preventing this kind of work on the part of the Japanese."[31]

Van Deman enthusiastically reinforced Bandholtz's assumptions and conclusions. Back in 1901, Van Deman replied, he had "unearthed" two Japanese military officers in Manila, whom he was able to drive out. They were "active members of the Japanese-Filipino Party which was formed in Japan by J. A. Ramos alias J. A. Ishikawa." Particularly since Van Deman was in the midst of preparing a report on Japan for President Roosevelt, he was enthralled by Bandholtz's observations. "I wish you would keep me posted as to what is going on in the line of Japanese activity in the Philippines for I am deeply interested in the subject," he wrote back. "There is no doubt but that the Japanese-Filipino Party I spoke of was formed for the purpose of drawing closer together the people of the Philippines and those of Japan for the purpose of aiding the Filipinos in throwing off American rule when the time should be propicious [*sic*]." Japan's designs seemed self-evident. "She proposes to control Asia and intends first to unite the peoples of Asia under her protection and then eat them up as she has recently done with Korea," Van Deman stated confidently. With his own views confirmed, Bandholtz could hardly contain himself. "Like all Orientals, the Jap is a good waiter and eliminates time from all consideration," he warned. Bandholtz hoped the US government would "boost our navy as rapidly as possible and deliberately provoke war with Japan and destroy her sea power before she makes it."[32]

Bandholtz took pride in that "we are finding out more in the Constabulary about Japanese plans and intentions than they are in the Information Division of the Army," but the various agencies of the US security apparatus were becoming centralized and integrated, in ways that at once magnified and deflected attention from Filipino struggles against the US empire. On the ground, the Constabulary's foremost concern remained Filipino resistance. Distress over Filipino cries of *Fuera los Americanos!* (Away with the Americans!) appeared in the same reports as Japan's reputed imperial designs. At MID headquarters in Washington, DC, those reports were then filed and assimilated with reports on Japan from around the world. In June 1907, a US agent in St. Petersburg, Russia, transmitted a confidential letter on "a private affair and in a private cabinet, at which only English and Japs were present." The "proverbially silent" and "devilish sly" Japanese, the letter began, opened up once alcohol started flowing. One reportedly said, "Gentlemen, you hear it said that Japan will take the Philippine Islands when she desires and is ready. *She is ready now* and to take the Sandwich Islands as well . . . I tell you *we will make a Japanese colony of California and of the Pacific Coast of America, Alaska included.*" Japan, the inebriated official said, would never forget or forgive "the enemy who has insulted us and our children merely because we are Japanese." By way of Russia and elsewhere, Filipino resistance became enmeshed in a vast Japanese conspiracy.[33]

Military intelligence, in due course, pieced together fragmented accounts of the Philippines and Japan into a racial narrative of US national security. Undoubtedly with Van Deman's assistance, Lieutenant Colonel T. W. Jones, the MID chief, authored in November 1907 perhaps one of the earliest global surveys of US national security interests, titled "A Report Compiled from Reports and Other Data Showing the Activities of Japanese and Japanese Officials in Relation to the

United States and Her Possessions." In the "confidential" report—equivalent to "classified" later—Jones stressed the need to move beyond "diplomatic utterances," particularly since Japan's "diplomacy is Oriental with a strong mixture of Russian methods." Having made that racial distinction clear, he assured the War Department's chief of staff that "care has been taken to state nothing as a fact which cannot be proven by reference to the mass of documents, reports, etc., on the subject on file in the Second (Military Information) Division of the General Staff." Because Japan's relations with the Philippines was the oldest and highest "in importance" among US "possessions," Jones devoted more than half of his report to Japanese relations with Filipinos in Japan and in the Philippines. It was also where a history of revolution and insurgency was fresh and alive, as in Cuba, where, according to Jones, Japanese agents were likewise "gathering military information" and possibly "engaged in fomenting insurrection." Japanese presence further made Cuba a matter of US national security.[34]

Defending US security around the world came to be equated with preventing a revolution, a national project that, in effect, elided and advanced the US empire under the guise of international relations and racial conflict. The ties between Japan and the Philippines dated back to the Philippine Revolution against Spain, Jones argued, when José A. Ramos sought refuge and support in Japan in 1896. Japan's government demonstrated every inclination to support Filipino exiles and revolutionaries against Spain, but, once the United States entered the scene, its policies could not be so brazen. Gearing up for war with Russia, Jones surmised, Japan did not want to risk a conflict with the United States, but its officials maintained close communications with Filipino revolutionaries in Manila and Hong Kong. Jones summed up Japan's grand designs, which he claimed became manifest by 1899. "Japan has, for many years, desired to unite the people of Asia, with herself as the dominant and controlling power," he stated. "She believes that she has a Heaven-sent mission to control the affairs of the Extreme Orient and all her efforts have been directed to this end for a long time back." It was in Japan's interest, therefore, to assist Filipino revolutionaries, for "a Philippines governed and controlled by Filipinos, especially when that control was acknowledgedly acquired with the aid of Japan, would be much easier to dominate than a Philippines governed by an European nation or by the United States."[35]

Completely disregarding Filipino grievances against US colonial rule, Jones fixated on Japan's racial and imperial ambitions. Through diplomatic channels and at times military personnel, he explained, Japan actively aided and abetted the Philippine insurgency against the United States in a mission to make "Asia for the Asiatics." Over the course of the Philippine-American War, according to Jones, "there were frequent rumors current among the Filipinos to effect that Japan was about to intervene in their behalf: that a Japanese army was about to land in the Philippines, etc. etc." Discounted at the time as a stratagem to encourage Filipino forces, he now believed that there was substance to those widespread rumors. "Nor have these rumors ceased with the suppression of the insurrection," Jones added, "but have been more or less constant up to the present time." Echoing Bandholtz almost verbatim, he stated that Japan's strategy was "to incite the Filipinos to frequent uprisings and disturbances in the hope of creating such a disgust in America that our government would be willing to get rid of the Islands at any price, and as near as I can see, our government is not well equipped for stopping or preventing this kind of work on the part of the Japanese." Since Japan's antipathy to the United States in particular stemmed from a "feeling of injured national and racial pride," Jones predicted that "racial antagonism" would remain "a very delicate and difficult" issue for the foreseeable future.[36]

If a potential revolution in the Philippines consumed Jones's attention, his global survey ultimately rendered the Philippines and Filipinos minor footnotes in a racial struggle between two "big nations." After surveying Japanese presence on the "Pacific Slope" of North America and the US-Mexico border, Jones took comfort in the normalcy of international espionage. "The evidences [sic] of the gathering of military information within our borders are numerous," he noted. "Every nation of any size or importance in the world does this kind of work on a greater or less scale." The Japanese stood out for their "notoriously cautious and secretive" nature, with their efforts in and against the United States "remarkable" for their relative conspicuousness. "It must always be remembered, too, that every Japanese, male or female, is a government spy, whether in their own country or in a foreign one," Jones cautioned. That collective determination, combined with Japan's renewed investments in the military, led Jones to an ominous conclusion about Japan. "Whatever her plans may be, we may rest assured that . . . whatever policy she has adopted will be carried out to the bitter end," he wrote. "We may be sure that her people will accept cheerfully any sacrifice which will aid their country to place herself where they believe she properly belongs in the congress of nations, and we may also rest assured that no treaty obligations or past declarations will stand in her way when she has once determined on her line of action."[37]

CONFRONTING THE US SECURITY STATE

The Philippines might have remained there, in the footnotes of history, but Filipinos mobilizing against the US empire made sure that their struggles retained the spotlight. When the Philippine Commission prohibited the display of the Katipunan flag in 1907, *El Renacimiento,* an independent newspaper that had exposed Constabulary abuses two years earlier and survived criminal charges of libel, was "frothing at the mouth," according to the chief of the Constabulary. In column after column in 1908 and 1909, the newspaper laid bare America's history of brutality and hypocrisy. "Colonization invariably means absorption, even though they make a pretense of hiding it under golden fetters," an editorial read. "The bread of slavery is hard and bitter." Filipinos had once looked to the United States for inspiration, *El Renacimiento* pointed out, but not anymore. "We believed that the dawn came with the Statue of Liberty, (of New York) and the Constitution and the example of Lincoln encouraged the hope," another editorial stated. "The prism is broken!" Likening the position of Filipinos to Seminoles and other Indigenous peoples of North America, *El Renacimiento* called on Filipinos to awaken to their circumstances. "How have the Indians come out in their life with the Yankees?" it asked. "To quiet them the whites called on the troops . . . it is not certain but that the very noble of Lincoln was the one who said that it was a virtuous action, a worthy action, to shoot all Indians upon sight." Filipino struggles for liberation would mark "a cry against tyrannies."[38]

It was within that context of struggling against the US empire that the editors of *El Renacimiento* turned to Japan for hope and inspiration. A war between the United States and Japan would mean an immediate Japanese takeover of the island of Luzon, the newspaper predicted, a reprise of the Russo-Japanese War, except this time Japan would receive "the aid of the malcontents of the American sovereignty." *El Renacimiento* did not desire a new colonial master, but it adamantly opposed US colonial rule. "Filipinos, . . . we do not want Japan as ruler," an editorial counseled in December 1908, "nevertheless, we want her as a leader, as a redeemer, as a guide, as breath to the existence of the nations of the Orient and of a people gathered under the same name and united by ties of fraternity and of blood more or less strong." "The Orient for the Orientals!" exclaimed another column demanding the withdrawal of European and American interests "from the immense territory of Asia." Instructing Filipinos to "remain rebels at heart," *El Renacimiento* advised: "Perhaps we ought to learn the Japanese smile of concealing plans and chimeras." By the summer of 1909, sentiments against the United States had grown so widespread that the newspaper declared that the "dominion of the Pacific belongs to Japan." In a piercing editorial titled "Do you want more loyalty?" it asked US officials, "Why force harmonious relations upon the false foundation of a conquest?"[39]

From the perspective of US officials, Mariano Ponce's association with *El Renacimiento* helped to explain and intensify the newspaper's revolutionary agenda. Ever since Ponce returned from Japan and took over the editorship, Bandholtz believed, "the Japanese question has begun to forge to the front in the reports of my agents." Ponce, "the ancient patriot" who had served as Aguinaldo's emissary to Japan ten years earlier, and others were "daily turning out columns of rank sedition" that seemed to suggest an alliance with the Japanese government. "The hand of Japan is now apparent over here only through the writing of her agent Mariano Ponce in the 'Renacimiento,'" the Constabulary chief inferred. "I have no proof, but I a[m] convinced that the Japanese government owns or at least controls that paper." After the publication of another "certainly seditious and incendiary" editorial, Bandholtz concluded that "the Japanese are unquestionably doing their utmost to stir up racial hatred and feeling between the Americans and the Filipinos." Ponce's views in particular were deemed "the more intriguing and the more radical" among Filipinos with ties to Japan. His personal history, declared the head of the Constabulary's Information Division, left "no doubt but that his intention is not only the destruction of the American political power in the Philippines but contemplates the overthrowing of the whole political social and religious fabric not only in these islands but everywhere else, and in this, the Philippines would be merely a detail or so to speak a stepping stone towards his end."[40]

Resistance against the US empire continued to mount. In early 1909, workers began staging a wave of labor strikes, particularly against US firms. When sailors and stevedores on the docks and workers on the railroad and streetcar systems walked off their jobs in Manila, the Constabulary retaliated with "an old Spanish law" and outright intimidation. Bandholtz "quietly sent word" to Dominador Gomez and another labor leader that, "in case any intimidation or violence was resorted to, I feared they might be accidentally hurt." Gomez proceeded to try to organize a strike by Filipinos on Manila's police force, to demand the same wages as their American counterparts. Exploitation and repression also bred acrimony outside of Manila. The Constabulary officer in charge of southern Luzon found "a general feeling of insecurity" in March 1909. "There are all the elements in the Paracale district for a nice little labor and racial war," he reported. "Several big, husky Americans on the dredge work are accustomed to kicking and striking the Filipino workmen and the volume of G——D—— niggers, black S.O.B.'s etc. took me back to the days of '99." Under such circumstances, Filipino workers felt compelled to organize. "There is not much in the way of ladronism doing now," Bandholtz noted, "but our little brown proteges are getting more up-to-date, and strikes are taking the place of bandolerismo."[41] The state of affairs in the Philippines remained explosive.

What Bandholtz dismissed as "ladronism" also refused to fade into history. Since 1904 on the island of Samar, *pulajan* guerrillas, who combined a messianic religion with revolutionary nationalism, repeatedly foiled the Constabulary's "pacification" campaign. *Pulajan* units continued to engage, evade, and frustrate Constabulary and US Army forces for years. "The pulajanes are wild animals to whom it would be difficult or impossible to convey the idea of unconditional surrender followed by due Court process and later consideration by the Executive on the merits of the case," a Constabulary agent complained in April 1909.[42] Meanwhile, farther to the southwest, Jikiri and his elusive band of Muslim "Moros" refused to submit to imperial authority, wreaking havoc on US and British authorities in the Sulu archipelago and North Borneo. In July 1909, a US cavalry force cornered Jikiri and four companions in a cave near the island of Jolo. Though greatly outnumbered, Jikiri's small band exacted "a terrible price," killing and wounding dozens before being "exterminated." If his political agenda was not clearly articulated or organized, Jikiri's killing took on a wider political significance in the Philippines. "The progress of civilization, or to speak more correctly, North American domination," *El Renacimiento* announced, "found in Jikiri an obstacle to its establishing itself in the Jolo Archipelago and therefore he had to be suppressed." The newspaper concluded the eulogy with a poem incorporating Muslims into the Filipino "race": "The days will pass! The Empires and masters also!/Rest in peace, Jikiri! Thy race is praying!"[43]

At the same time in 1909, Filipino recruits in the Constabulary organized a mutiny on the island of Mindanao. For years, residents in and around Davao had witnessed growing tensions with the US colonial regime, particularly over the appropriation of lands and labor for plantation settlement and the assassination of the American governor in 1906. In early June 1909, twenty-three members of the Constabulary, fed up with the physical and emotional abuses meted out by their commanding officers, turned their guns against two of their superiors and later came into a skirmish with a group of Americans. Bandholtz, who happened to be traveling nearby, vowed to "fill Davao full to overflowing and scour every nook and cranny until we killed or captured every one of the mutineers." Although the armed uprising lasted only a few days, Constabulary and US military forces spent more than a month tracking down the insurrectionists. In part because they received assistance from local residents, five of the mutineers were never captured. Bandholtz tried to identify specific causes behind the mutiny—Mariano Ponce's recent visit and fiery editorials, abusive local commanders and Filipino officers ("the lax disciplinary ideas of an American captain of Semitic origin" and "a mestizo Filipino . . . very liberal in applying kicks and blows"), and "the peculiarities of character of some of the natives." His efforts to frame the mutiny as a "sporadic, purely local" affair, with "no political aspect whatever," reflected Bandholtz's wishes far more than the revolutionary climate sweeping across the Philippines.[44]

Toward the end of 1909, signs of insurrection and revolution appeared everywhere. "I dislike very much to say this, . . . however, it must be admitted that conditions can grow up in any district, similar, if not so bad, as those at Davao, without a district director knowing about it," a Constabulary officer wrote from Iloilo, Visayas, shortly after the Davao mutiny. "Especially when senior inspectors and other officers are not loyal to him and do not keep him informed." If members of the Constabulary could not be trusted, reports from Constabulary agents and informants painted a more unsettling picture. One confidential agent from Manila related, "The rumor of impending insurrection is constant and in nearly all places of the city they talk of nothing else; many families are preparing to leave the city. . . . It is said insistently that the insurrection will begin in the first part of January, and will be general throughout Luzon where they say people are already prepared for it." Commemorations of Rizal Day on December 30, 1909, were the biggest ever, another report noted. In Tondo, crowds gathered for five nights in a row. "Compatriots, let us imitate Rizal who shed his blood for his people," a speaker pleaded. "If you are fearful, we shall not secure our liberty, and if we do this we shall secure our independence." Another stated, "if America pays no heed to us, let us imitate what Andrés Bonifacio did."[45]

The revolutionary atmosphere seemed to grow more palpable, day by day, month by month. Though outlawed years earlier, seditious plays made a comeback. In January 1910, a Constabulary agent reported on the "very exciting" performance of *Ang Iskilang Partir sa Corregidor* (The Worthy Martyr of Corregidor) at Rizal Theatre on a Saturday night. In the second act, when the US governor-general refused to allow the protagonist's wife and daughter to visit him in Bilibid prison, the scene "provoked the indignation of the masses of laborers in the theatre and one shouted 'Fuera Americano' (Away with the American)." The play ended with the protagonist gaining his freedom, represented by "actors dressed in three colors" placing "themselves in a triumphal car of liberty, showing, with this group, the true Filipino flag." "The tendency of this drama is to provoke the hatred of the ignorant against the Americans and, for my part," the agent concluded, "I fear the consequences." The political mood harkened back to the Philippine-American War a decade earlier and perhaps even more so to the Philippine Revolution of 1896. "I know that the survivors of the Katipunan are just as fanatical in wishing to die for their country now as when Andrés Bonifacio was living," another agent observed. Reports of a "fanatic sect called 'Colorum'" spreading across the provinces of Luzon, particularly among women, likewise drew fear, because members were "re-organizing and preparing to take part in the insurrection."[46]

Amid the revolutionary rumblings, US officials revamped their surveillance of what they saw as an alliance between Filipino revolutionaries and imperial Japan. Describing Manila as "a hotbed of incipient insurrection" in October 1909, Bandholtz became convinced that the "Jap agents are doing everything in their power to stir up our little proteges to some kind of revolutionary activity." In his calculation, any "seditious and incendiary" expression was evidence that the Japanese were fanning "racial hatred and feeling between the Americans and the Filipinos." Bandholtz ordered Constabulary agents and informants to monitor Japanese officials and residents in the Philippines and their Filipino contacts, creating a dragnet that reinforced his presumptions. "I have lately picked up a man who, becoming scared at our watching him, came in voluntarily and admitted that he was in the employ of the Japanese agent Ysikawa," he reported proudly. The veracity of such confessions and reports mattered less than that US officials believed them to be true. When Bandholtz heard that the US ambassador to Japan did not believe the Japanese government to be involved in Philippine affairs, he did not reconsider his views. Instead, he likened the situation to the US position in Cuba, where "the American government took no action but in which its sympathies and those of the American people were with the Cuban insurgents." In Japan, he saw a mirror image of the United States, except without the latter's "humanitarian ideas." He had no doubt that the Japanese would aid a revolution if given the chance.[47]

After meeting with Bandholtz and other high-ranking US officials, Governor-General W. Cameron Forbes proposed to the US secretary of war a covert plan to "take certain precautionary measures with the object of creating among the Filipinos a public opinion distrustful of Japan, their methods and intentions toward the Philippines." The first step, he suggested, would be for the MID to dispatch "special agents," preferably Filipinos, to Formosa, Manchuria, and Korea to gather information on Japan's autocratic policies toward its "dependencies." That information could then be distributed in three different ways across the Philippines to mold "the general public opinion." A Filipino political party could be persuaded to adopt "a plank opposing aggression of any foreign power with the idea of changing the sovereignty over the Philippine Islands, and especially by any foreign power that has a monarchical form of government." Looking further into the future, Forbes suggested the organization of "a society among the Filipina school teachers which shall send out to the teachers the necessary letters and literature calculated to instill in the minds of the youthful Filipinos a rational distrust of Japan." The third method would be for the US government to purchase and control a newspaper, which was not to serve or appear as "an active government organ" but to be "at the same time actively and directly hostile to Japan." Since it was "a matter of United States strategy," Forbes asked for an annual budget of $25,000 from the president's "secret service fund" to carry out the operation.[48]

Within a month, in November 1909, Bandholtz began executing Forbes's plan to spread anti-Japanese propaganda. "I am having translated into Spanish all the anti-Japanese articles that the Military Information Division is sending me," he boasted, "and having them published in all the papers printed in Spanish excepting EL RENACIMIENTO which will not publish them." Focusing particularly on "Japanese abuses in Korea and Formosa," the articles, according to Bandholtz, frightened the "Japanese sympathizers" and created "quite a revulsion of feeling." He was especially delighted that some local newspapers were "becoming anti-Japanese" and accusing El Renacimiento of being a lackey to the Japanese. Although pressure was building against El Renacimiento, the newspaper took the offensive. A representative of

El Renacimiento met with Bandholtz to deny the accusations and to ask directly for the anti-Japanese articles for publication. Bandholtz soon realized that the newspaper would likely use his articles to publish an exposé of the US propaganda machine. "I am convinced this was a trap and I told him that, altho my position was an humble one," he recounted. "I was a government employee and my aiding in such a matter officially might be the cause of international difficulties." The US colonial security state nonetheless conveyed its message loud and clear that sentiments favoring Japan would be regarded unfavorably as seditious and insurrectionary.[49]

Toward that end, US officials decided to shut *El Renacimiento* down. After the newspaper published its infamous editorial on "Aves de Rapiña [Birds of Prey]" in October 1908, Dean C. Worcester, a zoologist who held the position of the secretary of the interior in the US colonial regime, became enraged. Without naming Worcester explicitly, *El Renacimiento* had mocked his scientific pretenses that camouflaged his true mission "to espy in his flight, with the eye of a bird of prey, where there are large deposits of gold." Worcester pursued criminal charges of libel against the newspaper. In early 1909, Bandholtz reported, "the relations between Filipinos and Americans here in Manila has been greatly stirred up by the Renacimiento trial." Not content with a guilty verdict, Worcester filed suit for damages. The ensuing judgment against the newspaper and the seizure of its property forced the newspaper to suspend operations in January 1910. If Worcester won in the courts, *El Renacimiento* prevailed in the court of public opinion. The newspaper's closure, a Constabulary agent reported, was "the favorite topic for all," framed across the Philippines as "a determined struggle between the honor of the Government and the dignity of the Filipino people." "It has also been said *sotto voce* that, as the suspension of a Korean newspaper cost Prince Ito his life," the agent continued, "it is very possible that the suspension of El Renacimiento may cost the Honorable Worcester his life." As in colonial Korea, the state could not eradicate anticolonial longings.[50]

In the Philippines, the anti-Japanese campaign had a feeble and ironic effect, as those demanding national independence embraced Japan as a potential ally. In late 1909, as during the Philippine Revolution thirteen years earlier, popular *espiritistas* (spiritual figures) began prophesying that war would commence between the United States and Japan within one year and that, if Filipinos sided with Japan, the islands would finally win independence. And growing numbers of Filipinos concluded that siding with Japan would make sense. At a meeting of the Columbian Society in November 1909, a group of *pensionados*—Filipino students who had received scholarships to study in the United States—debated the question of a possible war between the United States and Japan. When a speaker voiced a preference for America, a Constabulary informant reported, "the other members hissed the speaker so severely that he was forced to discontinue his remarks." By the spring of 1910, popular resentment against US colonial rule was inescapable. "I cannot recall when there was such a general feeling of distrust and dislike towards Americans on the part of Filipinos as there is today," observed Bandholtz. The imminent appearance of Halley's Comet intensified the anticipatory atmosphere. Felipe Salvador, a "pretty wily *hombre*" leading the Colorum movement, reportedly told his followers, "Just as soon as the comet shines in all its splendor, the era of the happy emancipation of the Philippines will be born." A Constabulary agent suggested that Salvador was working with Japanese military instructors and awaiting arms shipments from Japan.[51]

If the projection of a vast Japanese conspiracy reproduced racial narratives of US national security, the US colonial security state failed to dictate how stories of race and empire were told in the Philippines. A Japanese resident of Manila, a Constabulary informant stated, asked him "some important questions" on how Filipinos, specifically "the revolutionists," would respond to "hostilities between the United States and Japan." "The Filipinos ought all to know, that the Yankees will never give them any more autonomy than what they have already granted them," he reportedly said. "For our part, we like and esteem the natives of this part of the Orient as they are of nearly the same race and are of the same color, while the whites, or Americans, despise all persons of a colored race. See their history, how they have hated and exterminated the Pequod [*sic*] Indians, the Creeks and others in different parts of America and Africa." While the Constabulary released articles on Japan's abuses in Korea and Formosa, some Filipinos countered with stories of Japan's high regard of Filipinos. The Japanese, a speaker reportedly said at a clandestine meeting, "resemble the Filipinos in race and color" and recognize that "Filipinos are not in the state of savagery in which the Koreans are." Japan, he argued, took over Korea only to prevent a European power from doing so and would eventually grant Koreans independence to "form part of the league of the peoples of the Orient."[52]

Even as romanticizing imperial Japan reinforced the US security state's bifurcating logic, US officials could scarcely comprehend or contain Filipino revolutionaries. As early as November 1909, some Constabulary reports cast doubt on the notion that the vast majority of

Filipinos would support Japan. In a report on the widespread nature of "revolutionary agitation," a secret agent stressed that "Katipuneros prefer death to the Japanese." A Constabulary agent concurred later, concluding that "survivors of the Katipunan" were "enemies of the American government" *and* "infinitely more inimical to the Japanese and Japanophiles here." The formal annexation of Korea in 1910 further sullied many Filipinos' infatuation with Japan. Japan's actions, Pedro Mercado of the Constabulary reported, convinced Filipinos that "they can expect nothing good from Japan to judge from what happened to Korea and other peoples." Such reports should have comforted US officials, but the conflation of Japan and revolution had placed the Japanese and Filipinos on the same side of the color line. In that racial equation, it did not seem possible to reject the United States and Japan. As if talking to himself, Bandholtz denied his insecurities to protect his American manhood. "I don't want you to think that I am an hysterical old maid nor that we are at all rattled over the situation," he informed the White House. "Some of these little people can no more help conspiring than they can help fighting cocks; we are obliged to consider both as objectionable, but we should take neither too seriously."[53]

In spite of their growing security apparatus—or precisely because of it—US officials' surveillance of Japanese residents and Filipino "Japanophiles" hardly made US claims to sovereignty more secure. When Bandholtz decided to tour the northern provinces in January 1910, rumors circulated that he was leaving "for the purpose of catechizing the principal Japanophile leaders." "Many comments are made on this story everywhere," a Constabulary report stated, "and the Japanophiles, enemies of the government, laugh and make fun of these plans of the government for they say that . . . [the] mission will fail." Although US officials must have winced when they read that report, they craved and demanded information on anyone possibly affiliated with imperial Japan. And Constabulary agents supplied such information in bulk, providing sustenance to the idea of a Japanese conspiracy. In May 1910, a secret agent recounted his conversation with a Japanese physician about arms shipments and Japanese support of the Philippines. "We are all soldiers, even the women," the doctor reportedly said. "If the Americans declare liberty now there will be war just the same, for we shall take Hawaii and they will pay us. Only here there will be no more war, brother. Because when all we of Asia are one, we will make the whites look foolish here." Perhaps the Japanese physician truly uttered those words, but it was equally plausible that "Japanophiles" got another good laugh by making the Constabulary and the US state in the Philippines more paranoid, more distrustful.[54]

Fueled by Filipino revolutionaries and agents of the US colonial security state, rumors of an impending war between the United States and Japan ultimately bore witness to the US empire's insecurities. More and more Filipinos became emboldened to speak openly about national liberation. When Secretary of War Jacob M. Dickinson visited Lucena in August 1910, he was welcomed with a banner that read, "The Filipinos desire immediate Independence." When the secretary proceeded to deliver a speech on various improvements made by the US government—such as that the "Americans will not consent that the banner hoisted here be hauled down through offensive means"—he reportedly "made the people indignant, arousing heated comments." In the wake of the secretary's official visit, *El Mercantil* issued a candid editorial. "The Filipino people do not ask the Americans to lend them their capital, nor to give them their lights, nor to exploit their wealth, nor to govern them with justice . . . the only thing asked is that they go; a conclusive formula, the Basis and compendium of all their desires." The Philippine independence movement—and US state surveillance of it—expanded apace. That made an undercover agent nervous. "I believe that in order to be better informed it is necessary for me to join them," he confided in a report on various so-called Japanophiles, "but I fear that the authorities may take me for one of them, and therefore I consult you about it."[55] That was the folly of race, empire, and security at work.

MOBILIZING REVOLUTION AND SECURITY

Imperial insecurities, framed as a matter of national security and international relations, drove US officials across the Pacific. En route to the Philippines, Secretary Dickinson stopped over in Japan, where Bandholtz of the Philippine Constabulary greeted him. It was an occasion for Bandholtz to travel across East Asia and to enjoy fine meals—better than "the dyspepsia-encouraging Manila profusion"—and good company, first with British colonial authorities in Hong Kong and then with the highest authorities of Japan. At the first official dinner in Tokyo, the Japanese foreign minister deplored "a conspiracy to create misunderstanding between the United States and Japan" and forecast the continuation of "harmonious relations." Behind the scenes, Bandholtz informed the US ambassador and Japanese officials of "a situation that was not imaginary but real," with "the anti-Government outfit . . .

constantly preaching on the approaching war between Japan and the United States." The Japanese consul in Manila, he complained, encouraged "Filipino conspirators" like Mariano Ponce by consorting with them. Through diplomatic channels, the consul was replaced immediately, after which, according to Bandholtz, "our secret service reports in regard to Japanese activity dropped off seventy-five percent." Once back in the Philippines, Bandholtz nevertheless felt apprehensive about Japan's intentions. Official statements notwithstanding, he was convinced that "with oriental shrewdness she is attending to what she considers her more pressing needs and that with oriental patience she will bide her time and not attempt to eject us until she feels certain of success." Bandholtz despised those "Oriental" traits that betrayed his sense of proper manhood and national dignity.[56]

To US officials' consternation, Filipino travels on the same routes seemed to portend more immediate and revolutionary dangers. When Isabelo de los Reyes left for Japan in 1910, speculations of his collaboration with the Japanese government distressed US authorities. In March, a Constabulary agent learned that "the people of Ilokos" were refusing to pay their debts or to go to work because of letters sent by de los Reyes "advising them to prepare for war and to store up all they could, for war between America and Japan was inevitable and that at the latest, it would be in May." De los Reyes was busy in Japan, according to Constabulary reports, making arrangements for the shipment of arms, money, and "revolutionary pamphlets written by celebrated Spanish anarchists." By July, a secret agent learned that de los Reyes planned to return home soon to form a Socialist Party in the Philippines. "It is believed, and with reason, that if such Socialist Party is formed, it will be truly formidable," he stated. "Socialistic ideas are rooted here in popular sentiment. Only an organization to unify them is lacking." Another secret agent likewise reported that some Filipinos were talking about the need for "socialism or anarchy here, and thus the great Filipinos who surround the American government would not again play traitor to the people."[57] If the widespread demand for Philippine independence unnerved US authorities, the specter of anarchism or socialism leading the Filipino masses deepened their fears.

De los Reyes, for his part, understood the rules of confronting the US security state. When he returned to the Philippines, a Constabulary agent reported, he "does not by word or deed commit any illegal act and is very careful not to break the law." At a meeting with his associates from the Unión Obrera Democrática (UOD), a Japanese representative working with Ishikawa, and two unidentified Germans—in addition to the undercover Constabulary agent filling out a secret transcription of the meeting—de los Reyes reportedly stated:

> I do not believe that there can be a single traitor among us. Up to the present the agents of the government have accomplished nothing in their investigations, they hear noises but do not know where they come from and their heads are like bell-towers. They succeed in learning that arms have been landed but cannot learn where they are hidden, even the chiefs of police themselves make secret trips, incognito, to place themselves in contact with our principal persons, but they get nothing; our chiefs in Hongkong, Shanghai and Japan are aware of all the movements of the government agents since we have well paid employees to warn us, among the very secret police themselves. I myself, whom the Americans consider an irresponsible man, incapable of this kind of work, am constantly playing tricks on them, and when they talk with me they get nothing out of me, while I, with my insidious and seemingly innocent questions learn from them whatever I choose.

De los Reyes undoubtedly knew that his remarks were being recorded and that "several Tondo policemen were watching the vicinity." And he wanted US officials to know that he was not intimidated. Recalling his lessons on anarchism, he called on Filipino workers to rise up. "Until the laborers keep their strikes up to the end, following the proceedings of educated workers and responsible socialists, nothing good can come to them," he said. "Until the first bomb has been exploded they will not think of listening to the poor. Until they make themselves feared through violence they will be considered as ridiculous beings and peaceful lunatics." If anything, de los Reyes was engaging the US security state by mocking its futility and vulnerability. In 1911, when de los Reyes visited the offices of *La Vanguardia*, *El Renacimiento*'s successor, a Constabulary agent reported, an associate "entered and said 'Hello, Japanese,' at which they all burst out laughing." The vast Japanese conspiracy was, on one level, a joke.[58]

It was no laughing matter to the US regime. Artemio Ricarte's release from prison and banishment to Hong Kong in the summer of 1910 intensified the Constabulary's determination to uncover and suppress a conspiracy spanning colonized Asia and imperial Japan. Secret agent "26," charged with monitoring Ricarte's correspondence and contacts in the Philippines, heard that Ricarte and other Filipinos in Hong Kong were "very much preoccupied in planning how the principal government buildings in this capital may be reduced to ashes, in connivance with some Filipino politicians." In a letter castigating "radical politicians" for suggesting "the reduction or abolishment of the Constabulary and especially the Information Division," Rafael Crame, the superintendent of the latter, dwelled on the expanding network of Filipino revolutionaries and Japanese allies. He insisted that Felipe Salvador, who was recently captured, had organized his revolt through "his relations with the Japanese and Japophiles." Ricarte's deportation, he feared, was "a new encouragement to excite peoples' minds in favor of a new revolution." Ricarte planned to go to Japan, Crame exclaimed, "and there is no doubt that, united with the elements already in Japan and Hongkong and with those who will join them, they will form a nucleus which will engage in arousing the minds of people here and in pushing them toward a revolution." Constabulary reports assumed and stressed that Ricarte was conspiring with de los Reyes and Gregorio Aglipay, fellow Ilocanos who had established the Philippine Independent Church alongside the UOD in 1902.[59]

Beyond Ricarte's steadfast refusal to pledge allegiance to the United States, his movements and pronouncements seemed to epitomize revolutionary threats to the colonial order of things. Like Aguinaldo before him, he set up a revolutionary council of Filipino exiles in Hong Kong to incite and organize a radical anticolonial movement. In a letter intercepted by the Constabulary, Ricarte referenced Russian anarchist Peter Kropotkin to urge Filipinos back home, *"Liberties are not given, they are taken."* "I esteem the Japanese as friends or allies," he explained in February 1911, "but as dominators, Never! . . . Japan, by her admirable victories over Russia, is the first Oriental nation which has dignified the Orientals." In the context of rising tensions between the United States and Japan, he argued, Filipinos' only option was "to take advantage of that situation to shake off, once and forever, the hateful American yoke." A few months earlier, the Constabulary had learned that a "native of Guam," recently released from Bilibid prison, discussed similar objectives for Guam "in case of war between America and Japan." By June 1911, Ricarte appeared ready to execute his plans, announcing to his associates his imminent trip to Japan and his intention "to make the revolutionary movement before America and Japan come to blows." Toward that end, the Constabulary learned, Ricarte's revolutionary council decided to form "a section of anarchists" in the Philippines and to assassinate "all who are false to their oaths . . . without compassion."[60]

Tracking Ricarte's movements, in turn, entrenched the US colonial security state in the Philippines and beyond. In February 1911, the situation seemed dire enough to dispatch the Constabulary's secret agent 26 to Hong Kong to monitor Ricarte and his inner circle closely. Particularly

FIGURE 9. Bilibid Prison. Courtesy of Filipinas Heritage Library.

because Ricarte's associates knew that agent 26 had once been a guard at Bilibid prison, he had to work especially hard to gain their trust. Some became suspicious anyway. On his second trip to Hong Kong in May 1911, when Ricarte instructed agent 26 to study "the best places for landing arms," Ricarte's colleagues—including Constabulary officers recruited to join Ricarte's movement—began murmuring that agent 26 was, in fact, working for the Constabulary. The agent's superiors, in turn, concocted an intricate scheme to deflect those charges by making him appear to be a target of the Constabulary's surveillance, not its undercover operative. Felix Almarines, who was working with Ricarte, was shown fabricated Constabulary reports on agent 26 and others, including Almarines. Apparently assured that agent 26 could be trusted, Almarines instructed him "to warn all the members of the committee and other members of the Ricarte party that the Constabulary is very well informed about the organization, collections, and conspiracy which the people has [*sic*] attempted to make." About a week later, Almarines said the opposite, stating that the Constabulary had no "positive proof" in its case against "this attempted conspiracy."[61] Did Almarines trust agent 26? Or was he using the undercover agent to pass on false information to his bosses? Either seemed possible.

Perhaps above all else, reports filed by agent 26 reified and magnified Ricarte's movement and his alliance with Japan. On his first trip to Hong Kong, the agent met with a Japanese veteran "commissioned by the Tokio Government to confer with Ricarte." The Japanese representative certified his status by sharing "a photograph of himself in field costume taken in the Russian War" and claimed "he could deliver arms into the interior of any province, and even into Manila, whenever they were wanted." In addition to forging a partnership with Japan and organizing a revolutionary council in Macao, according to agent 26, Ricarte's coconspirators had "well converted the 600 Scouts in Lucena," developed plans for an uprising at Bilibid prison and the capturing of the Philippine Commission, popularized Ricarte's movement across the different provinces, particularly in Ilocos, and avowed that "the secret agents of the Japanese in the Philippines exceed those of the government in number and talent and that said agents are in connivance with Ricarte's followers." The Constabulary could not trust anyone. Pio del Pilar, a prominent military leader from the Philippine Revolution and the Philippine-American War, promised to Bandholtz to support the US regime by raising twenty thousand men "in case of war with Japan, or in case of any revolution," but agent 26 reported that the old general's true allegiance was to Ricarte's conspiracy. As against Spain, del Pilar planned "to turn on the government once they were armed." The Constabulary placed del Pilar and his "old revolutionary chiefs and soldiers" under surveillance.[62]

As the US security regime extended its reach to deter a revolution, its excesses ironically mobilized Filipinos, pushing them to welcome a war between the United States and Japan and to embrace Ricarte and Japan as harbingers of national liberation. In January 1911, a secret agent stated that the barrios of Tondo and Sampaloc were "the most agitated because they have direct correspondence with Hong Kong and Japan." Some residents said that "they hoped the Japanese would come at once to root up the abuses of the Americans, who disturb even the women who have done nothing but protect our interests." The agent was monitoring the situation, but he complained to his superiors that the Constabulary's wanton searches were proving counterproductive. "I tell you that these searches do nothing but excite the minds of the people and if you can," he suggested, "find me[an]s to keep the people from rushing into suicide." When the MID searched "the Japanese bazaar" weeks earlier, another agent reported, the "inevitable effect" was to increase predictions that "war between Japan and America is very near." As in years past, those predictions and animosity toward the US regime produced a combustible climate. Even in Bilibid prison, Crame reported, "they talk much of this war and are ready there to rebel at the first news of revolt." Discontent and anticipation were everywhere. "The Japanese bugaboo is still walking about the country," an unidentified source informed Bandholtz, "and, whether imaginary or real, the excitement among the lower classes is certainly real."[63]

The widespread surveillance of anyone possibly affiliated with Japan and Ricarte generated more surveillance, which simultaneously uncovered and engendered new revolutionary schemes. Toward the end of January 1911, Crame caught wind of a mass meeting at Manila's Opera House to organize a Filipino Carnival that brought together Isabelo de los Reyes, Hermenegildo Cruz, and many others implicated in Ricarte's movement. Within a day, he received an agent's detailed report of the meeting. Convened by the League of Filipina Women—presumed to be "a screen" and "a breastwork"—the meeting, the agent reported, displayed an intense hostility toward the American-sponsored Carnival that would eventually effect "a constant boycott here against everything American." A couple days later, another agent overheard de los Reyes discuss the Filipino Carnival's deeper significance. "When the Carnival is held, it will not fail to provoke the American and he will take vengeance and commit all kinds of abuses on the Filipinos who support the Carnival," de los Reyes said reportedly. "Then they will unite for all will bear the marks of the whip. This is the great work of union which is to spring from an innocent idea and that union is more terrible than Taal volcano, because they unite linked by misfortune and fatality and they will suffer themselves to be killed rather than disunite." The US regime would not wait to be provoked further. Manila's municipal board promptly refused to grant a permit for a Filipino Carnival.[64]

Perhaps not on the scale imagined by de los Reyes or the Constabulary agent spying on him, the short-lived Filipino Carnival movement helped to rally Filipinos against the US empire. When the American Carnival opened in February 1911, rumors began flying around Manila—that Filipino attendees would be beaten or killed, that the grounds would be bombed, that a Red Hand Society existed to carry out threats, that Americans "masked as devils" would attack Filipinos. The rumors might have been a ruse to enforce a boycott, a Constabulary agent wondered, but "I am of the opinion that we should not be absolutely confident for people's minds are greatly excited about this question of the Carnival and it seems that unity of ideas exist." Another agent became convinced that Ricarte and "the Hongkong Filipinos" had organized the Red Hand Society "to start a revolution," but he recanted two days later, claiming that everyone was too afraid of the Constabulary to organize so boldly. The rumors around the Carnival—and the Constabulary's incapacity to contain or verify them—attested to the popular rejection of US colonialism, the very reason for the Constabulary's birth and growth. Fear did not translate into submission. At a movie theater appropriately titled Empire Cinematograph, Crame wrote, "the American flag was hissed loudly by the audience." Under the cover of darkness, Filipinos expressed their solidarity and rage. Although the police were notified, the US security regime could do little but remark on the event's ordinariness. "Have seen thing at Majestic," Bandholtz scribbled on Crame's report.[65]

More than anyone else, Constancia Poblete of the League of Filipina Women captured the spirit of defiance behind the Carnival movement. She had first come to the attention of US officials in 1901 when she led a march of five hundred women for the release of Filipino prisoners of war. Eight years later, she began publishing *Filipinas*, a magazine that unabashedly criticized colonial rule. After the municipal board's decision, Poblete led another mass meeting at the Opera House to convey the news. She said that various responses were proposed—taking the municipal board to court, boycotting the American Carnival—but she "did not today wish to make public what we have decided in the matter, as it is a secret which the public will learn when it sees and feels the results." Particularly given her "spirited and threatening" demeanor, a Constabulary agent inferred that she meant "either a boycott of the American Carnival or an approaching insurrection." Poblete ended her speech by addressing the US security state. "Finally I must remin[d] you that for about one month I have been watched by secret agents, wherever I go, they follow me and watch me," she said, "but so far, they cannot say anything about me, but this does not make me afraid for I am resolved to forward with all the work I am doing for the sake of our people, and if it is necessary, to lose my life for our country, I would do it gladly."[66]

Poblete's contentious words resonated with Ricarte's fierce determination and his longstanding confrontation with the US security state. Over the next several years, Ricarte remained exiled in Hong Kong, trying to organize an armed revolution against the US empire. In August 1914, evidently while on a clandestine trip to Mount Halcon on the island of Mindoro, he penned a constitution for the "Rizaline Islands," a republic to be forged out of the Philippines and Guam. "The only desire of my life is to elevate you to the pinnacle of happiness, to make you free and great," he wrote to fellow Rizalines, "in order that other countries may see that you are not inferior to any of them in strength, science, and power." Assuming and inflating Ricarte's influence, the Constabulary, the Manila Police, and the MID infiltrated his network and monitored his contacts and activities. By Christmas Eve 1914, when an ill-fated insurrection was to commence in Manila, the colonial security state was ready, armed with machine guns aimed at a couple hundred of Ricarte's "army corps" gathered at the Botanical Gardens. With the quick suppression and dispersion of the uprising through warning shots, US officials set their sights on apprehending Ricarte and extinguishing the last vestiges of the Philippine Revolution. They convinced their British counterparts, who were growing wary of South Asian revolutionaries in Hong Kong after the outbreak of World War I, to expel him from that British colony. Empires had to work together.[67]

Ricarte's hope of allying with Japan continued to elude and contest the US empire. In March 1915, Constabulary agents followed Ricarte to Shanghai and secured an arrest warrant from a US extraterritorial court. After finally taking their old nemesis into custody, they placed Ricarte on a ship bound for Manila. At a stopover in Hong Kong, he managed to get away from his captors. Through his wife Agueda Esteban, who had also participated in revolutionary struggles against Spain and then the United States, and Japanese contacts, Ricarte made his way to Japan. He eventually made Yokohama his new home base, operating a restaurant with Esteban and teaching Spanish at a school in nearby Tokyo. Although he carried on the anticolonial struggle by publishing articles and books, the old Vibora faded as a focal point of revolutionary movements and imperial insecurities.[68] Dreams of Japan leading a pan-Asian movement against white supremacy and empire, however, lived on. The Philippine-American War and then the Russo-Japanese War had extended the US empire and the Japanese empire, two "gentlemen" recognizing and legitimizing each other's claims to sovereignty, but US officials increasingly came to see struggles for national liberation (sedition), social revolution (anarchism and socialism), and Japanese imperialism (pan-Asian solidarity) as one and the same. To support one was to support the other, a symptom of "Oriental" depravity and duplicity that seemingly demanded more resources to defend US national security, from San Francisco to Manila. Through that perverse logic of race, empire, and national security, imperial Japan and pan-Asian solidarity made the US empire defensible.

CHAPTER 3

Fighting John Bull and Uncle Sam

When the British declare that they are fighting for democracy,
even unborn children laugh at the humour of it. The dead rise
from their graves and mock at them, and say, Why so many
lies, O Englishmen? O Tyrannous Englishmen, who are
fighting for democracy, who have trodden under foot the
peoples of the world, who have broken promising buds or
have at least killed them by the darkness of tyranny.

—*Ghadar,* September 9, 1917

As Filipino revolutionaries confronted the US security state in Hong
Kong, Japan, and the Philippines, Har Dayal's anticolonial radicalism
caught the attention of the British security state. Born in 1884 to a literary caste (Kayastha) and a father in the colonial bureaucracy, Dayal's
intellectual accomplishments placed him on a trajectory to a career in
civil service. After earning his bachelor's and master's degrees in India,
he left in 1905 to study at Oxford University on a scholarship sponsored by the colonial government of India. Although his academic
achievements momentarily eclipsed his political activities, the British
Government's Investigation Department had grown concerned enough
to file a report in 1904 that "a sense of revolt had taken deep root in his
mind and had even permeated strongly a select circle of his friends."
Dayal engaged in formal historical studies at Oxford and informal
political studies with fellow colonized subjects in England. His outrage
against the British empire compelled him to "resign" his scholarship in
1907, as he put it, a year before he was expected to graduate with high
honors. The British colonial educational system, he would write the following year back in India, was "one huge octopus which is *sucking out
the moral life-blood of the nation.*" Hounded by British undercover
agents and repressive laws, Dayal left India in less than a year, returning

to England and then finding a home briefly among radical circles in Paris. There he edited a revolutionary newspaper, *Bande Mataram*, for South Asians everywhere, especially back home in India.[1]

Dayal soon sought refuge across the Atlantic, to recover from ill health and to regenerate his political philosophy and revolutionary organizing. Having grown tired of the socialist orthodoxy pervading the exiled left in Paris, he embarked in 1910 for Martinique, a French colony in the Caribbean. Dayal led an ascetic life on the island, evidently determined to bequeath a new religion to the world modeled on Buddha's life. His mission took him to the libraries of Harvard University via the Virgin Islands, Puerto Rico, and New York. A couple months in Cambridge were apparently long enough. Hearing that there were thousands of South Asian laborers on the Pacific Coast who might be organized in the struggle for the liberation of the Indian subcontinent, Dayal made his trek westward in the spring of 1911. The United States, he wrote then, was an "ethical sanitarium, where eternal sunshine prevails, and the wrecks of other climes are wrought into beautiful specimens of restored humanity." His love affair with America would be short-lived, but he was ready to make the San Francisco Bay Area home, at least for a while. After a short trip to Hawai'i, where he read Karl Marx and became friends with local Japanese residents, he received a temporary appointment as a lecturer of Indian philosophy at Stanford University. Dayal wrote and lectured widely on the British empire and revolutionary politics. He was ready to move back into the spotlight.[2]

Both the US intelligence and surveillance program, which had taken root in the Philippines, and the British system, which had originated in the colonial administration of India, took notice. By January 1913, William C. Hopkinson, in charge of monitoring South Asians for the Canadian government since 1909, established a transimperial network of state officials and paid informants to keep track of "seditious" activities in the Bay Area. The British consul general, whose government had urged Canadian authorities to dispatch Hopkinson, provided him with names of South Asian college students willing to provide information on Dayal. Hopkinson also made contact with US officials at the immigration station on Angel Island and the Department of Justice, all of whom promised cooperation and support in his investigation of "Hindu agitators." He attended Dayal's public lectures, which were featured regularly in local radical networks, trying to gather criminal evidence to pass on to his American colleagues. Like Stanford administrators who pressured Dayal to resign from his academic post, Hopkinson was

FIGURE 10. Har Dayal. Courtesy of Wikimedia Commons.

dismayed by Dayal's unflinching radicalism and adoring leftist audiences. "Of all the Indian agitators who have visited the States and of all those whom I have a knowledge," he reported, "I am led to believe that Har Dayal is the most dangerous."[3]

To those investigating Dayal's activities, he became more dangerous by the end of 1913, a busy year in which he rallied South Asian students and agricultural and lumber mill workers behind an anticolonial movement. In speeches across the Pacific Coast, he rebuked the hypocrisies and fallacies of the British empire. "In other countries the man of education is honoured and respected, whereas in India he is despised and degraded," he said. "Desist, therefore, from your petty religious dissensions and turn your thoughts towards the salvation of your country." With widespread support, Dayal was able to begin publishing a revolutionary newspaper, titled *Ghadar* ("revolt" in Urdu), in November. The first issue proclaimed that the newspaper would provide a "history of the present nationalist movement," "purely literary propaganda . . . to bring on the day when the whole nation shall rise up to overturn the existing political system in British India." In an article on a British official in India who commented openly that he did "not like black and yellow men," *Ghadar* offered a caustic rejoinder. "Our thought with regards to you is the same," Dayal wrote. "You do not like us and we do not like you; therefore, it would be proper for you to go to a distance from before our eyes. Take your white carcass to your cold and barren country, and leave our land for us." In quick succession, Dayal also announced the formation of a revolutionary party, also called Ghadar, and an ashram to educate revolutionaries.[4]

Dayal also continued to lecture on a wide range of topics before audiences beyond South Asians. On October 31, 1913, he delivered an address on the Russian revolutionary movement at Jefferson Square Hall in San Francisco, a speech that US immigration officials transcribed carefully and would soon use in their case against Dayal. Among "the living evil institutions" in the world, he said, "we have to reckon [with] the British Empire, called in other words the British Vampire, which is sucking the life blood of millions of people in Ireland, India and Egypt, called that empire the sun never sets on—because it does not find a decent place to set upon." Dayal praised Russian revolutionaries' incorporation of anarchism, feminism, and terrorism. "If a serpent were to throw itself around your neck you would not lose much time by deciding whether you would get rid of it by constitutional means, terrorism, or how," he argued. "You would crush it." Those revolutionaries, he noted, had supported Japan in the Russo-Japanese War, which he extolled as the dawning of a new age. "The victory of Japan has opened a new era for the Asiatic races by giving them self-confidence and respect," Dayal proclaimed. "The victories of Japan broke the spell; now the old color barrier is being thrown down everywhere." India was not immune. "I believe that the future of humanity depends on the great masses of humanity packed up in India and China," he said, "and the sooner the white people realize that the better."[5]

Dayal's intrepid rhetoric and anticolonial politics—and false reports of his close association with Emma Goldman, the most prominent anarchist in the United States—drove US and British officials to intensify their surveillance of Dayal and his comrades. In January 1914, Samuel W. Backus, appointed by US President William Howard Taft to head the immigration station on Angel Island, forwarded a copy of Dayal's Jefferson Square Hall speech to Commissioner-General of Immigration Anthony W. Caminetti and requested an arrest warrant. Time was of the essence. "The reason this subject is presented at this time is that from information received," Backus explained, "he has been in the United States nearly three years; and if the Bureau shall be of the opinion that he comes within the excluded classes, he may be arrested before the statute of limitation operates and then his case can be considered at leisure." Caminetti complied immediately, securing a warrant for Dayal's arrest on February 10, 1914. "That the said alien is a member of the excluded classes in that he was an anarchist or person who believed in or advocated the overthrow by force or violence of the Government of the United States, or of all government, or of all forms of law," the warrant read, "or the assassination of public officials, at the time of his entry into the United States."6

The US bureaucrats' plan to deport Dayal backfired. Their failure to locate the exact date of Dayal's landing in New York—February 9, 1911— led them to miss the statutory three-year window by a single day, a fateful mistake that they tried to cover up by investigating if Dayal had subsequently left and reentered the United States. Not only did Dayal pounce on that error, he fought back, loudly. US authorities arrested Dayal at the conclusion of a socialist meeting in San Francisco's Bohemian Hall on March 25, 1914. The news stunned local South Asians, two hundred of whom accompanied Dayal as he was taken away to Angel Island for questioning the following morning. In his interview with an immigration inspector, Dayal refused to renounce or apologize for his political beliefs and activities. "As a general rule I believe that tyrannical government[s] should be over-thrown by mass uprisings," he replied at one point, "but this does not mean that I must condemn the assassination of public officials in all lands, in all ages, and under all circumstances, as a principle." He presented himself as an intellectual, denying that he was an anarchist three years earlier but admitting his espousal since of what could be called "philosophical anarchism." "I will never enter a country by denying my convictions," Dayal stated. After posting a $1,000 bond, he returned to San Francisco and proceeded directly to the Industrial Workers of the World Hall to deliver a lecture on "The Problem of Unemployment."7

Dayal's confrontation with US immigration authorities underscored the colonial roots of the modern liberal state. Propelled by global demands for migrant labor and a repressive colonial security state at home, South Asian workers and activists moved to all corners of the world, including the Pacific Coast of North America, where they forged an anticolonial movement in the opening decades of the twentieth century. But, as Dayal discovered, the US state would become intimately wedded to the British empire, in a wider project to secure imperial borders and racial hierarchies by silencing anticolonial critiques and criminalizing anticolonial activities. That project extended the reach of the US security state to encompass and conjoin British and US laws on sedition and immigration. The outbreak of World War I, in turn, unleashed a wave of transpacific visions of anticolonial revolution, visions that appeared to solidify and magnify racial and radical alliances emerging out of the Philippines and Japan and across colonized Asia. Fighting the British empire in the US empire enhanced and advanced the idea of pan-Asian solidarity as a means to contest empire around the world, particularly in and through a revolutionary Asia. The US state, in response, turned to racial caricatures of religious tradition, sexual deviancy, and revolutionary anarchism to categorize anticolonial South Asians as seditious threats to US national security. In the end, as the British empire and the US empire went to war together for "democracy," anticolonial South Asians laid bare that that democracy was nothing but a veneer for white supremacy and empire.

EXCLUDING SEDITIOUS SUBJECTS

South Asian migrations and British state power materialized hand in hand to expand the British empire in the nineteenth century. Anticipating financial and social calamities in the wake of slavery's abolition, sugar planters across the British colonies clamored for new workers from South Asia, bound to long-term indentures. They wanted a labor force, a prominent planter argued, to "make us, as far as possible, independent of our negro population." When the inaugural shipment of workers to British Guiana in 1838 produced charges of widespread abuse, British officials in India and London felt compelled to prohibit further migrations. As the secretary for the colonies explained, "I am not prepared to encounter the responsibility of a measure which may lead to a dreadful loss of life on the one hand, or, on the other, to a new system of slavery." With former slaves organizing strikes and planters lobbying doggedly for new sources of labor, state prohibition evolved into state regulation. Overseeing recruitment in India and transportation to and employment in the sugar colonies of British Guiana, Trinidad, Fiji, Mauritius, and elsewhere, the British imperial state ostensibly intervened to guarantee freedom for all. In practice, the state enforcement of indentures on behalf of the planters—and the lax oversight of extralegal methods like kidnapping, deception, and corporal punishment—far surpassed the state protection of workers' rights. The mass migration of South Asian laborers bound to five-year indentures became the centerpiece of the British empire after slavery.[8]

South Asian migrations to North America had little to do with sugar production, but they emanated from the British empire's demands for particular kinds of masculinized labor. Annexed by the British in 1849, the Punjab region in northwestern India bore the disastrous effects of colonial domination in the second half of the nineteenth century. In the wake of the Mutiny of 1857, the British increasingly relied on Punjabi recruits, particularly Sikhs, to man the British Indian Army, which was tasked with maintaining security on the subcontinent and in the far reaches of the British empire. At the same time, new irrigation projects and railroad networks facilitated the expansion of agricultural production in Punjab, causing socioeconomic transformations that drove increasing numbers of residents to join the army and to seek livelihoods elsewhere. British land and revenue policies fueled absentee landlordism and rampant indebtedness, a cyclical process that accelerated land sales and tenant farming, exacerbated class tensions and divisions, and sowed mass discontent against moneylenders and British officials. By the turn of the twentieth century, British officials were on high alert for signs of general insurrection in Punjab. They also dispatched Indian troops to China to quell the Boxer Rebellion and to Hong Kong and Singapore, where many remained after their tours of military duty. Especially from Hong Kong, Punjabis began boarding ships bound for Canada, a dominion within the British empire that seemed to afford relatively high-paying jobs and other opportunities unavailable back home.[9]

The migration of nonindentured South Asians generated intense debates that reified and reinforced racial hierarchies in the British empire. In claiming sovereignty over the Indian subcontinent in 1858, Queen Victoria had promised to treat all subjects under her rule equally, without regard to "race or creed." In the ensuing decades, however, London increasingly drew distinctions between "dominions," colonies granted the right of self-government in domestic affairs, and "Crown Colonies," which remained firmly under the authority of the British Parliament and the Colonial Office. Race marked the difference. While white settlers in "temperate" zones—colonies that would constitute Canada, Australia, New Zealand, and South Africa—were granted the right to form "responsible" governments, those living in the "tropical" colonies of the Caribbean, the Pacific, and India were deemed incapable of self-government. When white dominions objected to the migration of British subjects from South Asia, they brought to the fore the contradiction between imperial proclamations of equal citizenship and patently unequal access to political rights. White settlers found a sympathetic hearing in London. When the Natal government was considering restrictions on Asian immigration in 1897, the Colonial Office suggested that "the legislation be directed not against race or colour, but against impecunious or ignorant immigrants." Heeding the advice and following precedents in the United States—from Jim Crow laws in Mississippi and other southern states to federal immigration statutes under consideration—the Natal regime turned to a literacy test in a European language to exclude "undesirable immigrants" from Asia.[10]

When white residents of British Columbia reacted with similar venom against South Asians, Canadian authorities felt compelled to enact an exclusionary measure racist in practice, but not in name. By the time thousands of Punjabis began arriving in Vancouver in the first decade of the twentieth century, the Canadian government was long familiar with the nuances of legal subterfuge, having implemented a head tax on Chinese immigrants beginning in 1885. When that measure failed to eliminate Chinese migration, Canadian officials raised the tax, from fifty dollars in 1885 to one hundred dollars in 1902 and then five hundred dollars in 1903. British Columbia's provincial legislature also turned to the "Natal solution" to respond to Chinese, Japanese, and South Asian migrations, passing a series of literacy test requirements. Under pressure from British imperial authorities, who feared that additional restrictions would stir up discontent in India and threaten the Anglo-Japanese alliance, dominion officials in Ottawa disallowed British Columbia's literacy test measures. But racial violence swayed Canadian authorities to endorse racial exclusion. In September 1907, white mobs marched with banners reading "Stand for a white Canada" and "A white Canada and no cheap Asiatic labor" and descended on Vancouver's Chinese and Japanese neighborhoods, targeting their racial ire against all Asians. Knowing that nearly every South Asian arrived from Hong Kong or Shanghai, the Canadian cabinet passed in January 1908 an order-in-council prohibiting immigrants who did not travel on a continuous journey from their land of origin. South Asians were effectively excluded from Canada.[11]

As in the United States, Canadian officials cloaked racial restrictions on immigration in a language of national security. In March 1908, the Canadian government dispatched W. L. MacKenzie King, the deputy minister of labour, to London to confer with British officials on "the subject of immigration to Canada from the Orient, and immigration from India in particular." King received a warm response. "That Canada should desire to restrict immigration from the Orient is regarded as natural, that Canada should remain a white man's country is believed to be not only desirable for economic and social reasons," he reported, "but highly necessary on political and national grounds." Accustomed to "the conditions of a tropical climate, and possessing manners and customs so unlike those of our own people," King explained, South Asian migrants in Canada posed threats to their own safety and to the dominion's future. "It was recognized, too, that the competition of this class of labour, though not likely to prove effective, if left to itself, might none the less, were the numbers to become considerable . . . occasion considerable unrest among workingmen whose standard of comfort is of a higher order, and who, as citizens with family and civic obligations, have expenditures to meet and a status to maintain which the coolie immigrant is in a position wholly to ignore." And, in private conversations, King raised the specter of white workingmen turning to socialism or vigilantism if Asian migrations continued. Canada's security seemingly required racial exclusion.[12]

To British officials, working-class articulations of white supremacy appeared as threats to imperial security in western Canada. Days before the Vancouver riots in September 1907, hundreds of white residents of Bellingham, Washington, had waged attacks on South Asian workers employed in local lumber mills. Spurred by rallies led by organized labor and the Japanese and Korean Exclusion League, which soon changed its name to the more inclusive Asiatic Exclusion League, white mobs beat up individual South Asians walking on Bellingham's streets before systematically driving all of them out of the city. Many South Asians headed back to Vancouver, with the hope that their claims to British imperial citizenship would afford a level of protection. Prominent white labor and exclusion leaders from Seattle made the same journey north, inciting the white masses in Vancouver, as they had in Bellingham, to demand immigration restrictions and to expel Asian migrants in their midst. The influence of American "agitators" unnerved British authorities. In the wake of the Vancouver riots, a report for the Colonial Office highlighted "a constant and serious danger" that "the United

States may stand out on and through this question as the leaders of the English-speaking peoples in the Pacific as against the coloured races." The problem was not white supremacy per se but a working-class white supremacy attracting Canadians into the fold of the US empire. If a war between Britain and the United States over the US-Canadian border seemed less and less likely, British Columbia's secession and US annexation were not beyond the pale.[13]

Not to be outdone by their British and Canadian counterparts, US immigration officials decided to restrict South Asians from entering the United States when the de facto exclusion from Canada in 1908 shifted migrations southward. Nearly two thousand entered the United States in that year alone. Although a law explicitly targeting South Asians would not be enacted until 1917, US immigration officers had a range of excludable categories at their disposal. Summing up the litany of federal statutes passed over the previous three decades, the 1907 immigration law itemized the deviant "classes of aliens" prohibited from the United States:

> All idiots, imbeciles, feeble-minded persons, epileptics, insane persons . . .; persons likely to become a public charge; professional beggars; persons afflicted with tuberculosis or with a loathsome or dangerous contagious disease; . . . persons who have been convicted of or admit having committed a felony or other crime or misdemeanor involving moral turpitude; polygamists, or persons who admit their belief in the practice of polygamy, anarchists, or persons who believe in or advocate the overthrow by force or violence of the Government of the United States, or of all government, or of all forms of law, or the assassination of public officials; prostitutes, or women or girls coming into the United States for the purpose of prostitution or for any other immoral purpose; persons hereinafter called contract laborers, who have been induced or solicited to migrate to this country by offers or promises of employment or in consequence of agreements, oral, written or printed, express or implied, to perform labor in this country of any kind, skilled or unskilled.

The law included an exemption for persons, "if otherwise admissible, . . . convicted of an offense purely political, not involving moral turpitude."[14]

Particularly beginning in 1908, individual South Asian migrants faced hostile boards of special inquiry intent on discovering a "moral" reason to deny their legal entry into the United States. Anait, a twenty-two-year old Muslim who had lived previously in Oregon, applied for readmission to the United States in December 1908, after a brief sojourn in Vancouver, Canada. "If you were in India and your brother died," an immigration inspector asked, "would you take his wife[?]" Anait mistakenly tried to demystify Muslim practices. "The Mussulmen always take care of their brother's wives," he replied. "They do not marry them direct, but they bring them to their house and let them live there. If his wife should die then he would marry his brother's wife." His answer prompted a series of questions on Islam and marriage, especially around the practice of rich men marrying a second wife if the first failed to bear them children. "Well, it is all right, but I have no wife at all yet," Anait said plainly. "I will not get married to two." Feeling cornered by his inquisitors, he repeated again later, "My wish is only to marry once." The board summarily rejected his application nonetheless, concluding that he was "a believer in the practice of polygamy." Against the backdrop of contemptuous reports on resistant "non-Christian tribes" in the Philippines, US immigration officers disparaged Islam to exclude South Asians for "polygamy."[15]

South Asian migrants found demonstrating their economic fitness to enter the United States as elusive as explaining their religious practices. In October 1908, Mangal Singh probably figured that immigration officials would rule favorably in his case. Not only did he carry enough cash to reach his final destination near Seattle, but his cousin had already secured him a job at a lumber mill for two dollars per day. But before Singh knew it, his hearing was over. The board determined that he was a contract laborer who had been "induced to seek admission to the United States by an offer of employment." Lacking familiar contacts or tangible employment prospects in the United States, in contrast, resulted in the more widespread accusation of "likely to become a public charge," which was nearly impossible to disprove. In denying an appeal by Hira, a twenty-six-year-old "Hindu laborer" seeking a job in Portland, Oregon, the acting commissioner-general of immigration reasoned that "thousands of white men are now out of employment in that section of the country . . . owing to the deplorable labor conditions there existing and the prevailing feeling against members of the East Indian race, there is but little prospect of the man's finding employment." The absurdity of his logic—citing white supremacist feelings to sustain his white supremacist decision—did not deter other immigration officers from adopting it. Proving a status somewhere between a "contract laborer" and "likely to become a public charge" became a nearly impossible task.[16]

As US immigration officers fortified the border against South Asians, Secretary of Commerce and Labor Oscar S. Straus, who was in charge of the Bureau of Immigration and Naturalization, sought to systematize the identification and deportation of anarchists and criminals. In March 1908, he issued a circular to all commissioners of immigration and immigrant inspectors on the need to collaborate with local police departments and the US Secret Service regarding "alien anarchists and criminals located in the United States." Straus instructed agents to circulate the legal definition of those "excluded classes" and to point out his department's authority to deport such individuals within three years of entry. To effect deportation, he stressed, local and federal officials had to work together to gather evidence to demonstrate that "the person in question is an alien, subject to the immigration acts" and that "he is an anarchist or criminal, as defined in the statute," in addition to information on when and whence the alien arrived in the United States. If it was "impractical" to determine the alien's date of arrival, Straus added, immigration officials were to assume that it fell within three years. "It is desired that the above indicated steps shall be taken at once," he concluded, "and that no proper effort shall be spared to secure and retain the cooperation of the local police and detective forces in an effort to rid the country of alien anarchists and criminals falling within the provisions of the statute relating to deportation."[17]

Straus's circular represented the US state's recognition of the growing prominence and influence of radical movements, particularly in the western reaches of the incorporated United States. Among the most militant and vocal was the Industrial Workers of the World (IWW), a labor organization founded in 1905 "to do away with capitalism." The IWW's radical critique of capitalism and confrontational methods emerged out of and appealed to migratory workers, many of whom were immigrants from Europe. By 1908, those "alien anarchists" that Straus vilified helped to make the IWW into an unabashedly revolutionary organization, eschewing reformist politics of any kind in preference for direct action and anarcho-syndicalism. When a group of anarchists in Seattle heard about the federal government's concerted effort to keep their "foreign co-workers from entering this consecrated land," they wrote immediately to the local immigrant inspector in charge. "We are aware of the fact that the hirelings of the criminal organization known as the United States government," W. P. Lawson, Otto Bobsien, H. Arnold, J. Bernstein, G. der Hertag, and Abe Beyer wrote, "take advantage of the present hysteria of that mob of many aliases, the 'public' etc. to suppress every effort that is made on the part of thinking men and women to show the people that the only remedy for existing social evils is liberty." They were not afraid, they proclaimed, and hoped for a day when "the state would atrophy having lost its function, and we would have peace and social order."[18]

As Straus and US immigration officials reinforced the notion that anarchism and anarchists were inherently alien, their claims to jurisdiction over "alien anarchists" naturalized the borders of the US empire. When the commissioner of immigration in Puerto Rico received Straus's circular, he promptly requested information on "alien anarchists" from Wilhelm Lutz, the acting chief of the insular police force. With "two detectives employed in this special work," Lutz confidently provided a list of individuals affiliated with "the only alleged anarchist organization on this Island." The members were all Puerto Ricans, he stated, except for a Mexican and a Venezuelan who would "come within the law for deportation." The organization received anarchist publications every week from Barcelona, Spain, Lutz reported, and was then organizing a visit by prominent anarchists from there and Havana, Cuba. "All meetings of men referred to in this memorandum have been, so far, behind closed doors, and while their sessions were violent enough, so far as speeches are concerned, I do not anticipate that any harm will come to any one from those here as they lack entirely that reckless courage that a true anarchist is known to be pos[s]essed of." Lutz nevertheless promised to keep "a sharp look out" on "the reds," for European "firebrands" would find "plenty [of] material that would serve as tools" in Puerto Rico. That Puerto Ricans were susceptible to the influence of "alien anarchists" did not make them "Americans"—they remained "Porto Ricans"—but made them all the more subject to US state surveillance.[19]

In the same month that Straus penned his circular, the unruly politics of anticolonialism and anarchism that US officials monitored in Puerto Rico appeared to manifest in San Francisco. In March 1908, Durham White Stevens, a former US diplomat employed by the Japanese government to promote its colonization of Korea, was making his way across the Pacific to Washington, DC. "Japan is doing in Korea and for the Koreans what the United States is doing in the Philippines," he stated during a stopover in San Francisco. Stevens's published interview enraged the local Korean community, which held a mass meeting and selected four representatives to convey their outrage. When they confronted Stevens in the lobby of the Fairmont Hotel the next day, he refused to recant his statements extolling Japanese policies in Korea or to acknowledge the violence inflicted by the Japanese state. The four Koreans proceeded to beat up Stevens on the spot. The following day, as Stevens and the Japanese consul general approached a ferry station, a Korean man brandishing a pistol wrapped in bandage—like Leon Czolgosz seven years earlier in Buffalo—attempted to shoot Stevens. Because his gun jammed, the would-be assassin whipped Stevens with his pistol instead and started to run away. A fellow Korean nationalist, In Whan Chang, then stepped into the breach and gunned Stevens down. A white crowd apprehended the two Koreans and began screaming, "Lynch the yellow devils!" Stevens died two days later. Although Chang was not an avowed anarchist, he understood the power of propaganda by the deed.[20]

Stevens's assassination reverberated in Hawai'i, where Chang had lived and worked and where US officials interpreted Straus's circular letter on "alien anarchists" in relation to Korean anticolonial struggles. The immigrant inspector in charge of Honolulu reported, "Some little suspicion prevailed here that local Koreans were implicated in the killing of D. W. Stevens . . . and, further suspicion that, on account of some utterances made by him at this port, an attempt was to be made on the life of Bishop M. C. Harris of the Methodist Church, on arrival in San Francisco." Officials in Hawai'i had no concrete evidence on Stevens's assassination, he noted, but local rumors suggested that "he *would* have been killed in Honolulu, if the vessel by which he traveled had not been placed in strict quarantine and he had been allowed to come ashore." Harris, like Stevens, drew the ire of local Koreans for publicly praising Japanese colonialism. That Koreans in Honolulu transmitted Harris's statements to Koreans in San Francisco—and that US officials had intercepted that telegram—generated a coordinated effort by the Department of Justice, the US Marshals Service, and the Bureau of Immigration and Naturalization to ensure Harris's safe landing in California. The Honolulu Police Department, in the meantime, promised to cooperate with federal officials in the enforcement of immigration laws and the surveillance of Korean political activities. Police chiefs of San Francisco and Oakland likewise promised to keep a close eye on "suspected anarchists" and to dispatch special officers to attend their meetings.[21]

As Koreans in Hawai'i, California, and elsewhere rallied against Japanese colonialism, South Asians intensified and expanded their struggles against the British empire. Japan's victory in the Russo-Japanese War attracted widespread attention, awakening many to new political possibilities. In 1905, a Bengali newspaper announced that "the Asiatic race has broken the pride of the greatest power in Europe so thoroughly that not even hope of retrieval is left." In reaction to the rising unrest, the British colonial regime resolved to partition the province of Bengal, a measure that galvanized a new wave of anti-British protests across the subcontinent. Even the Indian National Congress, which had been seeking moderate reforms toward greater political representation, voiced opposition to Bengal's partition. With college students leading the way, demands for national independence turned increasingly militant and revolutionary in ideology and strategy. The *Swadeshi* movement, which called for the boycott of British and other foreign goods and the consumption of local products, effectively mobilized various segments of Indian society to participate in anticolonial politics. Some called for more radical steps, including armed struggle. In Punjab, Lajpat Rai advised farmers to engage in direct action by refusing to pay their taxes or to cultivate their mortgaged lands. The British responded to those challenges with the sweeping Prevention of Seditious Meetings Act (1907), prohibiting meetings, speeches, and newspapers that might promote sedition against British rule and empowering the state to arrest and deport those deemed seditious agitators. Rai was among those deported to an undisclosed location.[22]

What the British criminalized as sedition—which was similar to the US regime's definition in the Philippines, namely any kind of opposition to colonial rule—could also be used as legal grounds to exclude or deport noncitizens from the United States. Despite the exemption for "an offense purely political," US immigration law prohibited "anarchists, or persons who believe in or advocate the overthrow by force or violence of the Government of the United States, or of all government, or of all forms of law, or the assassination of public officials." Under that definition, In Whan Chang and all Koreans who came to his defense were, in effect, anarchists. So were the countless South Asians potentially guilty of sedition against the British empire. Within that context, US immigration officials made questions on political beliefs standard in interrogations of South Asian migrants. In November 1908, Rajoo, a twenty-seven-year-old man petitioning to move from Vancouver to Seattle, was asked if he believed in "organized government." His affirmative reply failed to satisfy one of his interrogators, who demanded to know if Rajoo had "heard of the plots in India to upset the present government." He replied, "No, I never heard that." Rajoo also steadfastly deflected questions on whether or not the Sikh religion allowed men to marry more than one woman. Unable to reject him as an anarchist or a polygamist, the board unanimously denied his application for entry because he was "likely to become a public charge." No matter what, he represented a "moral" affront to the US nation.[23]

South Asian migrants understood how they were supposed to answer questions at their immigration hearings, but their adroit answers failed to change the predetermined outcome. In January 1909, Guljara Singh decided to leave Vancouver, Canada, where work had grown scarce, to try his luck in Tacoma, Washington. Asked if he had a specific contact in Tacoma, Singh stressed that he had "no address cards or anything of that kind" to avoid being classified as a contract laborer. When he explained that he would avoid Bellingham, recalling the anti-Asian riots, the board of special inquiry related that Tacoma was no better. "There are so many of you heading for Tacoma they are liable to drive you out of there," an immigrant inspector said. "Twenty years ago they drove the Chinamen out and there has not been a Chinaman in Tacoma since." Singh replied in silence. Later in the interview, another inspector asked, "Are you satisfied with the existing state of affairs in India today—do you wish to upset that administration?" Singh responded simply, "No, I am satisfied." Around the same time, Babu, another South Asian in Vancouver, was asked, "Do you believe in all organized forms of government as administered in various countries, India particularly?" He answered, "Yes, if I should not be loyal to the king of my country, then I would be at fault before God." His enthusiasm mattered little in the end. Both Singh and Babu were rejected as "likely to become a public charge."[24]

With so many exclusionary options and discretionary powers, US immigration officials moved to exclude virtually every South Asian trying to enter the United States. Shut out of the Pacific Northwest, South Asian migrations shifted to San Francisco, where H. H. North, the local commissioner of immigration, appeared to provide them with a semblance of a fair hearing. North's refusal to reject South Asians across the board incensed the Asiatic Exclusion League, which mounted a campaign against him. In April 1910, Commissioner-General of Immigration Daniel J. Keefe, North's boss in Washington, DC, intervened. "It is true, of course, that there is no law directed at the exclusion of Hindus as a race," he admitted. And Keefe was not advocating "any consideration of the matter of race as a cause, ipso facto, for rejection." He, however, instructed North to recognize other means and reasons, noting the need for "a careful medical inspection of a detailed character," the strong opposition to "the immigration of Asiatics" in Canada, and the application of "likely to become a public charge" provision to European immigrants on the East Coast. "If this principle is sound . . . with respect to Europeans . . .," he concluded, "how much more apt is its application to the cases of aliens like those here under discussion, whose habits of life, religious and social beliefs and customs, etc., are so dissimilar to those existing in the United States, and with respect to whom there is known to be considerable prejudice."[25]

By the summer of 1910, racial and sexual anxieties reached a boiling point and placed immigration restrictions at the heart of white supremacy and national security. On July 4, 1910, in Reno, Nevada, Jack Johnson, the flamboyant Black heavyweight champion of the world, pummeled Jim Jeffries, the former champion representing the "Hope of the White Race." White mobs took to the streets, coast to coast. In San Francisco, *The White Man*, "an organ of the movement for Asiatic exclusion" and "for racial segregation and international equity," announced the fight's results: "Nearly one hundred killings as an aftermath; a national crusade against prize fighting, while we secretly pray for a white man who can slaughter the Ethiopian." White men could exact revenge immediately, though, through Asiatic exclusion. "The surrender of our lands and opportunities to Asiatics is a mark of national decay," the lead editorial implored. "The association of white women with Mongolians, Hindus and negroes is racial pollution." In August 1910, William R. Wheeler of the US Immigration Commission cited *The White Man* to demand, as Keefe had, the stringent application of the "likely to become a public charge" clause to all "Hindus." From Calcutta (Kolkata), the US consul general vowed to take all necessary steps to discourage emigration to the United States, including by determining if applicants "were in sympathy with sedition in India or not."[26] Keeping South Asians out meant keeping sedition out; keeping sedition out meant preserving the racial and colonial order of things. The United States stood for white supremacy, manhood, and empire.

REVOLUTIONARY POLITICS UNLEASHED

Although very few South Asian migrants would have identified themselves as anarchists—and definitely not in front of US immigration officials—their hostile encounter with the Canadian and US states cultivated a collective sense of injustice. In the last two months of 1910, US immigration officials in San Francisco admitted two South Asians while rejecting nearly three hundred. It had become virtually impossible to enter the incorporated states of the US empire. There were 5,424 South Asians in the United States in 1910, according to the census, with the vast majority on the Pacific Coast. As they traveled to the agricultural fields and lumber mills of California, Oregon, and Washington, they shared stories of their transpacific journeys, which often included stints in the British Indian Army, and bitter experiences in Canada and the United States. Over the summer, college students with different backgrounds joined their ranks. At the University of California, Berkeley, in 1912, recalled D. Chenchiah of his arrival, there were about thirty South Asian students, nearly all of them committed to the liberation of their homeland. "As to regards the methods to be employed for achieving the same, they were poles apart," he continued. "The Punjabee students believed in the overthro[w] of the British Rule in India by armed revolt and they were ready for all the sacrifices and sufferings involved in such a revolt. But, the Non-Punjabee students believed in non-violent methods." Out of those assemblages—Punjabi workers, militant Punjabi students, and perhaps less militant Bengali students—would emerge a revolutionary movement to challenge empire and white supremacy.[27]

Har Dayal provided the spark that brought South Asians together. He had entered the United States in 1911 through New York and quickly moved to the San Francisco Bay Area. In December 1912, he addressed a meeting of South Asian students at Berkeley, imploring them to realize the historic role they could play in overthrowing the British empire. "Prepare yourselves to become great patriots and wonderful warriors," he advised. "Great suffering and sacrifice are required of you. You may have to die in this revolutionary cause. Anybody can be a Collector, or an Engineer or a Barrister or a Doctor. What India needs today is warriors of freedom. Better death in that noble cause than living as slaves of the British Empire." J.N. Lahiri, a graduate student who had embraced revolutionary anticolonial politics back home in Bengal, supported Dayal's speech, but challenged him to do more. "Mr. Har Dayal: Don't you know that hundreds and thousands of Indians are living outside India?" he asked. "Don't you know that they are the best of fighters? Don't you know that during the last War of Independence in 1857, the Punjabees helped the British, and thus destroyed the chances of our freedom, our country's freedom? I dread to think of our fate in the coming war of Independence if the Punjabees will be against our freedom movements? Here is the wonderful [h]uman material for you to inspire them with patriotism!" Having won the students over, Dayal embarked on a tour to meet with Punjabi workers in 1913.[28]

Although Dayal was a galvanizing force, South Asian migrants had become politicized years before his arrival. In the context of race riots and immigration restrictions, they could not help but recognize the power of race, the worthlessness of British imperial citizenship, and the need for an organized response. Taraknath Das was among the first to try to forge a collective voice. Das had gravitated to revolutionary movements against the British empire as a college student in Bengal, eventually abandoning his studies to become a full-time organizer. In 1905, upon learning of his imminent arrest by the colonial authorities, he sought exile in Japan. When the British ambassador applied pressure on the Japanese government to silence and deport Indian anticolonial activists, Das hoped to find refuge in the United States and landed in Seattle in July 1906. He made his way down to California, taking on a series of physically exhausting jobs familiar to his compatriots—on the railroads and farms and in laundry and custodial work—and then enrolling at the University of California, Berkeley. With fellow South Asian students and workers, Das founded the Indian Independence League, which offered evening courses on American history and English to prepare South Asians to apply to become naturalized citizens. Because he needed to earn a living, he left Berkeley to assume a government position as a translator with the US Immigration and Naturalization Service in Vancouver, British Columbia. He arrived there in July 1907, two months before the anti-Asian riots.[29]

The riots in Bellingham and Vancouver mobilized South Asian migrants to band together. Reports from Vancouver indicated that Chinese, Japanese, and South Asian residents organized a joint labor strike to protest the violent attacks. The Japanese in particular gained a reputation for their steadfast defense of their communities, with guns, if necessary. A. E. Fowler, a leader of the Asiatic Exclusion League who had fanned the flames in Bellingham and Vancouver, declined to hold a rally in Seattle. After seeing what happened up north, he was convinced that the Japanese—"all of them trained soldiers, armed fanatics ready to die for their emperor and subject to the instant call of their local leaders"—could potentially overwhelm undisciplined white mobs. Fowler also feared for his life. "I am willing to be a hero," he said, "but I don't want to be a martyr."[30] Das, for his part, helped to establish the Hindusthani Association to demand justice for South Asians in Canada. In April 1908, he began publishing *Free Hindusthan,* a bimonthly newspaper unabashedly demanding "Swaraj—absolute self-government." Calling on South Asians everywhere to oppose immigration restrictions, he warned British authorities that exclusion would spell the end of empire. "The British government must be told in an active way that if Indians are not allowed to enter British colonies," he wrote, "Britishers will sooner or later be excluded from India." Pressed by British officials,

FIGURE 11. Taraknath Das. Courtesy
of Norwich University and South Asian
American Digital Archive (SAADA).

the US immigration bureau told Das to choose between his newspaper
and his day job. He chose his paper.[31]

From his college days in Bengal, the British security state monitored
and harassed Das, who found no sanctuary in the United States. When
he refused to cease publishing *Free Hindusthan,* Canadian agents tried
to have the "seditious and disloyal" publication impounded and banned.
Tired of the mounting pressure, Das moved back to the United States in
the spring of 1908, where he briefly resumed publishing his newspaper
in Seattle before enrolling in Norwich University, a military academy in
Vermont. Everywhere Das went, agents of the British state followed
him, dispatching alarming reports on his anticolonial activities. Upon
learning that Das was delivering anti-British speeches in New England
and encouraging other Indian students to apply to Norwich, British
officials lobbied successfully for his departure from the school. US officials "will always be in sympathy with us in matters of this kind," the
British military attaché stated, "as they have an idea that the education
which they are now giving to the Filipinos may tend to breed the same
class of agitator there." Empires had to stick together. In the meantime,
Das found a new home for *Free Hindusthan* in New York, with the help

of the editor of an Irish nationalist newspaper. As copies of his newspaper began circulating in Calcutta, British colonial authorities denounced *Free Hindusthan* as "revolutionary and anarchical" and appealed to the US government to suppress its publication. The US State Department asked New York officials to investigate if Das was violating any state law. He left for the Pacific Coast.[32]

As Das pursued academic studies at the University of Washington and the University of California, Berkeley, he remained committed to challenging immigration restrictions and colonial rule. In December 1910, he became involved in a case that would put into question US claims to sovereignty over the Philippines. On November 4, 1910, nineteen South Asians left Manila for Seattle, where immigration authorities summarily rejected them for being "likely to become a public charge" and, in the case of four individuals, believers "in the practice of polygamy." Herbert W. Meyers, an attorney representing seventeen of the individuals, appealed the decisions, arguing that his clients were able-bodied workers and that they had been admitted legally into the United States in the Philippines. "This country of ours has been heralded as the hope of the down-trodden," he pleaded, "but if we go out of our way to exclude men who have *once been rightfully admitted* in the country and who, under the law, should really not be rejected, we will soon find we have made a serious mistake." Meyers added that Das, "a college graduate and a writer of some repute," vowed to post bond that "these men will not become public charges" and to employ fifteen of them immediately. Although those migrants were interested first and foremost in gaining entry into Seattle, they exposed and exploited the contradictions of empire. The US government could not claim jurisdiction over the Philippines and, as Meyers put it, over his clients' "journey from one section of our country to another."[33]

US immigration authorities, in effect, concluded that they could do both. Ellis DeBruler, the commissioner of immigration in Seattle, affirmed the decisions, stressing the dangers of allowing "an open gateway to the mainland of the United States" and thereby flooding the market for "common labor." White workers, he continued, would not stand by idly, "and one of the ways in which these men would all finally become public charges would be the fact that the American laborers would drive them from the fields and the camps and then they would be for us to feed and not only to feed, but to protect from violence which would ultimately ensue." Commissioner-General of Immigration Keefe sustained DeBruler's views, but clarified that the migrants were not being denied entry but were being deported from the United States. "While ordinarily it is doubtless assumed that aliens admitted to so distant a part of the 'United States' as the Philippines intend to remain there, where climatic and economic conditions are very different from on the mainland . . . the matter takes on another aspect when viewed retrospectively in determining whether aliens who have not remained in the islands, but have attempted to move into a part of the country where conditions are dissimilar, are subject to deportation." Keefe allowed two migrants who had resided in the Philippines for longer than three years to land in Seattle, but all the others were to be deported to Hong Kong, "where they embarked originally for the Philippines."[34]

The particular migrants in this instance would find a reprieve from the deportation orders, but their legal appeals unwittingly reinforced US colonial claims over the Philippines. In March 1911, Secretary of Commerce and Labor Charles Nagel overruled the judgment of immigration officials. "No doubt deportation could be ordered and could be made effective," he reasoned, "but I can not bring myself to believe that such a course would be a fair enforcement of the law." More than fairness to the migrants, Nagel was unwilling to reverse decisions rendered by War Department officials in the Philippines, at least not without additional legislation authorizing his department to inspect such migrants independently. Nagel's decision sanctified the US state's claims to sovereignty in the Philippines, precisely at a moment of heightened imperial insecurities. Rumors of another Philippine revolution, in alliance with Japan, swirled in the Philippines, driving the US security state to monitor an ever growing number of potential revolutionaries. In June 1911, a Philippine Constabulary agent submitted a report on a South Asian peddler in Manila, "an intelligent man" who was leaving soon for Japan and China before returning to India. He concluded that the man was "an Indian political agitator." "He is a slick individual anyhow and I believe he could stand some close watching," the agent suggested. In 1911, the state authority to monitor an "agitator" in Manila and to admit South Asian migrants from Manila helped to make the Philippines a part of the "United States."[35]

The state surveillance of anticolonial revolutionaries expanded apace in North America. In January 1909, the Canadian government hired William C. Hopkinson, formerly an inspector of police in Calcutta, to monitor South Asians in Canada. He began tracking Das's movements and activities immediately and grew increasingly alarmed. When he learned that Das filed papers for naturalized citizenship in 1911—Das had been trying to secure US citizenship since 1906 to avoid being expelled, as he had been from Japan—Hopkinson initiated a campaign with his Canadian and British superiors to convince US officials that Das was an anarchist conspiring to overthrow the British empire. He built a close working relationship with US immigration authorities, receiving a promise from Seattle's inspectors that they would testify against Das's application. By the time Har Dayal set off on his speaking tour of the Pacific Coast in 1913, Hopkinson's surveillance network extended to every stop along the way. On June 9, 1913, Hopkinson rushed a telegram to the US immigration commissioner in Montreal, Canada, to ask for assistance. "Har Dayal, notorious Hindu revolutionist and anarchist, delivering course of lectures in Oregon and Washington; was in Astoria third instant," he wrote. "Would it be possible for any officers of your service to attend his lectures and take notes?" The commissioner requested that his boss, the commissioner-general in Washington, DC, send agents "to attend the lectures given by this man, with a view to determining whether he comes within any of the excluded classes." Commissioner-General Anthony Caminetti responded immediately.[36]

South Asian workers welcomed Dayal and embraced his unabashed critique of the British empire. Already organized into the Pacific Coast Hindi Association in Oregon before his arrival, they eagerly attended Dayal's speeches in 1913. In Astoria, the local newspaper reported, "a large delegation" greeted Dayal and others and escorted them to a large meeting of "the local Hindus." "You have come to America and seen with your own eyes the prosperity of this country," Dayal stated. "What is the cause of this prosperity? Why nothing more than this, that America is ruled by its own people." After discussing the proliferation of famines and plagues since the British occupation of India, he made a direct appeal to his audience. "What work you do, do it for your country. . . . Prepare now to sacrifice yourselves for your country. . . . You must collect funds whereby we can have books published, which will implant in the minds of all Indians an undying hatred of the British." Two nights later, at the Finnish Socialist Hall in Astoria, Dayal castigated the British before a multiracial crowd. A British intelligence officer captured the essence of the speech on the evils of British rule: "It could not be reformed and it must be abolished. . . . He called it the Brutish Vampire not the British Empire. In ten years revolution would be brought about by actual warfare." From those meetings with hundreds of South Asian workers across Oregon emerged the Ghadar movement.[37]

As Dayal set out to garner support up and down the Pacific Coast and to establish the movement's headquarters in San Francisco, Hopkinson warned US authorities of the vastness of South Asian revolutionary circuits. In August 1913, by which time he also served as a "Hindu interpreter" for the US Immigration Service, Hopkinson informed US officials that Madame Cama "in company with several anarchists is coming to the United States, in a short time." Madame Cama (Bhikaiji Rustom Cama), he explained, published *Bande Mataram,* a revolutionary newspaper "printed in Geneva, Switzerland, and sent to all parts of the world from Paris." "It is the intention of these people to join a Hindu anarchist named Har Dayal . . . who is known to be a close associate of Miss Emma Goldman," Hopkinson reported. Commissioner-General Caminetti instructed US immigration officers across the United States and Canada to be on the lookout for Cama and her comrades. Through an informant, Hopkinson also intercepted the correspondence between Taraknath Das and Guru Dutt Kumar, who had been active in organizing and publicizing revolutionary work against the British empire in Victoria, Vancouver, and Seattle. In May 1913, Kumar had left for Manila, where he hoped to establish a base, in his words, to "supervise the work near China, Hong-Kong, Shanghai" and "to export to South America, Mexico, Chili [*sic*], Peru and Brazil." "Information I have received is to the effect that Kumar was going to the P.I. with a view to encourage Hindu immigration into the United States," Hopkinson wrote.[38]

Hopkinson's reports reinforced US immigration officials' resolve to curb South Asian migrations from the Philippines. Since 1912, Hopkinson had framed the Philippines as the weak link in the regulation of US borders, an opening through which revolutionary ideas and anticolonial revolutionaries could enter. In June 1913, three months into Woodrow Wilson's presidency, his appointees formalized a new approach. Commissioner-General of Immigration Caminetti and Secretary of Labor William B. Wilson authorized immigration officers "to reject aliens coming from insular possessions unless it should appear that at the time of entry they were not members of the excluded classes or persons 'likely to become a public charge.'" In contrast to his predecessor, Secretary Wilson was willing to appropriate the authority to reconsider decisions made by US officials in the Philippines. As much as the US state had an investment in claiming the Philippines as a part of the "United States," it had a deeper commitment to demarcating a clear boundary between the US nation and its colonies. The decision to amend US immigration regulations followed the reasoning of Supreme

Court Justice Edward Douglass White, who in 1901 argued that "whilst in an international sense Porto Rico was not a foreign country, since it was subject to the sovereignty of and was owned by the United States, it was foreign to the United States in a domestic sense, because the island had not been incorporated into the United States, but was merely appurtenant thereto as a possession." The Philippines was likewise "owned," not "incorporated."[39]

South Asians from the unincorporated US possession of the Philippines would be "deported," not denied entry, but that legal distinction did nothing but underscore their subjection to British and US empires. In September 1913, more than seventy of the two hundred South Asians arriving from Manila received deportation orders in Seattle because they were deemed "likely to become a public charge." When they then appealed those orders in court, the local federal judge refused to grant them writs of habeas corpus. Immigration and deportation matters, he argued, rested with the executive branch, beyond the reach of judicial review. The deportation orders infuriated South Asians across North America. At a mass meeting in Vancouver, Rajah Singh articulated that collective rage by calling for vengeance. "All Hindustani, Mohomedans [sic], Sikhs should speak up for your rights, and I have to say this, that when these Canadians, Australians and New Zealanders do not allow us to enter into their country, why should we not drive them from India?" he exclaimed. "We should take those steps and we could start a struggle and exclude those people from our India, and I have great hope with our friends and our people that this work can be done." There was no question that "their country" now included the United States. "Hindustani Brothers, for what reason are we being deported?" asked another speaker, who had tried in vain to enter the United States with his family. He proposed to raise money to assist the deportees in Seattle and "to force the Indian Government to recognize our status." Attendees pledged $24,000.[40]

When Dayal began publishing *Ghadar* in November 1913, his unrelenting rebuke of empire and unremitting calls for collective action articulated and resonated with South Asian migrants' frustrations and aspirations. "It is fifty-six years since the Rebellion of 1857," he wrote, "now it is urgently necessary to have another." Dayal presented extensive reports on the many crimes committed by the British in India and the British criminalization of political activities, a combination of which, he argued, demanded concerted, direct action. In December 1913, *Ghadar* commemorated the attempted assassination of Lord Hardinge, the viceroy of India, one year earlier. "The echoes of that bomb have spread all over the world," Dayal argued, "for the newspapers in far distant countries published articles (about the incident) and asked what is wrong with the government of India that such a terroristic group has appeared." He spelled out the future course of history. "Similarly, all events clearly indicate that the rain storm of 'revolt' is about to burst on India soon, which sweeping away the debris of (the ruins of) centuries will establish a republic." For an audience trying to make sense of their migrations and persecutions, Dayal's words provided direction and resolution. "It becomes immediately the duty of every patriot who reads this paper to become a soldier of the Rebellion," he implored, "to join the regiment of the Rebellion; to prepare for the Rebellion; to see visions of the Rebellion; to wait impatiently for the day of the Rebellion." Copies of *Ghadar* soon circulated everywhere South Asians resided—in North America, Africa, India, and East and Southeast Asia.[41]

IMMIGRATION LAWS AND THE US SECURITY STATE

By January 1914, US immigration authorities were on high alert for South Asian migrants' revolutionary activities. Commissioner Samuel W. Backus, head of the San Francisco office, provided a comprehensive report on "Hindu colonies" in the United States, highlighting the locales where Dayal, Das, and many other individuals engaged in anticolonial politics. He expressed particular concern over college students, or those claiming to be students to gain admission into the United States, "whose primary purposes are to foment and foster a revolutionary movement in India, to prepare and distribute circulars and pamphlets inciting their countrymen to such a revolution, to prepare and train leaders for the uprising, and to collect funds for the promotion of their plans." Those congregated at the University of California, Berkeley, Backus noted, went so far as to conduct "rifle and revolver practice" nearby. They also supported *Ghadar*, which he described as "highly revolutionary in character" and "suppressed by the British Government in India." In addition to editing the newspaper, Backus reported, Dayal was delivering "periodical addresses at various points on the Pacific Coast under the same auspices wherefrom such agitators as Emma Goldman secure their support." He hoped soon to gather evidence of Dayal's "apparently anarchistic advocacies" to initiate deportation proceedings. Backus vowed to commit his office "to scrutinize with the greatest care all Hindu applications for admission in order that we may bring the fullest strength of the immigration laws against those who may be coming to join in the movement referred to."[42]

Dayal and his supporters struck back, for they realized the intimate links between the British and US states. In January 1914, Dayal wrote a letter to US Immigrant Inspector Charles H. Reily, stationed in Astoria, Oregon, to convey that he was, in Reily's paraphrasing, "aware of the plot of the British government and the United States Immigration Service to 'kidnap him' because of his activities in behalf of the Hindu Nationalist party." Unless Reily replied personally to suspend the plot, Dayal threatened to expose it to a San Francisco newspaper and to report to Reily's superiors of his receiving improper subsidies from the British government. Although Reily dismissed Dayal's letter, he could not so easily disregard a long series of threats from local residents. "At various times since June, 1913, at which time inquiry concerning these Hindus was first directed, I have been approached by Hindus who have warned me if any effort was made to find either Har Dayal or R[am] Chandra they would personally see that I was 'blown up,' or 'pushed off the dock at night,' or my family molested," Reily reported. "It was explained to me that the work of Har Dayal, and the interests of the Hindu Nationalist party were of such importance that rather than permit any interferance [sic] with their plans they would cheerfully dispose of me in some manner." "As evidence of their proficiency in the art of 'blowing people up,'" he added, "I was assured that most of the members of the Hindu nationalist party were also 'IWWs.'"[43]

As the revolutionary movement against the British empire mobilized increasingly against the US state, US immigration officials reacted to secure the United States from South Asian revolutionaries. At the end of January 1914, Commissioner Backus decided that it was time to arrest Dayal since he "has been connected with alleged revolutionary movements in this vicinity for some time" and "may be considered anarchistic." "This office has no definite information as to the exact period of his arrival," he admitted, "but it is believed that evidence can be obtained showing his presence in London, Paris and Martinique within three years, from which his movements can be traced to the United States." As Backus's request moved up the chain of command, Dayal arrived in Washington, DC, to appear before the congressional Committee on Immigration and Naturalization. He wished to voice his opposition to an immigration bill prohibiting Asian laborers. Commissioner-General Caminetti secretly informed Representative John L. Burnett, chair of the committee, of Dayal's impending arrest warrant so that "it may be possible to illicit [sic] some testimony from him which otherwise would not come to light." Dayal did not testify before the committee, but he evidently stopped by Caminetti's office to protest that "we are united with all idiots, imbeciles, feeble-minded persons, and so forth" in the bill. In his testimony before the committee, Caminetti conveyed Dayal's objection, identifying Dayal only as "a cultured man and a graduate of Oxford University," and suggested revising the bill's language to deflect criticisms from "some people of that race."[44]

Besides recounting his conversation with Dayal, who might have said a lot more in person, Caminetti lobbied fervently for a more stringent immigration law and a more expansive administrative state. Discretionary and emergency measures, such as the examination of aliens arriving from the Philippines, he insisted, were not enough. "We have not been able to exclude, under the present conditions of the law, more than 50 per cent." Like the Chinese before them, "Hindu immigration" had grown "stealthily" over the years, to number twenty to thirty thousand, according to Caminetti, far in excess of the official figure on legal entrants (6,656). "The question is, shall we allow this experience we have had on the Pacific coast to be repeated with the Hindu before we take action," he asked, "or shall we profit by the experience of the past and meet the question now?" In addition to a new immigration law, Caminetti appealed for greater resources from Congress to build "patrolling facilities on both borders and on the extensive coasts, east, south, west, and on the Great Lakes" and to improve "water patrol particularly in the Northwest," all in an effort "to protect ourselves from people who desire to come in surreptitiously." In his letter to Congress, Secretary of Labor Wilson transmitted the same message, arguing that indirect "expedients and makeshifts . . . to prevent a large and ever-increasing influx of laborers of that race, who to all intents and purposes are 'coolies' in the same sense that Chinese were regarded," now required explicit legislation and "direct methods."[45]

Using the confidential information he had received from Caminetti, Representative Burnett attempted to banish South Asian migrants as revolutionary anarchists. When Representative Denver S. Church of California's San Joaquin Valley testified to the criminality and deviancy of "Hindus" in his district, Burnett's colleagues on the committee used the occasion to ask about "crimes against nature" and "Hindu women dressed like men and working with men, side by side." Amid Church's harangues, Burnett asked, "Have you heard of any of the leaders teaching any anarchistic ideas?" Church conceded that "the Hindus down in my country" concentrated on obtaining jobs and sending money to India, but he nonetheless affirmed Burnett's assertion. During 'T'Ishi Bhutia's testimony, Burnett asked a similar question on anarchists and asked specifically about Dayal, although Dayal's name was omitted in the records. "The principles of anarchism are very far from India, because Buddhism prevents the shedding of blood," Bhutia, representing the Hindustani Association, answered. "We are socialists." Burnett persisted, quoting at length from Dayal's speech that Caminetti had shared with him. Bhutia's nimble responses—that Dayal had "the right to make a free speech" but that "he is not sanctioned or authorized by any of our organizations to make that speech," that his compatriots wanted to "assimilate the ideas of your democracy and then go back," that they hoped to effect change in India through "passive resistance," that Americans had once taken up arms against British rule—only fueled Burnett's and US immigration authorities' efforts to cast South Asians as menacing anarchists.[46]

As one of the most outspoken and visible anticolonial activists in the United States, Dayal came to represent the intensifying rift between the US state and South Asian communities. US immigration authorities arrested Dayal in March 1914 after his return to California, using a warrant dated February 10, 1914, based on the premise that he had arrived in "an unknown port, subsequent to the 26th day of February 1911." "For many months I have been spied upon by British secret service operatives," Dayal informed local newspapers, "but have gone about my affairs openly and have not tuned my statements or modulated my declarations because of their presence." He condemned the Wilson Administration for "licking the boots of England" and for demonstrating its "despicable pro-British subservience" by arresting him. "This is a political question and not an ordinary immigration case," Dayal stated. His case revealed the emerging alliance between Britain and the United States around race and empire. "It is simply ridiculous to think that I am being prosecuted in the United States and in the twentieth century because of my ideas," Dayal said. "I have broken no laws, and I have not advocated breaking of any laws. The only overt act I have committed is advocating the overthrow of the British in India by an armed revolt." He exuded defiance. "I am not afraid of any Government," he wrote in *Ghadar*. "If I am turned out of this country I can make preparations for the Ghadr in any other country."[47]

Dayal mounted a challenge that placed US officials on the defensive. "The Government of Great Britain has had no part in the matter nor has it either directly or indirectly requested either the arrest or the deportation of the alien," Caminetti announced, denying Dayal's accusations. Dayal's attorney, in the meantime, stressed in his brief that his client's articles and speeches were "incorrectly and most unfavorably translated . . . to give violent and anarchistic significance." "Mr. Dayal has never advocated terrorism," he explained, "but only a national rebellion." At root, what Dayal might have or might not have stated did not matter legally, his attorney argued, since he "had actually and continuously been a resident of the United States of America" for longer than three years. Dayal conveyed the same message directly to Caminetti. Within two days of Dayal's arrest, the acting commissioner of immigration at Ellis Island certified that Dayal had indeed arrived in New York from San Juan, Puerto Rico, on February 9, 1911, three years plus one day before the arrest warrant was issued. That he had sailed from an unincorporated US possession might have served as a bone of contention if the date of arrival had been even a day later—his attorney could have argued that Dayal had landed in the United States when he set foot on Puerto Rico on February 3, 1911—but, as it was, US officials knew that they had missed the legal window of opportunity by one day.[48]

Even with his legal argument in hand, Dayal could not ignore the power of the modern state to legitimize and consolidate race and empire. At the same time that Dayal was arrested in San Francisco in March 1914, Gurdit Singh chartered the *Komagata Maru* in Hong Kong to transport nearly four hundred South Asians to Canada, in defiance of immigration restrictions. At stopovers in Shanghai, Moji, and Yokohama, those affiliated with the Ghadar movement delivered fiery speeches against the British empire and circulated copies of *Ghadar* to passengers. The arrival of the *Komagata Maru* in British Columbia in May precipitated a standoff between South Asian migrants and Canadian officials that resonated with colonial subjects around the world. Refused entry and receiving deportation orders, the passengers lived nearly two months aboard the vessel in Vancouver's harbor, with their once hopeful outlooks and daily living conditions deteriorating week by week. The fate of the *Komagata Maru* consumed the attention of Canadian, British, and US authorities and South Asian communities, as it came to symbolize the revolutionary potential of Asia and the legitimacy of the state to restrict immigration and to suppress revolutionary movements. "The Hindusthanees, subjected to eternal hunger and maltreatment of every sort in their native land," Taraknath Das wrote, "want to be recognized as human beings and have equal rights to come to Canada

FIGURE 12. *Komagata Maru* in Vancouver, British Columbia. Courtesy of City of Vancouver Archives.

or any other place in the World just as others have the right to come to India." The impasse concluded in July with a Canadian naval cruiser forcibly escorting the *Komagata Maru* west toward the Pacific.[49]

In contrast to the drama unfolding in Vancouver's harbor, Dayal's stay in the United States ended on an anticlimactic note. In early April 1914, he sent a telegram to the Department of State to offer a concession. "Considering all circumstances we have decided to discontinue publication in this country of Hindu Nationalist anti-British paper and other similar propaganda here," he related. "No necessity now of persecuting educated political refugees." Commissioner Backus, in the meantime, was investigating rumors that Dayal had traveled outside of the United States after his initial entry. Dayal probably sensed that the US government was not going to allow the facts of his case impede his deportation. At the end of April, Backus demanded that Dayal appear before him for further examination, but no one could locate his whereabouts. A short time later, Backus learned from "an authentic source" that Dayal had left for Switzerland, a turn of events that drove him to seek revenge. Backus wanted to collect the $1,000 bond. His superiors disagreed. The commissioner-general stated, "At the time the bond was taken it had not been shown, nor has it since been established, that the three-year period had not expired—indeed, it seemed quite clear that it had at the time the proceedings were instituted." The Department of Labor canceled the bond. But the Bureau of Immigration refused to withdraw the arrest warrant, in case of Dayal's return, because "some advantage might result from not having absolutely closed the previous proceedings."[50]

Even as Dayal evaded US authorities, his departure underscored the growing authority of the modern state to secure nation and empire from racialized and radicalized subjects. Amid Dayal's confrontation with the Bureau of Immigration, eleven individuals in Delhi faced charges that they had conspired with one another and others, including Dayal, to commit murder against public officials. During their trial in May 1914, the prosecuting attorney reportedly "read an effusion of Hardyal's [sic] which was a mixture of religion and anarchy." He also read passages from *Ghadar* "to show the revolutionary trend of the publication." The US consul in Bombay (Mumbai), in turn, requested from British officials information on Dayal's "alleged anarchistic activities" and all "suspected or known to be anarchists" leaving India for the United States. The prosecution and deportation of anarchists, presumed to signify and include anticolonial revolutionaries, seemingly demanded transimperial and inter-state collaboration. In July 1914, Dayal explained from Geneva why he had decided to leave the United States. "I understood that my presence in the country was undesirable, as I was carrying on an active anti-British propaganda among the Hindus on the Pacific Coast, and certain unfounded charges have been preferred by the English Government against me with reference to incidents in India," he informed US officials. "I hope that the US government will not needlessly molest my poor and ignorant compatriots who live in the United States and cherish dreams of the freedom of their country." As Dayal knew from his own experience, that wish would not be granted.[51]

WAR, EMPIRE, AND SEDITION

By the time Dayal took up residence in Switzerland, Europe was on an accelerating path to World War I, but the roots of war extended far beyond Europe and farther back than 1914. Race and empire, W. E. B. Du Bois argued, sowed the seeds of war. "The Balkans are convenient for occasions," he observed in 1915, "but the ownership of materials and men in the darker world is the real prize that is setting the nations of Europe at each other's throats to-day." For Du Bois, the formation of the modern nation—"a new democratic nation composed of united capital and labor"—explained the new stage of "world-wide freebooting," where "the white workingman has been asked to share the spoil of exploiting 'chinks and niggers.'" What emerged was a "democratic despotism" rooted in "the color line," demarcated and enforced by immigration restrictions, segregation codes, and brutal violence. "All over the world there leaps to articulate speech and ready action that singular assumption that if white men do not throttle colored men," Du Bois stated, "then China, India, and Africa will do to Europe what Europe has done and seeks to do to them." The extension of "the democratic ideal to the yellow, brown, and black peoples" might bring about "real peace and lasting culture," he proposed. Otherwise, "these nations and races, composing as they do a vast majority of humanity, are going to endure this treatment just as long as they must and not a moment longer."[52]

Many South Asians in the United States and elsewhere concluded that the moment of reckoning had arrived. The declaration of war between Great Britain and Germany in the summer of 1914 appeared to portend a moment of revolutionary possibilities. "Germany, England, France, Russia, Italy, Turkey, Serbia, Austria, Belgium, Holland, Switzerland, Mexico, Morocc[o], Albania and China are in the throes of revolution," *Ghadar* proclaimed. "This is the time to mutiny in India too." Reporting that Indian troops were about to be dispatched to the frontlines of Europe, the newspaper offered a historical lesson to soldiers and readers. "The brave Sikhs fought for the British in Afghanistan, Afridistan, China, and Soudan," *Ghadar* stated. "The reward which they are today getting is that their beloved country is day by day going deeper into the abyss of slavery, and in Canada the Indians are regarded as less than dogs and cats." In a pamphlet addressed to Indian troops, the Ghadar Party pointed out the workings of white supremacy in the armed forces. "The white soldiers do not do the hardest of work, (but) make us to do that," it argued. "Therefore, O Indian soldiers! *Do not be slaves of the English.*" It was a moment like 1857, a moment for Indians everywhere to band together. "Open your minds. Store your wealth in the Ghadr office and register your name in the army of the Ghadr," the paper implored those in the United States. "Clean[s]e your blood. How long will you remain seated in lethargy?"[53]

Moved by such words, and remembering the *Komagata Maru* and countless other grievances over the years, many South Asian migrants made the decision to return home to foment a revolution. Almost immediately upon the beginning of the war, Jawala Singh, a wealthy farmer in California and a prominent figure in the Ghadar movement, resolved to donate his property to the Ghadar Party and to lead a group of revolutionaries across the Pacific. As about seventy of them were about to set sail from San Francisco, Ram Chandra, who had assumed the leadership of *Ghadar* and the Ghadar Party after Dayal's departure, urged them on. "Your duty is clear; go to India, stir up rebellion in every corner of the country, rob the wealthy and show mercy to the poor," he told them. "In this way gain universal sympathy. Arms will be provided for you on arrival in India; failing this you must loot rifles from police stations." Chandra and other Ghadar leaders traveled up and down the Pacific Coast to mobilize their compatriots. Mostly in small groups, more than a thousand South Asian revolutionaries left North America and joined thousands of others from Panama, the Philippines, China, and Hong Kong, all in a mission to liberate India from the British empire. Singh's contingent arrived in Calcutta in October 1914, aboard the *Tosa Maru*, which, according to British authorities, carried "173 Indian passengers, mostly Sikhs, from America, Manila, Shanghai and Hong Kong" talking "openly of starting rebellion on arriving in India."[54]

The ordeal encountered by returning migrants signaled that the British security state would fight wartime hopes of revolution as fiercely as any battle in Europe. Greeted by a military force, one hundred of the passengers on the *Tosa Maru* were transferred summarily to a special train to Punjab to be interned. "Of those who were not interned," a government report stated, "six were afterwards hanged for murderous outrages in the Punjab, six were convicted in various conspiracy cases, six were subsequently arrested and interned on account of their mischievous activities, two were chief leaders of the subsequent revolutionary movement and were admitted as approvers [government witnesses]." A month earlier, in September 1914, passengers aboard the ill-fated *Komagata Maru* had suffered a similar homecoming. Denied permission to land in Singapore and Hong Kong—because of British fears that stories of the passengers' plight would incite mutinies—the ship proceeded toward Calcutta. Forcing the vessel to dock in Budge Budge, an industrial town outside of Calcutta, to ward off public attention, British authorities instructed the passengers to board a guarded train to Punjab. After their long odyssey back and forth across the Pacific, most of the passengers refused and began marching toward Calcutta, only to be met by military troops and police officers. When ordered back onto the *Komagata Maru*, the passengers sat down and began praying, an act of collective defiance that police officers responded to with brute force. After the "riot," more than two dozen people lay dead, including twenty passengers.[55]

The mass harassment and internment of returning migrants were made possible through new laws enacted ostensibly to meet the exigencies of war. In September 1914, the government of India adopted the Ingress into India Ordinance, which provided the governor-general in council and local government officials with the authority to restrict and detain all persons entering British India "to protect the State from anything prejudicial to its safety, interests or tranquility." Passengers aboard the *Komagata Maru* and the *Tosa Maru* were the earliest victims of that wartime measure, which was subsequently applied to returning migrants wholesale. "The rule was that those from Canada, the United States, Hong Kong, Shanghai, and Manilla [*sic*] were restricted in all cases," a government inquiry stated later, "and that discretion was exercised only in regard to persons from the Malay States, the Straits Settlements and the Dutch East Indies." In March 1915, in the immediate wake of a Ghadar-inspired mutiny in Singapore and the discovery of a similar plot in Punjab, the government of India implemented the Defence of India Act, authorizing the governor-general in council to establish rules "to empower any civil or military authority to prohibit the entry or residence in any area of a person suspected to be acting in a manner prejudicial to the public safety, or to direct the residence of such person in any specified area." The law also allowed special tribunals to try revolutionaries, without access to judicial appeals.[56]

The British state in India quickly applied its new statute to punish those who dared to challenge the British empire, targeting in particular those affiliated with the Ghadar movement. In April 1915, it charged eighty-two individuals in Lahore, Punjab—half of whom were return migrants from the United States—with conspiring to overthrow the British government in India. During the first Lahore Conspiracy trial, key government witnesses, convinced to testify in exchange for pardons, detailed their personal journeys to the United States and toward the "seditious" politics of the Ghadar Party. Kartar Singh Sarabha, a former student at the University of California, Berkeley, recounted a similar story, except that he denounced the entire proceedings along with the British empire. He and six other defendants decided to accept full responsibility for the charges and to use the occasion to proclaim the righteousness of their cause. Sarabha enumerated the many indignities suffered by Indians under British rule, including the plight of the *Komagata Maru*, and refused to retract his statements. He declared that it was the "right of the slave to revolt." In September 1915, the trial concluded predictably with more than twenty of the defendants sentenced to death and another twenty-six condemned to life in prison. Most of the death sentences were commuted to life imprisonment, but

Sarabha and five others were hanged in Lahore's central jail in November 1915.[57]

British officials then lobbied the US government to investigate South Asian revolutionaries and their allies in the United States, the root cause of the Lahore Conspiracy as they saw it. Within months of the convictions and executions, the British Embassy in Washington, DC, forwarded "confidential papers" gathered from the "exhaustive appendix" of the trial's record to US federal officials. The appendix provided an extensive history of the Ghadar movement, stressing its brazen radicalism and its American genesis. "It is from the Pacific Coast of America that the present conspiracy derives its origin," it asserted. To British authorities, Har Dayal's arrival in San Francisco had defined the movement's intensity and popularity. "He appears while in England to have become i[m]bued with an extraordinarily passionate and unreasoning race-hatred and to have developed into a monomaniac," British officials claimed, "dangerous because he appears to have possessed a certain power of speech and because he thereafter devoted himself to inoculating others with the same views of intense race-hatred." His speeches infected "his hearers with political ideas" and spread the "flame of sedition" along the Pacific Coast. Perhaps most disconcerting of all, the Ghadar movement's influence appeared to be growing around the world. Having proposed Germany as a potential ally months before World War I, according to British sources, Dayal and fellow revolutionaries were working closely with "foreign enemies of his majesty." British officials had information to indicate "the very important part taken by the German Consular officials in America and the Far East in engineering and supporting the conspiracy."[58]

In the spring of 1916, a year before the United States entered World War I, the US Department of Justice initiated an investigation of its own against South Asian revolutionaries. Based on the materials forwarded by the British Embassy, department officials became convinced of a dire situation along the Pacific Coast. "This conspiracy for the overthrow of British rule in India," a department memorandum stated, "was, in fact planned, organized and financed in the United States." Recent reports, moreover, seemed to suggest a transpacific movement very much still in operation. "Movements of men and arms from California to various parts of the East but converging on India have been, and are still being noted," the same memorandum remarked, "and from time to time there has been evidence of German participation." As thousands of men heeded *Ghadar*'s call to return to India, they appeared to wreak havoc everywhere they stopped, "responsible en route for outbreaks or attempted outbreaks at Singapore, Penang and Hong Kong." In May 1916, Assistant Attorney General Charles Warren charged US Attorney John W. Preston of San Francisco to investigate potential violations of US neutrality laws. "The Indian Court was intent only on showing that the sentiments expressed in this paper were seditious and insurrectionary," Warren counseled. "It is therefore quite probable that an investigation with a view to showing sentiments of 'a character tending to incite arson, murder or assassination' would lead to productive results."[59]

As much as British officials pressured the US state to recognize possible criminal activities on American soil, they also exposed the colonial world order in which the United States had a deep possessive investment. Warren's instructions closed with a lengthy quote of the British ambassador, whose conclusions he hoped Preston would find "of service." "Since the Lahore trials further information has come to hand which shows that a world wide organization exists, the centre of which is in Berlin (where Har Dial [*sic*] is now living) and that the object of this organization is the destruction of the British in India," the ambassador had written. "It appears that some Irishmen are employed as agents and that efforts are being made to affiliate some of the Industrial Workers of the World, one of whom is now in Berlin." Forging new alliances and building on his old radical ties, Dayal, the "general director," seemed to work easily across racial and imperial borders. "America is one of the spheres of activity of this organization," the ambassador continued, "and money appears to be provided through German Consuls (as well as that raised by local subscriptions) for the purpose of sending parties to India and arming them." From hidden locations in the United States, according to the ambassador, the vast organization was plotting to ship arms and men to India through various points in colonized Asia. In a recent case, he noted, US customs officials in Manila had refused to clear a ship chartered to convey arms "probably to some point near Java."[60]

In the course of Preston's investigation and eventual prosecution of South Asian revolutionaries, he not only cultivated a strong bond with the British security state but helped to create and consolidate the US security state. By February 1917, when Preston was preparing to present evidence before a grand jury, Assistant Attorney General Warren explained how much the case meant to the British. "It seems that the activities of the Indians connected with the 'Ghadr' have given the British authorities grave concern and they are very anxious that the revolutionary

FIGURE 13. Bhagwan Singh. Courtesy of Surinder Pal Singh and South Asian American Digital Archive (SAADA).

movement in this country looking to the liberation of India should cease," he informed Preston. And Preston worked very closely with British officials. He could not have completed his work, Preston reflected later, without "the very able and exhaustive investigations that were conducted by the British agents in conjunction with our own." He never saw "more full, complete, accurate and intelligent reports than were produced by these Agents." Preston was equally impressed with his colleagues in the US government. "The cooperation that we received from the Department of Justice itself in gathering the data from the four quarters of the earth practically, was most remarkable," he added.[61] Tracing revolutionary movements rested on identifying, exploiting, and coordinating state resources near and far. Gathering information, especially from across the Pacific, rendered revolutionary movements visible and menacing. Criminalizing those movements, in turn, justified and expanded US imperial claims and interests in "the four quarters of the earth."

The investigation of Bhagwan Singh's movements exemplified how those transimperial relations and processes marked South Asian revolutionaries as racial and sexual threats to US national security. Singh, according to British police and intelligence reports, left India around 1909 for the British Federated Malay States "on account of having got into trouble through taking away a married woman." A religious leader (*granthi*) by training, Singh worked at a *gurdwara* until he came into a quarrel with local Sikhs for "preaching sedition." He moved to Hong Kong in 1910 and secured another post at a *gurdwara*. Singh's tenure in that British colony proved even more scandalous. "Bhagwan Singh had got himself into bad odour by consorting with loose Chinese women, which is a serious religious offence from the Sikh point of view," a British police officer reported, "and his preaching, although it could not at that time be proved to be actually seditious, was certainly directed against the British Government, and encouraged a considerable amount of loose talk." In May 1913, Singh departed for British Columbia, where he "openly preached sedition." He was deported in November 1913 for having given false statements when entering Canada. He sailed back across the Pacific to Japan and, in the spring of 1914, greeted the *Komagata Maru* as it stopped over on its way to Vancouver. The British Embassy in Tokyo related that Singh "sold a pistol to the leader of the expedition, Gurdit Singh . . . and made speeches of extreme violence to those on board."[62]

Singh's transpacific movements and connections distressed British and US officials. In Japan, he lived with Muhammad Barakatullah, who had been a professor of Hindi-Urdu languages at the Tokyo School of Foreign Languages and editor of *Islamic Fraternity,* a pan-Islamic newspaper banned in India. By the time Singh arrived in Japan, Barakatullah's anti-British politics had already led to the loss of his teaching position and the Japanese government's suppression of his newspaper. Barakatullah and Singh decided to devote their energies to the Ghadar Party in the United States, taking over leadership positions in San Francisco just as Dayal fled the United States. When war broke out between Britain and Germany, Barakatullah and Singh toured with Ram Chandra up and down the Pacific Coast to urge Ghadarites to incite a revolution in India. Singh himself left San Francisco in October 1914, traveling under a false name, and landed in Manila the following month in a journey that he hoped would lead back to India. In an interview published in the *Manila Daily Bulletin* in March 1915, Singh explained how state repression had forced him to move repeatedly. He said:

> For three years I officiated as a priest among my people in Hongkong. . . . I mingled among the Indian soldiers garrisoned there and preached revolution to them. They were all opposed to British oppression and gave me their

assurance that they were ready to fight for their country when the time came. . . . The British authorities finally became suspicious. They were afraid of my influence. A false charge was brought against me and I was place[d] under arrest. Their case against me, however, was so flimsy that they were obliged to order my release. Then I went to Canada and British Columbia. I began there as a teacher among the Indians in that country and when the British learned of my mission, I was ordered deported to Hongkong. I knew what would happen to me if I was taken back there, so I succeeded in escaping from the steamer in Japan. I was in Yokohama when the Yamagata [*sic*] Maru stopped there with the Indian[s] bound for Canada, who were afterwards deported to India, and I went aboard and delivered a lecture to them. Finally a secret service man who was sent to watch me told me that the British authorities were after me and advised me to go away. I then went to the United States and was working among my people there when the war broke out.

Reproduced, shared, and filed by US agents in Manila, Singh's interview underscored both the apparent necessity and the perpetual futility of state surveillance. British authorities could never quite contain his movements, his relationships, or his speeches.[63]

To US authorities grappling with anticolonial revolutionaries of their own, Singh's arrival in the Philippines generated anxiety and insecurity. In January 1915, unable to find a non-British ship to India, Singh left Manila to try to reach the Dutch East Indies by way of the southern islands of the Philippines. Suspecting that Singh was up to no good, an Englishman working as a US customs inspector in the Sulu archipelago arrested him for attempting to incite an insurrection among the Muslim "Moros." Singh was eventually transferred to Zamboanga on the island of Mindanao, where US authorities interrogated him. After a short time, an agent of the Philippine Constabulary and the customs office in Zamboanga reported, "I found out that he had not been talking, or had he in any way or manner had any connection with the moros [*sic*]." In his statement, though, Singh embraced revolution. "My business is to get all of my countrymen to assist in the general uprising which is about to take place (probably next month) in India against the English Government," he said. "It was for this purpose that I have visited the United States, Canada, and Mexico and am now here in the Philippines." Claiming to have been promised at least a million rifles by German agents, Singh stated that, once back in Punjab, he would command "an army of three or four hundred thousand men." He was not alone, he said, for there were anticolonial organizers like him "in all parts of the world wherever any of our people live."[64]

Released after being deemed "not a serious menace to public order though perhaps somewhat unbalanced mentally," Singh decided to test the bounds of political freedom in the Philippines. When he returned to Manila, he informed the governor-general that he was "working for the revolution in India." He also recounted his personal story to the *Manila Daily Bulletin* and declared that "the revolution has already begun." British authorities had heard enough. In May 1915, the US consul in Hong Kong related to the governor-general's office in Manila that British colonial authorities had approached him several times about Singh. The consul recommended strongly that Singh "be deported to Hongkong or Singapore and the authorities notified at the time of his deportation and the vessel by which he will arrive at either place." The Philippine Constabulary investigated the matter and concluded that there were "no grounds upon which to base legal proceedings against this Indian." When British officials demanded again a few months later that "Indian agitators in Manila" be deported to Hong Kong, US authorities refused politely. But they also had Manila's secret agents warn the "agitators" that they "could not permit any activity on the part of the Indians residing in these Islands looking to the creation of disturbances in a neighboring colony, and that further activity on their part would result in immediate steps being taken to rid the Islands of them." The US colonial government, with agents at "every meeting of the Indians in Manila," pledged to monitor revolutionary activities in the Philippines.[65]

Singh, for his part, continued to evade British and US authorities to advance his work against the British empire. In June 1915, he left Manila for Japan and reportedly established communications with German agents in Shanghai. Four months later, he and a compatriot traveled to Tientsin (Tianjin), "where they were nearly captured by the British." By June 1916, according to information gathered by British officials and shared with US officials, Singh was back in San Francisco, having "concealed his traces so skil[l]fully that it has not been possible to ascertain by what vessel he arrived." He quickly sailed to Panama, traveling under the alias B. Pritam, and thence to Cuba, from which he was forced to leave because of trachoma. Singh returned to Panama, staying at "a hotel and restaurant of more or less bad repute and which used to be a resort for Germans." "Pritam while in Panama formed secret meetings with the East Indians and collected funds for the purpose of starting a revolution to free India from British rules [*sic*]," the US minister reported. Nearly all four hundred East Indians in Panama "promised to support the movement." The British minister to Panama, the US minister noted, actively sought to have Singh deported, accusing him of being Turkish and pressuring the government of Panama to apply its immigration laws against "members of the Turkish race and certain other races." Given fourteen days "to prove he was not a Turk or leave Panama," Singh headed back to San Francisco.[66]

When US Attorney Preston decided to prosecute Singh and a host of other South Asian revolutionaries in San Francisco in 1917, there was no question that the movement against the British empire had to contend with the US empire and its expanding security state. In the wake of Singh's forced departure and local protests against it, US authorities in Panama maintained a "practically complete list of East Indians resident on the Isthmus of Panama in the vicinity of the Canal Zone," prioritizing "all members of the Ghadr (or Gadar) Party" and keeping the "leaders of these men" under "observation, and any information received . . . transmitted to the American Minister to Panama." Claiming authority over the Panama Canal Zone translated into monitoring South Asian revolutionaries. Returning to San Francisco hardly liberated Singh from state surveillance. In January 1917, he and his supporters charged Ram Chandra of using German funds for his own personal use, spurring bitter divisions within the Ghadar Party. As Singh assumed control of *Ghadar* headquarters—and Chandra set up a rival press likewise claiming lineage to the original newspaper—the US government's investigation of South Asian revolutionaries intensified. On the eve of US entry into World War I in April 1917, the attorney general sent a telegram to Preston ordering immediate arrests in the "Hindoo revolution matter." "Advise arrest in advance declaration War since fear escape Ram Chandra," he wired. He also suggested searching Singh's headquarters. Singh decided to flee to Mexico before it was too late.[67]

Once the United States entered World War I, various agents and agencies of the US state bolstered and coordinated their efforts to suppress revolutionary movements. On April 18, 1917, US immigration authorities in Naco, Arizona, detained Singh for appearing "very suspicious." At first, he reportedly claimed that "he was an English Jew by the name of William James" on his way to visit his white "sweetheart." Assuming Singh to be connected with the "Indian Revolution movement," the immigrant inspector immediately contacted the Bureau of Investigation (BI), the forerunner to the Federal Bureau of Investigation. When examined by a BI agent and the immigrant inspector the next day, Singh explained that he was planning to "preach" to "my people" in Mexico about "their duties as Hindus, about nationalism." Pressed by the BI agent if that meant "to teach your countrymen to raise up in arms against the English Government in India," Singh replied: "We are not allowed to speak anything in India; so we are getting new ideas in this country and so we are teaching them to our people so that they will not be behind." Not satisfied, the BI agent repeatedly asked if Singh was, in fact, "a revolutionist against the British Government in India." "If the English are going to oppress my people in India I am against them . . . I want to see India enjoy freedom and happiness like other countries," Singh responded. "If this is a crime, then let me be a criminal."[68]

The US state did indeed deem Singh a criminal and issued a warrant for his arrest, a turn of events that expanded and sharpened Singh's critique of empire. In July 1917, as he and dozens of fellow South Asian revolutionaries awaited trial for violating US neutrality laws, Singh wrote a piercing column on US claims to be fighting for "the protection of democracy." "If America has entered [World War I] with the purpose of emancipating small nations then what need is there for a revolution, for she will liberate all," he posed. "The question is, but will she fulfill her purpose?" Long before the Paris Peace Conference, Singh knew the answer. Having "never dreamt of endeavouring to secure the emancipation of smaller nations," he argued, the United States offered no hope, for "the cause of the evil existing in India to-day is the friendship of America and England." The contradiction between empire and democracy was too stark to ignore. "When a nation which keeps in subjection the Philippines and Porto Rico," he observed, "then her claim appears a matter of astonishment to the whole world." As Singh penned those words, US Attorney Preston was busy compiling them to prosecute him. That was the state of affairs South Asian revolutionaries faced around the world—in Punjab, in the Philippines, in Hong Kong, in San Francisco. By daring to confront the colonial roots and colonial objectives of the modern states flying the Union Jack and the Stars and Stripes, they bore the brunt of state repression.[69]

CHAPTER 4

Radicalizing Hawai'i

Infused by a wave of labor migrations and radical politics, Harlem was abuzz at the end of World War I. And no one demanded to be heard more than Hubert Harrison, the self-described "radical internationalist" whose West Indian roots had led him to see beyond Harlem, beyond the United States. "We must organize, plan and act, and the time for the action is now," he argued in 1921. "A call should be issued for a congress of the darker races, which should be frankly anti-imperialistic and should serve as an international center of cooperation from which strength may be drawn for the several sections of the world of color." His appeal for "a colored international" beckoned "representatives and spokesmen of the oppressed peoples of India, Egypt, China, West and South Africa, and the West Indies, Hawaii, the Philippines, Afghanistan, Algeria, and Morocco." Reframing V.I. Lenin's theorization of imperialism as "the monopoly stage of capitalism" by placing race at the heart of his analysis, Harrison argued that "capitalist imperialism" was the common enemy, "which mercilessly exploits the darker races for its own financial purposes . . . [and] which we must combine to fight with arms as varied as those by which it is fighting to destroy our manhood, independence and self-respect." He was calling for a revolutionary politics across racial and national borders, a kind of global and interracial solidarity that challenged the nation-state form. The US state kept a close eye on Harrison's activities.[1]

Hailing from a land colonized by Japan and toiling in cane fields owned by a coterie of *haole* (white foreigners), Korean workers in

Hawai'i knew firsthand the pernicious effects of capitalist imperialism. They seemed to embody the spirit of collective resistance against white supremacy and empire that Harrison was calling forth. But when plantation workers on the island of O'ahu staged a massive strike in 1920, their political allegiances seemed to be at a crossroads. Would Korean workers support the local strike and thereby ally themselves with Japanese and Filipino workers? The US military wanted to know. Some Koreans joined the strike right away, according to Lieutenant Colonel George M. Brooke of the Military Intelligence Division (MID), but, in the early days of the strike in January 1920, he was interested more in the popularity of the Korean National Association (KNA). With more than fifty branches and five thousand members in Hawai'i, he reported, Koreans appeared organized and unified. Those figures belied bitter divisions. At a raucous meeting attended by more than six hundred Koreans, Brooke observed a little later, KNA leaders expressing sympathy with the strike were expelled and replaced by a firmly "anti-Japanese faction." "We also passed resolutions placing ourselves irrevocably against the Japanese and the present strike," the revamped KNA announced. "We do not wish to be looked upon as strike breakers, but we shall continue to work in the plantations and we are opposed to the Japanese in everything." The debate grew so heated that the police raided the meeting hall.[2]

Not without divisions and contradictions, plantation workers in Hawai'i initiated a labor strike in 1920 that reverberated across the Pacific. Brooke grew increasingly alarmed. When a Japanese worker agreed to return to work on Aiea plantation, Brooke reported to his superiors in Washington, DC, his compatriots seized and carried him to a labor rally in Honolulu. "He was taken to the platform and compelled to sit there for fifteen minutes facing the audience, from which came fierce cries of 'Kill him!'" To Brooke, such confrontations illustrated the racial solidarity of Japanese workers, not their political differences. "This may be a case of labor against capital, but it sounds more like a declaration of final racial allegiance. . . . It is a reflection of Pan Asianism." For many workers, though, the labor strike represented a local expression of a wider struggle against capital and empire. "The strikers, therefore," a Japanese-language newspaper argued during the strike, "should be very careful in their conduct in making the present strike a lawful one to win the victory of industrial democracy over capitalistic imperialism."[3] As radical appeals against racial capitalism, critical of white supremacy and "capitalistic imperialism," echoed around the world, Brooke and his colleagues reacted vigilantly and adamantly. In

Hawai'i's labor struggles, they saw a wider campaign to challenge US claims to sovereignty.

Perceiving and framing the 1920 labor strike as a racial and international conflict between the United States and Japan proved indispensable to fortifying the US empire across the Pacific. The strike and its aftershocks revealed and represented a series of what Michel Foucault called "counter-conducts," acts that redistributed, reversed, nullified, and partially or totally discredited state domination. In laying bare histories of empire in and beyond Hawai'i through incipient, if fleeting, interracial solidarities, plantation workers engaged in "counter-conducts" that constituted an essential element in the ongoing genesis of the US security state.[4] Unwilling and unable to comprehend the complex roots of labor struggles in Hawai'i, planters and military leaders fixated on race, specifically a pan-Asian solidarity presumably led by imperial Japan, and projected its undue influence in undermining US national interests. Those contrasting and overlapping roots of the 1920 labor strike—plantation workers' struggles grounded in transpacific movements and localizing connections and the racialization of plantation workers through imperial circuits of knowledge—generated intense struggles that, in turn, rationalized and produced a US security state spanning the Pacific. As a result, in the years during and after World War I, the US state's capacity to monitor and criminalize revolutionary movements and interracial solidarities expanded conspicuously. If the 1920 labor strike in Hawai'i bore a momentary testament to "a colored international" that Harrison and others imagined possible, a revolutionary aspiration reflecting and exceeding pan-Asian solidarity, its brutal repression marked a new phase of the US empire, where "domestic" and "foreign" politics converged in a seemingly endless racial and international confrontation with imperial Japan.

FEARS OF A RISING SUN

Like many of his compatriots, Taraknath Das saw World War I as an opportunity to advance struggles against the colonial order of things. Soon after war broke out in Europe in 1914, he traveled to Berlin, where exiled South Asians were attempting to forge an alliance with German officials. As a member of the Berlin India Committee, Das attempted to persuade Indian troops fighting for Britain to switch allegiances, first among prisoners of war in Germany and then among soldiers stationed in the Suez Canal Zone. Neither mission yielded encouraging results or captured Das's imagination. After a stint carrying out publicity work in Constantinople, Das set his sights on East Asia, where the Berlin India Committee hoped to procure arms and to cultivate a pan-Asian movement. The US government stood in his way. Back in June 1914, despite great efforts by US immigration authorities to cast Das as an anarchist, a US federal court had granted him US citizenship, largely based on favorable testimonials by university professors. Two years later, US embassies in Europe, under pressure from British officials keeping tabs on Das's anticolonial activities, refused to grant him a new passport. When he finally secured an emergency passport from the Stockholm embassy, Das ventured back to New York and San Francisco before boarding a ship bound for Yokohama in August 1916. He was going to Japan and China, Das told a friend, to tend to "Pan-Asiatic affairs."[5]

By the time Das reached China in the fall of 1916, Shanghai, Hong Kong, and other cities were already integral sites of revolutionary organizing. Shir Dayal Kapur Khatri, a South Asian migrant employed by the customs department in Shanghai, had no interest in anticolonial politics until he began reading *Ghadar* in early 1914. "Numerous copies of the 'Ghadr' came to Shanghai," he recalled. "Every Indian shop and store got it. . . . The Gurdwara used to get 100 to 200 copies a week." Kapur himself joined the Ghadar movement around December 1914, when about seventy-five returning migrants from the United States stopped over in Shanghai, part of a larger contingent making its way westward across the Pacific. In Shanghai, the migrants rented a house in the French district and hosted a meeting attended by local South Asians like Kapur as well as German and Chinese supporters. Guru Dutt Kumar, the Ghadar leader based in Manila, began the meeting by noting how "auspicious" it was to be welcomed by fellow "Indian brothers" in Shanghai. A German speaker then explained that "Germany had gripped the sword, not to extend their own dominion over the w[ho]le world, but to raise fallen and oppressed races; now was the opportunity for Indians." When Kumar finally asked the audience who was "prepared to sacrifice their wealth, position and life itself for India," according to Kapur, they all raised their hands.[6]

Such scenes unnerved the British security state, which dispatched agents around the world to monitor and contain anticolonial movements and sentiments. Several months before Das's arrival, the Central Intelligence Department of India assigned an agent to Shanghai to survey and consolidate British antiradical measures across East Asia. The brutal campaign in India had a profound impact. "There is no organization to receive and support the plotters the moment they set foot on Indian soil," the agent reported. "While this is the case, the Germans and Indians in Shanghai, Manila or elsewhere may talk as big as they please regarding ships and guns and rifles and landings in India. It need hardly cause us a moment's uneasiness." That, however, did not mean that the British security apparatus could let its guard down. To the contrary, the state of affairs demanded greater resources. "We know all or very nearly all the persons in each place who represent the whole available machinery for setting of these 'schemes' in motion," the agent concluded confidently, "and I am inclined to think that in most cases, if we take care of the men, the schemes will take care of themselves." From the moment Das landed in Yokohama, British officials maintained a surveillance of his activities, characterizing him as "one of the most dangerous German agents," "a veteran conspirator," "one of the most important revolutionaries," and an "apostle of the Pan-Asiatic Movement." They tracked his movements to Peking (Beijing) and then Shanghai, growing wary of his pan-Asian political message.[7]

During his time in China and Japan, Das concentrated his energy on articulating and promoting a pan-Asian movement. As some Chinese officials and lay persons began lobbying for China to join the war against Germany, he wrote an article recalling China's subjection to foreign domination to argue otherwise. The course of China's future and the fate of Asian independence, Das contended, could not depend on an alliance with Britain and France. For a time, he also worked with H. A. Chen—a Chinese student that Chandra K. Chakravarty, the head of the Berlin India Committee in the United States, had dispatched from New York City—to try to smuggle arms from China to India and to popularize Chakravarty's Pan-Asiatic League. Those plans failed to bear much fruit, but Das's work in the realm of publicity and propaganda resounded around the world. Shortly before leaving Shanghai for Tokyo in the spring of 1917, Das completed *Is Japan a Menace to Asia?*, a book his former faculty advisor at the University of Washington lauded as reflecting "a great deal of research and deep thinking." Then, in June 1917, writing anonymously as "An Asiatic Statesman," he published *Isolation of Japan in World Politics*. Those publications immediately captured the attention of British officials, who banned *Is Japan a Menace to Asia?* across the British empire and pressured neutral and allied governments to prohibit its distribution. Das's writings, a British agent informed US Attorney John W. Preston, were "intensely anti-American and anti-ally" and "treacherous and treasonable."[8]

In *Is Japan a Menace to Asia?*, Das spelled out his extravagant hopes for a decolonized Asia. He dedicated his book to "the Asian youth," who would lead the world to "a day . . . when the idea of dominance of Asia by Europe or America will be abandoned by the present aggressors." "This can be brought about only through effective and vigorous assertion of Asia in all fields of human activity, especially Politics," Das wrote. "Every Asian youth—male or female—who possesses even a tiny bit of the feeling of self-respect should strive to achieve the goal of Assertion of Asia to the fullest sense of its meaning." If Asians were to look toward a better future, they also had to explore their history rather than striving to be a "mere imitation of the West." "Our ambition is to draw our inspiration from the glorious past of Asia and rising above its present degraded condition," Das implored, "preserving the best of our ancestral treasures from the attacks of vandals and assimilating the best of all that the modern world has to give to Humanity, to build up something higher than the best products of Modern civilization." Tong Shaoyi, the former premier of the recently founded Republic of China, concurred in his introduction: "Japan's demonstration of military strength forces the so-called superior nations to shake hands with her, though with great reluctance. Political assertion of Asia will make Europe and America more tolerant and respectful towards human rights."[9]

For Das, Japan's status in the world marked a lesson and a guide. Despite signing treaties and diplomatic agreements with the West, he noted, Japan has been represented as a "Menace to Asia," denounced "for being too aggressive and for trying to hurt China's interests and sovereignty." A series of humiliating anti-Japanese measures by the United States, Canada, and Australia and uneven revisions of the Anglo-Japanese alliance, Das argued, awakened "far-sighted Japanese statesmen" to recognize that Japan had "to establish a community of interests between all the yellow races (if not Asiatic people) and to begin with the strongest of them all—China." Behind the façade of international diplomacy was the hard truth, he explained, that "Japan faces the strongest opposition of Great Britain and [the] USA, both haters of Asiatic people." Europe's hypocrisy was too overwhelming to ignore. "When Japan, an Asiatic nation, makes progress, extends her commerce, and tries to extend her political influence," Das argued, "it is taken to mean a challenge to the European nations, especially to Great Britain, which has the largest interest in the Orient." Das's defense of Japan extended to the colonization of Korea, which he admitted was not "an ideal thing" but a necessary step to thwart "Russian aggression." "Really

Japan has taken away Korea from Russia," Das insisted, "and undoubtedly Japan has given Korea a better administration than Russia could have ever given." Korea was now "being developed for the benefit of the Japanese and Koreans and other nations."[10]

Beyond Das's all too eager apology for Japan's colonization of Korea, his ultimate mission was to challenge Japan to lead Asia against European domination, particularly toward Indian independence. If Japan aided Britain in blocking "the aspiration of 315 millions of people of Asia," he argued, then it would incur "the displeasure of the people of that country, which to-day forms a great market for her goods and may serve in future as a source of strength in case of conflict with other nations." And "India is not Korea," he warned," and "the India of the twentieth century is not the India of the eighteenth century." Accommodating to white supremacy, he reasoned, would lead only to more humiliation. "Japan is supposedly to be a First Class Power," he wrote, "but with all her army, navy, commercial development, she is nothing but a 'Pariah' before the European nations, specially the so-called superior Anglo-Saxon World." Japan needed to awaken to the future of pan-Asian solidarity. "May Japan be the true leader of Asia!" he appealed. "Japan is the pride of Asia; her achievements speak for Asia, and they demonstrate that China and India, under better environment, can at least do like Japan in all fields of human activity." Lest Japanese officials misinterpret his call for solidarity and alliance, Das added emphatically, "*let us forewarn the Japanese people that unless these words of friendship be accompanied by sincere acts of friendship, the result will be most demoralising for the interest of all concerned.*"[11]

Published in Tokyo by the Asiatic Association of Japan, *Isolation of Japan in World Politics* appealed more directly to the people of Japan. Identifying himself only as "An Asian Statesman" and "The Author," Das invoked a collective *we* to imply that he, too, was Japanese. "It seems to us that the Japanese nation is quite unconcerned about the future of the nation, and the men at the helm of the state are anxious to stick to the old beaten track," he wrote. "That we have to chalk out a new road for our national greatness is our conviction, and to demonstrate that we have penned these lines." Das betrayed his anonymity somewhat by using the last paragraph of *Is Japan a Menace to Asia?*—on the "three great problems in the Far East"—as the epigraph, but, more than the matter of authorship, his self-reference made it clear that *Isolation of Japan in World Politics* would extend and supplement his earlier work. In his foreword, Masayoshi Oshikawa, a member of the Japanese Diet, stressed the coherence of Japanese nationalism and pan-Asian solidarity. "We hope that every Japanese proud of his birthright will work to make Japan great politically, economically, morally, and spiritually, in order to save Asia from the bondage of the Whiteman [*sic*]," Oshikawa argued. "It is the work of the Almighty, it is the cause of true Justice and Humanity and it will be accomplished by the Divine Power which cannot be thwarted by evil and selfish influences from any quarter."[12]

Surveying Japan's relations with the world—nation by nation, empire by empire—*Isolation of Japan in World Politics* warned particularly against an Anglo-American alliance that sought to isolate Japan in the emergent world order. The United States entered World War I ostensibly for "Humanity and Justice," Das began, but "the truth is that this situation has been brought about by the gradual change of American policy toward Great Britain (because America herself has become Imperialistic to the backbone)," a shift inaugurated "the day Great Britain gave up her special claim in the Caribbean Sea." Anti-Japanese measures swept across the United States and British dominions and colonies, Das noted, making it "impossible to bring about an Anglo-American and Japanese Alliance" but leading to "closer relations between America and Great Britain." Das foresaw France joining the United States and Britain to contain Japan so as to preserve white colonial claims across Asia. "If France is to keep her possessions in Asia, the United States her Philippines, and Great Britain her Hongkong, Australia, and other islands to the east of India," he argued, "then these three Powers must co-operate." In that context, according to Das, Japan's hopes lay in alliances with Germany and Russia—he, however, refuted the notion that a "democratic Russia" would no longer harbor imperial aims, pointing to "democratic America," Britain, and France—but Japan had to hold fast to its interests by demanding, for example, Germany's colonies in the Pacific for "self-preservation."[13]

As in *Is Japan a Menace to Asia?*, Das's overriding message focused on the need for pan-Asian solidarity. "The time will come when Japan's prayer for aid to the western nations will not get any response," he counseled. "For that day of emergency, Japan should pave the way by an alliance with China and Free India." It was in Japan's long-term interest, Das argued, to support China in reforming its government and army. Das quoted Sun Yat-sen, who held that the "reform of Chinese conditions" would advance "the position of the Asiatic races in the world" and thereby "prove very advantageous to the national development of Japan." If Das prescribed reforms in China, he categorically dismissed anything less than a revolution in India. Brutal repression by the British secret police in India and around the world, he noted, was "not sufficient to cope with the power and fervor of patriotism of the Indian nationalists, who are throwing bombs, killing police officials, and carrying on armed robberies to acquire funds to keep up their campaigns against the British Raj." Das contrasted the revolutionary movement against "the most moderate of the moderates" calling for "Home Rule" in India, a "self-governing" status that Britain would exploit to maintain supremacy in Asia. "Free India means the rise of a new power which would be able to check European aggression in Asia. . . .," he stated. "Asia is never safe and Japan is never free from danger until India is free and all Asia united."[14]

In the end, framing the liberation of Asia around a revolution in India *and* an imperial state in Japan reflected—and failed to resolve—the contradictions of race, colonialism, and capitalism. Although Das did not address Korea in *Isolation of Japan*, he called on Japan to fortify its military forces and colonial holdings, particularly in the Pacific, since Europe and the United States "respect force and nothing else." For Japan to lead Asia, he added, it needed "economic strength," which could "only be obtained by expanding her trade in the undeveloped lands of millions like China and India." At the same time, capitalist development in Japan produced tensions and movements that he absurdly hoped the Japanese state would recognize and address. He wrote:

> The great menace that is facing Japan—and it has not received due attention of the nation—is that Japan is becoming prosperous, and this sudden prosperity has given rise to all kinds of abuses. With the increase of Japanese prosperity, we have seen an increase of strikes among the industrial classes. There has also risen a band of agitators which threatens to destroy the Japanese industries. The idea of a general strike and syndicalism is being spread in an alarming way. This is a real menace to a state. But the state should not be content in taking repressive mea[s]ures. It is not my intention in this connection to discuss the rights of the laborers of Japan, but I emphasize with all possible emphasis that the state should not only do her best to check the growth of these movements when Japan's international position is so delicate, *but should also take vigorous steps to conserve the human resources of the empire of the Rising Sun.*

Justifying, and indeed summoning, state repression in Japan while condemning state repression in India underscored Das's uninhibited infatuation with Japan. "Let all Asia gather around Japan to strengthen her for the final issue of Asian Independence," he declared. How strengthening an imperial state and its proclamation of an "Asiatic Monroe

Doctrine" would translate into "independence" for Asians was a question that Das left unanswered.[15]

Das, first and foremost an advocate of Indian independence, was by no means alone in inflating the emancipatory promise of Japan and pan-Asian solidarity. Lothrop Stoddard, a leading white supremacist intellectual, espoused the same premise, but drew very different conclusions on history and politics. Born to a patrician New England family, Stoddard earned his PhD in history from Harvard University in 1914 and went on to write numerous articles and twenty-two books, none more influential than *The Rising Tide of Color* (1920), his masterpiece. Published in the immediate aftermath of World War I, Stoddard cast his unabashedly imperial and white supremacist gaze across the Pacific to warn against a rising tide of revolutionaries arming themselves for a race war of all ages. "The white world's inability to frame a constructive settlement, the perpetuation of intestine hatreds, and the menace of fresh white civil wars complicated by the spectre of social revolution," he wrote, "evoke the dread thought that the late war may be merely the first stage in a cycle of ruin." That cycle, according to Stoddard, began with the Russo-Japanese War, which ended four glorious centuries of "imperial progress" that had "crushed down all local efforts at resistance." Japan's victory, followed by a greater war with a lasting "disgenic effect" amounting to "white race-suicide," he argued, awakened the "colored world" to new possibilities, leveling a death blow to "the legend of white invincibility" across the continents.[16]

The "brown and yellow worlds of Asia" led by "Mongolian Asiatics," in Stoddard's view, posed the greatest challenges to white world supremacy. Although "Asiatics do not seem to possess that sustained constructive power with which the whites, particularly the Nordics, are endowed," he believed, "the browns and yellows are yet gifted peoples who have profoundly influenced human progress in the past and who undoubtedly will contribute much to world-civilization." With Japan's "hegemony over China" in particular, Stoddard could envisage a day when "the white man may soon find himself economically as well as politically expelled from the whole Far East." He demanded the containment of Asians to Asia. "Our race-duty is therefore clear," he preached to fellow white folk. "We must resolutely oppose both Asiatic permeation of white race-areas and Asiatic inundation of those nonwhite, but equally non-Asiatic, regions inhabited by the really inferior races." The "peril of migration" was the gravest threat to human progress, to eugenics. The "wholesale Oriental influx" into the United

States "would inevitably doom the whites . . . to social sterilization and ultimate racial extinction." Stoddard called for the immediate prohibition of Asian migrations and the restriction of "lower human types" from "even within the white world." He clamored for white blood, "Nordic" in particular, to rule the United States and the world, the "clean, virile, genius-bearing blood, streaming down the ages through the unerring action of heredity, which . . . will multiply itself, solve our problems, and sweep us on to higher and nobler destinies."[17]

Stoddard's raging fears extended beyond race or, more precisely, included racial threats beyond blood. Asia was especially pernicious because it held the potential to foment and forge "Pan-Colored" and "Colored-Bolshevist" alliances. Bolshevism had recently ruined Russia, Stoddard argued, and was now enlisting "the colored races in its grand assault on civilization" that made V. I. Lenin nothing more than "a modern Jenghiz Khan plotting the plunder of a world." What Lenin heralded was, in his view, "anti-racial" and "anti-social." "Accordingly, in every quarter of the globe, in Asia, Africa, Latin America, and the United States, Bolshevik agitators whisper in the ears of discontented colored men their gospel of hatred and revenge," Stoddard warned. "Every nationalist aspiration, every political grievance, every social discrimination, is fuel for Bolshevism's hellish incitement to racial as well as to class war." Bolshevik influences, he claimed, could be found in "China, Japan, Afghanistan, India, Java, Persia, Turkey, Egypt, Brazil, Chile, Peru, Mexico, and the 'black belts' of our own United States." And Stoddard could imagine nothing more threatening than Bolshevism—"the renegade, the traitor within the gates, who would betray the citadel"—to white solidarity and white supremacy. "Civilization would wither like a plant stricken by blight," he predicted, "while the race, summarily drained of its good blood, would sink like lead into the depths of degenerate barbarism." As "the arch-enemy of civilization and the race," Stoddard concluded in one of his more incendiary tirades, "Bolshevism must be crushed out with iron heels, no matter what the cost."[18]

For Stoddard, Hawai'i stood as an example of the racial and sexual perils of Asian migration. "The mid-Pacific archipelago was brought under white control by masterful American Nordics," he stated, "who established Anglo-Saxon institutions and taught the natives the rudiments of Anglo-Saxon civilization." Determined to make the islands' "marvellous fertility to immediate profit," they imported labor from "the ends of the earth," particularly "Asiatic labor," since the "native

Hawaiians, like other Polynesian races, could not stand the pressure of white civilization, and withered away." Short-term profits turned into long-term woes, Stoddard argued, offering a "highly instructive" case study in eugenics. "These Asiatics arrived as agricultural laborers to work on the plantations," he observed. "But they did not stay there. Saving their wages, they pushed vigorously into all the middle walks of life." Through "ruthless undercutting," Asians, especially the Japanese, according to Stoddard, were taking over Hawai'i. "To-day the American mechanic, the American storekeeper, the American farmer, even the American contractor, is a rare bird indeed," he wrote, "while Japanese corporations are buying up the finest plantations and growing the finest pineapples and sugar." The results were racially catastrophic. "Fully half the population of the islands is Japanese," Stoddard cautioned, "while the Americans are being literally encysted as a small and dwindling aristocracy." Seeing their future reflected in Hawai'i, he noted happily, "the lusty young Anglo-Saxon communities bordering the Pacific—Australia, New Zealand, British Columbia, and our own 'coast'—have one and all set their faces like flint against the Oriental and have emblazoned across their portals the legend: 'All White.'"[19]

It was in the context of such hopes and fears of pan-Asian solidarity that the US federal government intensified its investigation of Das's movements in Asia. In March 1917, the Bureau of Investigation (BI) received word that he might be in Japan and, since the last renewal of his US passport in China had expired two months earlier, expected Das to contact a US government office in the near future. From "a very confidential source," the BI also learned that Das was attempting "to send arms to India through Chinese coolies." As the US government declared war on Germany in the first week of April 1917, its officials prepared to receive Das, hopefully at a US port of entry. "Would it not be possible to have a search made of Tarak Nath Das's baggage, under the customs supervision, on some alleged theory that he was engaged in the importation of opium or some other prohibited article and copies, photostatic if possible, taken of the important documents you find?" the BI chief suggested to his agent in San Francisco. "It is very important in this matter, however, that Das be ignorant of the true meaning of this search, since he will probably proceed, if unsuspicious, to get into communication with the men who sent him out and thus connect them with his enterprise, whatever it may be." The Attorney General's office simultaneously issued a warrant for the arrest of Das and other South Asian revolutionaries for violating US neutrality laws.[20]

Das's hopes for Japan and its government to lead a worldwide movement against colonialism contrasted sharply with his daily experiences on the ground. What he encountered toward the end of his stay in Japan was not pan-Asian solidarity to liberate colonized peoples but a transpacific pact to defend empire and to repress revolution. The Japanese police and British agents kept a close surveillance of his activities and correspondence, ironically carrying out the state repression of "agitators" that Das called for and applying the Anglo-Japanese alliance that he dismissed. In July 1917, the Japanese police banned the sale and the mailing of *Is Japan a Menace to Asia?* When Das visited the US Embassy to renew his passport, the US consul confiscated it, citing a pending request for his extradition to the United States. The Japanese government then evidently offered Das three options: a secluded life in Japan, Korea, or Formosa; an assisted passage to Russia; or a "voluntary" return to the United States. Das chose the last option to defend himself against "certain political charges" and in early August attended a farewell dinner, where he unrepentantly unfurled a banner for Asian independence. As he set sail across the Pacific aboard the *Siberia Maru,* officials in the US Justice Department feared that Das might take flight en route. They sent word to the secretary of war to put US authorities in the Philippines on alert and prepared for Das's stopover in Hawai'i.[21]

In Hawai'i, Das came face to face with the US security state. For months, US Attorney S. C. Huber had been corresponding with the attorney general and Preston, the US attorney in San Francisco leading the investigation and prosecution of South Asian revolutionaries. In June 1917, Preston informed Huber of the imminent arrival of Frieda Hauswirth, who had reportedly advised Das to stay clear of the United States to avoid prosecution. Followed and interviewed by "a plain clothes secret service man connected with the Navy," Hauswirth admitted to knowing Das and Har Dayal and expressed her willingness to hand over letters in her possession. She and her South Asian fiancé, who worked as a chemist on a Maui sugar plantation, both claimed to have "refused to take any part in . . . revolutionary matters." When the *Siberia Maru* docked in Honolulu on August 17, 1917, the same naval intelligence officer boarded the vessel to interview Das, who stated that he was on his way to San Francisco to surrender to US federal authorities. When the officer asked to search his baggage, Das demanded to see a search warrant. In the meantime, without a search warrant, a private detective confiscated Das's leather case, which, according to Das, contained a brief and other documents related to his defense strategy. With

Huber's promise to locate and return the brief, Das agreed to a search of his baggage, with some items removed and forwarded to San Francisco under the seal of the US marshal.[22]

To US officials, Das's pan-Asian message and transpacific circuits illustrated the need for a security state with more agents and greater influence in and across the Pacific. Even before Das's arrival, Hawai'i had become embroiled in the "Hindu Conspiracy." Two years earlier in 1915, the Ghadar Party and the Berlin India Committee had organized an ill-fated scheme to ship arms from California to India on two ships purchased with German funds. As the vessels continually failed to meet up—the original plan was to transfer arms from the *Annie Larsen* to the *Maverick* on Socorro Island, three hundred miles south of Baja California—the *Maverick* made its way westward to Hilo, Hawai'i. In Hilo, the crew evidently met with and received financial support from George Rodiek and Heinrich Schroeder of H. Hackfeld and Company, a sugar firm owned by a German family. In July 1917, a month before Das landed in Honolulu, Preston indicted Rodiek and Schroeder for "conspiring with others to carry on a military enterprise against India." Fellow *haole* families exploited the anti-German climate to take over Hackfeld and Company and increasingly banded together to secure their plantations and investments from Japanese workers. As agents of the US state likewise turned their attention to workers' struggles, they called for a bigger imperial presence in Hawai'i. In the words of US Attorney Huber, their work was "necessarily difficult and limited" by the dearth of federal agents. World War I and the 1920 strike would dramatically change the political landscape.[23]

STRIKING HAWAI'I

The 1920 labor strike in Hawai'i was decades in the making. Galvanized by commercial treaties between Hawai'i and the United States beginning in 1876, the sugar industry grew exponentially in the last quarter of the nineteenth century to dominate Hawai'i's physical and social landscape. That phenomenal growth—from 12,540 tons in 1875 to 289,544 tons in 1900—rested fundamentally on the backbreaking labor of workers under penal contract, beginning with Kānaka Maoli (Native Hawaiians) and Chinese migrants, followed by recruits from Japan. By 1902, Japanese workers made up 73.5 percent of the plantation labor force. It was a system of migrant labor widespread in sugar-exporting colonies around the world in the nineteenth century, predicated on lip service to freedom and formal rights and daily realities of superexploitation. The accelerated and expanded flow of sugar to the US market also rendered the Kingdom of Hawai'i increasingly dependent on the US empire, economically and politically. The US annexation of Hawai'i in 1898, following a coup d'état by the *haole* elite five years earlier, removed all legal vestiges of political independence, formalizing US claims to sovereignty over the islands the same year that the United States laid similar claims over the Philippines, Guam, and Puerto Rico.[24] America's colonial archipelago stretched around the world.

The passage of the Organic Act in 1900, which prohibited penal labor contracts in Hawai'i, generated a new wave of labor struggles among sugar plantation workers, as the frequency and scale of labor strikes increased dramatically. When Motoyuki Negoro, an attorney based in Honolulu, suggested the need for greater organization and immediate action in 1908, the Japanese community came together to form the Higher Wages Association (HWA). When sugar planters rebuffed the HWA's appeals for wage increases—to be on par with Portuguese and Puerto Rican workers—and better working conditions, seven thousand Japanese workers staged an islandwide strike on O'ahu beginning in May 1909. Hawai'i's sugar planters, unified under the Hawaiian Sugar Planters' Association (HSPA), retaliated vigorously and viciously, vowing never to concede to workers' demands. They evicted striking workers and their families, hired Kanaka Maoli, Chinese, Korean, and Portuguese strikebreakers, established an espionage network to monitor the HWA, and conspired with the police to arrest and imprison labor leaders. "I took the position in making these arrests," explained the high sheriff of the territory, "that the Higher Wages Association, together with its organ, the *Nippu Jiji* [a Japanese-language newspaper], was a criminal organization, organized in the first instance with the deliberate plan to violate the law in carrying out the purposes of that organization." The violent campaign of repression brought the strike to an end by August 1909.[25]

As the 1909 strike wound down, both planters and workers recognized that it was the beginning of a wider struggle. In July on the Waimanalo plantation, where the manager had declined "to discharge certain employees at the demand of the labourers," a "riot" erupted that "necessitated the intervention of the sheriff and ultimately of armed police." The official end of the strike a month later failed to ease planters' anxieties. On the Oahu plantation, Japanese workers returned to the fields, but collectively refused to lift a finger until a mechanical loader was removed from the premises. The management had no choice but to turn off the loader. Japanese workers, F. M. Swanzy of a leading sugar firm observed, "appear humble now, but they are not so humble as they look and do not consider themselves beaten." "We are told that the perfecting of a Japanese labour Union is now being done and that when the organization is completed it will have all the machinery and discipline of a well regulated army whose general issues orders which pass through all the officers until they reach the privates," he maintained, "who are expected to act in strict accordance with the instructions they receive." To ward off further trouble, Swanzy concluded, planters could accede to Japanese workers' demands on wages, housing, and other working conditions or recruit new workers "in sufficient numbers to offset the Japanese." He was disappointed that "large numbers of Filipinos" were not available immediately.[26]

The search for alternative sources of plantation labor cast Japanese workers as racial threats to US interests in Hawai'i. Before the House Committee on Immigration and Naturalization, which in 1912 was debating the addition of a literacy requirement in US immigration laws, political leaders from Hawai'i begged for an exemption. To counter the "growing predominance of the Asiatic," Jonah Kalanianaole, the territorial delegate to Congress, argued, Hawai'i's government had been subsidizing "Caucasian immigration," particularly from Portugal, but a literacy provision threatened to undermine such efforts "to keep these islands under American control." Without an amendment exempting Hawai'i, he insisted, Congress would "throw us more hopelessly and helplessly than ever back into the sweep of the apparently natural tide that is pulling Hawaii swiftly, if quietly, away from the United States and into the hands, control, and dominance and ultimate use, we fear, of Asiatic powers." The key to making Hawai'i "the center of both military and naval operations in the Pacific Ocean," another member of the delegation contended, was "a Caucasian citizen population for those islands." Having failed to attract "settlers" from the mainland, he explained, Hawai'i had no choice but to target "other Caucasian stock, who themselves will in time become naturalized citizens and whose children will all be educated American citizens." Otherwise, he suggested, the islands faced two "very much less desirable" options: "the present population," which will remain "predominantly Asiatic for all times to come," or "practically accepting the addition of population from Filipinos and Porto Ricans."[27]

Hawai'i's sugar planters concentrated their recruiting efforts on the Philippines. After years of lobbying US officials in the Philippines, the

HSPA had secured permission from the Philippine Commission in 1906 to transport Filipino workers under three-year contracts, with fixed wages, an arrangement that did not take root fully until the 1909 strike. The number of Filipino recruits skyrocketed afterward, rising rapidly from a mere 0.3 percent of Hawai'i's plantation labor force that year to 19.3 percent five years later. Upon hearing of the possible legal prohibition of Filipino emigration to Hawai'i by the Philippine legislature in 1914, William Matson of the Matson Navigation Company, which was owned and controlled principally by Hawai'i's big sugar firms, pleaded for a reconsideration. "If the Japanese see no new element ready to replace them," he explained, "their tendency to be overbearing will undoubtedly assert itself on all occasions, with the danger of strikes and other disturbances." It was "a matter of concern to the National Government . . . particularly from the standpoint of the Military authorities." Filipino migration continued. In contrast, the number of Japanese workers declined precipitously, as fresh memories of the strike and its brutal repression drove them off the plantations. By 1919, Japanese workers continued to form the majority of the sugar plantation labor force (54.7 percent), but the shift to Filipino workers (22.9 percent) was decisively underway.[28]

The stage was set for a bigger standoff between planters and workers. In response to the 1909 strike, planters had instituted a bonus pay system in 1911, whereby workers earned a bonus relative to the price of sugar—the higher the price of sugar, the higher their bonus payments. During World War I, when sugar prices soared to new heights, bonus payments increasingly made up a higher percentage of workers' annual earnings, from 5 percent in 1914 to 20 percent a year later. In 1917, when sugar prices continued to rise, Hawai'i's sugar planters decided to change course, unilaterally lowering the rate of bonus payments and, to discourage labor mobility, withholding half of all bonus payments until the end of the year (from a policy of withholding four-fifths of bonus payments every six months). Workers, in the meantime, received no increase in their basic wage rates and encountered ever higher costs of living. Sugar planters braced themselves for a bitter confrontation. Amid growing complaints by Japanese workers about high food prices and low wages in the summer of 1917, trustees of the HSPA voted to circulate to all members a letter on the growing popularity of the Industrial Workers of the World (IWW) along the Pacific Coast and its "doctrine of discontent and violence." "We have given much thought to the probable consequences of an introduction of IWWism into the Hawaiian Islands," the letter noted, "which we consider a very fertile field for

FIGURE 14. Japanese workers on a sugar plantation, ca. 1920. Photograph by Ray Jerome Baker. Courtesy of Bishop Museum Archives.

them to work." The HSPA recommended vigilant investigation "as a matter of preparation."[29]

Japanese workers organized, motivated by their distressed circumstances and stirrings on both sides of the Pacific. As in Hawai'i, food prices in Japan rose sharply during World War I, a situation created and exacerbated by the Japanese government's stockpiling of rice for the military. In the summer of 1918, a wave of "rice riots" engulfed Japan, as millions of ordinary working people stormed into the streets to protest high food prices and government policies. Protests rocked the incorporated states of the US empire a year later, as more than four million workers waged strikes from coast to coast, often coming into violent blows with state militias and federal troops. On plantations across Hawai'i, Japanese workers eagerly discussed those movements afoot across the Pacific and took stock of their own predicament. They congregated in many meetings facilitated through the Young Men's Buddhist Association, a socioreligious organization rooted in plantation communities. "THE JAPANESE LABORERS MUST BE PAID THE SAME WAGES AS THE PORTUGUESE AND HAWAIIANS in order that they may escape severe and unbearable hardships and what we say is not at all dangerous," the *Hawaii Hochi* stated. Through the fall of 1919, workers organized local plantation unions to demand higher wages and better working conditions, including the reformation or the elimination of the unpredictable bonus system, across the islands of Hawai'i. On December 1, 1919, the local unions converged in Honolulu to ally themselves into the Federation of Japanese Labor (FJL).[30]

Filipino workers likewise organized, though perhaps less so from the grassroots. The main force behind the formation of the Filipino Labor Union (FLU) in August 1919 was Pablo Manlapit, who had arrived in Hawai'i in 1910 as a plantation worker under contract. Born to a working-class family in southern Luzon, Manlapit worked a series of jobs as a teenager in the US-occupied Philippines, until he was fired for trying to organize a labor union. In 1913, he spearheaded a labor strike on the plantation where he worked on the island of Hawai'i, for which the HSPA promptly blacklisted him. Three years later, he joined an interracial longshore strike and received a beating for urging Filipinos to stop working as strikebreakers. While studying to become an attorney in his spare time in 1919, Manlapit talked with plantation workers on their plight and emerged as the FLU's president by the summer's end. Manlapit's message resonated with Filipino workers, whose complaints of contract violations mounted. And Manlapit saw readily the need to cooperate with the local Japanese labor movement. "Japanese and Filipino laborers should get together and work [for] their mutual benefit as the interests of both parties are practically the same," he stated before Japanese workers in October 1919. Two months later, the FJL and the FLU put forward to the HSPA common demands for wage raises, eight-hour work days, and regular bonus payments (75 percent paid monthly).[31]

The planters' reply precipitated the strike. Without officially recognizing the workers' collective voice, the HSPA immediately announced a policy on bonus payments in line with the workers' demands and established a new office to inquire into living conditions on the plantations. The HSPA flatly rejected all other demands. Both unions had already resolved to strike if their demands were not met, but they disagreed on how and when to move forward. The FLU wanted to strike immediately, perhaps as early as December 20, 1919. Heeding lessons from 1909, the FJL attempted to petition the HSPA once more and to bide some time until the late spring or early summer, when the grinding season (harvest) would be in full swing and their strike fund would be in better shape. The FJL was able to convince Manlapit and the FLU to postpone their strike deadline to January 19, 1920. When Manlapit tried to delay the strike again, following another request by the FJL, his message failed to reach the rank and file. On January 20, 1920, 2,600

Filipino workers and several hundred others walked off their jobs. With many Japanese workers refusing to cross the picket line, out of sympathy and fear, and the HSPA repudiating any move toward concession or conciliation, the FJL voted to strike beginning on February 1. Involving upward of 8,300 workers (77 percent of the plantation labor force on the island of O'ahu), the strained and fragile alliance of Filipino and Japanese workers brought sugar production to a halt.[32]

Almost everyone across the islands of Hawai'i understood that the strike marked a decisive moment in the social relations of sugar production. In the days following the largely Filipino walkout, plantation managers attempted to convince Japanese workers to stay on the job. The HSPA instructed all managers on O'ahu to inform workers that "they have not been excused from work by the Manager and will not participate in the bonus for this month unless they perform twenty days' work." As such threats made little difference, members of the HSPA voted in the last days of January to stand fast together, as in 1909, to share "all losses to property which may be occasioned by the resistance of strikes on any and all plantations arising out of controversies over wages." In response to hundreds of Japanese workers on the Honolulu plantation joining the strike in early February, the manager began "paying off" the striking workers and ordering them off the plantation grounds, "putting out of the best houses the leaders among the Japanese and Filipinos." When he evicted three of the Japanese leaders—US citizens, the manager noted—and their families, they protested bitterly but were nonetheless "put out." A fire ensued in the cane fields, a blaze the manager attributed to the recently discharged workers. A neighboring manager believed that "both the Japanese and Filipino organizations were becoming stronger" and now favored "taking some radical action." His Chinese workers, too, were "drifting away."[33]

Racial charges of anti-Americanism came forth almost immediately. "Manla Pit [*sic*] principal Filipino agitation," George M. Brooke of the MID telegrammed his superiors after the Filipinos initiated the strike. "It is expected that the Japanese will strike. By an intense campaign of agitation, the entire Japanese language press is encouraging the Filipinos and urging the Japanese to strike. . . . Shimpo urges a red flag parade of the Japanese in Honolulu. This agitation has the appearance of centralized propaganda. A general unrest, financial losses and anti-American feeling are the results." He became more alarmed two days later, after learning that Filipino workers, if evicted from plantation housing, would organize themselves into "military camps" by veterans of the US Army among their ranks and that some Chinese workers had also gone on strike. "Strongly suspect that the Japanese government is behind this movement, which is wide and concerted," Brooke surmised. "It expresses pan-American-*Asia*nisum [*sic*]." He requested "more white troops here" right away to preserve "safety." On the eve of Japanese workers joining the strike, Brooke grew more certain of its racial bases. "It is not too much to say that the study of this situation leads to the presumption that the Japanese Government is behind this movement . . . in order to weld together and to whip into line the oriental population of this territory in the furtherance of its Pan Asian policies. . . . We have, in other words, a powerful, potential and masked enemy in our midst."[34]

Brooke's hyperbolic rhetoric replicated and reinforced planter propaganda. "Is control of the industrialism of Hawaii to remain in the hands of Anglo-Saxons or is it to pass into those of alien Japanese Agitators?" asked the pro-planter *Honolulu Star-Bulletin*. The strike was nothing but "a dark conspiracy to Japanize this American territory," a threat the planters would fight "to the end, no matter what the cost, the delay, or the inconvenience might be." The stakes were too high for anything less, according to the newspaper. "A compromise of any nature or any degree with the alien agitators would be a victory for them and an indirect but nonetheless deadly invasion of American sovereignty in Hawaii," it proclaimed. The contention that the strike represented alien agitators' growing influence over Hawai'i quickly became the standard refrain of the strike's opponents. "Being steadfastly and unalternably [*sic*] opposed to any alien or nationalistic domination of the sugar industry within this American territory," the HSPA president argued, "we are resolved never to permit it under any guise or form." At the first territory-wide convention of the American Legion, which met in February 1920, its members adopted "100% Americanism" as their top mission, to promote it and to root out "disloyalty, alien propaganda and activities, lawlessness." "A clear understanding of these things is the sovereign antidote for anti-American propaganda of all sorts, for Bolshevism and all the rest," stated the leader of Hawai'i's American Legion.[35]

Anticipating such reactions that had already hounded striking Japanese workers in 1909, the FJL took great pains to deflect them from the outset. "We consider it a great privilege and pride to live under the Stars and Stripes," delegates to the FJL's inaugural meeting declared in December 1919, "which stands for freedom and justice, as a factor of this great industry and as a part of the labor of Hawaii." When a strike appeared imminent, the FJL stressed to its members the need for patience and peace. "*And In Particular,* if a strike of Japanese labor shall be called, our countrymen and countrywomen are requested and cautioned to quit their places in a quiet and peaceable manner, delivering tools to the plantations, and doing no damage to property," the FJL secretary cautioned, "and, MOST PARTICULARLY, to refrain from disputes with, or assaults upon either the remaining laborers, or the officers of the plantations, or any strike-breakers who may be engaged to take your places." Embracing and appealing to US nationalism—ironically, earnestly, or wearily—became a reflexive response to anti-Japanese and anti-Asian charges. "We want peace and order; we love labor and production," the FJL insisted in its final report on the strike. "But when we think of the group of capitalists who show no sympathy whatever toward the struggling laborers, turn deaf ears to their cries and reject their just and reasonable demands under the pretense that they are formulated by 'agitators,' we cannot remain silent. We must act. And so we went on strike . . . honorably and bravely, as laborers living under the great flag of freedom and justice."[36]

Facing an onslaught of planter propaganda, the FJL issued a statement to the public in February 1920, explaining at length the material conditions prevailing on the plantations. "We admit that laborers are furnished free houses," the FJL noted. "But what kind of houses are they? Many of them are such that they do not permit of sitting space when two beds are put in. How about the kitchen? There are stoves made of empty kerosene tins in them. And how about the toilet? They are hardly endurable." The strike was strictly about improving workers' laboring and living conditions, nothing else. "The present movement in favor of higher wages for labor is an economic movement, pure and simple," Japanese workers declared in refutation of the planters' and English-language dailies' charges. "It is entirely dissociated from any considerations of local or foreign politics, as well as from questions of the advantage or disadvantage to other groups of nationals resident in Hawaii. . . . The suggestion, frequently put forward in print, that 'the Filipinos are simply being used as a cat's paw by the Japanese' . . . has no more foundation in reality than any other untruth." Although the FJL would "receive with gratitude every act of assistance, whether material or otherwise," it had no interest in the "racial composition of our associates" or the Japanese government. "The Federation has no official connection (not even a backstairs connection) with the Japanese Government or any of its officials, whether resident in Japan or in Hawaii," the FJL stressed.[37]

FIGURE 15. Harvesting sugar cane, ca. 1910s. Courtesy of Prints and Photographs Division, Library of Congress.

On individual plantations, the strike, which commenced on the eve of the grinding season, produced a combustible climate. When two skilled workers were discharged and evicted on the Kahuku plantation, the entire labor force threatened to leave, compelling the manager to rescind his order. Around the same time in early February 1920, two fires flared up in the cane fields of the Waialua plantation, one suspected to have been ignited by Japanese workers and the other by Filipino workers. Japanese laborers warned that "further cane fire at this plantation might happen." Noboru Tsutsumi, the FJL secretary, had recently delivered a speech on the plantation to rally the striking workers. "When the weeds grow up in the canefield beyond control and should the Planters give up the planta- tions," he reportedly said, "we will walk in and take possession of same and will conduct the plantations ourselves." A week later, after consulting with plantation managers, the HSPA decided to take out an insurance policy on the ripened cane stalks of Oʻahu. "There have been incendiary fires on most of the plantations, but fortunately they were put out before any serious damage was done," the president of American Factors explained. "But we are none of us quite sure what a concerted movement to fire the cane might result in, especially if a strong wind were blowing." The policy was "quite a serious step"—costing upwards of $250,000 for three months—but it insured against catastrophic losses and would allow planters to consider mass evictions with less apprehension.[38]

EMPIRE STRIKES BACK

As a resolution appeared nowhere in sight, a committee of prominent *haole* and elite Japanese headed by Reverend Albert W. Palmer proposed a plan for the "common good." The Palmer Plan sought to remove the source behind "the widespread suspicion that the causes of the strike are not only economic but racial and nationalistic." Purportedly to restore "the spirit of aloha and good will between races," the plan called on the FJL to "recognize the unwisdom and peril of any such organization along racial lines and that it therefore call off the present strike" to help create another labor organization "inter-racial in scope." The committee asked the HSPA to establish through an election "an employees' committee" on each plantation "to confer with the plantation manager in securing the utmost cooperation between the management and the men." The FJL appealed to Acting Governor Curtis P. Iaukea to highlight the proposal's perversity. The Palmer Plan "proposes, in short, that we shall dissolve our organization, efface ourselves as a compact of laborers—throw up our hands, shout 'Kamarad'—and return to our work as before the strike, leaving the equities to be adjusted or not adjusted—by a series of fantastic committees . . . that will be (to a great extent) under the control of the plantation managers, and that will have no 'teeth' . . .," the FJL argued. "Workmen's sovi[e]ts, in short, but destitute of any of the powers of the soviet, as we have come to understand it."[39]

If the strike placed Japanese "agitation" and "invasion" in the spotlight, that racial framing hinged on acknowledging, indeed exalting, the US empire. Any talk of "Anglo-Saxon" dominance and "100% Americanism" could not but point to colonialism in Hawai'i, in the past and in the present. In a sermon on "The Strike Situation" to promote his plan, Palmer began by acknowledging the centennial of Christian missions in Hawai'i. "A hundred years ago a band of brave and devoted missionaries came to build a Kingdom of God in these islands, to bring justice, peace and brotherhood to savage tribes," he said. If those white Christians successfully fought off "tyranny, slavery and despotism," their descendants faced new forms of savagery in their midst. Palmer attempted to provide some credence to workers' complaints—"there must have been, on some plantations at least, real grievances or the agitators could not have gotten a hearing"—but he discredited the labor movement wholesale by bolstering the planters' racial charge that it had the appearance of "a nationalistic Japanese movement, using the Filipinos as tools, but aiming at Japanese control of the sugar industry and the islands." The strike's continuance would have dire consequences, according to Palmer, with the hastening of "moral degradation," the slowing down of "Americanization," and "the deepening and embittering of race antagonisms." "Organization will be driven into secrecy and a fertile ground will have been prepared for Bolshevist and other destructive and revolutionary social teachings," he preached.[40]

Belatedly and begrudgingly accepted by the FJL in principle and categorically rejected by the HSPA, which refused to engage the FJL in any way, the Palmer Plan fell by the wayside. The debates around the strike and the Palmer Plan, however, heightened the contradictions of race and nationalism, so much so that they compelled critiques of the US empire. A longtime diplomat for the Kingdom of Hawaiʻi before the *haole* coup d'état, Acting Governor Iaukea was accustomed to the sugar planters' duplicity and hypocrisy. Taking the helm of the territory during the *haole* governor's absence, Iaukea sought to work toward a compromise and commended the Palmer Plan as a step in the right direction. Unlike Palmer, Iaukea offered a sharp rebuke of the HSPA in the process. "I wish we had more such men [like Palmer] in this country," Iaukea stated, "for there would be no reason then for all this hullabaloo about 100 percent Americanism." Demanding concrete evidence of a Japanese conspiracy if there was one, he expressed his "mistrust" of the planters. "For quite a while there has been such pressure brought to bear upon me to petition the United States government to use its military forces against the strikers. . . . It is a matter of history that armed forces of the United States were used to overawe the Hawaiians at the time of the overthrow of the monarchy, and there seems to be a desire to repeat this measure of intimidation."[41]

Likening Japanese and Filipino workers to Kānaka Maoli—all subject to *haole* domination and potentially US military intervention—recalled a history of race and empire that the HSPA, the American Legion, and Palmer embraced but tried to erase. It was much easier to hide behind the cloak of "Americanism." Snubbed by the planters, Palmer attempted to disentangle race and "Americanism," an impossible task, particularly for this reverend. "Let us have faith, courage, grit, determination and make Hawaii 100 per cent American. . . . The Oriental who gives to Red Cross and Liberty loans and is capable of organizing a labor union (typically an Anglo-Saxon organization) is already far more Americanized," he pleaded. "Democracy in the public schools, the playground, the Boy Scouts, the church, and the utter denial of democracy in industry promotes Bolshevism and anarchy, not Americanism." Iaukea and others, in contrast, removed that cloak—the emperor's new clothes—to generate sympathy, however limited, for the striking workers. Iaukea could not understand the planters' call for "any military display . . . that might seriously endanger the relations of the United States and Japan." He continued, "Perhaps the kindliest construction would be to consider that, like the rest of capital, they are the first to resent government control of their property and the first to ask that government for aid when they think they are threatened." Another Kanaka Maoli politician underscored the incompatibility of "democracy" and "Americanism." "The fact is that Haoles draw the color line more than any other people," he said.[42]

The struggles of Filipino workers likewise brought to the fore a history of the US empire, even as they made claims on "Americanism" toward their own ends. Beginning in mid-February, the HSPA began evicting striking workers and their families en masse from their plantation homes, resulting in the displacement of 12,020 persons, including 4,127 children. The FJL responded by setting up makeshift homes, particularly to help contain an influenza epidemic spreading across Hawai'i. When three hundred Filipinos relocated to an old sake brewery, the Honolulu Board of Health ordered them removed for violating the city's sanitary code, a turn of events that shocked local residents. "Filipino people who are under protection of the Stars and Stripes are being threatened with 'actual killing' by the white Americans," the *Hawaii Shinpo* reported. That was the logic of race and empire pervading the US-occupied Philippines, but Filipinos tried to exploit it to demand some level of protection in Hawai'i. When Manlapit, the FLU president, announced an end to the Filipino laborers' strike on February 9, 1920, it did not mark his finest hour. But it was a moment of racial incongruities. Perhaps bribed by the HSPA, a charge he denied, Manlapit decried the Japanese as "an unscrupulous alien race" plotting to take over Hawai'i. "As Americans we cannot be parties to any such a program and it becomes our duty as citizens of the United States to help the people of Hawaii to break the strangle hold which the Japanese community is trying to obtain upon it," he stated.[43]

Although the Filipino rank and file pressed Manlapit to retract his call, engendering and sustaining interracial and working-class solidarities remained a daunting proposition. Distressed by declining access to food and shelter, individual Filipino and Japanese workers began returning to work. When several Japanese moved back onto the Oahu plantation in early March, a group of enraged striking workers attempted to intercede, but "were driven off when the police fired two shots in the air." On the Honolulu plantation, it was reported around the same time, three Japanese workers "were carried away last night by the strikers." A few days later on the Waialua plantation, the house of the Japanese riveter who had returned to work was set on fire in the middle of the night. As those tense confrontations played out from plantation to plantation, the strike's leaders decided to organize a parade, in Tsutsumi's words, "to expose the obstinacy of the HSPA and to inform the general public about our plea for justice." On April 3, 1920, approximately three thousand Japanese and Filipino workers, families, and supporters marched through the streets of Honolulu, carrying US flags and banners to minimize their radicalism and to maximize their "Americanism." "We Want to Live Like Americans," "We are NO REDS, God forbids. We are Brown workers who produce White Sugar," "We Believe in Lincoln's Ideas," they argued. A contingent of marchers carried their "American" message as far as it could go. "Hawaii's sugar plantation workers are still suffering under slave-like treatment," those carrying Lincoln's image wrote on their placards. "Free these slaves."[44]

The HSPA's entrenched position and racial pronouncements placed Japanese workers in particular on the defensive. Immediately after the parade, based on false rumors, the *Honolulu Star-Bulletin* accused the Japanese consul of supplying Lincoln's portrait and masterminding the rally. The pro-planter newspaper essentially vowed racial revenge. "Americans do not take kindly to the spectacle of several thousand alien Asiatics parading through the streets with banners flaunting their hatred of Americanism and American institutions and insulting the memory of the greatest American president since Washington," the *Star-Bulletin* warned. To counter such charges, the FJL amended its constitution in mid-April, renaming itself the Hawaiian Federation of Labor (or the Hawaii Laborers' Association) and proclaiming to be "free from any religious faith, racial and political party or creed." The union's foremost aim, the new constitution stated, was to "safeguard the industrial prosperity of Hawaii on the basis of capital-labor cooperation." At the same time, the constitution did not mince words when it listed another aim as to "work for the equal distribution of surplus-profits, and to safeguard the rights of the laborers," even as a later clause expressly prohibited membership to "those who have communistic, Bolsheviki, anarchistic, or any other radical ideas." Such desperate measures marked the strike's last gasps. The HSPA continued to refuse to recognize or negotiate with the FJL, no matter what it called itself,

and hired strikebreakers—Chinese, Koreans, Kānaka Maoli, Portuguese, Filipinos, and Japanese—to resume sugar production almost at
prestrike levels by the end of April.[45]

The return of more and more workers hardly relieved the strike's
mounting pressure. In early May, on the Honolulu plantation, "sticks
of giant powder, wrapped in an oil soaked bag and Japanese newspaper,
were found in cane field next to the field that was burned." Several
weeks later, on the Oahu Sugar Company's estate in Waipahu, nearly a
hundred acres of ripe cane were destroyed in the middle of the night. "It
is believed that an automobile containing strikers came from Waialua,"
a US military intelligence officer reported, "and that these strikers threw
inflammable materials into the ripe cane in several places." Japanese
merchants and other prominent Japanese individuals, in the meantime,
felt emboldened to denounce the strike and to try to facilitate its conclusion. A meeting in Honolulu between Japanese union officials and Japanese merchants concluded, according to a leading sugar firm, when "the
Federation Officials staged a small riot." After the meeting, S. Kanda
suggested that planters help their workers get rid of "the tyrannous
hands of the insincere radical leaders" and then agree to raise workers'
wages once "the present trouble is settled." Some planters agreed with
Kanda on the need for some kind of concession, if only to mollify Japanese workers' pride. In a letter that he wished "destroyed" upon deliv-
ery, Allen W. T. Bottomley of American Factors explained that the striking workers dreaded going back to work, where they would be "laughed
at by the Koreans and Chinese" after having "stayed out all these
months, lost all this money and got absolutely nothing" in return.[46]

Although the strike was limited to plantations on O'ahu, its impact
extended to the other islands. Without financial support from fellow
Japanese workers still at work, the strike could not have lasted as long
as it did. When A. W. Collins, a plantation manager on Maui, learned in
February 1920 that each of his workers planned to contribute one dollar
that month and then five dollars in March, he suggested that "some
action be taken on the outside Islands so as not to allow this money to
go to Oahu." Having failed to block the flow of money, Collins's boss
proposed in May "the idea of putting the head men and the collectors of
subscriptions off the plantations." Excepting perhaps "the most loyal
men" who were collecting funds pro forma, Collins advocated "the firing of some of these agitators." When Japanese workers on Maui caught
wind of the plan, they organized a near "riot." Tsutsumi, a member of a
union delegation visiting Maui, then delivered a speech before Collins's

workers. He had "his audience spell bound thruout," the plantation manager reported, "no one dissenting at all and all agreeing to raise the fee to $14.00 next month." Collins grew frustrated by the strike's pervasive influence and suggested the need for "something more drastic in the way of a lock-out." "The present situation is certainly an impossible one," he reasoned, "in that with the high bonus we are financing a strike that may last for a long time, a strike that is a rule of the minority."[47]

On July 1, 1920, Hosen Isobe, a Buddhist priest, convened a meeting between John Waterhouse, the HSPA president, and "about sixteen Japanese laborers" at a Honolulu hotel to negotiate an end to the strike. After being assured that no one was representing the FJL, Waterhouse declared that the HSPA "would not at the present time consider any change whatsoever in the wage or bonus schedule." And he was not about to negotiate with any of the representatives "because they were not at present employees of the sugar plantations." Waterhouse advised them to return to work, at which point "the Managers would meet them and discuss their problems with them in the future, the same as they had done in the past." He then shook hands with everyone and announced that the HSPA "bore absolutely no ill-will against the laborers, or the Japanese." The meeting lasted thirty minutes. Union representatives then held a rally at Aala Park to mark the official end of the strike. "The great controversy between capital and labor on the sugar plantations of Hawaii, which has lasted for the past six months," they said, "has been completely settled by the mutual and confidential understanding between the magnanimous capitalists and the sincere laborers." The statement praised the workers' resolve. "You have faithfully stood to the last this long strike, as inhabitants under the rule of the United States," it read, "respecting and obeying its laws, as members of this association, and as laborers, preserving your honor and dignity."[48]

The strike was officially over, but the solidarities forged through the strike persevered. Many workers figured that they had won—concluding the Aala Park rally with rounds of "Banzai!"—and dispersed to speak with plantation managers to claim their old jobs. To the managers' surprise, the returning workers were anything but repentant. They had a list of "certain demands," Bottomley recounted, "which included that they all be taken back; that they get their old jobs and their old houses back and that those Japanese who had gone back to work before the strike was ended should be fired." When the managers rejected those demands, many workers made "a good deal of grumbling" and continued to insist on their demands. Frustrated by the impasse, plantation managers posted notices the following week that "the Hawaii Laborers' Association has not been, and will not be recognized" and that workers would be reemployed on the old wage and bonus rates, with no guarantees of their previous houses or former positions. Any workers found to be harassing, maligning, or interfering with "the Japanese or other employees who have been loyal to the plantation," the notice warned, would be "summarily discharged and removed from the plantation." For weeks after the strike's end, managers refusing to reemploy all of their former workers encountered collective walkouts.[49] Although the strike failed to resolve plantation workers' grievances, their enduring solidarities continually distressed sugar planters and US officials, who increasingly saw in the plantation strike a deeper and vaster conspiracy to challenge the US empire in and across the Pacific.

As the plantation workers' strike gripped the attention of nearly everyone in Hawai'i, sugar planters and US officials simultaneously felt compelled to respond to indigenous claims to the lands they assumed as their own. Long-term leases of public lands, signed originally between the Kingdom of Hawai'i and various sugar corporations, were scheduled to expire in 1920 (or shortly before or after) and become available for general homesteading. Sugar planters' cheap and ready access to thousands of acres of rich agricultural lands appeared at risk. At the same time, and from a very different vantage point, elite Kānaka Maoli pressed the US Congress to "set aside suitable portions of the public lands of the Territory of Hawaii by allotments to or for associations, settlements, or individuals of Hawaiian blood in whole or in part, the fee simple title of such lands to remain in the government." Although not framed explicitly as a matter of colonial dispossession and Native Hawaiian sovereignty, the campaign for the "rehabilitation" of common Kānaka Maoli nevertheless summoned those histories and memories. "When the Hawaiians had everything they gave everything," a member of Hawai'i's delegation told the House Committee on Territories in February 1920, "and now that the United States has control of all the government lands, we come to the United States to-day and expect you to have the same feeling and the same liberality and the same liberal spirit, and return some of these lands to the Hawaiians."[50]

Race resolved the contradictions of those dual initiatives—to secure lands for *haole* sugar interests and to allot lands for Kānaka Maoli. Despite their discrete origins, the two measures came to be consolidated into a single congressional bill, with the debate shifting from contextualizing indigenous entitlement to public lands to determining who

among the Kānaka Maoli deserved state recognition and welfare assistance. Cast as a singularly benign, incompetent, and vanishing population, "full blooded" Hawaiians emerged in the deliberations as a racial
group requiring "rehabilitation," not as an indigenous group demanding reparations and justice. That racial construction, J. Kēhaulani
Kauanui argues, rested on the projections of "part-Hawaiians," particularly those of white ancestry, as "a virile, prolific, and enterprising lot
of people" and of the Japanese as utterly inassimilable and threatening.
In the end, the Hawaiian Homes Commission Act (HHCA) prioritized
and sanctified sugar planters' continued access to the most valuable
lands while restricting homesteading eligibility to marginal lands and
biological definitions of Kānaka Maoli (50 percent or more blood quan-
tum). Hawai'i's sugar interests prevailed again. If the legislative proceedings over public lands and homesteading implicitly exposed the
tenuousness of the US empire's claims over Hawai'i, the passage of the
HHCA, in combination with the violent repression of the 1920 labor
strike, legitimized US sovereignty and *haole* domination, solidifying
Hawai'i's place within the orbit of the US empire under the banner of
national security and white supremacy.[51]

Three months after the conclusion of the 1920 labor strike, MID
officer George M. Brooke decided to write a comprehensive report on
the "Japanese situation," reflecting on the local labor movement and on
the state of world affairs more generally. "All signs point to the approach
of a new crisis in the relations of Japan and the United States," he began
ominously. For Brooke, the Japanese influence extended well beyond
the Japanese community in Hawai'i. "Japan knows that if with the aid
of hosts of aliens, of radicals, of pacifists and of renegades of every sort
and description now rampant in the United States, as well as fermenting
under cover," he proclaimed, "that she may be able to aid in tying up
the United States with strikes, and that she may be able to make the
aliens, the radicals and the discontented working classes buck war, even
when war is necessary to preserve the vigor of our nationality." Fomenting unrest in the United States, Japan was simultaneously fostering "her
Pan-Asian propaganda throughout the Orient" to guide "the development in Asia of new conception of nationalism" and "a distinct lowering of the prestige of the white race." "Japan openly aspires to a dominant place in the Pacific," he concluded. "She aspires to leadership of
the colored peoples. She classes herself as colored when appealing to
colored races, but resents racial discrimination against herself, as a
question of color."[52]

Brooke distinctly saw the recent labor strike in Hawai'i as a phase of a worldwide problem, a racial problem. The Chinese, Koreans, Filipinos, and Kānaka Maoli in Hawai'i "would be not only of very little assistance to the United States," he cautioned, "but instead a practical impediment, excepting perhaps for the Hawaiians who are very easygoing people." The stage was nearly set for Japan to execute its global designs, Brooke argued. "Based on Asia she holds an island line from Korea to the mouth of the Amur. . . . She is firmly based in Formosa close to the Philippines. She has by her propaganda in the Philippines rendered possible insurrections on a small scale. . . . She is undoubtedly plotting with the Germans in Mexico. . . . She controls the lanes of the Pacific from Hawaii to the Orient. . . . She has extended her espionage net from Puget Sound to Panama." Brooke's apocalyptic vision went on and on, so much so that his superiors noted that the report was "a peculiar paper for an official document" that "reads more like a piece of propaganda."[53] His report was, in truth, an uncensored iteration of intelligence reports emanating from the Philippines, Hawai'i, and elsewhere. Concentrating on the "Japanese problem" drove the great expansion of the US security state and served to elide the ultimate source behind local struggles in Hawai'i: the US empire.

A COLORED INTERNATIONAL

By the time Brooke interpreted the global implications of the 1920 strike, the racial projection of the Japanese as agitators engaged in a global conspiracy to undermine US sovereignty had become engrained in military intelligence reports. Beginning in 1918, even before the strike, the Japanese in Hawai'i comprised a focal point of state surveillance. In a war between the United States and Japan, Major H. C. Merriam reported to the head of the MID in Washington, DC, "practically all the Japanese would side with Japan." The Japanese government, Japanese language schools, and Buddhist priests—all later represented as instigating the 1920 strike—were on a common mission, he claimed, to make all Japanese in Hawai'i loyal Japanese subjects, ready to wage war against the United States. The Office of Naval Intelligence (ONI) reinforced the MID findings, noting that a Japanese informant in Hawai'i had exposed the real object of Buddhist priests. "Buddhist priests in Hawaii, while ostensibly loyal to the United States," the informant stated, "are in reality doing everything in their power to undermine any American intelligence entertained by the Japanese in

Hawaii."[54] No matter what the local Japanese said or how they acted, their role within the US empire was predetermined or overdetermined: they posed the greatest threat to US national interests across the Pacific. The racialization of the Japanese as subversive and revolutionary agents, originally in the US-occupied Philippines and then in US-occupied Hawai'i, reflected and reproduced that conjecture and conclusion.

The expanding scale and scope of military intelligence and state surveillance in Hawai'i further classified the Japanese as disloyal and deviant. Working as the MID's assistant chief of staff in Honolulu, Brooke enlisted the *haole* planter elite to collect information on four distinct but increasingly indistinguishable categories: "Disloyalty"; "Radical activity, propaganda, literature, etc."; "Japanese activity or sentiment"; and "Any suspicious alien activity." Perceiving the growing influence of the Mormon Church and its possible links to the Japanese community at the conclusion of the 1920 strike, he demanded information on Japanese sexual practices—the prevalence of polygamy among the Japanese, the treatment of "illegitimate Japanese children," and the prominence of prostitution in the Japanese community, including "husbands selling wives and parents daughters for money consideration." "During the present unsettled relations which may be expected to continue for some months special watchfulness is necessary," Brooke explained. "Many straws rather than one show the way the wind blows." In December 1920, the Bureau of Investigation, a civilian federal agency that grew rapidly during World War I, dispatched A. A. Hopkins, an agent based in Los Angeles, to conduct "an under cover investigation of Japanese Activities in the Territory of Hawaii." Finding Brooke "very conservative and cautious" and wholly reliant on sugar planters for information, Hopkins echoed military leaders' call for a permanent BI office or agent in Hawai'i. "Our ignorance of the machinations, intrigues, and activities of the Japanese population in Hawaii," a US general stated, "is abysmal."[55]

As the civilian and military intelligence network prepared to gather information on the perceived threats posed by the local Japanese population, Hawai'i's *haole* elite fixated on containing and criminalizing the labor movement. During the 1920 strike, the HSPA had created its own Secret Service Department, with undercover agents and informants producing reports that dealt, according to Hopkins, "almost exclusively with Japanese Activities in connection with the strike and labor difficulties." The HSPA agreed henceforth to furnish the BI copies of all Secret Service reports and to extend its investigations to "Japanese Activities, Military, Political, Economic, and Radical." The territorial legislature buttressed the HSPA's interests and priorities, having already passed in 1919 a syndicalism law that prohibited "crime, sabotage, violence or other unlawful means of terrorism as a means of accomplishing industrial or political ends" and circulating by "word of mouth, writings or teaching the duty, necessity or propriety of those actions." In 1921, it added a law banning anarchistic publications, defined as any material "for the purpose of restraining or coercing or intimidating any person from freely engaging in lawful business or employment." As if to prove the connection between labor organizing and unlawful violence, territorial officials prosecuted and convicted fifteen FJL leaders in March 1922 of conspiring to plan, back in June 1920, a dynamite attack against a Japanese plantation employee opposed to the strike. The trial, during which prosecuting attorneys vilified the strike's motives and participants and offered no evidence beyond the testimony of two individuals who confessed to detonating the dynamite, depleted the union's meager funds.[56]

While the labor movement suffered one blow after another, the expanding US security apparatus dwelled on the racial dimensions of the 1920 strike. Three months after the conspiracy trial in 1922, the ONI reported that the "Japanese Labor Organizations are very quiet and many of them disorganized completely." The HSPA, in the meantime, remained on the offensive, establishing the Hawaii Emergency Labor Commission (HELC) through the territorial legislature to lobby the US Congress to exempt Hawai'i from Chinese exclusion. In response to the HELC's refrain on the need to counteract the "Japanese menace" in 1921 and 1922, President Warren G. Harding appointed a special commission to investigate labor conditions in Hawai'i. In December 1922, Major General Charles P. Summerall, the US military commander in Hawai'i, furnished the federal commission with a comprehensive "Summary of Data on Factors Bearing on the Japanese Situation in Relation to Our Military Problem." Framing the 1920 strike as a manifestation of Japanese racial solidarity, Summerall stated that all of the Japanese labor leaders' speeches "criticized everything American, condemned the American leaders of the community, American ideals and institutions." Believing that the Japanese government officially endorsed the strike, based on a false rumor spread by a strike leader, the Japanese community, according to the report, intimidated and assaulted those "loyal to the plantations" and eventually stood "whole heartedly behind the strike." It became a "racial movement," Summerall argued, binding "young Hawaiian born Japanese" and their parents alike to "the ideas of allegiance to the Japanese race."[57]

Summerall's contradictory views of the Hawai'i-born Japanese, a major focus of his report, served to reify and underscore the revolutionary and seditious potential of the local Japanese community. Plantation managers on O'ahu, he reported, agreed that "the young Japanese who were born here and received their education and training in the American public schools were the most radical of all the strikers." But the "absolutely unscrupulous" behavior of FJL leaders during the 1920 strike, Summerall asserted, opened younger Japanese eyes to the truth, leading "many of these Hawaiian born Japanese who otherwise would have remained loyal to Japan and to the Japanese race . . . to become better Americans." Racial allegiances, he believed, would not dissolve overnight, though. "The test undergone by the American born Japanese during the plantation strike of 1920 was the first real test that they have had as to whether or not they are becoming Americanized," he argued. "In this test they failed and it is believed that in similar tests that occur during the next ten years they will also fail." Partly because of the "race prejudice" exhibited by "the vast majority of the white race," Summerall did not think that the Japanese could ever be "fully assimilated," even if they might become "Americanized." In the end, he pronounced the Hawai'i-born Japanese—who would remain, he predicted, "neutral" until "local conditions" directed them to be "loyal to Japan or America"—as "a military liability to the United States."[58]

Military concerns over those local conditions and unreliable allegiances emerged and escalated in a US imperial context across the Pacific. As US military intelligence agents established a network of surveillance in Hawai'i, their colleagues in the Philippines likewise demanded greater resources to monitor the local population. Deeming the "Far East" essential to US interests, Captain Armin W. Riley, the MID officer in Manila, argued in March 1919 for "some degree of permanency in the intelligence organization which should last as long as our sovereignty over the Islands." Beyond the increasingly "Filipinized" government, he referred to "the presence of a large Spanish colony who are more or less anti-American, numerous East Indians, Turks, Russians, Germans, and other foreigners whose attitude and activities should be under constant observation." Even more unsettling was the high number of Japanese in the Philippines, about fifteen thousand and increasing every day, including through "illicit entrance." Spreading "their carefully arranged propaganda of blood brotherhood," establishing "Japanese-Filipino societies," and purchasing lands "to colonize locations of strategical interests," Riley stated, the Japanese required "serious study and constant observation." The Philippines, he suggested, served as a nexus of global movements against which "the representatives of other nations" constantly requested information and assistance. "For example, the Hindu conspirators who are threatening from the Philippines the peace of Great Britain," he noted. "Then there are the Bolshevists who are urging Natives to follow their lead and many other instances which will occur to anyone."[59]

If the Hawai'i-born Japanese seemed less than loyal to the United States, growing ranks of Filipinos, seemingly inspired by and allied with Japan, appeared again to be preparing for a revolution against US colonial rule. "The vigor with which the advocates of immediate independence for the Philippines have pressed their cause has resulted in the whole population becoming extremely disturbed in mind as to the future," Riley reported. The Philippine Constabulary and other Filipinos trained by the US Army, he explained, "could make up a nucleus around which a very effective insurrection unquestionably could be built." Under instruction from the commanding US general in the Philippines, Riley promised to continue "espionage among the Civilian population, but only where such espionage tends to disclose activities which reasonably could be supposed to lead to insurrection against the authority of the United States Government." Investigating the Sociedad Orientalista de Filipinas, which was founded in 1917 to cultivate friendly relations in the "Far East," evidently fell within that mandate. Stressing the organization's editorials favorable to Japan and hostile to the West, the MID cast the Sociedad as propagating a pan-Asian, revolutionary message. "Instead of the 'Yellow Peril' as portrayed by the Kaiser it is the 'White Peril' against which the 'Natives of Asia' must take care of their sacred possessions," the MID wrote in summary of the Sociedad's editorial from April 1918. Armed Filipinos, according to the MID, would then be justified in joining "the Chinese and Japanese to defend the Orient against Western aggression."[60]

The potential alliance between the Japanese and Filipinos against the United States appeared to warrant a more expansive US security state across the Pacific. Ralph H. Van Deman, whose fears of Japanese subversive activities in the Philippines dated back to his first tour during the Philippine-American War, lobbied assiduously for the permanent revival and institutionalization of the MID in the 1910s. Along with veterans of the Philippine Constabulary, he mapped the course of US military intelligence, helping to launch networks of combat intelligence on the US-Mexico border and then the European front and counterintelligence on the home front. By 1920, Van Deman was back in the Philippines, commanding an infantry division and contemplating the state of world affairs. Japan's global ambitions over the previous two decades, he believed, were "not in the least in doubt." "She proposes to make the Pacific a Japanese lake and to control the islands and Asiatic littoral and as much of the interior as she can," he informed a colleague. In that transpacific world, local disturbances—from calls for immediate independence to the "labor situation here in its relation to radicalism"— needed to be "watched by a man who has enough knowledge of the world situation to detect the real danger points." "The little local strikes seldom have any significance out here in relation to the present world movement," he noted. "However, you never can tell when that is going to be injected into the situation and the whole thing must be watched."[61]

Months later in May 1921, Van Deman remained frustrated by the US military's refusal to invest more in espionage and surveillance in the Philippines and across Asia. "There has been no one here in charge since the war began who really knew any thing about the larger aspects of the game," he stated in reference to World War I, "or who could realize that this office should be the collecting and distributing center for the Orient." Through intelligence agents, he argued, the US Army ought to be collecting "topographical data in China and northeastern Asia" and keeping tabs on Japan's maneuvers in that part of the world. "Don't think I believe we are going to have war with Japan in the near future," he added. "Japan is not ready yet." But Japan was preparing for such a conflict, in his mind, including in the Philippines. The "Japs," he reported, were "pretty active" in propaganda work, "revising the old 'Japanese-Filipino Association' which was organized in 1900, using it for the same purpose for which it was formed—to aid the Filipinos to immediate independence." As in MID reports on the Oʻahu strike, Van Deman was not particularly concerned about Filipinos per se. "There is little Radicalism in the Philippines just now nor do I believe that . . . there will be in the immediate future," he noted. "The Filipino character does'ent [sic] lend itself to things of that kind. It requires too much staedy [sic] planning and cooperation." Outside "agitators" were another story.[62]

Contrary to Van Deman's critical appraisal, the US state's capacity to monitor potentially subversive individuals and activities had grown considerably during and after World War I. When Van Deman referred to "agitators" in the Philippines, he pointed specifically to "'Captain' McKinney, a negro from Los Angeles." McKinney, he discovered, had been "active on the Pacific Coast in aiding Japanese propoganda [sic] against the California alien land law" and leading a "negro organization." "He is 'anti-white' and may stir up trouble along those lines also," Van Deman noted. On his way from California to the Philippines, McKinney claimed to have been feted by Japanese officials in Japan, but Van Deman did not know "how much negro bombast there may be in that story." Regardless, he learned that in Manila the Black veteran had met with the Japanese consul general—a "very bright and capable Jap"—and his "white wife who is bitterly anti-American." With the assignment of an MID agent to trail McKinney in the Philippines, Van Deman was confident that "we will know what he is up to in time to block him if it becomes necessary." His brief account of McKinney instantly generated MID memoranda to J. Edgar Hoover of the BI and to the MID office in San Francisco on "the endeavor of the Japanese to secure the support of negroes in the United States" and McKinney's probable plot "to start trouble" among his old segregated unit (Ninth Cavalry) in the Philippines.[63]

If Van Deman and other agents of the expanding US security state dwelled on the presumptively Japanese origins of radical and seditious influences, they sensed something perhaps more insidious in McKinney's movements and on Hawai'i's sugar plantations—the beginnings of what Hubert Harrison called forth around the same time, "a colored international" of the "darker races" around the world. When Van Deman reported on McKinney in the Philippines, a BI agent in Springfield, Massachusetts, kept an eye on M. Danchi Takeuchi, a "Hawaiian-Jap student at YMCA College," who accompanied another "Jap" and a Filipino college student to visit a local "negro leader" affiliated with Marcus Garvey's Universal Negro Improvement Association (UNIA). "My people are of mixed races. . . . Eighty per cent are of dark skin, Moro, Taga, Malay, Chino, Jap, Borno etc.," the Filipino student reportedly stated. "We are for complete independence." The mixing of races and politics disturbed the agent. "Many negroes attended picnic of Russian Club (Communists). . . . ," he noted. "They sang the Internationale as lustily as did the Ruskys." The agent tracked Takeuchi's movements closely—noting his meetings with UNIA officials and labor organizers of "radical tendencies" and "locally fraternizing with Russian and Italian radicals"—and inspected his mail from all over the world. Takeuchi, he learned, was soon planning a trip to Puerto Rico. His destination, another unruly site of the US empire, further convinced the agent that Takeuchi was working for the Japanese government.[64]

From the Philippines to Hawai'i to Massachusetts and New York, casting blame on imperial Japan for fomenting radical and interracial alliances had become an indispensable rationale to defending US claims across the Pacific and to assigning agents of the US security state across the "domestic" and "foreign" spaces of the US empire. In July 1921, a Black informant keeping tabs on Harrison and other Harlem radicals interviewed Sumio Uesugi, a Japanese resident of Harlem who had been speaking at UNIA meetings and in Black churches. "He told me that the white people were hypocrites who called themselves Christians, but always turn him down on account of his color," the informant reported to the BI. Uesugi declared that "everywhere he goes he will tell the negroes of the hypocrisy of the white race" and that he had forwarded literature on "the great strength which lies in Garvey's movement" to Japanese newspapers and to "his government." Whether or not Uesugi was, in fact, a representative of the Japanese government was almost irrelevant. What mattered was that the BI informant assumed the connection and that "Garvey's followers" seemed "enthused" by it.[65] Like plantation workers in Hawai'i who dared to go on strike, Uesugi's interracial activities were interpreted within a transpacific framework that fixated on locating anyone who might be affiliated with imperial Japan. In that endless pursuit, agents of US intelligence found fragmentary glimpses into a revolutionary, interracial critique of the US empire that they could not quite recognize or repress fully.

CHAPTER 5

Red and Yellow Make Orange

Having expanded dramatically over the course of World War I, the US security apparatus—including 1,700 employees in the Military Intelligence Division (MID), three hundred officers in the Office of Naval Intelligence (ONI), and 1,500 agents in the Bureau of Investigation (BI) by the war's end—produced countless reports on "Radical Activities," "Japanese Activities," and "Negro Activities." Those subject categories converged and overlapped so much that they often came to represent one and the same in many cases. In the summer of 1919, a BI report on the "Communist Convention and Communist Labor Party Convention" in Chicago stressed the imagined links between radical labor organizers and Japanese government agents. Bill Haywood, the prominent leader of the Industrial Workers of the World, met with a Japanese activist, it stated, "from whom it was learned that the 'Japanese People' are having some 'Missionary Work' done in America, with permission of the Japanese Government, and that the Japanese Agents are making their headquarters at 1947 Broadway, NY, Room 62, which is also used by Sen Katayama as the publishing office of the 'Heimin.'" What marked Katayama and others as Japanese agents in BI reports were their radical politics, racial backgrounds, and interracial "missionary work," a combination that simplified and magnified the role of the Japanese state. Haywood, moreover, was "closely working with the Bolsheviki Agents in America, Canada and Mexico" and expecting "something serious to happen in America before this year will be over." The specter of communism taking root in the United States kept the spotlight on Japan.[1]

The racial assumption that Katayama acted in collusion with the Japanese government was at best ironic. After a dozen years seeking higher education in the United States, Katayama had returned to Japan in 1896 and immersed himself in the incipient labor movement, which, modeled after the American Federation of Labor (AFL), was hardly revolutionary in ideology or strategy. The Japanese state nevertheless reacted punitively, revising the Public Peace Preservation Law in 1900 to decimate the labor movement and to proscribe leftist political organizations. When segments of the Japanese socialist movement critiqued militarism and championed anarchism and anarcho-syndicalism, they faced a barrage of recrimination, prosecution, and harassment. In 1908, after a violent clash between anarchists and the police, Katayama, whose brand of socialism remained largely reformist, noted that "there were two policemen always after me; one at the back of my house and the other opposite my house as a janitor in the school." Things turned much more violent in January 1911, when the secret trial of leading Japanese anarchists resulted in convictions for conspiracy to commit high treason. Shūsui Kōtoku and eleven others were executed for allegedly plotting to assassinate the Japanese emperor. A year later, Katayama fell victim to the Public Peace Preservation Law, spending months in jail for helping to organize a successful labor strike among Tokyo's transit workers. Katayama soon decided to seek refuge in the United States. "I am really driven out of my country because of socialism," he explained.[2]

After holding a series of menial jobs in California, where white supremacy and Japanese consular agents limited his political and professional options, Katayama moved to New York City, which for a brief moment served as a safe haven. He began publishing the *Heimin* in 1916, first in San Francisco and then in New York, to criticize the Japanese state on behalf of "the interest of workers and socialists in America and also in Japan." It was "the only publication of its kind in America or in fact anywhere . . . [to] speak out freely and preach the International Socialism and . . . criticize and attack injustices and oppression of the Japanese government that are constantly and increasingly heaped upon the workers of Japan," Katayama argued. In New York he found new opportunities for political expression and radical affiliation, including the eventual formation of the Bolshevik-inspired Communist Party of America in 1919, but the US government quickly cracked down on those opportunities. In August 1919, the BI director instructed his

FIGURE 16. Sen Katayama, 1925. Photograph from Seishichi
Iwasaki, *Ōbei Yūshō* (Tokyo: Atoriesha, Shōwa 8, [1933]).
Courtesy of Division of Rare and Manuscript Collections, Cornell
University Library.

agents to investigate all "anarchistic and similar classes, Bolshevism,
and kindred agitations advocating change in the present form of government by force or violence, the promotion of sedition and revolution,
bomb throwing, and similar activities," particularly "persons not citizens of the United States, with a view of obtaining deportation cases."
As the Palmer Raids targeted many of his communist comrades in New
York, Katayama went into hiding in January 1920.[3]

Having thrown his full support behind the communist movement,
Katayama would soon leave the United States for good, but leaving the
United States did not mean escaping the US security state's reach. In
1919, Bolshevik leaders in Russia organized the Third International and

invited Katayama to Moscow to represent Japanese socialists. Although he was not able to attend the historic meeting, the Communist International (Comintern, otherwise known as the Third International) accorded Katayama a significant role by dispatching him in 1921 to Mexico City to foster revolutionary organizing in Latin America. The BI tracked his activities there. He was busy, a BI report stated, "waging active propaganda amongst the laboring element . . . to bring about a General Strike." Katayama was not the only one hailing from the United States. Feeling persecuted north of the border for engaging in "radical propaganda," many Mexicans evidently returned to Mexico to provoke the US state and to build a global labor movement. "These men are of the opinion that, if a great movement of propaganda in favor of the proletariat be waged in Mexico and if the American government at some time in the future attempt intervention," the BI learned, "the American laboring element will aid the Mexican radical movement by impeding in every way possible the mobilization of troops." The returning migrants were convinced, according to the BI report, that "the 'mass' of the American laboring element will rise up against 'American Imperialism' because of the fact that a great discontent exists at present amongst the American 'poor.'"[4]

Katayama soon left Mexico for Moscow, the world's new headquarters for revolutionary politics. On December 14, 1921, Leon Trotsky, other Bolshevik dignitaries, and his Japanese comrades from New York City greeted Katayama's arrival in Soviet Russia. Over the next decade, he came to represent the promise of communist internationalism, often serving as the only non-European in the Comintern's inner sanctum. In 1922, he welcomed 150 delegates from across Asia to take a stand against colonialism, proclaiming: "The task of the Japanese proletariat is, for the present, to construct, together with the toiling masses of other lands in the Far East, a plan for a common struggle against the imperialists." The Comintern encouraged the formation of the Japan Communist Party, which promptly called for the dissolution of the Japanese monarchy, the imperial army, and the secret police, as well as the withdrawal of Japanese military forces from Formosa and other parts of Asia. The Japanese government retaliated violently, arresting and incarcerating communist leaders and labor organizers en masse in 1923 and then again in 1928 and 1929. Dispirited by the turn of events in Japan, Katayama and the Comintern attempted to retain the focus on linking proletarian movements and anticolonial struggles. At the Sixth Congress of the Third International in 1928, Katayama declared, "the time has come to prepare ourselves for the fight against world imperialism which threatens our fatherland, the Soviet Union."[5]

Through his movements, Katayama bore witness to the contradictions of race, empire, and state power around the world, placing the United States and Japan not in international opposition but in transimperial alignment. Back in 1919, while in New York, he challenged workers in Japan to renounce Japanese imperialism. "Don't serve any more the greedy and bloodthirsty Imperialists, but rise up and strike hard at your oppressors who made Japan infamous and the Japanese unpopular in the eyes of the world's proletariat," he wrote. "If you love your country the best, destroy Imperialism in Japan that made Koreans, Chinese and Siberians enemies of Japan and of the Japanese!" He advised them not to be seduced by the Japanese state's deflecting excuses. "Don't be consoled cheaply at a citation that England has her Ireland, Egypt and India and America her Negroes and practice of lynching and also her Mexico!" Just as America and Britain would "pay for what they are now doing," Japan would not be "immune from punishment for the crimes in Korea and Siberia."[6] Although the Comintern's directives from Moscow did not necessarily translate into concrete results on the ground, communist internationalism shifted and shaped the course of racial and anticolonial politics to make radical imaginings of "a colored international" into an institutional, global possibility. In particular, communism generated critiques, organizations, and movements that increasingly drew links between Black struggles against white supremacy in the United States and anticolonial struggles in Asia that paradoxically kept alive revolutionary dreams and counterrevolutionary fears of pan-Asian solidarity allied with imperial Japan.

INTERIMPERIAL ANTIRADICALISM AND
PAN-ASIAN ANTICOLONIALISM

The Japanese and US governments perceived Katayama and his fellow travelers as seditious subjects because of their transpacific associations with both Japan and the United States. In his weekly report on "Japanese Activities" in December 1921, the ONI agent in San Francisco noted the arrival of Kensan Suzuki, a Japanese labor organizer investigating "the Japanese socialists in Europe and America and their connections with those in Japan and with the Russian Bolsheviks." Operating "all in the dark in a way," Suzuki reportedly stated, the Japanese "radical movement" had forged networks across Japan and around the world, with roots in New York, "home of the world's radical movement." "The Japanese radical leaders came from New York as Trotsky came from there," he said, according to the ONI. "There are something like five or six hundred Japanese who are now on the Government black list in Japan; among them many are those who were educated in America or who resided there." Japanese workers in Hawai'i likewise encountered hostility from the Japanese government. Recalling earlier military intelligence reports alleging the Japanese government's influential role behind the 1920 strike, a BI agent in Los Angeles reported that the "home Government" decided to cut its ties to the Hawaii Laborers' Association because of the union's "bad reputation." The Japanese government, the BI agent observed, seemed to possess "a natural distrust of the Socialist and Radical element that has developed among the leaders of the Labor Association."[7]

Indeed, Japanese government officials collaborated with their US counterparts to identify and contain radical movements. In January 1920, BI officers in New York City discovered Yojiro Nakadate's name during a raid on the Communist Party headquarters and telegraphed the Los Angeles office to arrest him as a member of the Communist Party, for possible deportation to Japan. The Japanese consul in Los Angeles, BI agents reported, immediately agreed to assist in the investigation as the consul had "previously expressed his willingness to do anything in his power . . . to the stamping out of bolshevism, or extreme radicalism." He, however, was unable to find any evidence against Nakadate. The *Nippu Jiji,* a Japanese newspaper in Hawai'i, in the meantime, defended Nakadate, a former school teacher there, as "a very good-natured man" and "a strong Christian." Nakadate, for his part, denied being a communist and admitted only to receiving and subscribing to two radical publications and to contributing to the Industrial Workers of the World (IWW) Defense Fund, the "sole evidence" in the case, which the immigrant inspector ruled insufficient for deportation. While Nakadate was able to elude the anticommunist crusade waged by Attorney General A. Mitchell Palmer and J. Edgar Hoover, then in charge of the BI's new antiradical division, the Japanese government took inspiration from the Palmer Raids. In December 1920, the head of Foreign Affairs of the Police Bureau in Japan's Department of the Interior toured the United States to study "government control of Bolsheviki and other radical movements" and, through diplomatic channels, requested a personal meeting with Hoover.[8]

If the Japanese government engaged in any kind of "missionary work" in the United States, its mission fixated not on promoting anticolonial radicalism but on fortifying antiradical colonialism. In August 1919, a BI agent in Chicago learned through his confidential informant that "several citizens of Japan," in possession of IWW literature, were suspiciously occupying a hotel room and "interviewing other Japs." Proceeding cautiously to avoid "any possible embroilment with the State Department," the agent conferred with the Japanese consul, who told him that the room's occupants were members of a government delegation studying "labor conditions" and "radical movements." Toward that end, one of them had joined the IWW in Seattle and collected IWW pamphlets to be included in "a report which he was compiling for his government on radical activities here." And when U. Tokinaga, the secretary of the Japanese colonial regime in Korea, visited the United States in the summer of 1920, he called on Frank McIntyre, chief of the Bureau of Insular Affairs, a division within the War Department in charge of the civilian administration of the Philippines as an "unincorporated" territory of the US empire. Tokinaga inquired specifically on the US colony, McIntyre noted, asking for "publications bearing on our work in the Islands," in particular "school readers" on "the relation of the people to the government and instruction in governmental matters." He, in turn, shared with McIntyre pamphlets on administrative reforms in Korea and thanked his American colleague for his "kindness and further offers of service."[9]

Beneath the apparent alliance between the United States and Japan during and after World War I, transpacific tensions festered. In addition to continuing fears of a Philippine revolution against the United States, presumably aided and abetted by Japanese agents, Japan's seizure of German colonial claims in China (Shandong) and the Pacific and its encroachment on Manchuria convinced many US officials of Japan's nefarious designs. To President Woodrow Wilson and his administration, the Allied intervention in revolutionary Russia, including the deployment of US and Japanese troops to Siberia in 1918, likewise appeared to portend an impending conflict with Japan rather than a lasting coalition against Bolshevism. If anything, military intelligence reports over the previous decade pointed to a likely alliance between Japan and the Bolsheviks. In September 1918, upon hearing of "a list of radical Anarchists and rabid Socialists who have been congregating in Japan recently, probably for the purpose of getting into Russia," the War Department's Office of the Chief of Staff contacted ONI's director to "furnish us with a copy of this list for our information." As the list circulated among military intelligence agencies, the MID commented that at least some of "these radicals are in enemy pay and all are dangerous agitators." Although a naval attaché in China would dismiss the report as a "nonsensical piece of false information," the racial assumption of Japan's revolutionary ties and objectives lived on.[10]

Those fears and anxieties proliferated in a world of new political possibilities, a world where challenges to race and empire took center stage in world affairs. In 1917, V.I. Lenin published *Imperialism*, in which he theorized that imperialism marked "the monopoly stage of capitalism," signified by the global concentration and domination of "finance capital" and "the territorial division of the whole world among the greatest capitalist powers." As he led the Bolshevik Revolution, Lenin challenged that world order, speaking boldly of "self-determination" and "the liberation of all colonies; the liberation of all dependent, oppressed, and non-sovereign peoples." Not to be outdone, President Wilson framed US entry into World War I in 1917 as a cause "for democracy, for the right of those who submit to authority to have a voice in their own governments, for the rights and liberties of small nations." His ambivalent statements specifically on colonialism paled in comparison to Lenin's forthright language, but Wilson moved to embrace "self-determination" as "an imperative principle of action," championing the ideal to thwart—not to advance—revolutionary movements. Although he proved adept at co-opting anticolonialism, Wilson's position on race was another matter. When Japan's delegation demanded in 1919 a clause on racial nondiscrimination in forming the League of Nations, Wilson, as the head of postwar negotiations in Paris, maneuvered to defeat the measure.[11] Beyond tensions among nominal allies, diplomatic debates over race and empire served to reinforce the US security state's longstanding conflation of Japan and revolution.

Regardless of the Japanese government's antiradical ethos, agents of the US security state continued to focus on imperial Japan's presumed mission to subvert the United States. The US government needed to pay attention to "the activity of the Japanese among the revolutionary labor circles" in the United States, a confidential informant told the Department of Justice, particularly since "the tendency of hostile Governments to embar[r]ass the United States by backing the radicals in this country is a matter of record since the World War." The Japanese were prominently represented in the Socialist Party, the IWW, and other radical organizations, he noted, including at an international banquet in Los Angeles "attended by all those 'who had a kick to register against the United States,' as one of the speakers put it." In the same weekly report in November 1921, an "oratorical mass meeting" of Japanese students at the University of Southern California also distressed the ONI. All of the speeches, an agent reported, "consisted of sneer and sarcasm of American institutions and politics, especially concerning the American attitude and policies toward the Japanese Empire and the Japanese, even seasoned with bitterness and ferocity which are the racial traits of the Islanders." Individual speakers referred to America's "limitless greed" and "capitalistic imperialism" that had "usurped the country from the helpless Indians through brute force and deceptory bargains." Though "educated in America" and "supposed to be Christians," the report added, the speakers were "bitterly against everything American and everything Christian."[12]

Weeks later in Berkeley, a group of speakers at a New Year's celebration concentrated their attacks on the world's colonial order. The Tamalcraft Club, an association established to promote the arts, hosted a banquet that, an ONI agent stated, "was marked by a radicalistic air of agitation of the weaker and smaller nationalities against the stronger and larger nations generally called powers." After a Chinese speaker addressed the "forced foreign concessions in China" and "his still unshaken faith in the future of China and . . . the moral aid of America," the president of the Hindu Club recounted "the bitter experience of nearly three hundred years first as the enemies of Great Britain, then as the 'friend' of Great Britain and finally as the Subject of Great Britain." The president of the Philippine Club, described as "smooth, smiling and somewhat persuasive," then spoke of Filipino yearnings for independence. "Even though we know what America has done for us, even though we are thankful for it, even though we are loyal and friendly to America," he said, "we want independence just the same." He recalled a broader history of anticolonial resistance. "Besides the Philippines have historical leaders who died for the freedom of their nation and their memory is very dear to us," he continued. They were determined to finish the work, not through violence but through appeals to the US Congress, he concluded ironically, "since we know the American sense of justice and fair-play."[13]

The evening's program suggested a budding pan-Asian, anticolonial consciousness that conjointly critiqued Britain, the United States, and Japan. The ONI informant, in this instance, was a Korean who felt compelled to deliver a speech rebuking all three empires, in part to protect his secret identity as an agent of the US state. If he said what he said to appease his audience, his remarks nonetheless served to position Britain and the United States as Japan's allies in ravaging Korea. "Korea has come to a point where she is about to lose entire faith in all 'Powers,' perhaps even including America," he said, reminding his audience of the

Portsmouth Treaty negotiations and the US government's swift recognition of Japanese claims over Korea. Koreans were determined to win independence, the Korean informant stated, meeting Japan's policy of "assimilation or entire racial extermination" with a struggle for "political self-determination or racial extermination" and exposing "Japanese duplicity" to the American public. After speeches by an "Egyptian speaker" and a "Turkish speaker," the president of the Tamalcraft Club "announced that America should look out for the Pan-Asiatic Empire now in the making lest America and the white race should be made the victim of the little son-of-Heaven." His joke drew "the greatest clapping of the evening." Even if the audience of "all sorts of people" appreciated the mockery of Japan, the Chinese, Filipino, South Asian, Korean, and other students in the crowd must have taken delight in the idea of a "Pan-Asiatic Empire" bringing down "the white race."[14]

The surveillance of college campuses, particularly their propensity to facilitate interracial alliances and radical ideas, was very much a part of the Red Scare. In March 1920, a professor of military science at Syracuse University informed the MID that Cosmopolitan Clubs at leading US universities were disseminating "foreign radical propaganda" amounting to "a real national menace." Agreeing on "the great menace to our country which can be brought about by the organized propaganda among the young college men of to-day, who in fifteen or twenty years will be the leaders of national life," MID officials convinced the BI to launch an investigation of Cosmopolitan Clubs across the United States. The organization, most BI agents reported, sought only to foster "inter-national friendships" between foreign and American students. There were signs of potential subversion, though. The president of the University of Michigan chapter was described as a Russian Jew from China belonging to "Bolsheviki and IWW—very Radical." The dean of undergraduates at the University of California, Berkeley, related that his campus's chapter had "many Japanese, Chinese, Hindus and Russians, one or two Canadians and . . . some from the Dutch East Indies." Although the South Asian students, including the chapter president, were all "anti-British" and many members held "strong socialistic views," he noted, the club existed "primarily for social purposes." The BI agent based in Cleveland, Ohio, discovered a similar scene at Oberlin College, with a chapter welcoming Asian and pro-Bolshevik students and advised by a "radical" sociology professor.[15]

Around the same time in April 1920, the BI agent in Springfield, Massachusetts, became aware of two Chinese students radicalized by their wartime experiences. S. C. Wang and W. L. Wang had enrolled initially at the International YMCA College (now Springfield College) four years earlier, but left for France in 1918 to assist the Chinese in France during World War I. Before their year-long sojourn, according to the college president and a local high school teacher, they had demonstrated "excellent" deportment, "rapidly absorbing American principles of Government." Upon their return to Springfield in 1919, however, Wang and Wang talked like "wild eyed crazy headed Bolshevists." "They declared that they hated this Government and its institutions," observed the teacher, who had befriended the Chinese students, and "expressed very strong anti-American sentiments . . . saying: 'The Japanese and Chinese are classed with the negroes, the United States abuses the negro and classes all dark-skinned peoples as negroes.'" Things had been different in France, where the two men felt "treated as equals by the white people." "They spoke greatly in favor of the Japanese," the BI report stated, "and made declaration that they were to return to China, and tell their people that the United States and the people therein were not friendly to China or the Chinese." In Springfield after the war, moreover, Wang and Wang were on "very friendly terms" with two French female students, who were being sponsored by the French government to study in the United States and who shared their "radical views."[16]

INTERRACIAL BLACK INTERNATIONALISM

The contradictions of race, war, and democracy that the two radicalized Chinese students experienced and articulated corresponded to Black veterans' struggles. In the segregated US military camps of France, African American soldiers—numbering two hundred thousand, with only about a fifth allowed to serve as combat troops—continued to suffer the humiliating and grinding effects of Jim Crow, but their encounters with the world beyond the camp gates and beyond America's shores stirred new political imaginaries. Even as French officials attempted to reinforce racial boundaries as much as their US counterparts, historian Adriane Lentz-Smith argues, they concentrated on disciplining French colonial subjects from Africa, the Caribbean, and Southeast Asia, not on targeting Black soldiers from the United States. That context proved foundational to the formation of the "New Negro" during and after World War I, driven by an idealized vision of freer race relations in France and a radical critique of the United States. Among Black soldiers and Black civilians, who readily recognized the hypocrisy of Wilsonian democracy, there emerged a variety of internationalisms—from Marcus Garvey's Universal Negro Improvement Association (UNIA) to W. E. B. Du Bois's Pan-African Congress and Cyril V. Briggs's African Blood Brotherhood (ABB)—that refigured Black political subjectivity beyond the US nation-state. Returning home in 1919 after working in France as a volunteer sponsored by the Young Men's Christian Association, Kathryn Johnson seethed at having to submit to racial segregation in the steamer's dining room. Sitting with Black and Asian passengers, she understood why the "world's darker citizens" despised America.[17]

Not unlike France, Japan figured prominently in cultivating Black internationalist sensibilities and the New Negro movement. The introduction and rejection of Japan's racial equality clause at the Paris Peace Conference in particular called attention to white supremacy's global scope. "This question would not bear the slightest examination by the American peace commission which has its vexatious Negro problem and which excludes Japanese immigrants by a gentlemen's agreement," A. Philip Randolph and Chandler Owen argued in the *Messenger*. "Nor could Great Britain face the issue with her West Indian colonies and her India. Australia, a British dominion, excludes both Negroes and Asiatics." Garvey praised "the yellow man of Asia" for preparing to fight "the war of the races" and implored "the Negro" to do likewise, "so that when the great clash comes in the future he can be ready wherever he is to be found." Upon hearing rumors of an impending war between the United States and Japan, perhaps in alliance with Mexico, notably in the bloody context of race riots in the Red Summer of 1919, Briggs made it clear on which side the New Negro stood. "The Negro who fights against either Japan or Mexico is fighting for the *white man* against himself . . . and for the perpetuation of *white domination of the colored races . . .*," he argued, "in opposition to the principle advocated by Japan of Race Equality, and . . . that . . . *no loyal* Negro will do."[18]

Such unabashed utterances in favor of Japan enhanced the specter of widespread sedition and revolution. In October 1919, the BI office in Los Angeles responded quickly to a white citizen complaining about a Black man engaging in "considerable inflammable talk." Brandishing a revolver, the man, named Tom Brady, supposedly talked about Japan planning "trouble with Mexico against the United States" and "inlisting [sic] and promising certain things to the colored people on this coast if they will join in with Japan and Mexico when the trouble is begun herein [sic] California." A BI agent learned that the complainant had gained the information through a family member who knew a laundrywoman who worked next to Brady, a "negro bootblack." The agent interviewed Brady, who explained that a young Japanese customer had asked him why he was wearing a US Army cap. When Brady told him that he had been "an overseas soldier," according to the BI report, "the Jap spoke sneeringly of that fact and asked him 'what he got out of it,' and then told him that the right thing to do was for the colored people to 'stand in with the Japanese' who in a few years were going to take California, and then the negroes would be 'treated right.'" The BI agent dismissed the matter as "nothing but a lot of loose talk on the part of this negro," warning Brady of "what he might expect if he was caught intriguing with anyone," but he felt that the case warranted being "kept open."[19]

In the following months and years, agents of the US security state attempted to keep tabs on potential interracial and anticolonial alliances that might align African Americans and Japan against the United States. When W. E. B. Du Bois lectured on "The Future of the Darker Races" in Boston in December 1920, a BI agent was there to summarize and transcribe the speech. Du Bois, the agent noted, "devoted considerable attention to England, who, . . . under the guise of elevating inferior races, invariably exploited those races for profit and cloaked commercialism in a mantle of Christianity." In the same vein, Du Bois condemned the US military's deployment and occupation of Haiti. "Japan is pressing the question of race equality and no one can blame her to retain her armaments so long as the present attitude of the white race exists," he said, according to the BI agent. "There is no place in the world where there is so much disgust with the white race today as in India. . . . In Egypt it is the same. . . . There was open rebellion in the Sudan, of which little has leaked out to the world." The "colored people of the world," Du Bois reportedly concluded, were beginning to see the need to "take sides with the labor element of the white race." And those sentiments and perspectives seemed to be reflected in Du Bois's audience. "A number of Chinese and Japanese, presumably students, were present," the BI agent noted.[20]

In Harlem, the center of Black radicalism, an undercover informant provided almost daily reports on a growing range of individuals, organizations, and meetings, often highlighting their foreign and interracial character. In October 1920, he attended a UNIA meeting, where W. S. Basuma, a "Hindu," read a pamphlet denouncing "the white races" as "the natural enemies of mankind . . . that should be fought tooth and nail." By the following spring, the informant became convinced that "nearly all these Negro radicals carry the Bolshevic [sic] red card," noting that most were "West Indian men who have not been naturalized or even in possession of their first papers." The BI office ordered him to look for "a Japanese preacher in Harlem" commingling with Black radicals, among whom the BI informant considered Hubert H. Harrison the most dangerous. At street meetings that attracted huge crowds "which even block traffic," the informant reported, Harrison predicted war between Japan and the United States and instructed African Americans not to fight for Uncle Sam until lynchings and race riots ceased. "Harrison is a fellow who never works but lives on his wit and has a wonderful method of telling negroes to learn the use of TNT, guns, fires, etc., so as to kill white men if attacked," the informant stated, "but he has practiced a way of clothing his dangerous advice in such subtle words and phrases that his audience understand[s] him while at the same time he seeks to evade the clutches of the law."[21]

Across the continent in San Francisco, ONI and BI agents observed and investigated similar sentiments and movements. The UNIA's secret mission, an ONI agent reported, was to rouse "racial and political hatred against the Whites and against the existing American government." With branches in "every city of the United States and in various places in Africa and elsewhere," he continued, the organization was communicating with "'colored races' other than the black." "The Japanese agents are playing an important part of the role, and evidently there are Hindus who are busily engaged in aiding the novel and disastrous propaganda," the agent noted. "And, too, the ultra-socialistic doctrine enters into the actual work of the propaganda." In the waning weeks of 1921, a secret informant met with George Farr, the reputed leader of the UNIA branch in the Bay Area, in a dive run by a Korean. Even Farr's appearance and demeanor seemed to transgress racial boundaries. The ONI did not believe his claim to being "a negro." He had "a little accent—not the Southern accent that is common to all Negroes, but the accent similar to that of an American-educated Hindu." And, according to the agent, Farr's "facial color and the shape and structure of his face is also more like a Hindu than an American Negro." Farr's background would remain a mystery, but in nine years he might have reinvented himself in Detroit as Fard Muhammad to found the Nation of Islam.[22]

Before then, Farr's remarks to the secret informant underscored the possibility and the inevitability of interracial solidarity against white supremacy. "All Negroes—indeed all other colored peoples as well—should wake up to the wrongs done to them, planned against them, by the white race and should rise and stand up in a solid body against the whites," he reportedly said. "Why, the colored people all taken together, which numbers about four times as many as the whites, will not forever remain under the slavery of the whites." Farr pointed to Japan as an inspiration, "a mighty nation to-day" and "the pride of all the colored races." There were two Japanese delegates at the UNIA convention in New York a while back, he added, along with several visitors from Japan. "I know quite a number of the Japanese who are sympathizers of our cause—even in this town there are quite a number," Farr related. "I think most of them are. You know how the Japanese, Chinese and Koreans are treated in California and in other states of the Union. How can they help themselves from being against the whites?" Their common mission was clear: "'Down with the whites!' is our aim. Of course at present we cannot and must not say that." Over the next few weeks, Farr reportedly organized meetings at the same Korean dive and at other restaurants, pool halls, and hotels where Black and Asian workers congregated, specifically soliciting support from local Japanese residents.[23]

Jothar W. Nishida likewise traversed racial boundaries and engaged in radical activities that alarmed the US security state. Described as a "Japanese-Turkish half-breed" fluent in eleven languages, he was under the ONI's surveillance by 1918 for being "an extreme radical" with IWW connections. Nishida reportedly admitted to an ONI agent that he was "stirring the Hawaiians to action" and sending all of his correspondence to Honolulu surreptitiously via Japanese sailors. His name surfaced in the BI files during the Palmer Raids in January 1920, as a subscriber of *The Communist* jailed in Los Angeles for violating California's law on "criminal syndicalism." Having operated the Red International Book Shop, Nishida seemed in clear violation of the 1919 statute against promoting "any doctrine or precept advocating, teaching or aiding and abetting the commission of crime, sabotage . . . or unlawful acts of force and violence or unlawful methods of terrorism as a means of accomplishing a change in industrial ownership or control, or affecting any political change." Not satisfied with his guilty plea and five years' probation, the BI office in Los Angeles attempted to indict Nishida with a federal charge of failing to register for the military draft, but could not "gather sufficient evidence." The office then turned him over to US immigration authorities to deport him as an "alien anarchist," only to be foiled by Nishida's evasive responses on his background. Although he claimed to be at different moments "Hindu, Turkish and Japanese," British, Ottoman, and Japanese consuls "all disowned him."[24]

Nishida moved back into the spotlight and into BI reports a year later, in Miami, Florida. In the spring of 1921, a Miami detective reported that "a negro had been stirring up Colored Town for three nights," delivering speeches recommending the *Messenger*, the *Negro World*, and other publications and referring to "the Japanese question in California, where . . . the white people were afraid to draw any color line." Nishida "styled himself as a 'COSMOPOLITAN INTERNATIONAL SOCIALIST'" and boasted of having spoken in Egypt and the Caribbean and developed "an intimate knowledge of political conditions in Europe and the Far East." He also ridiculed "churches and religions," according to the detective, except for Islam, which he proclaimed as "the real religion." Based on the detective's account, the BI office in Miami launched an investigation to locate Nishida. Perhaps sensing the BI's pursuit, Nishida checked out of the "colored" hotel he had been staying at—he had registered as originating from Hawai'i—and told the owner that he was leaving for the Bahamas. Unable to find Nishida's name on various passenger lists, a BI agent stayed a couple nights in "Colored Town," where he was able to compile a description of Nishida: "Looks like a Hawaiian, with long black hair; is about 35 years old, and weighs about 170 pounds; he speaks several languages." Nishida's "radical" speeches, the agent learned, had been "sponsored by the UNIA, most of whose members in Miami are Bahama negroes, which number about 7,000."[25]

Although Nishida's racial identity remained ambiguous, his speeches in Miami explicitly addressed the struggles of Black folk. "I am looking into the faces of the Young and New Negro," he said in a speech transcribed by a "Bahama negress," who shared her work with a BI agent after he threatened to take her to the federal building. "I am so glad I do not belong to that race that is always blowing hot air." After speaking to the beauty of Africa, Nishida challenged his audience to look around and within, for the "hand that holds you down is a poison hand, that hand is the hand of the Black American itself." "The black hand represents the soul, the soul that you rob, the soul that is misinformed by the traitors called Negro leaders," he preached. "The only way to protect that soul is to protect that bo[d]y, feed, cloth[e] and house that body." Nishida contrasted the "hard times" suffered by African Americans to the Japanese in California, whose "religion" was to own the best vegetable markets in the world. He ended his speech by publicizing Garvey's movement and its symbolic colors—red, black, and green. Green, he claimed, represented "unity" and the Islamic "signal of war." Red, he continued, stood for the "blood that must be spilled by the men, women and children of the African race." And black, Nishida concluded, symbolized "the suffering that must be suffered by you, like the suffering of the Russians."[26]

After his spectacular speeches, Nishida disappeared, eluding US authorities coast to coast. The BI chief instructed the Los Angeles office "to investigate reports that Japanese Consuls had received instructions from Japanese Government to cover negro movements in this country and establish any connections of NISHIDA therewith." Those connections did not exist, the investigation determined, but BI agents elsewhere continued to pursue Nishida with the information that he had been born in Honolulu to a Japanese father and a Turkish mother. Upon learning that Nishida was traveling by ship from Key West to Galveston, Texas, a Houston-based BI agent hurried to the pier to greet the vessel's arrival. None of the ship's officers, however, could recall seeing "any person having the appearance of a Japanese" on board. "Agent closely scrutinized each passenger leaving the vessel," the agent reported, "but failed to note any person having Japanese appearance or characteristics." Racial profiling failed him. After conferring with the ship's officers in greater detail, he compiled "a more accurate description" of Nishida: "About 5' 10"; 180 lbs; very black kinky hair; small black mustache." The BI agent located and followed a man fitting that description in Galveston and alerted BI offices of Nishida's departure by train to Brownsville and his plans to return thence to Los Angeles. Weeks later, a BI agent in San Antonio was still looking for Nishida, who evidently announced in Brownsville "his intention of crossing into Mexico" to work for a radical publication in Mexico City.[27]

All of the fears and anxieties motivating and extending the US security state immediately after World War I—communist internationalism, imperial Japan, Black radicalism, and interracial anticolonialism—came together in Nishida. If he ventured to Mexico, BI agents and US customs and immigration authorities along the US-Mexico border, who were on the "lookout," failed to detect his crossing. Perhaps they were looking for someone who appeared Japanese. "The truth is that he is an American or Jamaican negro trying to pose as a member of another race," a BI agent in Los Angeles argued, "and thus obtain social privileges not granted to negroes." Whatever his racial background, Nishida's radical message seemed to hold the potential to bring different peoples together. In Miami, his coworker at a cabaret told the BI that Nishida "was an advocate of armed revolution in order to overthrow the government, not only from the viewpoint of the negro, but from the viewpoint of a cosmopolitan who viewed any kind of racial prejudice as wrong, regardless of the race or color." The agent did not know if Nishida had "perfected any organization of radicals in Miami," but the BI called for greater vigilance by having "members of the UNIA covered who were interested in his speeches here." From Los Angeles, another BI agent stated that Nishida's relocation to Mexico City and likely affiliation with the Third International would make him "a dangerous radical force." The BI marked Nishida as "dangerous" because he was defiantly Japanese, Black, and red.[28]

REVOLUTIONARY NATIONALISM AND COMMUNIST INTERNATIONALISM

Long before Manabendra Nath (M. N.) Roy made his circuitous journey to Mexico City, he was a seasoned anticolonial revolutionary, accustomed to the state surveillance of his movements. As a youth in Bengal at the turn of the twentieth century, he joined the Swadeshi movement against British rule, including underground plots to raid armories, build bombs, and assassinate colonial officials. Like his Ghadar counterparts in North America, Roy envisioned Germany as a potential ally during World War I and left India to arrange for shipments of German arms and funds, "determined not to return without the precious cargo which, we fondly believed, was floating somewhere on the Pacific Ocean." In the Dutch East Indies (Indonesia), Roy could "extract a fairly large sum of money" from German officials, but little else. He soon sailed to Japan, "still full of hope." There, he encountered South Asian and Chinese revolutionaries smitten by imperial Japan's anticolonial pretentions. "We must have faith in the leader of Asia and wait patiently for our chance," he was told. Roy had his doubts. "From the day that I had landed at Nagasaki," he wrote, "I was under strict surveillance." Feeling the need "to shake off the Japanese bloodhounds," Roy made his way to Korea and then to Tientsin (Tianjin), China, where British authorities prepared for his arrival and quickly detained him. Escaping and eluding the British dragnet, he decided to venture across the Pacific to discuss matters with the German ambassador to the United States.[29]

Roy would find no political freedom in the United States. "I was . . . curious to make the acquaintance of the famous Indian revolutionary exiles in America, of whom we had heard so much at home," he recalled. "But to cross the Pacific was a tough problem. I had no proper passport, and the American immigration law was particularly discriminating about the Asiatics." Managing to make his way to Japan, alongside Ghadar Party leader Bhagwan Singh, and to secure a US visa with a fake passport, Roy landed in San Francisco in the summer of 1916. Within months, he was in New York City, where he befriended Lajpat Rai and "frequented the New York Public Library to read the works of Karl Marx, and discovered a new meaning in them." As the US government entered World War I and arrested South Asian revolutionaries and German agents in the "Hindu Conspiracy" in April 1917, the Department of Justice identified Roy as a target. Because Roy was living outside "the territory or jurisdiction of the United States" when he took part in the alleged conspiracy, potentially a stumbling block to criminal prosecution, the US Attorney General suggested detaining him for violating US immigration laws. Roy had entered San Francisco as a Christian missionary from Pondicherry (Puducherry)—a "French subject; West India race." After attending Rai's lecture at Columbia University, Roy recounted, "half a dozen hefty fellows pounced on me out of the surrounding darkness; a couple of pistols were actually pointed at me." Along with his bride from California, Evelyn Trent, he faced intense interrogation.[30]

Roy sought refuge in Mexico, the place that he would later call "the land of my rebirth." With "nerves steeled by years of terrorist activities," he frustrated the US district attorney's attempts to intimidate him. "I thought America was the land of liberty," Roy shot back during an interrogation. Indicted for entering the United States illegally and placed "under strict surveillance," he resolved to flee the United States when he was released "on personal security." "I left the Court with the grim determination not to come there again," Roy wrote. "To court imprisonment had not yet become a revolutionary virtue." He secretly caught a train to San Antonio, passing through the Jim Crow South but encountering "no difficulty on account of my brown skin," and crossed over the Rio Grande and laughed "heartily for having called the American bluff." Witnessing the political turmoil and unremitting poverty amid the Mexican Revolution awakened Roy to the limits of "national independence"—that it "was not the cure for all the evils of any country." He saw India in a new light. "The liberation of the Indian masses, therefore," he reasoned, "required not only the overthrow of British imperialism but subversion of the feudal-patriarchal order which constituted the social foundation of the foreign political rule." For months at El Chino, a small Chinese restaurant in Mexico City, Roy discussed Marxism with "the passionately anarchist and fanatically syndicalist convictions of the leaders of the Socialist Party." He moved more and more to the left.[31]

It was in Mexico where Roy expanded his anticolonial critique to the US empire. An article in the newly adopted Mexican Constitution of 1917 made all subterranean resources the national property of Mexico, potentially subjecting foreign mining and petroleum companies to confiscation and nationalization. The prospect of another US military intervention appeared imminent. As much as Roy enjoyed and learned from his conversations with Mexican anarcho-syndicalists, he was "taken aback" by their indifference to rumblings of impending war, a matter they dismissed as a "quarrel between two bourgeois governments." Roy felt otherwise. "Might we not organise working class action to protest against, and eventually to resist, the threatened American intervention?" he asked of the Socialist Party. When word of the Bolshevik Revolution reached Mexico in 1918, stirring "the imagination of all who dreamt of the proletariat capturing power," Roy worked with sympathetic contacts in the Mexican government, including President Venustiano Carranza who had refused to extradite him to the United States, to mobilize and organize the Socialist Party of Mexico. With Mikhail Borodin, a Russian Bolshevik also in exile in Mexico, he then led the reconstitution of the Socialist Party into the Communist Party of Mexico, aligning it with the Third International and emphasizing "the anti-imperialist struggle of the oppressed and subject peoples." In November 1919, after two and a half years in Mexico, Roy left for Moscow to attend the Second Congress of the Third International, having experienced "a revolution in my mind—a philosophical revolution which knew no finality."[32]

In Moscow, Roy found an audience receptive to his efforts to ground Marxism in anticolonial struggles. "There are 1.25 billion people who find it impossible to live in the conditions of servitude that 'advanced' and civilized capitalism wishes to impose on them," Lenin said in the opening session of the congress. On behalf of the 70 percent of the world's population, he argued, the Comintern had "to elaborate or indicate the practical principles that will enable the work, till now carried on in an unorganized fashion among hundreds of millions of people, to be carried on in an organized, coherent, and systematic fashion." When Roy read Lenin's preliminary draft of "Theses on the National and Colonial Question" in advance of the gathering, he was impressed by its theoretical reasoning, but he questioned the Bolshevik leader's "ignorance of the relation of social forces in the colonial countries." In private conversations, Roy pressed Lenin to see that national liberation movements in

FIGURE 17. M. N. Roy (center on steps), V. I. Lenin (front left), and other delegates at the Second Congress of the Third International, 1920. Courtesy of Wikimedia Commons.

the colonies might not lead necessarily to "bourgeois democratic revolution" but toward "ideologically reactionary" ends. Lenin, in turn, invited Roy to articulate and circulate his ideas. In his "supplementary theses," Roy observed pointedly that "modern capitalism" rested on the "super-profits gained in the colonies." The Comintern, therefore, ought to "establish relations with those revolutionary forces that are working for the overthrow of imperialism in the politically and economically subjugated countries." The congress adopted both sets of theses.[33]

The Third International's "Theses on the National and Colonial Question" positioned Washington, DC, and Moscow on opposing trajectories in global politics. The document rejected the League of Nations and the entire notion of "national equality," calling instead for the recognition of "the oppressed, dependent nations, unequal in rights" apart from "the oppressing, exploiting nations with full rights," to expose "the bourgeois-democratic lies which conceal the colonial and financial enslavement of the vast majority of the world's population by a small minority of the wealthiest and most advanced capitalist countries that is characteristic of the epoch of finance-capital and imperialism." In attempting to bridge and distinguish between "revolutionary liberation movements" and the "proletarian movement," communist parties had no choice but to "give direct support to the revolutionary movements among the dependent nations and those without equal rights (e.g., in Ireland and among the American Negroes), and in the colonies." "We knew very well that the imperialists of America, Japan, and Britain would under no circumstances be so generous as to give up the advantages that the colonies accord them," a Korean delegate stated in support of the theses. With the Comintern's lead, he argued, communists around the world recognized that "the day of the social revolution" would arrive "only when all these colonial peoples rise up in revolt, when the western European proletariat deals the deathblow to its bourgeoisie, when the colonial peoples strike the western bourgeoisie in the heart."[34] The United States stood for empire and capitalism; Soviet Russia represented anticolonialism and revolution.

Disaggregating nations ("oppressor" and "oppressed"), nationalisms ("petty-bourgeois" and "revolutionary"), and internationalisms ("international capitalism" and "proletarian internationalism") placed racialized subjects of empire potentially at the forefront of a worldwide communist movement, but the Comintern's framing relegated race to false consciousness, an obstacle to ultimate revolution and liberation. Race was, on one level, an expression of "petty-bourgeois national prejudices"—examples included "race hatred, stirring up national antagonisms, anti-semitism"—that could be overcome by transforming "the dictatorship of the proletariat from a national dictatorship (i.e., a dictatorship existing in one country alone, and incapable of conducting an independent world policy) into an international dictatorship (i.e., a dictatorship of the proletariat in at least a few advanced countries, which is capable of exercising decisive influence in the political affairs of the entire world)." A worldwide overthrow of capitalism would be a long historical process, in which "the class-conscious communist proletariat of all countries" would have to acknowledge and accommodate "national feelings, in themselves out of date, in countries and peoples that have been long enslaved . . . to remove this distrust and prejudice the more quickly." Race was, on another level, a means to rally oppressed peoples to spurious global movements. "It is necessary to struggle against the pan-Islamic and pan-Asiatic movements and similar tendencies," the Comintern warned, "which are trying to combine the liberation struggle against European and American imperialism with the strengthening of the power of Turkish and Japanese imperialism and of the nobility, the large landlords, the priests, etc."[35]

John Reed, who had published *Ten Days That Shook the World* on the Bolshevik Revolution the previous year, attempted to elucidate the incompatibility of race and revolution by assessing the plight of "ten million Negroes in America." Immediately following Roy's introduction of his supplementary theses, the American journalist stood before the congress to recount the brutality of segregation and lynching. "This is mob murder, which commonly takes the form of drenching the Negro with oil, hanging him from a telegraph pole, and setting him on fire," he explained. But until the Spanish-American War, when Black soldiers "fought with extreme bravery," he said, African Americans "showed no aggressive consciousness of race." World War I accelerated Black mobilization, Reed argued, with returning soldiers and industrialized workers leading Black communities—"armed, well organized, and absolutely unafraid of the whites"—against white mobs "for the first time in history." "But while Communists should energetically support the Negro defense movement," he cautioned, "they should discourage all ideas of a separate, armed insurrection by Negroes." Dismissing "Back to Africa" movements of the past, Reed insisted that Black people "consider themselves first of all Americans at home in the United States." That made things "very much simpler for Communists." "For American Communists the only correct policy toward the Negroes should be to see them primarily as workers," Reed concluded. Forming interracial labor unions, he insisted, would be "the best and fastest way to break down race prejudice and foster class solidarity."[36]

Despite such contradictory efforts to consign colonialism and racism within the fold of nationalism, the Comintern's reckoning with the contradictions of empire and race ignited hope among anticolonial revolutionaries around the world. In Paris, Nguyen Ai Quoc (later Ho Chi Minh), whose petition for Vietnamese independence went nowhere at the Paris Peace Conference in 1919, had a visceral response to Lenin's straightforward language. "What emotion, enthusiasm, clear-sightedness, and confidence it instilled into me!" he exclaimed. "I was overjoyed to tears." Raised in a household grappling with the expansion of French colonial rule—his father worked as a civil servant in the colonial administration while expressing bitter opposition to the French—Nguyen and his compatriots looked abroad for inspiration and organization. For years, Japan had provided a base for Vietnamese mobilization, but Nguyen headed west in 1911, first to Europe and then to Africa and the Americas, including the United States, before longer stays in England and France. After reading the Comintern's "Theses" in 1920, Nguyen helped to found the French Communist Party and later the Intercolonial Union, an anticolonial organization that brought

FIGURE 18. Nguyen Ai Quoc (later Ho Chi Minh). Photograph by Agence de Presse Meurisse. Courtesy of the Department of Image and Digital Services, Bibliothèque Nationale de France.

together French colonial subjects from Indochina, Madagascar, Martinique, and Guadeloupe. In June 1923, he escaped the surveillance of the French police to make his way to Moscow, where he challenged the communist movement to tackle colonialism head-on. "You all know that today the poison and the life energy of the capitalist snake is concentrated more in the colonies than in the mother countries," he said before a Comintern meeting.[37]

Many African Americans traveled on the same circuits of empire and revolution, recognizing that racism, like colonialism, could not be theorized into historical oblivion. Born in South Omaha, Nebraska, in 1898,

Harry Haywood and his family were driven out of town in 1913 by a gang of white vigilantes. As he recalled, "Our whole world had collapsed. . . . Now we were just homeless 'niggers' on the run." After working a series of jobs that young Black men could secure—bellhop, porter, busboy, and waiter, the same jobs that Nguyen worked in his travels—Haywood enlisted in the US Army in 1917, joining a Black regiment known for its "racial solidarity." Unable to escape racial segregation and racial violence in the US Army, Haywood was grateful that his unit was incorporated into the French military. "The French treated Blacks well—that is, as human beings," he noted. At the end of World War I, a group of Black soldiers gathered to share news from home. Jim Crow segregation and lynching, they related, were "rampant, worse than before." "Now, they want us to go to war with Japan," one of them said. "Well, they won't get me to fight their yellow peril," another quipped. "If it comes to that, I'll join the Japs. They are colored." Everyone in the group felt the same way. Back in Chicago in 1919, Haywood and fellow Black veterans prepared for war, not against Japan but against white gangs invading Black communities during that city's bloody race riot.[38]

By the following year, when the Comintern issued its "Theses on the National and Colonial Question," Haywood set out to find answers to comprehend what he was experiencing and confronting. "I renewed my search for a way to go," he vowed, "pressed by a driving need for a world view which would provide a rational explanation of society and a clue to securing Black freedom and dignity." Haywood did not find his answers in Garveyism, but he was intrigued by its mass appeal. In particular, he was struck by "a grass-roots nationalism of the masses, the uprooted, dispossessed soil-tillers of the South; their poverty-ridden counterparts in the slum ghettoes of the cities." "These masses saw in the Black nationalist state fulfillment of their age-old yearnings for land, equality and freedom through power in their own hands to guarantee and protect these freedoms," Haywood observed. It was a political lesson that he carried with him, first to the ABB and the Young Workers (Communist) League and eventually to the Workers (Communist) Party and Moscow. Garveyism, he realized, was "the US counterpart of the vast upsurge of national and colonial liberation struggles which swept the world during the war and post-war period." Haywood began to see the Bolshevik Revolution and the Third International as "the focus of the colonial revolution." In 1926, a year after formally joining the Workers Party, he traveled to Moscow to enroll in the Communist University of Toilers of the East (KUTV).[39]

Established in 1921, the KUTV reaffirmed the Comintern's commit-ment to anticolonial struggles around the world. When Haywood arrived in Moscow, he marveled at the sheer variety of humanity at the univer-sity, a "national and ethnic diversity . . . hard to imagine." Designed to foster cadre leadership across the colonized "East," students represented the outer reaches of the Soviet Union—the former "colonial dependen-cies" of the Russian empire stretching from the Caucasus region to Mongolia—and parts of Asia, Africa, and the Americas. Joining the Eng-lish-speaking group that included African Americans, South Asians, Koreans, Japanese, and Indonesians, Haywood became close friends with Asian anticolonial revolutionaries, many of whom hailed from the United States. Among the "most interesting and brilliant" students he met was Dada Amir Haider Khan, known as "Sakorov" to Haywood and others at the university. Khan's familiarity with white supremacy and Black struggles in the United States led to an instant friendship. He looked and talked liked someone from back home. "He knew first hand the plight of Blacks in the United States," Haywood remembered, "and as a dark skinned Indian, he had experienced much of the same type of racial abuse while there." Although utopian dreams often collided with the daily regimen of Marxist-Leninist orthodoxy and Soviet ethnogra-phy, on top of harsh and unfamiliar living conditions, attending the KUTV exposed aspiring anticolonial revolutionaries to new worlds of radical knowledge and worldly networks of camaraderie.[40]

Haywood was following the lead of other Black radicals, who pressed the Comintern to tackle racism more forcefully. In 1922, Otto Huis-woud, the national organizer for the ABB, and Claude McKay, the famed poet, had attended the Third International's Fourth Congress and worked with Katayama, in charge of the Comintern's Eastern Commis-sion which housed the Negro Department, to explore the "Negro ques-tion." In his address, McKay called out the US delegates for dismissing race and practicing white supremacy, arguing that "they first have got to emancipate themselves from the ideas they entertain towards the Negroes before they can . . . reach the negroes with any kind of radical propaganda." The resulting "Theses on the Negro Question" placed African Americans at the forefront of "the liberation struggle of the entire African race." Enslaved for centuries "under the lash of American overseers" and facing "racial persecution, lynching, murder, deprivation of franchise," Black people in the United States engaged in "revolts, disturbances, and subterranean methods of gaining freedom," only to be "savagely suppressed" at every turn. "The Communist International

AN INTERNATIONAL GROUP INCLUDING A CHINESE, RUSSIAN JEW, NEGRO, RUSSIAN
GENTILE, BULGARIAN, HINDU, AMERICAN MULATTO, AlGERIAN, JAPANESE, ARMENIAN,
KOREAN, AND WHITE AMERICAN

FIGURE 19. The promise of interracial communist internationalism. Photograph from Claude McKay, "Soviet Russia and the Negro," *The Crisis* 27, no. 2 (December 1923): 62.

notes with satisfaction the resistance of the exploited Negro to the exploiters' attack," the resolution read, "for the enemy of his race and the enemy of the white workers are one and the same—capitalism and imperialism." Highlighting Black struggles in the United States and linking them to movements in Africa and across the Americas, the Comintern pledged "to support and promote the international organization of Negroes in their struggle against the common enemy."[41]

Two years after John Reed's screed on treating African Americans simply as "Americans" and "workers," the Fourth Congress reflected the Comintern's renewed determination to address race more critically and globally. Even as the "Theses on the Negro Question" concentrated on the United States—America was deemed "the centre of Negro culture around which the Negro protest crystallizes"—the Comintern likened Black struggles to those waged by "workers and peasants of Europe, Asia, and America" and implored "communists to apply the *Theses on the colonial question* to the Negro problem also." Calls for the solidarity and equality between Black and white workers, presumably within the bounds of the United States, were juxtaposed against references to "the oppressed coloured workers" of India, China, Persia, Turkey, Egypt, and Morocco "fighting for the same objects as the Negroes—political, economic, and social emancipation and equality." Underscoring the limits of formal political rights in US history—African Americans "had to kill and be killed for 'democracy'"—the Comintern nonetheless vowed to "fight for the equality of the white and black races, for equal wages and equal political and social rights." But Black struggles had to exceed the US nation-state, including "a world Negro congress or conference" to be sponsored by the Comintern. The ultimate objective was not national rights but "the proletarian revolution and the destruction of capitalist power," struggles toward which "the Asiatic coloured peoples in the semi-colonial countries" and "oppressed black fellow beings" would play "absolutely essential" roles.[42]

In the "Theses on the Eastern Question," also adopted by the Fourth Congress in 1922, the Comintern elaborated on the dynamics of race, nation, and revolution across the Pacific. While "the proletarian united front" defined struggles in the capitalist West, the resolution proclaimed, the "slogan" to mobilize "all revolutionary elements" in the "colonial East" was "the anti-imperialist united front." As a matter of expediency and strategy, communist parties of "colonial and semi-colonial countries" had to exploit "all the contradictions in the nationalist bourgeois-democratic camp" for national independence, all the while realizing the need for a worldwide revolution. The Comintern paid special attention to the "imperialist rivalry" emerging across the Pacific that threatened to erupt in "a new world war" involving Japan, the United States, Britain, and other capitalist states. To thwart such a calamity through an "international revolution," workers had to combat "antagonisms between nations and races" that capitalists took advantage of, in particular over "the immigration question and the question of cheap coloured labour power." White workers ought not demand the national exclusion of "coloured workers"—motivated, for example, by the recruitment of "indentured labour" from India and China to work "the sugar plantations of the south Pacific area"—but include them in "the existing trade unions of white workers."[43] Beyond the dim prospect of interracial solidarity in and through the AFL, the Comintern neglected to address perhaps the most visible targets of white exclusionists and the US security state in the 1920s: Japanese workers in Hawai'i and North America.

If Japan as a "colored" imperial power posed a global anomaly, the two theses from the Fourth Congress laid the foundation for a more vigorous application of the "colonial question" to the "Negro problem."

By 1927, Haywood had graduated to the Lenin School, which offered a more advanced course of study and introduced him to intense debates over race and revolution. At KUTV, he had learned from Katayama that Lenin viewed African Americans as an "oppressed nation," but Haywood steadfastly viewed Black people in the United States like Jews of the Soviet Union—"a national minority" and "an oppressed race." In preparing for the Sixth Congress of the Third International in 1928, with economic crises and anticolonial uprisings in the news, Haywood joined a subcommittee on the "Negro question" to review the Comintern's stance on race, nation, and empire, particularly concerning the status of African Americans. In the subcommittee's deliberations, he interrogated his own assumptions, expressing his qualms about the prevailing categorization of Black nationalism as inherently "reactionary." Rejecting Black nationalism wholesale because of Garveyism was like "throwing out the baby with the bathwater." "Afro-Americans are not only 'a nation within a nation,'" Haywood reasoned, "but a captive nation, suffering a colonial-type oppression while trapped within the geographic bound of one of the world's most powerful imperialist countries." Tapping into those Black nationalist impulses, he argued, had the revolutionary potential to strike at the heart of the "common enemy" of revolutionary struggles: US imperialism and capitalism.[44]

Overcoming various factional disputes, including his older brother raising the loudest objections to his proposal, Haywood and his allies convinced the Comintern to adopt the "Black Belt" thesis in 1928. "The Negro working class has reached a stage of development which enables it, if properly organized and well led," the resolution began, "to fulfill successfully its double historical mission: (a) to play a considerable role in the class struggle against American imperialism as an important part of the American working class; and (b) to lead the movement of the oppressed masses of the Negro population." Concentrated in the "Black Belt" of the US South, it continued, the "great mass of the Negro population are subject to the most ruthless exploitation and persecution of a semi-slave character." That concentration and oppression ("slave remnants"), the Comintern argued, provided "the necessary conditions for a national revolutionary movement among the Negroes." In addition to struggling "under the slogan of full social and political equality for the Negroes," the Communist Party had to "come out openly and unreservedly for the right of Negroes to national self-determination in the southern states, where the Negroes form a majority of the population." Placing the United States in the wider world, the Comintern hoped that a "strong Negro revolutionary movement in the USA" would "influence and direct the revolutionary movement in all those parts of the world where the Negroes are oppressed by imperialism." Racial oppression, the Comintern determined, could motivate a revolutionary nationalism against the US empire.[45]

Pronouncements from Moscow did not produce local struggles against white supremacy and colonialism, but they spurred new imaginaries and mobilized revolutionaries around the world. Upon learning of Lenin's death in January 1924, Nguyen Ai Quoc reflected on the Bolshevik leader's significance to colonized subjects. "It is true that the black or yellow people do not yet know clearly who Lenin is or where Russia is," he wrote. "But all of them, from the Vietnamese peasants to the hunters in the Dahomey forests, have secretly learned that in a faraway corner of the earth there is a nation that has succeeded in overthrowing its exploiters and is managing its own country with no need for masters and Governors General." They also heard that Lenin "called upon the white peoples to help the yellow and black peoples to free themselves from the foreign aggressors' yoke." In the ensuing months, Nguyen published articles on the brutality of lynching and the Ku Klux Klan in the United States and state violence in the Pacific, where, he argued, Japan, the United States, Britain, and France were waging imperial conflicts likely to lead to "a new world conflagration." Those global contexts framed Nguyen's revolutionary dreams for a free Vietnam, dreams that dared to theorize and confront the contradictions of race, empire, and capitalism.[46] As Nguyen led Vietnamese struggles against the French, Japanese, and US empires over the next half century, the US security state assumed and projected that yellow, brown, and black were dangerous and seditious variants of red.

FIGHTING SEDITION AND REVOLUTION

On the eve of US entry into World War I, an armed revolution against white supremacy and empire materialized along the US-Mexico border. Inspired by the anarchist publications of Ricardo and Enrique Flores Magón, Mexican brothers in exile in the United States, and mobilizing around the Plan de San Diego of south Texas, Mexican *sediciosos* (seditionists), as they came to be known, declared in January 1915 "the independence and segregation of . . . Texas, New Mexico, Arizona, Colorado, and California, of which states the Republic of Mexico was robbed in a most perfidious manner by North American Imperialism." Prefiguring the "Black Belt" thesis, they invited African Americans to join the armed uprising and promised to extend the campaign to win the independence of an additional "six states of the American Union" for Black people. While targeting Anglo residents, the Plan de San Diego formed the "Liberating Army for Races and Peoples" and welcomed explicitly those belonging to "the Latin, the Negro, or the Japanese race." A revised plan a month later, titled "Manifesto to the Oppressed Peoples of America," denounced lynching and the segregation of "the Mexican, black and yellow" from "the savage 'white skins'" and called openly for a "social revolution" and the redistribution of land to "proletarians." The revolutionary struggle, the new Plan de San Diego stated, would encompass Nevada and Utah and aspire to attract "all oppressed people of all despised races" to the ultimate objective of "universal fraternity."[47]

For a year beginning in the summer of 1915, armed bands of *sedicio-sos* orchestrated raids on ranch estates, railroad tracks, and other targets that turned the Rio Grande Valley into a war zone over race, nation, and empire. Whether or not beholden to the Plan de San Diego, *sedicio-sos* continued to highlight their determination to confront the US empire. "The moment has come to shake off the iron yoke," a handbill stated. "Let us destroy but at the same time build . . . War to Capital, War to the Clergy, War to the State, [to] everything that smells of oppression, War . . . to the *gringos. ¡Basta Ya!*" Though not always in complete alignment, the counterrevolutionary forces defending US claims over Texas—white vigilantes, Texas Rangers, and US federal troops—showed little restraint, making all Mexicans vulnerable to state violence and mob violence, including mass lynchings. On the other side of the border, President Carranza of Mexico collaborated with the US government to suppress the uprising and to convict the Flores Magón brothers, all in his drive to win recognition from the Wilson Administration and to solidify his own government against insurgencies led by Pancho Villa and Emiliano Zapata. Tension along the border intensified. When Villa launched a raid on Columbus, New Mexico, in March 1916, a raid unrelated to the Plan de San Diego, Wilson dispatched General John Pershing on a "punitive expedition" into Mexico. Carranza, no friend of Villa, objected to the US state's flagrant breach of Mexico's claims to national sovereignty.[48]

Although the Plan de San Diego emerged first and foremost out of local traditions of colonial violence and anticolonial resistance, US officials found its interracial overtures and international connections particularly worrisome. Not only did the discovery of individual African American and Japanese participants in the uprising spawn rumors of wider conspiracies involving Germany and Japan, fears of a potential alliance between Mexico, Germany, and Japan spurred the United States to war in Europe. In February 1917, when Wilson withdrew US troops from Mexico, his administration learned from British authorities that Germany had invited Mexico to forge an alliance against the United States. In that infamous telegram, Arthur Zimmermann, Germany's foreign secretary, promised Carranza financial support and "an agreement on our part for Mexico to reconquer its former territories in Texas, New Mexico, and Arizona." Zimmermann also asked Mexico to contact Japan to join the pact. That tripartite alliance did not come to pass, but its latent possibility seemingly demanded greater scrutiny after the United States declared war against Germany in April 1917. The BI Special Agent in Charge in San Antonio, Texas, instructed fellow agents "to be on the lookout for any *Japanese* who may have entered recently the *United States*, presumably from Mexico." Following those instructions, a BI agent trailed and searched a Japanese merchant in Port Arthur, Texas, in October 1917, only to learn that he was "a harmless Jap." The merchant reportedly took the incident "good naturedly," given "the abnormal conditions prevailing at this time."[49]

Those "abnormal conditions" justifying racial surveillance became normalized during World War I. Rumors of Germany, Mexico, or another "foreign intrigue" inciting the Black masses against the United States, for example, generated and rationalized more and more investigative reports on African Americans, whose protests against white supremacy came to be categorized as "Negro Subversion." After the bloody race riot in East St. Louis in July 1917, BI agents focused not on identifying white mobs responsible for attacking and killing African Americans but on tracking down the author of a leaflet that condemned the racial roots of empire, which "gobbled up practically the entire earth's surface, exterminated or subjugated the natives, seized, exploited their land and resources, and denied all colored races rights and citizenship; ALL in the name of Christianity, Civilization and Religion." On behalf of "Japs, Chinese, Hindus an' 'Niggers,'" the leaflet stated that "dark-skinned people the world over" now demanded "a re-apportionment—a redistribution of the earth's surface." The author, a Black physician from Springfield, Illinois, was arrested and charged with violating the Espionage Act (1917), supposedly by fomenting racial violence and interfering with the military draft. A. Philip Randolph and Chandler Owen of the *Messenger* faced the same charge in August 1918 for publishing "Pro-Germanism among the Negroes," an article that pointed to American hypocrisy, not

German propaganda, to explain Black discontent. To add irony upon irony, a US commissioner refused to believe that two Black men could write such an intellectual analysis and ascribed its authorship to white socialists.[50]

The US state's evocation of nefarious German designs to suppress Black radicalism during World War I paralleled its prosecution of Ghadar Party members. Between November 1917 and April 1918, South Asian revolutionaries and German consular agents stood trial in San Francisco for conspiring to violate US neutrality laws, in a courtroom drama that pitted the US and British governments against their common enemy in the battlefields of Europe—Germany. But the real target was the Ghadar movement. As the conviction of Ghadar activists in Lahore, Punjab, had demonstrated over the previous several years, war proved to be a convenient context to criminalize anticolonial politics under the pretext of "sedition" and "conspiracy." "It will be a highly interesting trial," US Attorney John W. Preston wrote days before it was to commence. "The evidence is in very good shape. The British Agents have worked very hard in putting the evidence in accessible form, and I have every reason . . . to believe that the case will result favorably as to all important defendants." Relying heavily on information gathered by British agents, he described a transpacific web of South Asian revolutionaries and German consuls—stretching from California and Hawai'i to the Philippines, China, and Japan—determined to organize an armed overthrow of British rule in India. Beyond specific plots to ship arms, Preston attacked the Ghadar Party's revolutionary message, delivered through *Ghadar* and "inflammatory speeches," beginning with Har Dayal, a "rank, out-and-out Anarchist" who believed in "revolution everywhere."[51]

Perhaps more than the tactical partnership between South Asian revolutionaries and German authorities, US officials saw in the "Hindu Conspiracy" disquieting traces of racial and radical alliances against the US empire. In the summer of 1917, with Roy in Mexico and with British reports of Ram Chandra, the indicted leader of the Ghadar Party, en route there, BI agents sought to disallow South Asians from finding refuge south of the border. They requested that US immigration authorities detain "all Hindus attempting [to] cross into Mexico." During the trial, a witness testified that Hari Singh, a defendant, had said that he was "praying every day that Mexico and the United States would get into open war" and "studying Spanish to start a revolution against the United States" to prevent US arms shipments to Europe. And, as if to substantiate the Zimmermann telegram, the US State Department requested from

Preston all evidence tending "to show the Japanese connection with the Hindu plotters in this Country." In particular, US officials grew alarmed by references to Hideo Nakao, who, according to another "most secret" telegram from Zimmermann, was sent to the United States with "important instructions" from Berlin. He was to receive $50,000 to execute "his plans in America and Eastern Asia" and to dispatch reports via German diplomats in China. Nakao's movements drew more suspicion. When he landed in New York in April 1917, he listed Russia as his last permanent residence and the "General Consul of Japan" as his destination. In May, he boarded a ship bound for Veracruz, Mexico.[52]

As the US state interpreted the Ghadar Party's links to Germany, Mexico, Japan, and Russia as evidence of sedition against the United States, South Asian defendants attempted to put the British empire on trial. Through Har Dayal's letter to Alexander Berkman and Taraknath Das's to Trotsky, Preston insinuated a "Hindu-Bolshevik" plot brewing in the United States. It was a pivotal moment in US and world history, he argued, when "we must stamp out anarchists and revolutionary sects that are fanning themselves into flames of hate and disregard for our laws, or the day will come when we will have no country to defend." To counter such charges, George McGowan, the lawyer defending Ram Chandra and others, argued that "a revolution or rebellion against the established rule in India" predated "the present war in Europe." It was a just revolution, he argued in his opening statement. "We shall show you that that is manifested by numerous acts of the British Government in India in suppressing newspapers, in imprisoning editors, in banishing people from the country for acting in the line of obtaining for the people of India some voice in the representation of the government of that country." Recalling the violent rejection of South Asian migrants in South Africa, Canada, and across the British empire, McGowan did not deny that some individuals voluntarily returned to India to fight the "tyrannical abuse on the part of the British crown." But those were "unorganized" acts, he contended, not an organized "military enterprise."[53]

The defense team strove to depict South Asian revolutionaries as rightful heirs to the American Revolution. "Well, thankfully in this country, we have liberty of the press, we have liberty of speech," McGowan stated. In the pages of *Ghadar*, he continued, were portraits of George Washington, Abraham Lincoln, Woodrow Wilson, and Patrick Henry and accounts of why America's founders rose up against the British empire. "That may be seditious to the British crown," he said, "but it is not seditious to publish that paper in this country, and it is not seditious against the laws of the United States to send that paper, a paper of general circulation, all over the world, through the mails of the United States." Chandra, as editor, never hid his activities to publicize "just exactly what the truth is within the British Empire," McGowan explained, even as "almost from the very day that he entered the United States [he] has been hounded by these minions of the British government." That was an extension of "British justice in India." "They may not blow them to pieces from the mouths of cannon today, gentlemen of the jury, but they did before," he declared. "They have their firing squads, they have their hangman's noose, they imprison people for life. They do all those things today." McGowan pleaded with the "American jury" of "American citizens" to stand with "the three presidents of the United States, and justify these people in the court of public opinion of the world, as they should be justified."[54]

Hopes for an "American" judgment against the British could not surmount white supremacy and empire at the heart of the Anglo-American alliance. Years of persecution by British, Canadian, and US authorities and five months of prosecution by Preston and the US Department of Justice took their toll on the defendants. The pressure reached a boiling point on April 23, 1918, the trial's last day. Ram Singh, who had traveled earlier to China, Japan, and the Philippines on behalf of the Ghadar Party, became convinced that Chandra was profiting personally from funds donated to the party. He shot Chandra dead in the courtroom, before being shot fatally by a US marshal. The day concluded with the jury finding all but one of the surviving twenty-nine defendants guilty of conspiring to violate US neutrality laws. Basking in his victory, Preston used the occasion to reflect on South Asians generally. "The Hindus are a very crafty and cunning people, but so far they have not become embittered against the United States," he wrote after the trial. "All they have done to us is to recklessly disregard our law, but they have not become . . . in such a state that they are willing to commit murder of American officials, although murdering English officials seems to be an easy thing for them to do." To a friend who sent him a congratulatory note, Preston related that he thought the verdict would have "a good moral effect on the community" and that he appreciated the note, which had "American patriotism oozing from every pore."[55]

Preston's vindictive measures after the trial deepened the Anglo-American alliance and sowed South Asian bitterness against the United States. The "German-Hindu cases," Preston noted to the US Attorney General, were "important to this country and more important to the

British Government." British agents, he related, "stood at my elbow during the entire trial, and whenever any point of information was desired, it was forth-coming immediately." Preston by no means considered his work finished with the convictions, particularly concerning Taraknath Das, Bhagwan Singh, and the twelve other South Asians fined and imprisoned for their roles in the conspiracy. Less than a month after the verdict, Preston heard from a US Army intelligence officer that the Ghadar Party planned to resume publishing political material. "I would ask you to use your influence to dissuade these people from carrying out any further propaganda work," he wrote immediately to McGowan, "as otherwise I shall be compelled to take severe action against them." When a South Asian compatriot in Portland, Oregon, broached the idea of parole for Das and Singh—sentenced to twenty-two months and eighteen months, two of the longest prison terms—Preston grew irate. "I would as soon advocate the release of a tiger on a band of defens[e]less children as to recommend parole for either of them," he replied. Having expended nearly $3 million on the "Hindu Conspiracy" trial—$450,000 by the US government and $2.5 million by the British government—the Anglo-American alliance stood together not only against Germany but against sedition and revolution.[56]

Preston's colleagues, also in the pursuit of defending US national security, likewise sought to silence and punish South Asian revolutionaries. After four of those convicted, including Das and Singh, were shipped to the federal penitentiary on McNeil Island, Washington, the immigration commissioner in Seattle contacted Preston right away. "These cases will be investigated with the view of deporting the aliens, when they have served their sentences," he proposed. The commissioner requested more information on the South Asian prisoners, particularly "whether they were found to be advocating or teaching the unlawful destruction of property, or advocating or teaching anarchy, or the overthrow by force of violence of the Government of the United States, or of all forms of law, or the assassination of public officials." Though not convicted as such, sedition implicated anarchism and deportation, a logic inscribed firmly in US immigration law. The defense attorneys, in response, objected vehemently to the prospect of their clients' deportation to India, where British authorities could apply their draconian methods. In the least, they asked that their clients be deported to Japan, to their last port of embarkation before entering the United States. Preston was not moved. Categorizing some of the South Asian convicts as "anarchists of a dangerous variety," he pressed for deportation to India.

The US State Department agreed. The "Indians convicted in this case may well be considered undesirable aliens and . . . should be deported to India, not Japan," Secretary of State Robert Lansing concluded.[57]

IMPERIAL JAPAN, SOVIET RUSSIA, AND THE US EMPIRE

Those passing references to Japan in the trial's aftermath underscored the ambiguous contradictions that Japan embodied. Like its wartime allies, the United States and Britain, Japan was an empire driven to suppress anticolonial movements. When Preston was attempting to locate defendants living in Japan before the trial, the Japanese government proved to be a reliable ally. Japanese officials had already ordered the deportation of South Asian revolutionaries out of Japan and then pressured Das to return to the United States. During the trial, Preston shared with the Japanese consul in San Francisco reports on Das and Hideo Nakao, an act of interimperial solidarity that the consul appreciated. That common mission to suppress anticolonial radicalism guided the US Department of Labor, in charge of immigration matters, to favor postprison deportations to India over Japan since "it is not at all likely that the Japanese Government would allow them to land at those ports or to remain in Japan after they had been convicted in this country and following conviction deported." Japan, however, also symbolized a threat to the US empire. In justifying plans to revoke Das's naturalized US citizenship and to deport him, the Justice Department stressed that he was "an out and out revolutionary and very active." Das was deemed a revolutionary, in part, because he had possessed "a large numbers of copies of a Russian Bomb Manual of the most dangerous description" and publicized that "Germany, Japan and Mexico should unite against the United States and Great Britain."[58]

South Asian revolutionaries' links to Russia and Japan seemingly magnified the prospect of sedition and revolution against the United States. In May 1918, Ralph H. Van Deman, the head of military intelligence who long feared Japan's malevolent influence in the Philippines, forwarded to the Labor Department a comprehensive report on "Hindu-German activities and suspects," warning that "the Hindus are preparing to take an active part in strikes and other anti-war demonstrations fomented by the IWW, Bolsheviki . . . in this country, about May first." In identifying "Hindu suspects" involved in "creating a revolution among the East Indians with the ultimate intention of throwing off British rule"—the list included individuals based in the United States, Mexico, Germany, Panama, Trinidad, and elsewhere—the report recommended that "all Hindus coming to this country from any foreign port" be interrogated closely. *Ghadar*, the newspaper, supposedly had no qualms about advocating "murder, arson, rape, sedition, seduction and other atrocities, to be visited upon the British in India that can possibly be thought of." In addition to plots with Germany and correspondence with Soviet Russia, the Ghadar Party's global reach, especially across the Pacific, unnerved US authorities. It had "representatives in Japan and China, and in fact, most of the foreign countries," where they incited "the discontented natives . . . to revolt against the constituted authority of their respective countries." The report suggested that generating "great publicity" on the leaders' personal faults, particularly financial and sexual in nature, "would have a bad effect on their propaganda."[59]

The Anglo-American alliance, in the meantime, grew stronger during and through the legal and extralegal war against sedition and revolution. US military and civilian personnel continued to cooperate with British officials to contain anticolonial struggles. In August 1918, US Army and British intelligence officers were dispatched to the San Francisco waterfront, where they examined fifteen South Asian passengers seeking to return to India. Eleven of them, including two women, were allowed to sail to Hong Kong, but the four Sikhs on the docks were ordered to the immigration station on Angel Island until a boat sailing directly to India arrived. "The British agents feel certain that these four men realizing that they would be arrested immediately upon there [*sic*] arrival in India intend to leave the boat at some port in Japan," a US Army intelligence officer reported. By February 1919, when Gopal Singh, the first of the prisoners on McNeil Island was scheduled to be released and then deported, the Ghadar Party issued a public letter to stop America from "deporting him to Death." Listing the many individuals executed or sentenced to life imprisonment upon their return to British India, the letter appealed to Wilson's wartime call for democracy. "We, on behalf of our countrymen in the United States, appeal to your sentiment and sense of plain justice," the Ghadar Party wrote. "We know Americans love fair play when their heart can be reached."[60]

Those ironic petitions to American ideals notwithstanding, the US government's prosecution of anticolonial revolutionaries in San Francisco and then its rejection of anticolonial appeals in Paris devastated and fueled the Ghadar Party. Reeling from the mass conviction of its leaders, the party had gone underground during the war. "The Ghadr

Party is still working quietly," the party headquarters informed a sup-
porter in Chile. "All the brethren living in the different localities are still
helping the cause." In September 1920, the party emerged from the
shadows of war by publishing the *Independent Hindustan*, a "Monthly
Review of Political, Economic, Social and Intellectual Independence of
India." "Breathes there a man or a woman with heart so dried and intel-
lect so cracked who never rejoices over the prospect of a glorious day
when the Banner of Freedom will be unfurled over Ireland, India, Persia, Egypt, China, Russia—over the suppressed and oppressed world?"
the opening editorial asked. In the same issue, Taraknath Das continued
to make the case for pan-Asian solidarity against the British empire,
calling on Japan to renounce its postwar claims in Shandong. "Anything that weakens any of the Asian powers weakens the cause of Asian
independence," he argued. Several issues later, Das challenged the
United States to reject the British empire, lest it be "classed with Britain
in the minds of the oppressed of the earth, and the subject peoples will
know that they must fight both Great Britain and the United States."[61]

Bearing the brunt of the Anglo-American alliance, members of the
Ghadar Party gravitated to communist internationalism to advance
their anticolonial movement. In 1919, Muhammed Barakatullah, a veteran Ghadar leader who had worked in Japan, the United States, and
Afghanistan, met with Lenin in Moscow. "I am an irreconcilable enemy
of European capital in Asia whose main representative is the English,"
Barakatullah stated afterward. "In this I concur with the communists
and in this respect we are genuine allies." Das agreed. Soviet Russia, he
argued, was "avowedly an enemy of imperialism in any form" that
would "inspire and unite with the Indian people to destroy the British
Empire." For many in the Ghadar Party, the coincidence of the Bolshevik Revolution and the conspiracy trial drove them to look to Russia for
political lessons. Santokh Singh, one of those convicted, studied Marxism while in prison and then helped to reorganize the Ghadar Party
after his release. He reached out to the Third International, which
invited him to attend the Fourth Congress in 1922. Many Ghadarites
from the United States and around the world followed Singh's footsteps
to Moscow, most of them as students enrolled at KUTV. The "Sikh
intrigues with the Comintern," head of the Intelligence Bureau in British India believed, revived a "practically moribund" party. "Early in
1926 it was observed that the shutters had again been taken down,
money was plentiful, enthusiasm was unbounded, fresh members were
joining up," he reported, "and activity was everywhere discernible."[62]

With headquarters still in San Francisco, the Ghadar Party attempted to resolve and exploit America's nationalist conceits and Soviet Russia's anticolonial bravado. In July 1923, the party rechristened the *Independent Hindustan* as the *United States of India*, albeit with the same subtitle. Praising the work of Mahatma Gandhi and the Indian National Congress, the new monthly appeared to shun anticolonial radicalism and to endorse US republicanism. "Our aim has been, and now is, the attainment for India of a form of Government such as America has, with some modifications befitting India," the inaugural issue proclaimed. "We want to have the UNITED STATES OF INDIA." But the emergent United States of India, unlike the United States of America, despised Britain and allied with Soviet Russia. After quoting a Soviet government note calling on the British to deal with "other states on equal ground," the journal gleefully translated it into Marxist vernacular: "Flourish your whip over the capitalist countries which you conquered, whose bourgeoisies cower before you. But we, the first proletarian state, we do not cower before your whip, however much we may desire peace. We are anxious for peace, and therefore we make concession, and do not rattle our sabres, but if you, lords of the world's capital, imagine that you can fasten your yoke upon our shoulders, then just come and try it!" There was no doubt that the journal sided with "a proletariat which has emancipated itself from its own oppressors" against "the victorious aggressors of the world."[63]

Those working to stop the US government's deportation of convicted South Asian revolutionaries likewise straddled between appealing to US nationalism and anticolonial internationalism. In March 1919, Agnes Smedley—who had earlier met Ghadar Party members in California and, beginning in 1917, immersed herself in the cause of Indian independence with Lajpat Rai, M.N. Roy, Evelyn Trent, Sailendranath Ghose, and, eventually, Das in New York City—helped to launch the Friends of Freedom for India (FFI) to organize a nationwide campaign against the deportations. With the first cases pending before the US Department of Labor, the FFI focused its campaign on labor organizations, including the historically anti-Asian AFL. Refuting charges of having been convicted of a crime involving "moral turpitude," Ghose and a labor organizer from New York informed Samuel Gompers that the charge was "contrary to American traditions and principles as it is to common understanding." "Surely it should be unnecessary to point out that we do not regard George Washington and the American Revolutionists as guilty of moral turpitude," they argued. In the summer and fall of 1919, Gompers, the

FIGURE 20. Agnes Smedley, ca. 1914. Courtesy of Agnes Smedley Photographs (CP SPC 330), University Archives, Arizona State University Library.

AFL, and throngs of labor and progressive organizations, in addition to liberal intellectuals and private individuals, responded with collective resolutions and irate letters condemning what they considered a gross violation of America's traditions. Smedley, a driving force behind the FFI campaign, was more forthright in radical circles, calling the Ghadar Party "the real voice of India." She challenged her "comrades" to be "truly international" and support "the Hindus in America."[64]

Those affiliated with the FFI, in turn, became targets of the US government, which had passed sweeping laws on sedition and immigration. Amid their organizing efforts, Smedley and Ghose were arrested for violating the Espionage Act, with Smedley facing another local charge of circulating information on birth control. The Sedition Act (1918) widened the scope of proscribed political beliefs, making it a federal crime to "utter, print, write or publish any disloyal, profane, scurrilous, or abusive language about the form of government of the United States . . . any language intended to . . . encourage resistance to the United States, or to promote the cause of its enemies." The US Congress also had passed a comprehensive immigration bill, over Wilson's veto, that bolstered the government's authority to exclude and deport noncitizens. In addition to previously excluded categories and a new literacy requirement, the Immigration Act of 1917 created an "Asiatic Zone"—a vast swath from South Asia to the Pacific, including "islands not possessed by the United States"—from which immigration was prohibited. The law broadened the list of persons liable to "be taken into custody and deported," including aliens convicted of "a crime involving moral turpitude" within five years of entry and "any alien who at any time after entry shall be found advocating or teaching the unlawful destruction of property, or advocating or teaching anarchy, or the overthrow by force or violence of the Government of the United States or of all forms of law or the assassination of public officials."[65]

Although the FFI campaign succeeded in halting the deportation orders, it could not avert an avalanche of laws and legal decisions that further racialized Asians as threats to US national security. Under mounting pressure, Assistant Secretary of Labor Louis F. Post dismissed the deportation proceedings against Gopal Singh, Santokh Singh, and Bhagwan Singh in May 1920. Within the same month, however, Congress specifically authorized the Labor Department to deport aliens convicted of violating US neutrality laws, undermining any legal protection afforded by Post's decision. Four years later, the Immigration Act of 1924 prohibited the admission of "aliens ineligible to citizenship" and rendered aliens subject to deportation if found "at any time after entering the United States" to have entered unlawfully. For "aliens ineligible to citizenship," the legal potential of deportation became a life sentence. The US Supreme Court supplemented the legislation by granting the federal government practically unlimited latitude in deportation proceedings and, through *Ozawa* (1922) and *Thind* (1923), categorizing all Asians racially as "aliens ineligible to citizenship." The Justice Department used the *Thind* decision to initiate denaturalization proceedings against Das and other South Asians who had earlier obtained US citizenship. Das was able to retain his citizenship, but, by 1927, sixty-five individuals had lost theirs. Stripped of his US citizenship, Vaishno Das Bagal committed suicide in March 1928, declaring to "the world at large" his refusal to live as "an interned person" inside "a free country." He blamed himself and the US government for his unbearable predicament.[66]

The US government's repressive onslaught compelled the Ghadar Party to look beyond the United States and the liberal nation-state, to pursue a communist internationalism rooted in anticolonial struggles. By way of Moscow, Santokh Singh returned to Punjab to found a communist newspaper, while Roy, Smedley, and many others shifted their activities to China, where Nguyen Ai Quoc organized the International Union of Oppressed Peoples of the East in Hankow (Hankou) in 1925. The congregation of South Asian, Korean, and Vietnamese anticolonial revolutionaries in China seemed to bring the Comintern's theses into reality, a movement against empire and white supremacy that likewise motivated Latin American, Asian, and Black delegates—including Barakatullah, Roy, and Katayama—at the founding conference of the League Against Imperialism in Brussels in 1927. After the Brussels conference, the Ghadar Party adopted resolutions that redoubled its commitment to revolutionary nationalism and communist internationalism. Dismissing "the opportunist leaders of the Indian National Congress," the party praised the "rank and file proletarian revolutionary leaders . . . organizing the masses on the basis of their class demands and converting them into a decisive factor in the anti-imperialist struggle." It condemned the brutal violence and the punitive legal apparatus of the "British Imperialist Government" that led to mass murder, imprisonment, and deportation. Appealing for "Dominion Status" within the British empire, which was founded on "colonial oppression and racial domination," would "drag the liberation movement on to the path of complete capitulation to British imperialism."[67] That was akin to individual South Asians having faith in US citizenship. Those were liberal conceits, paths to self-destruction, not liberation.

As Soviet Russia eclipsed imperial Japan in justifying the US state's repression of the Ghadar movement, Japan remained front and center in the Philippines. Members of the Philippine Scouts, reported a US Army intelligence officer in November 1919, were circulating "Anti-white propaganda in the interest of Japan." An operative had related to him the essence of that propaganda: "The power of Japan is pictured as enormous and close at hand. Americans abuse dark people, and America is far off. All India is united regardless of 'caste' to throw off the 'white yoke.' Filipinos are urged to forget tribal differences and unite under the slogan of 'The Orient for the Orientals.'" A military survey of "Japanese

Activities" in the same month found similar results, highlighting the "rapid and aggressive development of Japanese interests in Davao" and Japan's propaganda campaign across the archipelago. Informing the "natives" of an impending war between Japan and the United States, the survey reported, the campaign advanced "the usual arguments regarding the line-up of the yellow and brown against the white race and the necessity of Japan protecting the entire Orient." The commanding US general confirmed that military intelligence officers were devoting "a very large share" of their work to Japanese propaganda, but claimed that "Filipinos as a race" were mostly "loyal to the United States." Outside influences were another matter. "In the dissemination of racial propaganda the Japanese find willing agents among the East Indians who have penetrated into the remotest parts of these Islands," he related.[68]

Agents of the US security state detected not only Japan's determination to arouse seditious sentiments against the US empire but also its potentially revolutionary associations with the Ghadar movement and Bolshevism. In October 1919, a military intelligence report from Panama on a Ghadar activist, who would "not hesitate in doing anything possible against the United States and especially the local authorities," dwelled on his frequent visits to the Japanese consulate. That Japanese fishermen had "an intimate and thorough knowledge" of Panama's Pacific waterways and that Japanese barbers located their shops all over Panama City, according to the report, seemed to suggest an insidious plot against the US empire. Two years later, a broad military survey of Asia conducted by Manila's MID office highlighted the Ghadar Party's impending revival, based on exchanges with "the radical element in Europe and Asia" and "a substantial subsidy" from Soviet Russia, and the suspicious movements of Japanese residents in the Philippines. That racial perception of Japanese incursion prompted many US state governments to pass laws prohibiting "aliens ineligible to citizenship" from owning real property, a largely anti-Japanese measure likewise adopted in the Philippines. In response, a Japanese newspaper in Seattle published an article from Japan proposing an alliance with Russia and Germany "against the capitalism of Europe and America." "Bolshevism proclaims doctrines of the brotherhood of the four seas, insisting that labor knows no national boundaries," stated the article, which was translated and filed by the MID. "In this sense Bolshevism is superior to capitalism."[69]

Such reports spanning the Pacific reinforced accounts from Hawai'i. Alarmed by the level of American dependence on Japanese labor, the

MID warned in February 1921 that "a general strike by the Japanese would . . . practically paralize [*sic*] the industries of these islands." The "slightly inconsistent" messages in Japan's propaganda campaign—an amalgam of "Americanization, Pan-Pacific, Imperial Japanistic, pro-Colored and anti-White and Proletarian"—seemingly reflected its mission of global domination, a scenario that the US Army's War Plans Division (WPD) had been preparing for since 1906. Beginning in 1921, in concert with the MID, ONI, and BI, the WPD stressed the need to contain the "Japanese problem" in Hawai'i, specifically by recommending the internment of "enemy aliens" in case of war. During the military buildup, a local Japanese newspaper observed that "Oahu has become an island of big guns and soldiers, a nest of man-of-war and aeroplanes." "It may be splendid from an economical viewpoint," the newspaper noted. "But somehow there is an atmosphere of militarism and it is not good. What will be the effect on our second generation which is growing up in this atmosphere? Alas!" The MID classified the editorial as evidence of "an alien and unassimilable race" destroying a "democratic form of government." In its plans, the WPD designated nations by color, not by name. Japan was "Orange"; the United States was "Blue." It is not clear why, but, in the combustible mixture of red and yellow around the world in the 1920s, agents of the US security state clearly saw Orange.[70]

CHAPTER 6

Collaboration and Revolution

And Joe, revolution is brewing. . . . I have my ear to the
ground. It will be a miracle if we can get past the 15th of
November without. . . . The thing is growing. I'm sensitive to
this sort of thing, and I tell you that revolution is afoot here.

—Frank Murphy, Governor-General of the Philippines, to Joseph
Ralston Hayden, Vice-Governor of the Philippines, October 7,
1935, a month before the scheduled inauguration of the Commonwealth of the Philippines

Toward the end of World War II, US military intelligence officials issued
a disquieting report on the Hukbalahap, a guerrilla force fighting Japanese imperial troops in the Philippines. Though organized in 1942 after
Japan's invasion and occupation, the report began, the Hukbalahap
movement had deeper roots and grander objectives than resisting the
Japanese. "Actually, the war merely afforded the opportunity," US
Army intelligence officials stated. "It created a militant organ out of a
rumbling minority." The Hukbalahap, the report continued, harkened
back to agrarian movements of the 1920s and 1930s, most notably the
Sakdalista uprising of 1935 when "the Sakdal leaders appealed to fundamental emotions, nationalistic patriotism, racial antipathy and class
antagonism of their ignorant, illiterate, naive and religiously fanatic followers." After the failed uprising, the Sakdals evolved into the Ganaps,
a "pro-Japanese" organization before the war, and then the Makapili,
"a militant, armed society formed by the Japanese in December 1944 to
fight the Americans." To US officials, the Hukbalahap and the Makapili, as heirs to past agrarian movements opposed to US colonial rule,
shared common lineages that threatened the US mission to reclaim the
Philippines. Espousing "socialistic and communistic sympathies," the
Huk leaders were already organizing a "United Front movement."

"Though the Hukbalahap as an organization is anti-Japanese," the report concluded, "it is also anti-American insofar as American policy may affect adversely the future of the United Front." In a global war with seemingly clear allies and enemies, the specter of Japan and communism joining forces against the US empire lived on.[1]

Weeks earlier in February 1945, Luis M. Taruc, head of the Hukbalahap, had attempted to reassure US officials of the Huks' allegiance to the United States and its pledge of Philippine independence. "Politically, the aims of the Hukbalahap are to assure Philippine independence already promised by the American people, and to preserve democracy from the insidious attacks of the Japanese fascists and their puppets," he informed Douglas MacArthur, the commanding general of the US Army Forces in the Far East (USAFFE), and Sergio Osmeña, the president of the Philippine Commonwealth, a colonial status that implied eventual independence. "The Hukbalahap recognized the United States government as the supreme authority in the Philippines and the United States forces of Liberation as a part of a world United Front movement against Fascism; and the Hukbalahap is trying its level best to cooperate with the United States forces." But the "reactionary redbaiters" fomented tension and division between nascent allies by branding "the Hukbalahap as communistic organization with intentions to seize power and confiscate all private properties." Based on such "lies and misrepresentations" spread by a "few reactionary elements notably among the landlord class" that had collaborated with Japan, Taruc argued, US forces were disarming and mistreating Huk units, particularly in the province of Pampanga. He pressed for the return of Huk weapons and the recognition of Huk service. Lest MacArthur and Osmeña misinterpret his ultimate allegiance, Taruc explained the Hukbalahap philosophy. "The army needs the masses," he wrote, "and all its activities must be for the benefit of the people."[2]

Born in 1913 to a peasant family in San Luis, Pampanga, Taruc's political journey revealed the conjoined and contradictory roots of anti-colonial and communist struggles in the Philippines. Frustrated by a political and economic system run by landlords and their cronies and working multiple jobs as a "houseboy" to pay for his schooling, Taruc became awakened to a wave of labor strikes beginning in 1932, including a fatal confrontation with the Philippine Constabulary in Pampanga. In the funeral procession for the two killed workers, he saw that "the peasants carried red flags." For a time in 1934, he grew intrigued by the Sakdalista movement, attending meetings and reading and distributing copies of the newspaper *Sakdal*. "Peasants, looking for a way

FIGURE 21. Luis M. Taruc (holding newspaper) and the Hukbalahap. Photograph by Otto Bettmann. Courtesy of Getty Images.

out, flocked to the Sakdal banner," Taruc recalled later, "just as they had joined the Tangulan and any other movement promising change." In those meetings Taruc heard the word *imperialism*, which the fledgling revolutionary had to look up in a dictionary. After a "hunger parade" in Manila in 1936, he met an American socialist who laid bare US imperialism's malevolent effects. Taruc moved back to Pampanga to join the Socialist Party, founded by Pedro Abad Santos in 1933. By the time Japanese forces invaded the Philippines on December 8, 1941, the Socialist Party had merged with the Communist Party and Taruc had emerged as a leading organizer. The Constabulary used the occasion of Japan's invasion to raid Abad Santos's headquarters, accusing Filipino communists and socialists of conspiring with Japan.[3]

Whereas Taruc strove to advance the communist movement and to ally with the United States to liberate the Philippines from Japanese occupation, the Philippine political elite, under the tutelage and authority of the US empire, condemned communism as a grave threat to their aspirations for national recognition within the US empire. José P. Laurel, a justice of the Philippine Commonwealth's Supreme Court, wrote an urgent letter in May 1941 to Manuel L. Quezon, the first president of the commonwealth. Linking Abad Santos and his party to the Third International (Comintern),

TRY TO FIND an American or a Philippine flag in this picture. There aren't any. But there are plenty of Communist banners. In Floridablanca the Red flag was also lavishly displayed.

FIGURE 22. Communist rally in Pampanga. Photograph from "This Has Gone Far Enough," *Philippine Free Press*, January 18, 1941. Courtesy of American Historical Collection, Rizal Library, Ateneo de Manila University.

Laurel called for the revocation of a communist candidate's election in Arayat, Pampanga, and the repression of communism across the Philippines. Communism in Pampanga, he argued, was "an extension of communism in Russia, professing the same principles, devoid of patriotism and love of country, and is completely a destructive and subversive organization which can not and should not be allowed or tolerated to exist." He advised, "Vigorous and drastic action should, therefore, be taken to wipe out this organization which is rapidly gaining ground not only in the province of Pampanga but also in the provinces." To Laurel, the state's authority to protect its existence, including through violence, was its raison d'être; if it failed in that mission, the government might as well surrender to "a triumphant revolution." "A weak government is a contradiction in terms and is perhaps worse than no government at all," Laurel reasoned. He recommended singling out Abad Santos in particular, though without making him into a "Gandhi" or a "martyr."[4]

When Laurel assumed the Philippine presidency two years later, under the tutelage and authority of the Japanese empire, he elaborated on his yearnings for a strong government. After thanking "the honored guests" from Japan for "the liberation of Asiatic peoples from foreign domination," he stressed the need to maintain "peace and order." "In the ultimate analysis, all government is physical power and that government is doomed which is impotent to suppress anarchy and terrorism," he argued in his inaugural address. "The Constitution vests in the President full authority to exercise the coercive powers of the State for its preservation." His administration, Laurel declared, would focus on "the training, equipment and support of an enlarged Constabulary force strong enough to cope with any untoward situation which might arise." He demanded the cessation of "guerrilla activities"—recalcitrants would soon be categorized "public enemies of our government"—and the economic development of the Philippines through "benevolent paternalism" and "the spiritual ways of the East" over "rugged individualism" and "excessive materialism." Toward that end, the Philippine government might even consider a "socialistic policy" of establishing acreage limits on land ownership. Laurel prioritized "duties" over "rights," including the revival of patriarchy in "the Filipino family under the Republic" and "the improvement of the racial stock." That racial and sexual project ought to extend to prohibiting "the marriage of diseased individuals" and "the sterilization of imbeciles and lunatics." Laurel appealed for "national unity" behind "the Flag, the Constitution, the National Anthem and the President of the Republic." Fascism had arrived in the Philippines.[5]

All of those appeals and denunciations before and during World War II—for and against communism, anticommunism, fascism, antifascism, liberation, collaboration—generated a cacophony of nationalist claims through which revolutionary struggles against empire could be heard and silenced, somewhat incoherently and always incompletely. The allure of promised inclusion has historically constituted and elided the US empire, at once animating and eliminating movements for radical change. The US colonial project has involved provisionally enfolding peoples historically excluded from the nation-state, Jodi A. Byrd argues, to create "a cacophony of moral claims that help to deflect progressive and transformative activism from dismantling the ongoing conditions of colonialism that continue to make the United States a desired state formation within which to be included." As the United States and Japan prepared to go to war in the 1930s, both states competed unevenly to include a Philippine nation-state in their transpacific empires, with imperial Japan increasingly appropriating pan-Asian solidarity as its official policy.[6] Movements led by and otherwise identified with communism exploited the interimperial conflict to advance anticolonial critiques. The US security state, in turn, monitored and maligned those movements, in part by projecting their affiliation with communist internationalism and imperial Japan. Even as fighting fascism eclipsed fighting communism, compelling antifascists like the Huks to ally with the United States, fighting empire proved more elusive and enduring. In the end, radical movements on both sides of the Pacific excavated deeper histories of empire and revolution that nourished dreams of a different world, against and beyond the Japanese empire and the US empire.

COLONIAL "FILIPINIZATION" AND ANTICOLONIAL COMMUNISM

Deferred promises of Philippine independence rested fundamentally on perpetuating racial hierarchies and managing imperial insecurities. A hastened phase of "Filipinization" of US rule in the Philippines, inaugurated under Woodrow Wilson's presidency, cultivated a Philippine political elite to occupy more seats in the colonial regime. Buoyed by Wilson's gestures toward greater autonomy, Quezon, then a resident commissioner to the US House of Representatives, lobbied the US Congress to adopt the Jones Law in 1916 to lay a path toward eventual independence. Despite the creation of an elected bicameral legislature, the law simultaneously reinforced US sovereignty in the Philippines by preserving for the US president and his appointed executive in Manila, the governor-general, the authority to veto any legislation. The appearance of increased independence, in turn, allowed US authorities to attribute social and political ills plaguing the Philippines to Filipinos' supposed unfitness for democracy, yet another reason to deny and delay national independence. If Filipinos were incapable of self-rule, they were presumably also ripe for external influences that threatened the US empire. In May 1924, the Bureau of Investigation (BI) circulated a report on the Third International's ties to revolutionary movements in the United States and in the Philippines. Through "a strictly confidential source," the BI learned that the Comintern's executive committee had directed the Workers Party of America to publicize "the present agitation for the divorcement of the Philippine Islands from this Government." A recent labor strike in Manila, the BI added, "was a result of a plan for revolutionary work in the Philippines."[7]

Signs of unrest and revolution indeed cropped up across the US empire. Exalting and deifying José Rizal, Andres Bonifacio, and other nationalist figures, the Colorum movement helped to equate millennial deliverance with national independence in the Philippines, a fusion of religion and politics that resonated with the rural masses and unnerved US officials. In defense of a government crackdown, the *Manila Daily Bulletin* editorialized that any "opposition to constituted authority will under no circumstances be tolerated." In northeastern Mindanao, the Philippine

Constabulary attempted to monitor and infiltrate the movement and thereby provoked a series of fatal skirmishes in January and February 1924 that killed approximately thirty-seven among its ranks and two hundred Colorums. The ensuing conviction of about the same number of Colorums for murder and sedition failed to stem the tide of discontent, even among soldiers responsible for defending the Philippines from foreign invasion and domestic insurrection. Influenced by a surge of labor organizing in Manila, hundreds of Philippine Scouts stationed at nearby Fort McKinley formed the Secret Soldiers' Union and, days after a mass walkout by civilian workers at the Cavite Navy Yard on July 1, 1924, refused to appear for duty. The US Army headquarters in Manila promptly blamed "bolshevistic emissaries" of trying to take "advantage of any fancied discontent among the troops." General Douglas MacArthur, who commanded two Philippine Scout regiments in his brigade at the time, swiftly oversaw the court martial of more than two hundred participants, for which he received praise and promotion.[8]

In Hawai'i, Filipino plantation workers staged a strike across the islands that pitted them against sugar planters, US territorial authorities, and Philippine officials. Led by Pablo Manlapit and other veterans of the 1920 strike, Filipino workers reorganized themselves in 1923 to struggle for higher wages, eight-hour workdays, collective bargaining rights, and other demands. The planters' refusal to acknowledge their petitions spurred the Filipino union to commence a rolling strike in April 1924, involving a "direct strike" by some and a "silent strike" (a slowdown) by others. The Hawaiian Sugar Planters' Association (HSPA) prepared for a violent standoff, shipping funds and arms to local sheriffs and "special deputies" to suppress the strike that culminated in a fatal confrontation in Hanapēpē, Kaua'i, in early September. Sixteen workers and four police officers were killed. Filipino workers faced an increasingly hostile state, an emblem of their colonized status in Hawai'i and in the Philippines. At the planters' behest, prosecutors doggedly pursued Filipino labor leaders and striking workers, unreservedly applying a host of laws at their disposal, including territorial statutes passed after the 1920 strike that had essentially criminalized the labor movement. Meanwhile, Cayetano Ligot, the Philippine resident labor commissioner appointed by Governor-General Leonard Wood, also sided vocally against the workers he was ostensibly assigned to protect. With the support of Wood and the Philippine political elite, he implored Filipino workers "to disband as strikers, go back to work wherever you may find it, and to work faithfully in restoring the good name of Filipinos in Hawaii."[9]

Though led and mobilized by Filipino workers, the strike, as four years earlier in 1920, evoked longstanding racialized and gendered projections of imperial competition and national security that conflated radicalism and Japan. On behalf of "liberty-loving and law-abiding Americans," the *Honolulu Star-Bulletin* called "for law and order and against the criminal labor agitators and all their ilk." The pro-planter newspaper drew a menacing picture of "alien nationalism," fomented by Japanese language newspapers, and "IWWism," spread by "professional agitators" of the Industrial Workers of the World (IWW). "Besides the soft-handed and soft-living Filipino 'leaders' of the Manlapit type, and besides the Japanese who are encouraging the Filipinos and hoping the strike will win," an editorial declared, "there is a heterogeneous group of 'reds,' 'pinks' and yellows—'wobblies' and communists and crack-brained demagogues—who have aligned themselves with the strikers and are doing their bolshevik best to turn Hawaii into anarchy." It was supposedly an immense and underground plot, a toxic and explosive blend of race and radicalism, in which Filipino workers again were merely passive "catspaws." Before sentencing fifty-six men convicted of a barrage of crimes in the aftermath of the "Hanapēpē Massacre"—rioting, assault and battery, kidnapping, and vagrancy— the judge in charge implicitly claimed Hawaiʻi and Filipino workers as subject to the US empire. He denounced "the radicalism of some of your most prominent leaders." "You cannot have a government of your own in these fair islands and expect to get away with it," he preached to Filipino workers. "That would be dangerous and un-American."[10]

Through its trade union organ, the Red International of Labor Unions (RILU, or Profintern), the Third International took steps to build on the momentum of local labor movements by highlighting the intimate links between colonialism, race, and labor in and across the Pacific. Meeting in Hankow (Hankou), China, in May 1927, after being harassed by anti-communist authorities in China, Japan, Hong Kong, and elsewhere, delegates at the first Pan-Pacific Trade Union Conference sought to forge a common movement among workers encircling the Pacific, a condition made possible and necessary by empire. "The growing rivalry between the great powers in the Pacific and the undoubted imminence of war originating in this quarter . . . involving not only the Pacific, but the whole world," the RILU report began, "have forced all the advanced elements in the International Labour Movement to pay special attention to this section of the imperialist front." The conference disparaged the American Federation of Labor (AFL) and other elitist labor organizations as mere exponents of empire, white supremacy, and warmongering and called on workers "to transform the threatening imperialist war of races and nations into a war of classes, a war of the exploited against the exploiters." More than listing "ten economic demands," including "equal wages for equal work," the conference focused on imperialism, with banners demanding "Independence for the Oppressed Peoples from World Imperialism." In particular, delegates passed resolutions against British imperialism in India, Japanese imperialism in Korea and Formosa, and US imperialism in the Philippines.[11]

Those imperial contexts and anticolonial aspirations drove Crisanto Evangelista's politics leftward in the 1920s. Rising through the ranks of the Philippine labor movement, Evangelista helped to organize in 1913 the Congreso Obrero de Filipinas (COF), which unified and replaced the last remnants of the original labor federation Unión Obrera Democrática (UOD) and its rival Unión del Trabajo de Filipinas. Although he became critical of the labor movement's continuing reformist impulses, Evangelista attempted to work within and through the COF and Quezon's Nacionalista Party. In 1919, he joined Quezon in a mission to the United States to lobby for national independence and, in his particular role, to meet with Filipino workers and American labor leaders. That trip to the metropole awakened him to other political possibilities. Rebuffed by Samuel Gompers's defense of the US empire and white supremacy and repulsed by fellow Filipino representatives' insouciance and narcissism, Evangelista found the IWW and the emergent communist movement more intriguing and promising. He returned to the Philippines a Marxist, ready to try to steer the labor movement and the independence movement toward communist internationalism. In 1925, he and other leftist labor leaders abandoned the Nacionalista Party to revive and radicalize the Partido Obrero (Labor Party), originally founded by Antonino D. Ora in 1922. "It is not a party of social parasites," they declared. "It urges the workers—those who work with brawn and brain—to take economic and political powers away from the capitalist class, and to abolish all class divisions and class rule."[12]

Borne of wider struggles against the US empire, the budding communist movement in the Philippines embraced and exploited the Third International's theoretical treatises and political initiatives. Although Evangelista was not able to attend the Pan-Pacific Trade Union Conference in Hankow, he vowed public support to its mission. "It is therefore now our duty to work out a plan for assisting the active movement of workers and peasants all over the world and especially along the broad

FIGURE 23. Crisanto Evangelista. Photograph from Crisanto Evangelista, "The Birth of the Philippine Labor Movement," *Pan-Pacific Monthly* no. 28 (July 1929): 22. Courtesy of Joseph Ralston Hayden Papers, Bentley Historical Library, University of Michigan.

shores of the Pacific," Evangelista wrote, "where imperialism is endeavouring to establish its dread power." He remained influential in the COF, attempting to work within the labor federation to galvanize the Philippine labor movement around industrial unionism and communist internationalism. After the COF voted to affiliate with the Pan-Pacific Trade

Union Secretariat (PPTUS), an outgrowth of the Hankow conference, Evangelista headed a small contingent in 1928 to represent Filipino workers and peasants at a PPTUS meeting in Shanghai and the Fourth Congress of the Profintern in Moscow. His trip across the Soviet Union deepened Evangelista's conviction that communist internationalism would advance his hopes for labor mobilization and anticolonial liberation. Upon his return to Manila, he dispatched three Filipino workers to study at the Communist University of Toilers of the East (KUTV). At the same time, tension and division mounted within the COF, as Evangelista and other leftist leaders, in line with the Comintern's growing hostility to bourgeois nationalism, waged a withering attack on the Nacionalista Party and its politics of collaboration and compromise.[13]

Evangelista and his allies soon formed their own organizations to mark the official birth of communism in the Philippines. At the COF convention in 1929, anticommunist rivals, particularly those with close ties to Quezon, surreptitiously packed the meeting with their supporters to outnumber the "red danger" in their midst. Denouncing the "Congreso Obrero of Capitalists' Agents and Politicians' Lackeys," Evangelista and other leftists walked out and, within days, announced the inauguration of the Katipunan ng mga Anak-Pawis sa Pilipinas (KAP, the Proletarian Labor Congress), a new federation committed to industrial unionism. With a leadership closely overlapping with the Partido Obrero, the KAP declared through a manifesto on May Day 1930 its plans to form a "mass political party" of workers and peasants and to join the "world proletariat" in defense of the Soviet Union against an impending "imperialist war." In August 1930, to coincide with the anniversary of the beginning of the Philippine Revolution, delegates from KAP-affiliated unions held the founding convention of the Partido Komunista sa Pilipinas (PKP). Three months later, on the anniversary of the Bolshevik Revolution and amid the Great Depression, a rally of six thousand people at a plaza in Tondo, Manila—chanting "Down with Imperialism!" and "Down with Capitalism!"—officially launched the PKP. They set out to organize the masses against the US empire and the Philippine elite. "When the time comes," a peasant leader told members of the Constabulary and Scouts in December 1930, "you should desert and aim your rifles not at the communists but at your chiefs and imperialists."[14]

The US colonial regime monitored the communist movement in the Philippines from its inception, highlighting its global networks as particularly threatening. In a memorandum on "Red activities among certain Filipino labor leaders," C.H. Bowers, head of the Constabulary's

Intelligence Division, noted the radicalizing effects of Evangelista's trip to Moscow in 1928 that included stops along the China coast and in Berlin and Paris. Immediately upon their return to the Philippines, he reported, Evangelista and Jacinto Manahan, a fellow delegate leading the peasant movement, "became active in spreading Bolsh[e]vistic propaganda and organizing labor unions." In Shanghai, they had met with another Filipino labor organizer, who afterward "proceeded to Hawaii where after a conference with labor leaders in the Islands, continued his trip to San Francisco where he conferred with Pablo Manlapit and other IWW leaders in California." Without explaining his methods, Bowers reported to the Constabulary chief that his office was "fortunate enough to inspect Manahan's private papers and to photograph or obtain copies of the most important." Among his discoveries was Manahan's support of the 1924 strike in Hawai'i. "That cause of yours we are defending here as if it were our own," Manahan had written to Manlapit. Manahan's "considerable correspondence" with the All-America Anti-Imperialist League (AAAIL), a communist organization founded in 1925 to challenge imperialism across Latin America and the Caribbean, also captured the Constabulary's attention. The distribution of the league's anti-American "inflammatory pamphlets," Bowers feared, "cannot be otherwise than detrimental of the American prestige in the Islands."[15]

As the COF split into factions in 1929, the radical wing's pan-Asian and transpacific ambitions appeared as a pernicious threat to the US empire. For decades, the Philippine labor movement, not unlike the white labor movement in the United States, had adopted Chinese exclusion as a central tenet. Evangelista grew to repudiate that position and to ally with the Philippine Chinese Laborers' Association (PCLA), a local organization in sympathy with the Chinese Communist Party in its intensifying rift with the Guomindang (Kuomintang). In February 1929, the PCLA and leftists in the COF hosted a "Class Solidarity Night" to proclaim their united front against capitalism and imperialism. Objections to the accreditation of Chinese representatives at the COF convention three months later prompted Evangelista and his comrades to walk out. "The conservative faction standing for protection and nationalism as against radicalism and bolshevism," Bowers wrote of the proceedings, accused "the radical faction of attempts to introduce Red ideas and Chinese membership into the organization." The KAP then published resolutions, according to the Constabulary, that included: "to work for the freedom of the Philippines"; "to foster friendly relation between laborers in all countries bordering the Pacific Ocean"; "to protest strongly against the exclusion of Filipinos in California" and "against condition of Filipino laborers in Hawaii." Whereas Evangelista had lost faith in Philippine missions to Washington, DC, Bowers noted, he had sent delegates to "Russia and Japan for the purpose of obtaining recognition of their Independence movements in the Philippines."[16]

The communist movement's blunt criticisms of Philippine political leaders as accomplices of the US empire raised discomfiting questions that roused nationalist attacks on communism. Although Domingo Ponce, a major figure in the labor movement, identified as a socialist and welcomed contact with the Comintern—so much so that the Constabulary planned to keep "a close watch" on his activities—he became wary of Evangelista's radicalism, which he found increasingly incompatible with the struggle for national independence. Unlike Evangelista, Ponce retained his faith in the Nacionalista Party. In January 1929, Ponce contacted Quezon, the president of the Philippine Senate, to express his anxieties over Evangelista and the "red" movement in the Philippines. Explaining that Evangelista received generous financial support from Ora, a wealthy labor leader, Ponce suspected a nefarious scheme devised by the US state. He was convinced that Ora worked as an "instrument of American imperialism," enlisted to spread communism in the Philippines to provide the US Congress a reason, a new "danger," to discredit the independence movement and to prolong US colonial rule. On behalf of the Nacionalista Party and national independence, Ponce pledged to keep close tabs on "all of the 'red' plans and activities in these Islands." Quezon, for his part, fomented and encouraged anticommunism within the COF, in part to deflect the radical faction's forthright criticisms of his leadership. He coordinated public messages against communism and privately used a mixture of political favors and personal pressure to make labor leaders distance themselves from Evangelista and the Partido Obrero.[17]

By January 1931, two months after the PKP's official establishment, the US colonial regime prepared for a counterrevolutionary campaign. A peasant revolt in Tayug, Pangasinan, placed authorities on edge, as *insurrectos* overwhelmed the local Constabulary post, took control of the town plaza, and set ablaze many buildings and land and tax records. Although the PKP played no role in the short-lived uprising, the Constabulary blamed "Colorums" infected by communism, reporting that "Central Luzon [was] ready for an uprising, need leadership only," and that "the oppressed will soon right things with the bolo." Two weeks later on January 25, 1931, Ora's funeral procession attracted tens of thousands of people, defiantly flying red flags, to the streets of Manila. In their tributes to

Ora, who had died in an automobile accident, PKP leaders declared their resolve to press on. "We want to destroy this order by means of a revolutionary explosion which will at the same time be the eruption of truth, justice and equality," Manahan said. Sensing conditions ripe for such an explosion—rabid communists joining forces with "ignorant religious fanatics" and unemployed workers—Governor-General Dwight F. Davis supported a plan to arrest and prosecute PKP leaders for sedition. He made arrangements with Filipino officials—the secretary of justice and the secretary of the interior—to execute the plot while he was away "to remove any possibility of confusing the issue by injecting the element of racial prejudice." That was "Filipinization" at work, to sustain white supremacy and empire under the guise of independence.[18]

CRIMINALIZING COMMUNISM FOR EMPIRE

As during the Philippine-American War three decades earlier, charges of sedition rang across the Philippines. Beginning in February 1931, Manila's prosecutor, "on behalf of the People of the Philippine Islands," filed a series of charges against PKP leaders that framed sedition as organizing against the US empire. Lengthy translations and quotations of PKP documents railed against American imperialism and Philippine politicians, whose only purpose, the PKP proclaimed, was "to rise into power and exploit, with independence or not; to enrich themselves and strengthen the control of a government which is procapitalist and proimperialist." PKP leaders committed a crime, according to the prosecutor, when they "willfully, feloniously" delivered:

> seditious words and speeches, such as, that the laborers in the Philippines had a common cause with the revolting peoples of the colonies of the different nations and they must prepare to fight in getting the Government into their hands and to run it by themselves and for themselves like the poor people in Russia; . . . that when the laborers were united, neither the Constabulary, nor the United States Army, nor the imperialist Governor-General could stop them when they rose up as one body in order to free themselves from slavery by the capitalists; . . . that the Constabulary and the police were the ones who made troubles to the laborers because they were the agents of the American imperialists in the Islands.

Those statements were therefore "highly seditious" by inciting "rebellious conspiracies," instigating "others to cabal and meet together for unlawful purposes," and obstructing "the lawful authorities in executing their office."[19]

Philippine authorities turned to colonial laws passed in the throes of revolution and war to prosecute PKP leaders. The law against sedition, passed originally in 1901 and amended in 1907 by the Philippine Commission, provided a sweeping mandate to prohibit virtually all anticolonial expressions and anticolonial organizations. The law criminalized:

> every person who shall utter seditious words or speeches, or who shall write, publish, or circulate scurrilous libels against the Government of the United States or against the Government of the Philippine Islands, or who shall print, write, publish, utter, or make any statement, or speech, or do any act which tends to disturb or obstruct any lawful officer in executing his office or in performing his duty, or which tends to instigate others to cabal or meet together for unlawful purposes, or which suggests or incites rebellious conspiracies or which tends to stir up the people against the lawful authorities, or which tends to disturb the peace of the community or the safety or order of the Government, or who shall knowingly conceal such evil practices from the constituted authorities.

For good measure, prosecutors charged PKP leaders additionally of violating a Spanish Royal Decree from 1897 that prohibited "illegal associations," defined as those whose "purpose or circumstances, are contrary to public morals or whose object is to combat the fundamental bases of social order or to alter the regularity of its functions."[20] Empire rested on law and order, unquestioning deference to the state.

If local discontent concerned US officials, their fears became magnified by the prospect of global connections beyond the Philippines. In March 1931, the US secretary of state forwarded to the War Department a distressing article published in the *New York Times*. "A society of 4,000 members, largely composed of Reds, was discovered, it is reported, awaiting arms from Japan, after receipt of which hostilities were expected to open," the article stated from Constabulary reports from Pangasinan. Secretary of War Patrick J. Hurley and the Constabulary dismissed the account, but they also supported local efforts to contain communism in the Philippines. Governor-General Davis wanted to do more. After visiting Kuala Lumpur and Singapore in March 1931, he observed that colonial authorities all across Southeast Asia feared "the influx of Chinese" and "the question of Bolshevist activities." He requested the authority to communicate directly with US State Department officials and with colonial counterparts to check the communist movement. "For example, if we should learn of any particular activity which was planned against the British, the French, or the Siamese governments by communists acting directly or indirectly from Manila," he explained, "it might be too late to take effective action if the matter was reported to Washington and then reported back to this part of the world." Conversely, he wanted to receive reports that "might be of value to us in Manila, particularly if the whole movement is headed up in one place." Empires needed to join forces against a common enemy, international communism.[21]

Refusing to be intimidated by the anticommunist campaign, Evangelista carried on with his organizing work. Already marked as "the most active Red Leader among Filipinos" before the PKP's founding, he saw Constabulary agents everywhere he went. When Agnes Smedley, who had earlier championed South Asian struggles against the British empire, crossed paths with him in a seaside village in the spring of 1931, she noticed that "uniformed military police, armed with guns and bayonets," were monitoring a mass meeting of about 1,500 fishermen. Booked on charges of sedition, Evangelista had arrived straight from jail. Smedley found him to be "one of the strangest and most interesting characters in Asia" and "perhaps the only Filipino Marxian theoretician," whose "gentleness and wistfulness" inspired "devotion and love in the hearts of the workers." "He is no agitator, no demagogue," she explained. He taught history to the crowd, "of the causes of the revolutions against Spain, of the workers and peasants who fought in the revolution—and of the compromise signed between the American military invaders and the Filipino leaders—a document of the betrayal of the revolution." Evangelista also offered a lesson on Marxism. "Through his Tagalog language came such words as 'Karl Marx,' 'Lenin,' 'surplus value,' in English," Smedley noted. After spending more than three hours with Evangelista, many in the audience were ready to join the PKP, despite his caution "of what suffering would be in store for them if they became Communist Party members."[22]

The anticommunist crackdown proceeded apace, but it simultaneously threatened to expose the US state's colonial roots. In April 1930, the Philippine secretary of the interior approved a wholesale ban on communist meetings. Because the PKP was "seditious and illegal," a circular informed provincial governors, municipal presidents, and police officers, "any gathering or meeting under its auspices, whether held in public or private premises, or even in the very homes of its members, may be prohibited if not yet convened, or dissolved if already commenced, by the authorities." Filipino officials proved enthusiastic collaborators in the anticommunist campaign. US officials, however, felt ambivalent about collaborating with European colonial authorities. On the one hand, US Secretary of State Henry L. Stimson expressed a keen interest in learning "the ramifications of communist international revolutionary activities" and endorsed a Dutch proposal from Batavia (Jakarta) to share information on communist movements. On the other hand, Governor-General Davis's proposal to organize a transimperial network across Southeast Asia drew some skepticism. The US State Department approved of consular communications on "any information concerning criminal designs against the peace and security of foreign governments," but opposed a "system" specifically targeting "Communist activities." "Our position in Asia differs substantially from that of the European colonial powers," the State Department concluded, "and this ipso facto enjoins upon us an attitude of aloofness toward proposals envisaging the institution of a special police regime toward any particular aspect of Asiatic politics."[23] In that respect, image mattered more than substance.

Not surprisingly, Evangelista and other PKP leaders were found guilty of sedition and illegal association in September 1931. The defense attempted to deny the seditious characterization of PKP speeches, noting that they had "advocated a change of regime by peaceful and constitutional means," that they had not created "excitement, tumult or disorder" at meetings, and that they had spoken in Tagalog, which Constabulary agents translated inaccurately into English for the trial. The defendants also alluded to the Jones Law, and its guarantee of the right of peaceful assembly, and declared that communism was "not forbidden in any part of the civilized world," including in the United States. Judge Mariano A. Albert of Manila dismissed all of those arguments in his decision, stating that "the court cannot understand how a communist government as that of Russia, which is taken as a model, could be established in the Philippines by peaceful means, when the Russian Bolsheviks had to use force and . . . other violent means in order to accomplish their aims." Citing KAP's affiliation with PPTUS, an organization based in Moscow to spread "International Communism" to "several countries washed by the Pacific," Albert concluded that the PKP's mission—to incite a revolution against the government and "the so-called capitalists"—inherently constituted "illegal association." For the crime of sedition, he sentenced Evangelista, Manahan, and twelve others to prison terms of four months to a year. For violating the old Spanish decree on illegal association, Albert banished twenty PKP leaders to specific provinces for eight years and a day. Evangelista was sentenced to the Mountain Province.[24]

Evangelista and his PKP comrades used their legal appeals to sharpen the contradiction between US claims to democracy and US colonial rule in the Philippines. After the Supreme Court of the Philippine Islands, comprised of five white American and four Filipino judges, unanimously upheld the convictions in October 1932, the defendants filed a motion for reconsideration. Through their attorney Maximo Abaño, they disputed the "misleading" English translations of PKP documents and speeches—noting, for example, the difference between "revolutionary means" and "armed revolution"—before invoking and quoting the US Declaration of Independence. "Overthrowing the government by peaceful means though revolutionary is not a crime punishable by law," Abaño insisted. "If the Communist Party is not declared illegal in the United States," he continued, "why should it be declared illegal in the Philippine Islands while this country is a colony under the American flag?" Prohibiting the right of assembly, the defense contended, placed the US empire alongside the Spanish empire. "The old days of the 'GUARDIA CIVIL,' 'VETERANA' and 'FRIARS' seem to have revived in these days of 'FREEDOM OF THOUGHT,' 'FREEDOM OF ASSOCIATION AND ASSEMBLIES' and 'FREEDOM OF SPEECH,'" Abaño argued. The illusion of democracy in the Philippines accordingly reflected the fallacy of "bourgeois democracy." Evangelista stated in his personal testimony, "The present government because of its double character, capitalistic and imperialistic, its democracy, if there be any at all, is very narrow and limited." The "American-brand democracy" compelled "the toiling masses" to engage in "the broad use of extra-parliamentary action."[25]

Unrepentant in their commitment to communist struggles against the US empire, PKP leaders mocked the entire notion of sedition. For May Day 1931, because of Manila's ban on communist gatherings, the KAP had organized a rally just beyond the city limits, in Caloocan, only to learn that the municipal president rescinded the permit. Tens of thousands of people showed up anyway. In the appeal, Abaño included excerpts from the testimony of a Constabulary officer dispatched to disperse the crowd. The officer allowed Evangelista to address the crowd, ordering him to limit his speech to tell everyone to return home. "The first thing Evangelista did was to raise the hand with the fist closed, a sort of salute," the officer testified, "which was followed by the whole mass with the outcries of 'Mabuhay' [Long Live]." Evangelista then announced the permit's revocation. "This shows that the big ones are persecuting and oppressing us, who are small, which they have no right to do," he said. Sensing "an aggressive attitude" and hearing

cries of "Let us fight them," the Constabulary arrested Evangelista—
along with an attendee who allegedly screamed "Let us fight them until
death"—and doused the crowd to disperse it. "Now, what were the acts
and speeches branded as seditious?" asked Abaño. "Was it Evangelista's
raising of his closed fist which was imitated by fifty thousand workers
and peasants participating in the demonstration? Was this interpreted
to be a challenge to the constituted authorities?"[26]

Recognizing that the legal appeal would be denied, Evangelista used
the spotlight to situate the PKP within wider struggles against empire.
He submitted a treatise on "Communism and Capitalism," based on his
earlier testimony before the Philippine Supreme Court, to supplement
Abaño's legal arguments. "This high court knows that the working class
of this country has engaged in no less than a revolution for the sole
purpose of freeing this country from the yoke of foreign power," he
began. They would continue to fight for "freedom, unlimited freedom
. . . to the finish." He offered a challenge to, and a rebuke of, Philippine
collaborators masquerading as inheritors of revolution. "The prosecution itself, by the irony of history, now stands for and upholds the
present government which is a direct product of American Revolution
against the British rule, and the Philippine Revolution first, against the
Spanish rule, and second, against the American rule," Evangelista
argued. "The prosecution 'defends' and at the same time 'fights' revolution." Echoing V.I. Lenin and the Third International, he condemned
"finance imperialism" as "the last stage of capitalism" that suppressed
"the right of self-determination of all colonial and semi-colonial peoples." Whenever the masses organized, he explained, "the capitalist and
the government combine together through the use of force—police,
constabulary, gangsters—and . . . by intimidation, terrorism and brutal
force they ruthlessly crush the struggle of the workers." That was the
PKP's struggle in and against the US empire.[27]

Through its brash rhetoric and trenchant critique, the communist
movement expanded and complicated anticolonial politics in the Philippines. Evangelista and his comrades derided the US state's demand of
loyal collaboration and, in the process, imagined and pursued a world
beyond the US empire. That world, in many ways, looked bleak. In
Asia, Evangelista identified an interimperial conflict brewing that threatened to "degenerate into a world massacre, a world bloodbath, to be
staged along the Pacific in the immediate future." Japan's invasion of
Manchuria and Shanghai, he pronounced, was a symptom and a product of "finance imperialism," which "always leads to imperialist war

for the incessant partition and repartition of colonies and semi-colonies and the markets of the world." If empires shared an investment in advancing capitalism, racial contradictions pitted Japan against "America, Great Britain, France or other imperialist powers." Evangelista theorized and hoped for worker solidarity across national and imperial borders, arguing that those who stood to suffer the most in the bloodshed had to organize together to reject war—to refuse to produce and transport arms, to refuse "to fight against our fellow workers." For such views, the Philippine Supreme Court reaffirmed the convictions in November 1932. Legal and financial aid from the American Civil Liberties Union (ACLU) in the appeal effort, including potentially to the US Supreme Court, could not avert the criminalization of communism in the Philippines. From Washington, DC, to Manila, the US state took note of the ACLU's support of the PKP. The PKP went underground.[28]

If worker solidarity around the world represented the ultimate aspiration, the communist movement also articulated an insurgent pan-Asian consciousness that contested the US empire's racial order. In October 1928, by which time the Constabulary was monitoring Evangelista's activities, he spoke before an audience of Chinese workers at the Asia Theatre in Manila's Chinatown. They were there to celebrate the anniversary of the founding of the Chinese Republic, which emerged out of a revolutionary struggle led by Sun Yat-sen, whom Evangelista praised as the greatest "leader the Asiatic race has ever produced." But the "Kuomintang fascists," Sun's successors, thwarted that revolution. Aside from sharing parallel histories of revolution and betrayal, Evangelista argued that the Chinese and Filipinos were "racially . . . kinly related to each other." But immigration laws in "white capitalist countries, or colonies of imperialist countries," including in the Philippines, created racial divisions profitable to white capitalists. Meanwhile, those capitalists, Evangelista argued, shipped their "surplus capital" to China, India, and the rest of Asia "to monopolize the exploitation of inexhaustible cheap labor in those countries." In that context, he insisted, Chinese workers and Filipino workers had to form a united front, which would eventually include Japanese workers. "Under this Labor Understanding between the Chinese, Japanese and Filipino workers," he concluded, "I earnestly believe that there is no valid reason why they cannot unite in one common purpose, why they cannot strengthen their class ties, and why class solidarity between them is not but natural and possible."[29] In the US empire, those views rendered communism seditious and revolutionary.

INTERRACIAL SOLIDARITIES AND
ANTICOMMUNIST DEPORTATIONS

Anticommunism followed Filipinos across the Pacific. The emergence of the communist movement in the Philippines coincided with the mass migration of Filipino workers to the incorporated states of the US empire. Exempted from the Immigration Act of 1924, which prohibited the entry of "aliens ineligible to citizenship," Filipinos, as US "nationals," increasingly came to fill jobs historically associated with Chinese and Japanese workers, in the agricultural fields of California, Oregon, and Washington and in the salmon canneries of Alaska. Like the Japanese before them, thousands made the journey eastward from Hawai'i, particularly after the violent repression of the 1924 labor strike. Pablo Manlapit was among those who left for California. He suffered the wrath of the territorial government in September 1924, when he was convicted of conspiracy for subornation of perjury, a charge stemming from the strike. After serving more than two years in prison, Manlapit secured parole in 1927, conditional on his immediate departure from Hawai'i. "My offense was not against any law of morality or against any political statute," he wrote, "but against a system of industrial exploitation." His reputation—and the security state—accompanied him to Los Angeles. In February 1928, the local police arrested and questioned him for three hours on the suspicion that he was planning again to form "Filipino Labor Unions" and to organize "huge strikes" in California. Though released without charge, rumors of Manlapit's affiliation with the Third International and his recruitment of Filipino, Mexican, and Japanese workers circulated widely across the US empire.[30]

By the time Manlapit and other Filipinos arrived in California, Sadaichi Kenmotsu was busy organizing Japanese workers into the communist movement. Having entered the United States in 1923 as an aspiring student, he enrolled for a time at the Oakland Technical High School, even though he already had a college degree from Waseda University. His formal education ended within six months, but he soon helped to transform an Okinawan study group into the Los Angeles chapter of the Japanese Workers' Association (JWA, or Rafu Nihonjin Rodo Kyokai), a leftist organization driven by those who had joined the Workers (Communist) Party (CP). Like Kenmotsu, most members worked in gardening, agriculture, and domestic service during the day. At night, they turned to revolutionary theories to make sense of the world around them. "We intend to organize all Japanese workers in the US and carry

FIGURE 24. Sadaichi Kenmotsu.
Courtesy of Karl G. Yoneda Papers,
Department of Special Collections,
Charles E. Young Research Library,
University of California, Los Angeles.

on economic and political struggles," the JWA proclaimed. "We will work together with all anti-capitalist groups such as trade unions and socialist, communist, anarchist, and syndicalist organizations; we refuse to work with pacifists, reformists, and the like . . . we are against nationalism, imperialism, racism, as well as colonialism and semi-colonialism . . . we will teach and advocate to the proletariat how to achieve this transition from a capitalist to a socialist society . . . the JWA declares that our work cannot be accomplished without the support and help of all working people." Kenmotsu focused on spreading that revolutionary message, including as the editor of *Kaikyusen* (Class War).[31]

Kenmotsu and the JWA inherited a radical tradition begun two decades earlier by early Japanese migrants. Building on anarchist and socialist critiques of the Russo-Japanese War (1904–5) in Japan, a group of radicalized Japanese in the San Francisco Bay Area had organized the Social Revolutionary Party (Shakai Kakumeitō) in 1906. The party's newspaper, *Kakumei* (Revolution), openly embraced anarchism and direct action, extolling the "bomb" as "the means to harvest the revolution." In November 1907, on a Japanese holiday commemorating the emperor's birthday, some members penned a public letter mocking myths of his divine origins. "When revolutions arise, it is not because someone brings them about; they arise naturally," they warned. "And terrorism comes at the end of the process." Promising to study anarchist tactics employed in Russia and France, the letter concluded with a threat. "Mutsuhito, pitiful Mutsuhito, your life will not be long," they wrote to the emperor. "A bomb planted beside you will soon explode. Farewell!" Although the letter offended most Japanese living in the United States and led to internal divisions and state repression, including the Japanese consulate's call for deportation, the Social Revolutionary Party's brief existence helped to launch in 1908 a labor movement among Japanese agricultural workers in Fresno, California. With upwards of two thousand members, the Labor League challenged the labor contracting system, allied with the IWW, and published *Rōdō* (Labor), integrating pragmatic organizing and revolutionary theorizing. "We must go one more step forward and destroy the private property system which always spawns unemployment and poverty," *Rōdō* stated.[32]

The communist movement revived those incipient efforts at radical politics and labor organizing that resonated with a new generation of activists. Born in 1906 to Japanese parents who had fled plantation labor in Hawai'i, only to discover the grueling labor of California's agricultural fields, Karl G. Yoneda spent his adolescent years in Japan, where he became acquainted with anarchism, Marxism, and the labor movement. With his US birth certificate in hand, he returned to California in 1926 to escape military service. "To me," he recalled later, "I was leaving for a big, rich, and far away imperialist country where I could take temporary refuge from the Japanese Imperial Army." When a fellow resident at a boardinghouse introduced Yoneda to the JWA, he felt an instant affinity. Soon afterward, he attended a CP meeting on May Day 1927, where he heard speakers rail against "the dirty tricks of US imperialists in China, Mexico, and Nicaragua." Yoneda joined the party right away, "with a feeling of ease among the JWA members and hundreds of whites, Mexicans, and Negroes, men, women, and children." With fellow Japanese, including many women, Yoneda organized a Japanese branch of the International Labor Defense (ILD), a CP-affiliated organization devoted to the legal defense of victims of state repression and racial violence. And, inspired by Saturday night lessons on the history of the Fresno Labor League and plantation strikes in Hawai'i, the JWA began a campaign to organize agricultural workers.[33]

In southern California, as in valleys up and down the Pacific Coast, Yoneda and fellow organizers contended with a shifting racial landscape in the late 1920s, with white labor leaders and armed white mobs targeting Filipino workers in particular. "The Filipinos are probably more objectionable than either the Chinese or Japanese," argued Paul Scharrenberg, a California labor leader spearheading the anti-Filipino movement. They carried "many diseases" and claimed "an unlimited right to enter the country." Although some Japanese residents felt an "uneasiness" about becoming displaced by Filipino workers, Scharrenberg wondered why others believed that "friendship between the two peoples is possible and that it will be mutually beneficial, particularly to the Japanese." The specter of Japanese-Filipino solidarity resurfaced, now on the other side of the Pacific. While Scharrenberg lobbied for Filipino exclusion, within the AFL ranks and in political circles, white vigilantes in the Yakima Valley, Washington, decided to "deport" Filipinos in their midst. Enraged by rumors of Filipino men harassing and seducing white women and white girls in the fall of 1927, armed gangs descended on Filipino workers and warned them that "they would be hung if found in the valley after dark." Almost immediately, members of Kapatirang Magsasaka, a peasant organization popular in Bulacan, Pampanga, Tarlac, and Nueva Ecija in central Luzon, passed a unanimous resolution protesting the racial violence against their compatriots and called on US President Calvin Coolidge "to take the necessary action to remedy the deplorable condition of the Filipino laborers" in Yakima.[34]

To address the anti-Asian forces that Japanese and Filipino workers faced, the JWA attempted to forge a pan-Asian movement. Its members formed the Japanese Agricultural Workers' Organizing Committee (JAWOC) in 1928, in part because the CP leadership exhibited little interest in organizing agricultural workers and focused instead on trying to work with and through racist AFL unions. Though centered on organizing Japanese workers, the JAWOC recognized immediately the need to form interracial alliances. "Despite language barriers," Yoneda observed, "we also made contact with workers in Filipino and Mexican camps and learned of the working conditions in them." After the campaign yielded notable wage agreements in southern California, the JWA demanded greater support from the CP. At a district convention in January 1929, Kenmotsu expressed his frustration with the CP leaders in California. "I ask now, on behalf of the Asiatic races and exploited workers," he said, "that the CEC [Central Executive Committee] representative report the situation to the NO [National Office] and urge that in the future a strong effort be made to build a real revolutionary Asiatic [sic] Movement in the US of America, and establish a District here with a District organizer capable of fulfilling his revolutionary and Communistic duties." In the meantime, Kenmotsu corresponded with Sen Katayama in Moscow, keeping the veteran communist apprised of struggles in the United States. Under pressure from the Comintern and the Profintern, and with JWA representatives present, the CP launched the Trade Union Unity League (TUUL) in September 1929, a more radical union project potentially encompassing Japanese and Filipino agricultural workers.[35]

In addition to shared daily struggles in agricultural work, Kenmotsu sought to highlight a transpacific critique of empire to cultivate a pan-Asian consciousness in the United States. In the spring of 1929, he proposed a "Pan-American Fraction Convention" of Japanese workers across North America and Hawai'i, hoping that the movement would soon "spread among the Asian workers along the Pacific Coast" who were largely "unorganized, and from colonies or partial colonies." When a regional conference of the All-America Anti-Imperialist League (AAAIL) took place in San Francisco, Kenmotsu tried to organize a local "Anti-Imperial Alliance," with "a number of delegates from the Asian community—party fraction members from China, India, the Philippines, Korea, and other places." He also maintained connections with communist movements across the Pacific, arranging for the publication of pamphlets and handbills in Japanese to ship to comrades in Japan, where violent anticommunism arose alongside imperial militarism. Kenmotsu and the JWA organized and participated in a series of rallies and actions against Japan's military campaigns in China, including handing out antiwar leaflets to members of the Japanese Imperial Navy docked in Seattle, San Francisco, and San Pedro. In August 1929, at an antiwar rally in Los Angeles, thousands of people—"about twenty-five hundred workers, students, housewives," according to Yoneda—shouted "Down with US and Japanese Imperialism" and "Fight Against Imperialist War." In San Francisco, Kenmotsu helped to lead demonstrations against Japanese imperialism in China and US imperialism in Haiti. He was arrested on both occasions.[36]

Though a distinct minority among CP members and within Japanese American communities, the JWA's radical efforts at pan-Asian solidarity and anticolonial mobilization caught the attention of law enforcement agencies. Especially over the previous decade, in cities like Los Angeles, local police departments had established "red squads" to monitor, harass, and repress leftist organizations and labor activists. On July 27, 1929, after a public street meeting in Japantown, Yoneda went to Tetsuji Horiuchi's room to discuss their plans to distribute antiwar leaflets to Japanese naval crews. All of a sudden, Yoneda recalled, William "Red" Hynes and his notorious red squad (formally the Intelligence Bureau) of the Los Angeles Police Department "burst into the room, confiscated the leaflets, and took us to city prison where we were

FIGURE 25. The Los Angeles Police Department attacks Karl Yoneda (also known as Karl Hama). Photograph from "Police Have Dampening Influence on Red Demonstration on Main Street," *Los Angeles Times*, February 11, 1931.

charged with vagrancy." "Too bad, you were born here," Hynes reportedly told Yoneda, "otherwise, we'd send you back to Japan." A judge later dismissed those cases, but other JWA members confronted another set of charges because they had been born in Japan. After Kenmotsu's arrest in December 1929—by a San Francisco police officer "assigned from the office of the chief to assist in ferreting out and deporting all aliens who fall into the toils of the law"—his case was transferred to US immigration authorities. Police repression, Kenmotsu stated, was becoming "extreme," with anyone presumed to be a foreign-born CP member facing arrest. The seizure of an ILD address book made matters worse. "Since then," he observed, "the dogs' [police] searching has turned evil and has intensified more than ever."[37]

Like Chinese and Filipino communists in the Philippines, radical Japanese activists in the incorporated states of the US empire became ensnared in laws on sedition and immigration dating back to the Philippine-American War era. Kenmotsu was charged with violating an immigration law passed in October 1918, toward the end of World War I, that reinforced the US state's authority to exclude and deport "anarchists." Reinforcing the earlier proscription of anarchists in 1903, the law targeted:

aliens who are members of or affiliated with any organization that entertains a belief in, teaches, or advocates the overthrow by force or violence of the Government of the United States or of all forms of law, or that entertains or teaches disbelief in or opposition to all organized government, or that advocates the duty, necessity, or propriety of the unlawful assaulting or killing of any officer or officers, either of specific individuals or of officers generally, of the Government of the United States or of any other organized government, because of his or their official character, or that advocates or teaches the unlawful destruction of property shall be excluded from admission into the United States.

There was no statute of limitation in the new law, making it "applicable to the classes of aliens mentioned in this Act irrespective of the time of their entry into the United States." Two days after his arrest in December 1929, in San Francisco's city prison, Kenmotsu readily admitted to his CP membership, but did that affiliation make him deportable?[38]

US immigration authorities sought to cast the CP's stand against imperialism and militarism as an act of sedition against the US government. When T. V. Donoghue, the examining inspector, asked what the CP did, Kenmotsu replied matter-of-factly that it "teaches the people to contradict the present social system." Donoghue took advantage of that answer to frame the CP as a seditious organization that strove "to change the form of Government in the United States." "It desires to change the form of Government not only in the United States but all over the world," Kenmotsu responded. "If the United States were in war today would you take arms to fight for the United States?" Donoghue followed. Kenmotsu equivocated. The CP, he believed, "would teach the people the cause of the war" and, if "it was a war just against the interest of the workers, the people would not support the war." Donoghue concluded the interrogation by introducing a series of placards displayed at the CP rally where Kenmotsu was arrested, including those that read "Answer the bosses' attack; join the communist party" and "Trade Union Unity League Organizes the Unorganized." The case against Kenmotsu rested foremost on a single placard: "Turn Imperialist War into Civil War Against American Imperialism." Asked to explain what that sign meant, Kenmotsu did not equivocate. "Imperialist war is a war against the working class," he said. "Therefore that war should . . . be turned into a civil war against American Imperialism."[39]

Kenmotsu's steadfast repudiation of national allegiances sealed his fate. He did not hesitate to affirm Donoghue's paraphrasing of his views—that "a civil war of the working class be waged against the policies of the American Government, known as American imperialism." In a supplementary interrogation, Kenmotsu clarified that he had "never been in a civil war or had any connection with one." But the struggle against imperialism, he believed, meant "not only the United States but the whole world." To Kenmotsu and other JWA members, communism stood for a transpacific movement against empire, but, to Donoghue and the US state, anticolonialism represented sedition. If the United States entered a war that CP members considered "imperialistic," Donoghue asked, would they "encourage the workers of the United States to arm themselves against the Government with the object of overthrowing it?" "I do not know what the party will do in the war but I do know that while I am a member I will do what the party says," Kenmotsu replied. US immigration authorities had heard enough. That the CP used the same anticolonial and antiwar placards elsewhere, as Kenmotsu's attorney pointed out, did not matter. On March 4, 1930, the secretary of labor's office issued a warrant for Kenmotsu's deportation to Japan. Denied a writ of habeas corpus by a federal district court and then the circuit court of appeals over the next nine months, Kenmotsu was running out of options. If deported to Japan, he knew that he would face "extreme penalties."[40]

Ordered out of the United States and fearing a return to Japan, Kenmotsu searched desperately for a new home. He initially petitioned "to go to Germany at his own expense," to study "German methods" of commerce. Assured by the Japanese consul, who had been inquiring about his case, that Kenmotsu, as a known communist, would only "be questioned and be under surveillance continually" in Japan, the US commissioner general of immigration denied the request. In March 1931, the US Supreme Court declined to review Kenmotsu's appeal for a writ of habeas corpus. In addition to filing a second petition for a writ of habeas corpus, Kenmotsu then requested permission to leave voluntarily for the Soviet Union, a request the commissioner general rejected summarily. Although the court system continued to rule against Kenmotsu and the Japanese consulate refused to extend his passport or to issue a visa to the Soviet Union, US immigration authorities grew tired of the case. They wanted Kenmotsu out of the United States, expeditiously. In November 1931, Kenmotsu received permission "to depart voluntarily from the United States to Russia at his own expense," provided that he surrender immediately to local immigration officers, pay for his detention and transportation until the final departure, and leave the United States within thirty days. Kenmotsu spent his last days in the United States imprisoned at the immigration station on Angel Island—for which the US government billed him $27.61—before boarding a ship on December 16, 1931, bound for Germany and thence to the Soviet Union.[41]

Though isolated on Angel Island, Kenmotsu appreciated that his personal struggles related to a wider, collective struggle against imperialism. In late November 1931, CP members from California sent him a telegram with "proletarian greetings" and reminded him of the party's work to release "all class war prisoners," including the "Scottsboro Boys." Kenmotsu was especially grateful for the ILD's legal work to save him "from the deportation to Japan, the fascist country." On his last day in the United States, he penned a letter to his ILD comrades. "I realize by this that I am in the hands of you, namely, I belong to you— to the revolutionary movement," he wrote. "I pledge here to continue the revolutionary movement up to the end." He was excited that "Japanese imperialism" had stirred "the Chinese masses" and that he was headed to the Soviet Union, "where workers and farmers rule." He was going home, far from the place of his birth and the place of his incarceration, "to Our Fatherland upon whom every imperialist country is preparing to attack." He was ready to defend, "with you in America, Our Workers' Fatherland against the Imperialism." In Kenmotsu's eyes, Japan and the United States looked like a common enemy, two capitalist and anticommunist states advancing empire across Asia and the Pacific. But he remained hopeful. "US Government succeeded to deport me due to the reason that I belong to our Communist Party," he stated. "But the government is unable to 'deport' our party and its movement which has the historical necessity and importance."[42]

During the US government's pursuit of Kenmotsu's deportation, anti-Filipino violence took a deadly turn in California that brought to the fore the colonial status of Filipino workers. Cries of Filipino men as a racial and sexual menace to white workers and white women grew louder in the last months of 1929, when the stock market crash symbolized and precipitated a global crisis in capitalism. Near Watsonville, California, the opening of a new taxi dance hall, featuring white female dancers and catering to Filipino male workers, in January 1930 infuriated local white residents, hundreds of whom organized themselves into "Filipino hunting parties." Roving gangs of armed white men threatened to burn down the dance hall—while calling police officers in their way as "Goo-goo lovers"—and unloaded their weapons at bunkhouses full of Filipino occupants and, in one instance, Japanese occupants. On a ranch three miles south of Watsonville, Fermin Tobera was shot dead. Filipinos sent telegrams to Philippine and US officials in Washington, DC, pleading for immediate protection. "Every home and club were attacked by rioters; property destroyed and lives endangered," a group of Filipinos wrote from Watsonville. "Authorities cannot stop. Your immediate attention is most urgent to protect our lives." In addition to Tobera's death, others reported that wounded Filipinos were "mistreated at hospital by doctors and nurses." Within days, Pablo Manlapit organized a mass meeting of Filipinos in Los Angeles to demand intervention by US and California officials because "the Filipino people cannot protect themselves by reason of having no national government."[43]

Through the Young Communist League (YCL), the CP of California attempted to address the violence in Watsonville, but its didactic class analysis failed to critique the pressing reality of white supremacy and empire that had defined the communist movement for many Filipino, Chinese, and Japanese workers across the Pacific. Like Manlapit, the YCL arrived in Watsonville shortly after the mob attacks, to assess the situation and to organize agricultural workers. "The dancing hall incident was only the smoke screen," a YCL circular stated. "The Watsonville attack on the Filipinos arises out of the bosses' schemes, to incite them against one another in order to split the workers' forces, to keep them from organize [sic] together and demand for better conditions in the fields." The circular ironically fixated on the distinction between "Filipino workers" and "American workers," explaining how "farm owners" used "the Filipino workers as a means of forcing down the standard of living of the American workers," even as it noted that Filipino workers were "militant" in their struggles for Philippine independence and labor unionization. In the end, the YCL's parallel messages to "Filipino workers" and "American workers"—not to organize against the other but to recognize their common enemy, the "owners of the fruit companies and the big farms and their tools"—scarcely captured the urgency of what Filipino workers were experiencing. They were scared for their lives. Almost the last thing they wanted to hear was that "AN INJURY TO THE AMERICAN WORKERS IS AN INJURY TO THE FILIPNO WORKERS!"[44]

The communist movement around the world meant different things to different peoples, shaped by the contradictions of local histories, revolutionary theories, and grassroots solidarities. To Kenmotsu and the JWA, the communist movement afforded them an opportunity to reject Japanese imperialism and to cultivate pan-Asian solidarities in California and across the Pacific. Incongruous edicts from CP leaders in the United States to subsume their efforts to the national organization's agenda—to break up the "nationalistic isolation of foreign-born workers," a perverse variation of "Americanization"—and to focus on supporting the Japanese Communist Party did not necessarily mesh with their immediate priorities, their lived experiences. What resonated with them were the ILD's legal work against deportations and TUUL's organizing work among agricultural workers. Shortly after Kenmotsu's deportation, Hynes and his squad raided a CP meeting in Long Beach in January 1932 and arrested the participants en masse. Although criminal charges of "unlawful assembly" against forty-five individuals were dismissed, US immigration authorities decided to deport eleven of those without US citizenship, including nine Japanese and Okinawans. With the ILD's support, the nine subjects of the Japanese empire were able to follow Kenmotsu's path to the Soviet Union. At the same time, TUUL-affiliated Agricultural Workers Industrial League (AWIL) galvanized the labor movement, counting Japanese, Mexican, and Filipino workers in California among the most ardent and militant members. In the throes of political repression and racial violence, those aspects of the communist movement gave them hope, a hope exceeding the bounds of white supremacy and empire.[45]

KILLING A REVOLUTIONARY UPRISING

The news of Tobera's murder in January 1930 incensed Filipinos across the US empire. From provinces all over the Philippines, they registered their outrage through public resolutions and collective organizing. The Veterans of the Revolution in Silay, Negros Occidental, stated sarcastically that "if the Filipinos stayed and looked for jobs in California, it is because the American Flag and the Constitution of the United States gives them and guarantees them the right to do so, as long as the Filipinos continue to be under the well known American philantrophic [sic] regime." In light of the "atrocities" in California, they resolved that the US Congress "admit the failure of our relations between countries and between races and to agree with the Filipino people that the most appropriated [sic] resolution for the American leadership and idealisms in the Philippines is the granting of immediate and absolute independence of these Islands." Even the Chamber of Commerce of the Philippine Islands called for "such measures as may be necessary to check such abuses and to indemnify, if possible, the damages caused." In Manila and in towns across central Luzon and California, thousands of Filipinos gathered on February 2, 1930, to honor Tobera and to commemorate "National Humiliation Day." Fifteen thousand people showed up at Manila's Luneta Park. As Tobera's remains crossed the Pacific, popular condemnations of the US empire grew louder, augmented by thousands of Manila high school students who staged walkouts and rallies against an American teacher who had called Filipinos "savages."[46]

Benigno Ramos, a staff member in the Philippine Senate with ties to Quezon and the Nacionalista Party, joined the protests, feeling and articulating the anticolonial sentiments around him. Forced to resign from his post when he refused to follow Quezon's order to discontinue his anti-American and antigovernment speeches, Ramos began publishing *Sakdal* (To Accuse) in June 1930, a newspaper written mostly in Tagalog to reach a wider audience. Ramos and his newspaper soon received the support of Artemio Ricarte, then exiled in Japan, a personal association that bolstered Ramos's invocation of the 1896 Philippine Revolution. Over the next several years, Ramos and his allies and supporters organized boycotts of foreign goods, formed a loosely organized political group called Malayang Bayan (Free Nation), and joined forces with others demanding immediate and complete independence, including the PKP. When the US Congress passed the Hare-Hawes-Cutting Act in December 1932 and then overrode a presidential veto a month later, the nascent Sakdalista movement raised funds to send Ramos to Washington, DC, to protest the law's terms of measured and limited independence, underscored by a ten-year transition as a "commonwealth." In March 1933, Ramos left for the metropole, passing through Shanghai, Yokohama (where he met with Ricarte), Honolulu, and California, and finding at every stop Filipino audiences receptive to his message against compromise and gradualism. Largely ignored by US politicians, Ramos returned to the Philippines six months later, determined to challenge Quezon, his former mentor, and the political status quo. He announced his plans to organize the Sakdalista Party.[47]

Amid rival claims to champion national independence, the Sakdalista Party emerged quickly as a popular alternative to established fixtures in Philippine politics. While anticommunism had driven the PKP underground, debates over the Hare-Hawes-Cutting Act split the Nacionalista Party into two factions—"Antis" and "Pros"—that culminated in the Philippine Legislature's rejection of the act in October 1933. Quezon, who led the "Antis," soon departed for Washington, DC, to try to negotiate a better agreement. Attacking the political elite and wealthy landowners, the Sakdalista Party promised to work toward immediate independence and legal reforms to aid indebted peasants and other common Filipinos. Within months, Sakdalista chapters appeared across central and southern Luzon and spread to parts of Ilocos, Bicol, and the Visayas. In the election of June 1934, despite a literacy requirement and other obstacles to the ballot, Sakdalista candidates made an impressive debut, winning three seats in the national legislature, the governorship of Marinduque, and many municipal offices in Laguna, Bulacan, Nueva Ecija, Rizal, and Cavite. Shortly before that election, the Philippine Legislature had endorsed the Tydings-McDuffie Act, the law enacted by the US Congress and President Franklin D. Roosevelt in March 1934. Though touted by Quezon, the terms of the new agreement toward "complete independence" differed little in substance from the Hare-Hawes-Cutting Act. The United States retained "supreme authority" over the Philippines during a ten-year "commonwealth" phase, but, in response to growing calls for Filipino exclusion, Filipinos immediately became "aliens" from a "foreign country" in immigration matters. The Sakdalista Party opposed the Tydings-McDuffie Act.[48]

Even as the Sakdalista Party engaged in electoral politics, Sakdalista politics encompassed rhetorics and tactics that disrupted political norms legitimizing the US empire. Electoral rallies in June 1934 turned into fiery demonstrations against the Tydings-McDuffie Act, where Sakdalista leaders urged their supporters to boycott the upcoming election of delegates to draft a constitution for the Philippine Commonwealth. With Quezon's forces firmly in control of the legislature and the constitutional convention, which was in session from July 1934 to February 1935, the transition to commonwealth status appeared inevitable, but Philippine officials became wary of Sakdalista influences on ordinary Filipinos. The number of students enrolled in public schools in San Ildefonso and San Jose del Monte decreased sharply, a superintendent of schools reported from Bulacan, because of the Sakdals' "very pernicious objectives and procedures." Their "propaganda" instructed residents not to pay taxes, not to attend schools using English, and not to cooperate "with the present government so that a change in the form of the present government can be brought about." Ramos's absence from the Philippines also caused consternation. In December 1934, contrary to his earlier announcement of making another trip to the United States, Ramos relocated to Japan and began consorting with prominent exponents of Japanese fascism and imperialism. The days of pleading with the US empire were over, he declared. As with Ricarte earlier, reports and rumors of Ramos's designs to secure weapons from Japan to incite an armed uprising in the Philippines began to circulate.[49]

Long before then, US colonial authorities and their Philippine collaborators had classified the Sakdalista movement as seditious. In its early days, the newspaper *Sakdal* shared with the PKP the same printing press and similar hopes for Philippine liberation and defended PKP leaders as they faced state surveillance and criminal prosecution. The anticommunist crusade did not bode well for the Sakdalista movement. In 1931, the director of the Philippine Bureau of Posts banned the mailing of *Sakdal,* a decision upheld by the Philippine Supreme Court. In response to the ACLU's complaint that the freedom of the press ought to protect calls for Philippine independence, the US War Department refused to intervene, based on a report that "the paper preached sedition by advising hauling down American Flag, non use of Coat of Arms of United States on Court papers, getting rid of American Army and Navy and notifying the Governor General he no longer is Governor General but a guest." Writing for the department, Chief F. LeJ. Parker of the Bureau of Insular Affairs also referred the matter as falling within "local autonomy." Charges of sedition likewise dogged the Sakdalista Party. Quezon, for his part, unleashed personal attacks against Ramos, particularly after the June 1934 elections. "All you have done is cause the death of Filipinos," Ramos shot back in an open letter, "preparing them for total slavery, filling the hands of the greedy, and stealing money that should rightfully go to the people." The Philippine Constabulary kept close tabs on Sakdalista meetings and speeches.[50]

On the eve of a plebiscite on the new constitution, scheduled for May 14, 1935, the Sakdalista movement intensified its condemnation of the Tydings-McDuffie Act and the colonial order. In part to evade repeated postal bans, a new Sakdalista publication appeared on April 1, 1935, titled *Free Filipinos,* that scoffed at the absurdity of "independence" under US sovereignty. "How many 'Ten Years' does the US government need to kill our independence and to confiscate all the lands of the Filipinos?" the newspaper asked pointedly. "How many 'Ten Years' does this 'very benevolent' government need to Hawaiianize our country?" Calling Governor-General Frank Murphy "Frankenstein" who would lose his "princely life" after Philippine independence, another column derided Quezon and other Philippine politicians as "slaves" of "American interests." The Philippine Commonwealth would be a farce, conferring "*independence* for these suckers and *slavery* for the masses." Consistent with the Sakdalistas' more recent efforts to distance themselves from the proscribed communist movement, *Free Filipinos* proclaimed its opposition to communism, even as it acknowledged anticommunism as a ruse "to prepare the ground for future persecutions of the real defenders of Filipino Liberty." Rather than Moscow, communist internationalism, and proletarian revolution, the Sakdalista movement looked to Japan, pan-Asian solidarity, and cultural tradition. "The Sakdalistas stand for revival of Filipino oriental family tradition, oriental culture and civilization," *Free Filipinos* declared, "and for the attainment of a strong and eternal union between all countries of the Far

SOME OF THE FILIPINO PATRIOTS AND HEROES WITH
DR. JOSE RIZAL IN THE CENTER

Brave and patriotic—like the Samurays of the old—these Filipinos gave their lives for the Freedom of their Country. The independence movement of the Filipinos is a series of long unceasing struggles, hardships, sacrifices, tears and bloodshed. Dr. Rizal was called a stupid agitator and shot by the tyrants of the Philippines, and even if now he is recognized as the national hero, still persists this stigma cast upon his name by the foreign domination for his country is under foreign subjugation. The fourth man in the last row is General Malvar of Batangas who fought the Americans and assumed the title of President of Philippine Republic after the capture of Aguinaldo.

FIGURE 26. Filipino "Samurays"? *Free Filipinos*, April 1, 1935. Courtesy of Joseph Ralston Hayden Papers, Bentley Historical Library, University of Michigan.

East." A pantheon of "Filipino Patriots and Heroes" were likened to "the Samurays of the old."[51]

In the US empire, as in the past, possible affiliations with Japan, even in insistently heteronormative terms, evoked something sinister, an "Oriental" menace that Ramos and the Sakdalista movement exploited. "I will not go any more to Washington," Ramos stated in *Free Filipinos*. "That is not the place for me nor for any Filipino who is really working for his country's freedom. I may go to Europe, South America, India, East Indies, Indo-China, China and other places and return again here to Japan, but never to United States. As long as we are under American control against our will, the United States *is not the place for us*." Ramos called out the US empire. "The United States destroyed the Filipino republic, tried to convert our people in[to] contented slaves, and their illegal government is showing to us what really they are to the Filipinos—real enemies." If Evangelista and the PKP were guilty of uttering seditious ideas, Ramos and the Sakdalistas were equally defiant, if not more so. *Free Filipinos* suggested that government operatives were spreading rumors of "a general uprising" to prosecute Sakdalistas. "But, we say now, if you do that, be careful, please," the newspaper warned. "For your folly might ignite the little fuse and cause the whole conflagration. The friars did that before in 1896 with the intention to complicate their enemies (the defenders of Filipino Emancipation), but history has it that they were the ones who opened their own graves. So be careful."[52]

The Sakdalistas' refusal to abide by the US empire's rules of political engagement frustrated and frightened those invested in collaborative colonialism. On April 2, 1935, Secretary of Agriculture and Commerce Eulogio Rodriguez sent a dire, confidential warning to Acting Governor-General Joseph Ralston Hayden—Murphy was in the United States for medical treatment—about "the intensive campaign of propaganda that the Sakdalistas, the Reds and other radicals are waging against the Government and its leaders in the city of Manila and in the provinces around and near it." In "seditious speeches," Rodriguez reported, they preached that "the people should revolt and drive away the leaders on December 31, 1935, and this should be accomplished by unity of the Filipino people who should stand and fight." Citing the successful repression of the communist movement, he recommended "a policy of firm and strong hand against these radical organizations by arresting all who may actually be committing violations of the law." Without vigorous and coordinated action "to counteract this wave of radicalism," Rodriguez feared that "the ignorant and the discontented elements" would be aroused to create "a situation which will be very difficult for the Government to cope with." The arrest of seven Sakdalistas in Tayabas for sedition, allegedly involving a plot to assassinate Quezon, raised the state of alarm. Then, on May 2, weeks and months ahead of most intelligence reports, Chief Basilio J. Valdes of the Constabulary learned of "a very serious situation." The Sakdalistas were about to wage an armed insurrection that very night.[53]

The Sakdalista uprising shook the Philippines in 1935, revealing a revolutionary, anticolonial yearning that had persisted and percolated under US colonial rule. Across fifteen villages and towns in Laguna, Bulacan, Cavite, Rizal, Nueva Ecija, and Tarlac, thousands of Sakdal members and their allies decided that the time had come to declare again the independence of the Philippines and to take over municipal governments before eventually moving onto the seat of the colonial regime in Manila. Beginning on the afternoon of May 2, Sakdalista insurgents mobilized with mostly makeshift weapons at their disposal— bolos and other knives, clubs, and some guns—and cut telegraph lines and blocked roads and railroads, confiscating guns and ammunition from cars that they stopped. As darkness fell, they captured municipal halls in Cabuyao and Santa Rosa in Laguna and San Ildefonso in Bulacan and replaced the Stars and Stripes with flags representing the Philippine Republic and the Sakdalista Party. "We came in because we understood that if we captured the town we could have our independence," explained Nasario Javier. "The Jones Law promised independence so we came in to take it." They had grown tired of waiting and compromising. "I want immediate independence so we can show ourselves on equal terms with other countries," Isabelo P. Fuentes, a fifty-three-year-old man, stated. "It would be sweet to my heart to have independence, even if I with my children suffer every kind of hardship. I am a Sakdal, don't know why I was arrested."[54]

If the Sakdalistas faced formidable odds, they concluded that their odds would not improve under continued US colonial rule as a commonwealth. "We were faithful to the old leaders a long time," Salud Algabre, a Sakdal leader, explained. "We contributed to Quezon to get independence," she said. "We wanted to see independence before we die, so we changed leaders." To many in the Sakdal movement, that was a more viable option than retaining a faith in a politics of collaboration. "I am opposed to the Constitution because they say we won't get our independence under it," said Eriberto Jaurigue, a young farmer. "I'm opposed to the leaders who promised independence for 27 years and didn't get it." Beyond mounting frustration with US officials and Philippine politicians, the Sakdalistas saw a ray of hope in Ramos's exile in Japan and in armed Filipinos within the US security apparatus. Shortly before the uprising, Algabre's brother, another Sakdal leader, met a man "introduced as a captain of Scouts," who said that "Ramos would come with 100 airplanes and plenty of arms and ammunition" by the morning of May 3 and that "the Scouts and Constabulary would assist in taking over the government." And history seemed to be on their side. In Cabuyao, the Sakdalista rebellion took place in the shadow of a prominent statue of José Rizal and a street named after Father José Burgos. The memorials to the two martyrs served as daily reminders to Cabuyao's residents, even if only subconsciously, of a long anticolonial tradition.[55]

The spirit of Rizal and Burgos failed to sway the Constabulary in Cabuyao, where the exhilaration of revolution quickly gave way to the horror of counterrevolution. With cries of "Mabuhay ang Republica Filipina (Long Live the Philippine Republic)," hundreds of Sakdalistas took over the town plaza and drove away the police. After spending all night stopping cars and confiscating weapons, Algabre set out to prepare food with other women to feed fellow revolutionaries early in the morning on May 3. The revolution seemed at hand. They felt euphoric. In the meantime, Governor Juan Cailles of Laguna, who had once fought against US forces, led a Constabulary detachment to Cabuyao and instructed the insurgents to surrender. The Sakdalistas refused and retreated to a church yard protected by a stone wall. Positioned behind the Rizal statue and a band stand, Cailles and thirty-two soldiers and five officers of the Constabulary unloaded their arsenal. "When the firing came I laid on my face because I was afraid," a Sakdal said. "I couldn't run because those who stood up were falling down after being shot. All standing up near me were shot down." Journalists who arrived soon afterward saw "one of the ghastliest scenes": "Dying and wounded with agony written all over their faces, mutilated bodies, torn breasts, ripped thighs and ghastly figures of those who succumbed in the fight." In less than two hours of fighting, the Constabulary killed fifty-three Sakdalistas and wounded nineteen others. It was a bloodbath, a massacre.[56]

The armed uprising and its brutal repression alarmed US officials, whose fear of radical anticolonialism competed with their hope for collaborative colonialism. An investigative committee of US military officers appointed by Acting Governor-General Hayden reflected those seemingly complementary objectives in a rushed report, completed in less than two weeks' time. Chaired by Major George C. Dunham, the committee blamed the "radical wing" of the Sakdalista Party, "the leaders of which do teach that the ratification of the Constitution and the establishment of the Commonwealth Government should be prevented by force, if necessary." Most of the insurgents, the committee argued, were "simple barrio folks, ignorant of political matters, and easily swayed by emotional appeals however illogical such appeals may be." Although the report criticized local police and municipal authorities for abandoning their duties, it generally praised the Constabulary's "discipline" and "efficiency." "No instance of inhumane treatment by the Constabulary could be found," they concluded. Dunham, however, dissented in a minority report critical of the Constabulary's resort to excessive and lethal force in Cabuyao, a response that he feared "would inflame the general population and engender a widespread hatred of the constabulary and the government and by increasing the number of adherents and sympathizers of the radical movement increase the resistance to government authority." Edward G. Kemp, Governor-General Murphy's longtime confidante, was thankful at least that Filipino soldiers had carried out the violence. "With bloodshed apparently inevitable," he informed Murphy, "it is perhaps fortunate that it was entirely on Filipino responsibility and not American."[57]

Censuring "radical" Sakdal leaders and negligent Filipino soldiers reinforced the racial premise of Filipinization that shielded and vindicated US colonial rule under the banner of benevolent tutelage. In his appendix on the "Political, Economic and Social Background of the Filipino People," Louis J. Van Schaick of the investigative committee celebrated what he saw as "vast changes" enabled by US colonialism: "The groups of naked, potbellied, underfed children with loathsome skin diseases that lined the mudhole trails disappeared. . . . The standard of living for a majority of the people has been raised enormously; and benefits have accrued to all in transportation, education, mail and the protection of civil rights." Despite that progress, Filipinos had "been taught to look forward to complete, absolute and immediate independence," Van Schaick added, with "the more ignorant of the masses hav[ing] grown to think of independence as a remedy for all their ills." He simultaneously respected and disparaged the Philippine elite, casting them as realistic and opportunistic. "The whole Filipino people want independence," he believed, "but the upper classes recognize the difficulties." The elite, however, were not yet ready to rule. In response to *Sakdal's* "disloyalty," US officials "adhered to the American principle of free speech and free assembly," but "local governments" simply prohibited Sakdal gatherings. In the end, Van Schaick found fault with "an aristocracy of office holders and land owners who find it necessary to exploit the poor to keep going." They had created the "fertile ground" that made the "barrio people" susceptible to the Sakdalista message.[58]

If the Sakdalista uprising helped to uphold the belief that the Philippines was not yet ready for independence, it also drove the colonial security state to reify longstanding perceived threats to the US empire: communism and Japan. The Dunham committee, for its part, admittedly could not find "any evidence of communism or radical socialism." The Philippine Constabulary projected otherwise and suggested instantly an insidious connection between Sakdalism and communism. Estimating 68,000 members across the provinces, G. B. Francisco, the Constabulary's chief of staff, insinuated that the Sakdalista Party had "communistic tendencies" and shared "the same fundamental principles as communism." "They believe in equal or common ownership of property and in the division of big land holdings of rich land-owners," he argued, implicitly in defense of the US state and capitalist development. In a separate report submitted to the Constabulary's adjutant general shortly before the Dunham committee report, Lieutenant Colonel Miguel Nicdao highlighted the unsettling messages that he had received days before the uprising. Sakdal leaders, he reported, had stated that "Japan is the only nation interested in the freedom of the Islands, and is the only country interested to see an independent Philippines." As news of "impending trouble" spread, Nicdao warned Constabulary officers to be ready. To the officer in charge of Bulacan, Pampanga, and Nueva Ecija, which were "apparently free from Sakdalism," he warned against a potentially wider rebellion, in case "the Communists . . . make a common cause with the Sakdals." Sakdalism raised the specter of Japan and communism joining forces against the US empire.[59]

A secret Sakdalista letter, written in the wake of the uprising, appeared to corroborate those fears, particularly in signaling a convergence between Sakdalism and communism. In an open letter addressed to "Comrades"—and recovered and translated by US officials—"Your Comrades of Bulacan" demanded "mass retribution" for the killing of "our brothers . . . by the mercenary forces at the service of this capitalistic Philippine Government, a government of thieves, hypocrites and successful bandits." They proposed the assassination of elite Filipinos—

"Mestizo adventurers," "organized robbers," "political degenerates"—as a means "to hasten the revolutionary explosion of truth and justice." The Sakdalista movement, the letter explained, would continue to recruit "among the ranks of the municipal police and the Constabulary soldiers," those "minor tools of capitalism" who were "exploited human beings like ourselves." The letter's authors anointed Ramos "the living incarnation of the revolt of the masses against man's inhumanity to man" and ridiculed Quezon as a "demagogue par excellence," "born embezzler," and "incest[u]ous animal" who sold "the people of the Philippine Islands . . . to the bosses and fat pigs of Wall Street." They recalled a history of "revolution and bloodshed," including the French Revolution and the American Revolution, but derided "American Democracy" of "degenerating into organized gan[g]sterism." The Bolshevik Revolution, in contrast, stood as "the glorious beginning of the Soviet ascendency, the boundary line between two ages." The Sakdalista uprising, they concluded, would likewise mark "the opening chapter of our social and political emancipation."[60]

THE EAST IS RED

As the US empire institutionalized collaborative colonialism and criminalized anticolonial communism in the Philippines, Sakdalism kept alive radical histories of anticolonial struggles. Perhaps more than the communist movement, Sakdalism attempted to reach ordinary Filipino working peoples, including efforts to recruit women. Evangelista had recognized the PKP's need to attract women, "to strengthen our movement and make it more lively," but his overtures yielded meager results. Though not a labor union, working peoples of the Philippines found in the Sakdalista movement new possibilities out of their past. On the eve of the uprising, the Sakdal publication, *Free Filipinos*, addressed Filipinas in particular by featuring photographs of women who had led the "people's revolt" in Tayug against "American domination" in 1931. Women like Salud Algabre, in turn, read and shared such articles with their neighbors and friends. "We talked to our friends," Algabre recalled. "We read copies of *Sakdal* to them and discussed common problems. We also spoke out against injustice." She emphatically rejected Japan's potential support as a factor behind the Sakdalista movement. "We did not expect help from Japan or from anywhere else," she explained. "It would be utter foolishness to lead the nation to war, particularly a war between America and Japan." In Algabre's mind, it was a local, organic

Land-grabbing, pauperization-system are the striking characteristics of American domination in the Philippines. The uprising in Tayug, province of Pangasinan which occurred on January 1st, 1931 was only one of the direct consequences of the people's stifled rights. Women assumed the leadership in this people's revolt, and these pictures show that they prefered death than to see their country still agonizing under American domination. Their bodies are no more, but their defeat in unequal struggle, their bravery and courage had open the eyes of the people in order to see the naked truth that even if there are Filipinos in this government, it is not Filipino government but American government, the enemy of the Filipinos welfare.

FIGURE 27. Tayug Uprising. *Free Filipinos*, April 1, 1935. Courtesy of Joseph Ralston Hayden Papers, Bentley Historical Library, University of Michigan.

uprising. "What we did was our heritage, from our fathers and our fathers' fathers," she argued. "My family has always resisted." She refused to believe that the Sakdals had failed. "No uprising fails," she insisted. "Each one is a step in the right direction."[61]

In the wake of the May uprising, Sakdalism, communism, and Japan seemed to fuse into a revolutionary menace against the US empire, a creation of Filipinos' unrelenting demands for liberation as much as the US security state's recurring charges of sedition. Ramos, for his part, welcomed support from Japan and anywhere else that might support Philippine independence. Days after the uprising, he told the Associated Press in Japan that he was contemplating a return to the Philippines. "I am confident I would be able to return without being caught," he said. "They can't catch me because they won't see me." Ramos dismissed the possibility of his extradition. He planned to go to Europe or South America, "where the common Spanish culture provides bonds of sympathy with the Philippines." The Japanese consul in the Philippines soon stated that Ramos would not be extradited, placing his case next to "several Hindus who are wanted by the British government." Those potential alliances beyond and against the US empire frightened officials in the US security apparatus, who began circulating reports of an imminent Japanese attack, in coordination with Sakdalistas and under the pretext of protecting "Japanese subjects" in the Philippines, and a revolutionary movement against the commonwealth's inauguration involving Sakdalistas, socialists, and communists in Manila and surrounding provinces. "It is also said that should the Governor-General refuse to heed their petition that the communists in the city will stage some kind of an uprising similar to that done by the Sakdalistas," a confidential memorandum warned.[62]

The legal repression of the Sakdalista movement could not contain the anticolonial rage fermenting in the Philippines. The mass arrest of more than a thousand Sakdalistas immediately after the uprising for sedition, rebellion, and other charges only added fuel to the rage. "I am ready to offer my life to the bosom of the Mother Country if it is forbidden by law to show heroism and love for freedom and independence," a Sakdalista leader proclaimed in a Cavite courtroom. Following Quezon's election to become the inaugural president of the Philippine Commonwealth in September 1935, hundreds and then thousands gathered at the home of Emilio Aguinaldo, who had waged a presidential bid as the head of the National Socialist Party. His campaign had reached out to Sakdalistas. "Agents report seditious talk and speeches and threats upon the life of Quezon, Osmeña and others," Vice-Governor Hayden learned. As Quezon surrounded himself with an elaborate security detail, rice shortages led to "rice riots" north of Manila. "Of course the communists, Sakdals, and other trouble makers are making the most of this situation," Hayden rued. Major Dunham predicted "a wave of revolt" that was "bound to break soon." The rural masses in the Philippines, he told Hayden, "see the Commonwealth as 10 years of exploitation by the gang in power (which means Quezon), with American soldiers suppressing any revolt against abuses." "The worst of it is," Hayden admitted, "that their picture is pretty nearly a true one."[63]

Hayden's lament exposed and underscored the racializing logics and colonizing dynamics of the US empire that had justified its violent reproduction for more than a century and that would guide its continual recalibration in the twentieth century. To advance "democracy," the US empire needed to protect the "natives" from their own impulses, characterized now in the Philippines by political corruption under Quezon or revolutionary anticolonialism affiliated with imperial Japan and communist internationalism. That defined US hegemony, a transpacific formation that amalgamated colonialism, anticommunism, and, in time, antifascism: both allies and enemies had to be contained. Hayden, a longtime academic expert on the Philippines, recognized the "wide and deep foundation of injustice and abuse, economic and political." "There is no remedy except economic and social changes that go to the very roots of Filipino life," he argued. But the Filipinization of politics, he believed, had left US officials "utterly incapable of affecting these changes." US claims to sovereignty over the Philippines seemingly made no difference. "After 36 years of sovereignty we put a group of Filipinos in virtually complete control of the government where they will operate a system that exploits the common man and where they will have to be maintained by American bayonets!" Hayden concluded. "And we shall be responsible for their actions." The maintenance of "American bayonets" and the installation of Quezon as the commonwealth's president would mean that the US empire, in power but somehow powerless, could deflect responsibility for the colonial order of things—to Quezon, to communism, to Sakdalism, to Japan.[64]

Quezon's dual attempts to appease and to criminalize Sakdalistas and communists amplified the cacophonous politics of the US empire. Rumors of another uprising haunted the first year of his presidency, punctuated by a series of bombings in October 1936 that some Sakdalistas hoped would incite a wider revolution. Quezon predictably turned to mass arrests, but he also periodically issued pardons to convicted Sakdalistas to win them over to what he began calling his program for "social justice" on behalf of the "common man." In addition, at the urging of communist leaders from the US metropole, he agreed to release imprisoned PKP members, including Evangelista. In the municipal and provincial elections of December 1937, the Sakdalista Party and the PKP worked with Aguinaldo's National Socialist Party and other anti-Quezon parties under the banner of the Popular Front. The anti-Quezon coalition, which included Nuclio Totalitario Filipino, a fascist organization, failed at the ballot box, a victim of its irreconcilable differences as much as Quezon's public gestures toward social reforms. Meanwhile, Ramos attempted to collaborate with Japanese fascists as a fellow "Oriental people," but, particularly after Japan's intensifying war against China in 1937, he became wary of Japan's imperial designs. Through secret channels, Quezon encouraged and facilitated Ramos's return to the Philippines in 1938, in an effort to enfold the Sakdalista movement into commonwealth politics. Ramos's renovation of the Sakdalista Party into the Ganap Party had that effect, but his statements favoring "Asia for the Asians" continued to suggest affiliations beyond and against the US empire.[65]

The reemergence of the PKP from the underground in 1938 also created strange bedfellows and strident condemnations that tended to repress revolutionary yearnings for freedom. As an emissary of the Communist Party of the United States of America, James S. Allen attempted to steer the PKP away from its "deeply sectarian and 'Leftist'" ethos toward a coalition politics against fascism, encouraging a merger with the Pampanga-based Socialist Party and a partnership with Quezon. At a national convention in October 1938, the PKP and the Socialist Party formally joined forces in the wider struggle against the "rapacious fascist and militarist powers" that were "engaged in a crusade against the democratic and peace-loving peoples." Communists in the Philippines henceforth vowed cooperation with the US empire, "one of the most democratic powers on the Pacific." In that Manichean world, Ramos could be little more than "an agent of the Japanese military-fascists," an enemy of "democracy," heralded now by the United States and Quezon. Irony reverberated everywhere. Soon driven from power and to the US metropole, where he would die in 1944, Quezon placed his faith in the US military during World War II. "I want also to assure you that the time of your redemption is fast approaching," he told fellow Filipinos. "America is gathering her strength in the Pacific, and soon General MacArthur will start the reconquest of our homeland."[66] But generations of revolutionaries struggling against the US empire knew the difference between redemption and reconquest. Communism, fascism, and "democracy," alongside anticommunism and antifascism, competed against one another for conquest and empire.

Conclusion

America Is Not in the Heart

For purely tactical purposes, the nisei will have to abandon
whatever pretext they have had for democracy, and to come
out unequivocally for the democracy we have left—which in
reality is only a superficial reality—and the ironical thing
about all this is that the whole program of "Americanism"
which we exhort so damn much is in essence a preliminary to
the very thing we are ostensibly fighting against—fascism.

—Hisaye Yamamoto, quoting K., January 5, 1941

When Carlos Bulosan, the Filipino author and labor organizer, heard
about Japan's bombing of the US colony of Hawai'i, he became filled
with dread and sorrow. He knew that the Philippines, a US colony called
a "commonwealth," would suffer a similar fate. Looking at a friend's son
in Los Angeles, Bulosan was reminded of his own childhood in the Philippines. "Will another war wreck your life?" he thought. "Will you be
another lost person on the earth?" Bulosan's account of those days and
weeks after the attack on Pearl Harbor contrasted sharply against the
buoyant optimism he had felt beforehand. Talking with a group of cannery workers—"Japanese, Mexicans, Filipinos, and white Americans"—
Bulosan realized that "we were all fighting against one enemy: *Fascism.*"
Through that struggle, he sensed that revolution and democracy were
within reach, "the one and only common thread that bound us together,
white and black and brown, in America." The war shattered that dream.
Childhood memories of the Philippines mixed together with "the frustration and bitterness of our life in America" to recall a history of racial
violence that had shaped Bulosan's life in the US empire. When Filipinos,
after being rejected as "aliens," were finally allowed to join the US

military, Bulosan wrote, "we had found a release for our desires." One by one, they enlisted, full of grief, not bluster. "I'm not going on a world-wide crusade to save democracy," Bulosan's brother told him as he joined the US Army "the day Corregidor fell to the Japanese."[1]

Though traveling in the same radical labor circles, Karl G. Yoneda reacted to the same news with conviction, even fanaticism. On behalf of a leftist Japanese American newspaper, he immediately drafted a telegram to President Franklin D. Roosevelt, to "pledge full cooperation in all endeavors to secure victory for the democracies." "We stand ready to join the ranks of the fighting forces under your command to defeat the vicious military fascists of Japan," the statement read. Before he could send the telegram, the Federal Bureau of Investigation (FBI) rounded up Yoneda and other prominent Japanese Americans, based on the suspicion of seditious activities. Upon his release three days later, he learned that the leadership of the Communist Party of the United States of America (CPUSA) had expelled all Japanese American members. Though "stunned" by the "anti-working class, racist edict," Yoneda decided not to protest. He kept his focus on the task at hand, "to help smash Japan's fascist-imperialists who were knocking at our very door!" As the US federal government moved closer and closer to incarcerating Japanese Americans en masse, Yoneda reiterated his commitment to US nationalism. "If deemed a military necessity that all . . . should be evacuated from military areas," he wrote to a congressional committee, "we are ready to go." He felt that Japanese Americans had "no choice but to accept the racist US dictum at that time over Hitler's ovens and Japan's military rapists of Nanking." "We would thrash out the question of our rights after victory," Yoneda rationalized.[2]

Months before the Japanese empire and the US empire went to war, Yoneda's communist affiliation had caught the US security state's attention. The FBI classified him as most likely a "secret agent for Japanese government" in April 1941 and launched an investigation three months later into his communist activities and his "criminal record for Criminal Syndicalism." Although he had been born in the United States, Yoneda's citizenship was listed as "not established" and "not known." The FBI also followed up on reports that he had been "deported in 1932, and that he illegally re-entered this country." Yoneda and his wife Elaine Black, a "well known Communist," were accordingly to be considered "for custodial detention in the event of a national emergency." On December 8, 1941, FBI agents surrounded their apartment with submachine guns and then arrested Yoneda and delivered him to the

Immigration and Naturalization Service. With his US citizenship confirmed, the Justice Department concluded that there was "not sufficient evidence upon which to institute a criminal prosecution against the subject at this time." But the department requested a "complete investigation" of Yoneda's communist connections, which were translated as support for Japanese fascism and imperialism. FBI Director J. Edgar Hoover instructed the special agent in charge of the San Francisco office to conduct the investigation with "preferred and expeditious attention." The FBI learned that Yoneda worked "all around the waterfront and on most transports" and that "the subject has been passing as a Chinaman."[3]

Yoneda's work on the waterfront and in the labor movement, work that necessarily involved close association with Filipino workers, magnified the perception that he posed a threat to US national security, which was US imperial security. On Christmas Eve 1941, the Office of Naval Intelligence (ONI) circulated a confidential report on the Cannery Workers and Farm Laborers Union (CWFLU), a union affiliated with the Congress of Industrial Organizations (CIO) that Yoneda, Bulosan, and legions of Filipino and Japanese workers had organized before the war. "While the Japanese membership of subject union . . . is numerically inferior to the Filipino," the report stated, "it is obvious that the Japanese are in control of key positions and have utilized the union as a front for activities far removed from the demands of normal cannery business." Listing Yoneda's name atop the list of union officers under suspicion, the ONI suggested that "the union's connections with the West Coast Japanese consulates, Army and Navy agents . . . and other suspects have been more than coincidental." The union appeared to be part of "a highly integrated and specialized intelligence network" established by the Japanese government. "Under such circumstances," the report concluded, "Japanese nationals and pro-Japanese *nisei* who are well settled in normal and yet strategic occupations are likely to be the mainstay of Japanese espionage-sabotage operations in this country." In Yoneda and the CWFLU, as in the Philippines for decades earlier, the US security state saw a pan-Asian movement against the US empire.[4]

Rather than disrupting the racialization of Japanese Americans as a seditious threat, Yoneda's unmitigated support of the US government had the opposite effect. Beginning in December 1941, Yoneda served as a voluntary informant to the FBI, offering, unsolicited, "several reports to the San Francisco office of Japanese individuals whom he believed pro-Japanese in sympathies." His incarceration in Manzanar, one of the concentration camps operated by the War Relocation Authority (WRA),

FIGURE 28. Karl Yoneda and family, April 17, 1943. Courtesy of Karl G. Yoneda Papers, Special Collections, Charles E. Young Research Library, University of California, Los Angeles.

failed to loosen Yoneda's embrace of US nationalism. In the summer of 1942, he pleaded with WRA officials to segregate Japanese Americans by "loyalty" and citizenship, prefiguring and promoting WRA policies that aligned with his bifurcating worldview of enemies and allies. "I believe that the government has made a serious mistake in putting American citizens of Japanese ancestry together with undesirable enemy aliens," Yoneda argued. "I would say that 90 percent of the Issei are for Japan and no self-government democratic set-up will change their

FIGURE 29. Carlos Bulosan, ca. 1940s. Courtesy of Special
Collections (UW2710), University of Washington Libraries.

views." He recommended that the WRA allow only US-born Nisei to
become "block leaders," construct separate camps for "enemy aliens"
and "loyal Americans," and prosecute "anti-America pro-axis activities" committed by Japanese Americans. "In general, I think operation
of camp is satisfactory in spite of many shortcomings," he noted,
"thanks to the democratic government of the United States." Japanese
Americans had a name for informants like him—*inu*, a dog, a collabo-
rator. Although the WRA and the FBI welcomed Yoneda's reports, they
remained convinced that he was a "dangerous red." Inside a concentration camp, they continued to monitor his "subversive activities."[5]

On the other side of the Pacific, Artemio Ricarte, the old Filipino
revolutionary exiled in Japan for a quarter century, continued to place
his faith in imperial Japan to liberate the Philippines. Soon after Japanese forces attacked Hawai'i and the Philippines in December 1941,
he agreed to return home aboard a Japanese military plane. He was

seventy-five years old. When Ricarte landed in the Philippines, he raised the Japanese flag and delivered a speech advising Filipinos to cooperate with their Japanese "liberators." He later helped to organize the Makapili—a Filipino military unit fighting with the Japanese against Filipino guerrillas, US forces, and over time Filipino civilians—but his efforts failed to mobilize the Filipino masses to side with Japan. Ricarte passed away on July 31, 1945, shortly before Japan's surrender. For decades after the Philippine-American War, Japan, like the United States during the Spanish-American War, had served as a symbol of alternate possibilities rather than a force of radical change. During World War II, with Japanese forces claiming and occupying the Philippines, Japan and the United States seemingly traded places. The United States was cast again as a potential means toward anticolonial liberation. To his last days, Ricarte said that he was always "ready to answer the call of the Fatherland," but, in collaborating with Japan, just as if he had pledged allegiance to the United States, he worked to advance empire.[6] The fundamental contradiction was never between the United States and Japan. It was between empire and democracy.

Through his semifictional autobiography, Bulosan attempted to resolve that irreconcilable contradiction. Saying goodbye to his brother bound for the US Army, he felt a momentous shift that he found both inspiring and dispiriting, at least initially. "We belonged to the old world of confusion," Bulosan lamented, "but in this other world—new, bright, promising—we would be unable to meet its demands." The next day, he boarded a bus out of California, "to catch the last crew of cannery workers in Portland." As he rode past Filipino migrant workers in the fields, Bulosan saw his world collapse in time and space, with memories and dreams somehow crystallizing into an epiphany that "the American earth was like a huge heart unfolding warmly to receive" him. "It came to me that no man—no one at all—could destroy my faith in America again," he wrote, now suddenly and inexplicably full of hope. "It was something that grew out of the sacrifices and loneliness of my friends, of my brothers in America and my family in the Philippines—something that grew out of our desire to know America, and to become a part of her great tradition, and to contribute something toward her final fulfillment." That cloying sentiment was a prelude to the last sentence of *America Is in the Heart*. "I knew that no man could destroy my faith in America that had sprung from all our hopes and aspirations, *ever*," he concluded.[7]

For a brief moment, the FBI hoped that Bulosan, like Yoneda, could serve the US security state. In July 1950, four years after the publication of *America Is in the Heart,* the FBI launched an investigation into Bulosan's communist affiliations. Several months into the investigation, the special agent in charge of the Seattle office checked out Bulosan's book from the Seattle Public Library and skimmed it enough to recognize that Bulosan had been "the associate of persons connected with the Communist Party." A secret informant, who was involved in Filipino labor organizing, likewise affirmed that Bulosan was close to "many writers of left wing tendencies in Hollywood, California," but he felt that Bulosan held promise as an informant. The agent agreed. Though not able to provide a "thorough review" of *America Is in the Heart,* the Seattle agent was struck by the book's last passage, the ode to America that he quoted at length in his report. "The Bureau is requested to authorize this office to conduct a discrete [*sic*] interview with subject for the purpose of determining his attitude in the matter of cooperating with the Bureau," the agent proposed. "It is believed that a safe contact could be had with him by using that approach to talk to him about the books which he has written, it being well known that as far as Filipinos are concerned, they are quite susceptible to any manifestation of appreciation for their accomplishments." And Bulosan, he believed, could provide "exceptionally productive" information on "Filipino activities."[8]

But the deeper FBI agents dug into Bulosan's political connections, the more unsettled they became by his radical politics that extended far beyond the US nation. At the beginning of the investigation, FBI field offices up and down the Pacific Coast scoured their records to locate all references to Bulosan. The San Francisco office discovered a letter dating back to May 1943, written by the chief of the Counter Intelligence Branch of the Western Defense Command, US Army, that "pertained to suspected members of the Sakdalista, a Filipino labor organization then believed to be pro-Japanese." Bulosan was listed as "the leader of the Sakdalista Party with headquarters in Los Angeles." In January 1951, through an informant in Los Angeles, the FBI learned that Bulosan had delivered in 1943 a speech before the League of American Writers, a Popular Front organization affiliated with the CPUSA, that addressed the racial dynamics of World War II. "In the past I have been friendly with the Japanese," he reportedly said. "In America they were a kind people and generous. They were not ashamed of my friendship and received me gladly. Today they are gone and in my Islands they are my enemies." Bulosan, however, did not consider the enemy of the enemy of the Philippines an ally, remarking that "the white people here in California are no more my friends than before." Bulosan's potentially pro-Japanese and anti-American views appeared to reject simplistic wartime loyalties and to exceed the impassioned US nationalism seemingly at the heart of his autobiographical account.[9]

Far more than his wartime views and communist connections in the United States, the FBI became especially alarmed by Bulosan's engagement with ongoing struggles in the Philippines. Early in the FBI investigation, in July 1950, the Seattle office came across information that Bulosan had been in touch with Luis Taruc, "said to be the leader of the Communist Party in the Philippine Islands," and that "the Communist revolution in the Philippine Islands would start in 1951." Bulosan purportedly planned to send Chris Mensalvas, Ponce Torres, and Ernesto Mangaoang—all Filipino labor organizers in Seattle—to the Philippines to join the revolution. In December 1950, the special agent in charge of the Portland office in Oregon interviewed Pio del Pilar V. Soriano, who admitted to having been a member of the CPUSA. In a recent visit to Portland, Soriano stated, Bulosan "appeared to be very well versed in Asiatic affairs" and most likely "received information regarding Communist aims in Asia in advance of the local newspapers." Although he did not know for certain, Soriano "suspected that Bulosan might have some contact with the Hucbalahaps [sic] in the Philippine Islands." Informants from Los Angeles to Anchorage reinforced those findings, circulating reports and rumors of Bulosan's correspondence with Taruc and Amado V. Hernandez, the Filipino writer who had organized the leftist Congress of Labor Organizations (CLO) after World War II, and Bulosan's efforts to organize a revolutionary "world movement."[10]

Taruc and Hernandez represented the kind of revolutionary, anticolonial politics that "Filipinization" was supposed to divert and disperse. In June 1948, Hernandez wrote a public letter to Taruc, the Hukbalahap leader, to unite industrial workers and rural peasants in the Philippines—those following "Andres Bonifacio's upraised right hand that points the path to take for a people who strive to live under the blessings of democracy." For a rally in August 1948, as head of the CLO's Executive Committee, Hernandez contrasted "a truly democratic peace"—"a decent means of livelihood for everyone, a home for every family, opportunities for education and the enjoyment of leisure and freedom of belief and freedom of expression for all"—and the "kind of peace which the reactionaries and the neo-fascists are trying to establish." "It is a 'mailed fist' peace maintained by guns and bayonets, by terror and gangsterism, by irresponsible and depraved secret agents, by ruthless mercenaries," he argued. "It is a brutal sinister peace; it is the cowed conformism inside a concentration camp; it is the kind of peace that not so long ago, the Japanese fascist-militarists tried, with all cunning and ruthlessness, to enforce in the Philippines." Hernandez was relentless in his critique of the "farce" of "the so-called independence of the Philippines" inaugurated on July 4, 1946. In his committee report to the CLO's convention in 1949, he insisted that the imposition of military bases and trade agreements made Filipinos into "beggars," subject to "masters in Washington" and Wall Street.[11]

The US security state took note. Hoover and the FBI became interested in the Hukbalahap toward the end of World War II, particularly after the special agent in charge in San Francisco debriefed a US corporal returning from the Philippines with his two young children in January 1945. Hailing from North Dakota, the corporal had been stationed in the Philippines since 1938, married to a Filipina (whose father was "an American civilian employed by some Governmental agency"), and then captured by Japanese forces in 1942. After his escape, he served as an arms instructor to Huk guerrillas. Based in Pampanga and surrounding provinces in central Luzon, the corporal stated, the Huks had organized remote communities "entirely according to the Communist rule." The agent related that "the propaganda of this group is to incite the Filipinos to join with them after the Japanese have been defeated" and then "to request immediate freedom from the United States of America" and "to set up their own form of government following the principles of STALIN." Hoover forwarded the information to authorities in Australia and New Zealand, intimating that the Hukbalahap would attempt "to spread such doctrines to the nearby areas" and "constitute an additional problem during the reconstruction period." And when Taruc spoke at the fifteenth anniversary of the founding of the Partido Komunista sa Pilipinas (PKP) in Manila months after the war in November 1945, N. J. Alaga, the "Acting FBI Liaison Officer in Charge," was there to report directly to Hoover.[12]

The US security state, which had emerged and expanded in part to secure the US empire against revolutionary, anticolonial movements across the Pacific, carried on that mission after the end of Japanese occupation and then direct US colonial rule in the Philippines. The FBI opened its file on the CLO in May 1949, almost three years after the formal independence of the Philippines, when its Honolulu office discovered a CLO pamphlet at the local headquarters of the International Longshoremen's and Warehousemen's Union (ILWU), a radical union at the forefront of organizing Filipino workers in Hawai'i and the Pacific

Coast. Six months later, an agent of the Hawaiian Sugar Planters' Association (HSPA) in Manila forwarded Hernandez's CLO committee report, which ended up at the ONI and then the FBI. The HSPA was troubled by "how closely the CLO program and philosophy parallels those of the ILWU." The CLO positioned itself as part of a "labor movement throughout the world . . . on the move, militant and alert," laying bare the colonial edifice of the "Tower of Babel delusion that is now 'The American Century.'" "Imperialism and fascism which were supposed to have died with the defeat of Hitler and his gang are again rearing their ugly heads and threatening freedom and happiness of the working class," Hernandez's committee declared. To the CLO, that was America: a beacon of imperialism and fascism, on guard against "liberation movements in Asia" led by "the forces of China, Indonesia, Viet Nam, Malaya, Korea, Burma, and the Philippines."[13]

As the US state and the Philippine state collaborated to wage military and legal battles against the Huks, the CLO, the ILWU, and the CWFLU (which became ILWU Local 37 in 1950) for their "un-American" and "un-Filipino" activities, Bulosan gravitated to a revolutionary politics beyond the nation-state. In October 1951, through the Philippines' National Bureau of Investigation, the FBI received copies of Bulosan's rumored letters to Taruc and Hernandez, both dated December 1, 1949. Bulosan apprised Hernandez of the redbaiting of the Filipino labor movement in the United States, including the recent arrest and looming deportation of Mensalvas, Mangaoang, and other CWFLU leaders. He blamed the FBI—in cahoots with the Philippine consulate, "Filipino labor racketeers," and agricultural employers—for trying to destroy the "militant union created solely to organize the unorganized agricultural and factory workers." Bulosan related that he knew that he was "being watched too." "But this you must remember: You and the Filipino workers have many friends in America," he added hopefully. It was a moment of radical possibilities, perhaps the beginnings of that "new, bright, promising" world that he glimpsed in *America Is in the Heart*. "Don't sidestep or weaken your resistance: this is the right time to strike," Bulosan advised. "Everyday now the headlines in the nation are about the revolting workers and the Huks under Luis Taruc. The imperialistic are getting hysterical, and the American people are waking up to the realities of our present world."[14]

Bulosan's support of the Huk rebellion against Manuel Quezon's political heirs and the US empire allowed him to imagine a different world, a world beyond the bounds of empire. "There are many times when I had the impulse to return to the Philippines and join your movement," he wrote to Taruc. "But always I was paralyzed by the thought that I'll be more valuable here." Bulosan related that he was working on a fictional account of Taruc's life that he hoped would be made into a Hollywood film once "the sudden resurgence of fa[s]cist activities here . . . die down." Bulosan longed for a different time, a different place. "I can't leave the United States now because I'll never be able to come back if I do," he noted. "I think you know the reasons why I'll be there some day soon to work with you. I'm playing with time." Before then, he wanted to connect with Taruc, to support the movement he was leading to liberate the Philippines on behalf of Filipino peasants. Bulosan promised to send books by way of Hernandez. "What size of shoes do you wear? and shirts?" Bulosan asked. "I'm a very small man, only five feet and two inches, and I weigh not even a hundred pounds. But if there is anything I can do for you and your movement—if it is only the use of my name—please feel free to do so. I am not afraid of the *fa[s]cist* bastards at home."[15]

The fascist bastards in the seat of empire haunted Bulosan. In June 1954, Bulosan requested an interview with the FBI to try to clear his name. In an FBI car parked next to the King Street Station in Seattle, Bulosan, who was then employed as the publicity director for ILWU Local 37, talked to several FBI agents about his personal history. He said that he had become interested in the Hukbalahap movement during World War II "because it represented a movement on behalf of the people instead of the rich land owners." He also related that he had never met Taruc in person or known that Taruc was a communist, at least not until "it was publicly announced in about 1949." Bulosan denied membership in the CPUSA, adding that he had read Karl Marx's *Capital* "twice without understanding the theory." When asked by agents "how he could claim innocence with regard to following the CP line when by his own books and publication he seldom deviates from that line," Bulosan "shrugged his shoulders and displayed no interest in answering that or any specific questions concerning Communism." Hoover was not satisfied. He had heard months earlier that Bulosan had boasted of a vast communist communication network linking San Francisco, Honolulu, Saigon, Paris, and elsewhere. In September 1954, Hoover personally forwarded FBI reports on Bulosan to the Immigration and Naturalization Service and the Department of Justice, "for consideration as to possible deportation." The FBI continued to monitor Bulosan actively through May 1955.[16]

In the end, though, Bulosan's radical politics haunted the FBI and the US empire, even after his death. In his last years, he lived with Josephine

Patrick, a self-identified communist, and her young children. "He was very beautiful," she recalled. "He was small and delicate and he had a very soft voice . . . and he was funny; he had a marvelous sense of humor." In his last days, Bulosan was working on a sequel to *America Is in the Heart,* provisionally titled "My Letter to the World." After passing out drunk in front of the King County courthouse, he succumbed to pneumonia on September 11, 1956. The FBI took note of his death, but his file remained open. In November 1959, a confidential informant told the FBI that Filipino labor leaders who had traveled to the United States the previous summer—on US government funds, no less—had returned to the Philippines radicalized, adopting the "Communist way of thinking" to "become anti-American." The informant identified Bulosan specifically as a person "in touch" with the labor leaders while they toured the United States. There was nothing the FBI could do with that information, except to place it in Bulosan's file.[17] That was a fitting coda, a metaphor for the US empire: the US state's claims to security and sovereignty were always greater than its capacity to kill revolutionary struggles for freedom and democracy. Bulosan had the last laugh; he had a wonderful sense of humor. America was not in his heart.

LOOKING BACK, LOOKING FORWARD

During a rushed visit to the Philippines in October 2003, US President George W. Bush butchered the past to conceal and secure the US empire for another generation. "Together our soldiers liberated the Philippines from colonial rule," he said before the Philippine Congress. "Together we rescued the islands from invasion and occupation." Bush conveniently skipped over US colonial rule in the first half of the twentieth century, preferring to draw attention to joint battles against imperial Japan during World War II. The United States and the Philippines, he stated, shared a commitment to capitalism ("free enterprise, disciplined by humanity and compassion") and democracy ("the only form of government fully compatible with human dignity"). To wrest support for the recent US invasion and occupation of Iraq, Bush declared a global war against a "new totalitarian threat." "Like other militarists and fascists before them," he argued, "the terrorists and their allies seek to control every mind and soul." Echoing Theodore Roosevelt's war against anarchism a century earlier, Bush vowed to carry out "the war on terror" and demanded collaboration. "Every nation in Asia and across the world now faces a choice," he said. "Nations that choose to support terror are complicit in a war against civilization. Nations that try to ignore terror and hope it will only strike others are deluding themselves, undermining our common defense, and inviting a future of catastrophic violence. Nations that choose to fight terror are defending their own safety and the safety of free people everywhere."[18]

Bush's speech made a mockery of history and democracy, but it reflected major historical shifts in US colonial rule over the first four decades of the twentieth century. Through the Spanish-American War and the Philippine-American War, the US empire extended across the Pacific, claiming unilateral sovereignty over the archipelago's peoples and lands on racial grounds. The benign language of "benevolent assimilation" and the ruthless tactics of genocidal violence operated hand in hand to racialize Filipinos as "goo-goos" requiring state violence, state surveillance, and colonial tutelage. But Filipinos refused to submit to the US empire's dictates, engaging in guerrilla warfare, labor strikes, and revolutionary movements that the US security state criminalized as sedition. Securing empire through a legal discourse of sedition reified the nation-state form and national security, a discourse that the Philippine elite embraced and exploited in their appeals for national independence. Simultaneously repressing revolutionary movements and fostering collaborative colonialism, the US state passed the Jones Law and then the Tydings-McDuffie Act to offer the liberal promise of a Philippine nation-state through the US empire. Race made democracy and empire compatible, a contradiction Bush articulated in his speech. He promised "democracy" in Iraq, even though "skeptics" surmised that "the culture of the Middle East will not sustain the institutions of democracy." By becoming "the first democratic nation in Asia," Filipinos, guided by US benevolence, had proven wrong earlier doubts about "the culture of Asia." The backward peoples of Asia and the Middle East would follow America's "liberation" to discover "peace" and "democracy."[19]

Even as agents and agencies of the US security state spread across the Pacific, the US empire never realized the security that was its mission. Those monitoring and suppressing Filipino resistance not only detected widespread rejection of US colonial rule, they produced countless reports on interracial alliances and revolutionary conspiracies against the US empire. That state of affairs characterized the apparent necessity and the perpetual futility of national security. As political scientist David Campbell argues, "Ironically . . . the inability of the state project of security to succeed is the guarantor of the state's continued success as an impelling identity."[20] Fighting for "democracy" and weeding out "sedition" (later to encompass "terror") around the world, a never-ending racial project, came to define and legitimize the impelling identity known as the United States of America. In the Philippines, in Hawai'i, in California, and elsewhere, particularly after the Russo-Japanese War, imperial Japan materialized as an omnipresent menace, an international rival that portended the radical possibilities of pan-Asian solidarity. The formation of seditious Asians, an elusive racial and interracial figure presumably led by Japan's "Oriental" deceits to threaten everything that the USA stood for—the global status quo of capitalism, colonialism, heteropatriarchy, and racism marketed as "democracy"—sustained the US empire and subjected more and more peoples of Asia to state surveillance, immigration restrictions, deportation orders, criminal prosecution, and premature death. The catastrophic violence of the US state could not but generate more anticolonial rage among aggrieved peoples around the world.

For a time, it appeared possible for Filipino *insurrectos,* Ghadar activists, plantation workers, Sakdalista proponents, communist organizers, and many others living in or passing through the Philippines, Hawai'i, and North America to imagine and pursue pan-Asian solidarity as a viable means to contest the US empire. To many, imperial Japan was a potent symbol, a hopeful harbinger of what could be, a world beyond white supremacy and empire. Into the 1920s, despite the Japanese state's coalition with the British empire and the US empire to champion antiradical colonialism, anticolonial movements continually invoked a potential alliance with Japan to challenge the racial and colonial order enforced by the British empire and the US empire. Once the Japanese state began appropriating pan-Asianism in the 1930s to justify its imperial ambitions—including the establishment of Manchukuo in 1932, three years before the Philippine Commonwealth—pan-Asian solidarity increasingly ceased to be a revolutionary possibility.[21] Although colonized subjects continued to theorize and advance revolutionary nationalism, expectantly toward communist internationalism, the antifascist alliance heralded by the Popular Front largely foreclosed radical possibilities against and beyond liberal democracy and the nation-state. That history of race, nation, and empire affords no easy solutions. As racialized and radicalized subjects of the US empire grappled with the messy contradictions of racial capitalism and colonial rule before and during World War II, we have no choice but to do the same.

To point out the obvious, a "democracy" rooted in empire and white supremacy is not democracy. That is American democracy.

The US empire lives on, but its fragile and overwhelming existence rests on imperial insecurities. The US state's repression of anticolonial movements ultimately exposed and reinforced the racial and colonial edifice of the modern liberal state, which became indispensable to preserving empire in the name of national security. Over the first four decades of the twentieth century, the colonizing and racializing discourse of security marked Asians as seditious subjects that the US state had to monitor, exclude, deport, assimilate, and kill. Tracing the transpacific origins of the US national security state uncovers a history of colonial claims and anticolonial struggles, within which the multicultural project of insisting on the "Americanness" of Asians can be understood as the US empire's latest iteration of collaborative colonialism. An immense challenge before us is to reckon with history, white supremacy, and empire, in terms that refuse to naturalize nations, nation-states, and citizenship. The Philippines is no longer a colony of the US empire, but Philippine citizens, like Iraqi citizens and Asian Americans, remain racialized subjects of the US empire that the US state tries to claim and contain as "friends" and "enemies." As Bush uttered his vacuous truisms about "democracy" in 2003, to rounds of applause from Philippine lawmakers, the US Secret Service prepared for a quick departure. Sensing the anticolonial rage that dates back more than a century, agents of the US security state deemed the Philippines unsafe for an overnight stay.[22] As in the past, that anticolonial rage will find creative expressions and innovative movements around the world because empire and democracy cannot coexist.

Notes

PROLOGUE

1. Dada Amir Haider Khan, *Chains to Lose: Life and Struggles of a Revolutionary: Memoirs of Dada Amir Haider Khan,* edited by Hasan N. Gardezi (Karachi: Pakistan Study Centre, University of Karachi, 2007), 1–136 (quotes from 60 and 62). I am grateful to Junaid Rana for sharing his copy of Khan's memoir.

2. Khan, *Chains to Lose,* 137–247 (quotes from 140, 227, 236, 243, 245). Ghadar was also spelled *Gadar* and *Ghadr.*

3. Khan, *Chains to Lose,* 249–80 (quotes from 251, 264, 273, 274, 277).

4. Khan, *Chains to Lose,* 291–447 (quotes from 301, 302, 326, 327, 323, 395). On *U.S. v. Bhagat Singh Thind* (1923), which excluded South Asians from naturalization, see Ian F. Haney López, *White by Law: The Legal Construction of Race,* rev. ed. (New York: New York University Press, 2006), 61–65.

5. Khan, *Chains to Lose,* 441–522 (quotes from 444, 445). On the Shanghai massacre, see Hung-Ting Ku, "Urban Mass Movement: The May Thirtieth Movement in Shanghai," *Modern Asian Studies* 13, no. 2 (1979): 197–216. On the legal and political movement to defend Ossian Sweet, see Kevin Boyle, *Arc of Justice: A Saga of Race, Civil Rights, and Murder in the Jazz Age* (New York: Henry Holt, 2004).

6. Khan, *Chains to Lose,* 516, 531–619 (quotes from 536, 537, 589, 617–18).

7. Khan, *Chains to Lose,* 613, 638–742 (quotes from 613).

8. Hasan N. Gardezi, "Introduction" and "Prelude to Independence and Life in Pakistan," in *Chains to Lose,* vii–xii, 743–60. Khan was first arrested by Pakistani authorities in 1949.

9. Gardezi, "Prelude to Independence and Life in Pakistan," in *Chains to Lose,* 760–66 (quote from 760–61).

INTRODUCTION

Epigraph: W. E. B. Du Bois, *Darkwater: Voices from within the Veil* (New York: Washington Square Press, 2004 [1920]) 1–2; Alex Hing, "The Need for a United Asian-American Front, 1970," in *The Columbia Documentary History of the Asian American Experience,* edited by Franklin Odo (New York: Columbia University Press, 2002), 373.

1. Pedro B. Bunuan [*sic*] to the Congress of the US Government, n.d. [received by the White House on April 9, 1927], Box 928, File 19861, Records of the Bureau of Insular Affairs, General Records, Record Group 350 (RG 350), National Archives, Washington, DC (NA); Pedro B. Bunoan to Secretary of Labor, June 6, 1935, File 55874, Records of the Immigration and Naturalization Service, RG 85, NA.

2. Du Bois, *Darkwater,* 35, 27, 33, 36 (emphases in original).

3. Jack O'Dell, *Climbin' Jacob's Ladder: The Black Freedom Movement Writings of Jack O'Dell,* edited by Nikhil Pal Singh (Berkeley: University of California Press, 2010), 129, 134.

4. *Oxford English Dictionary,* 3rd ed.; V. I. Lenin, *Imperialism: The Highest Stage of Capitalism* (New York: International Publishers, 1939 [1917]), 88–89; William Appleman Williams, *The Tragedy of American Diplomacy* (Cleveland: World Publishing Company, 1959); Walter LaFeber, *The New Empire: An Interpretation of American Expansion, 1860–1898* (Ithaca: Cornell University Press, 1963); Thomas J. McCormick, *China Market: America's Quest for Informal Empire, 1893–1901* (Chicago: Quadrangle Books, 1967). Lenin was building on the work of J. A. Hobson, *Imperialism: A Study* (New York: Gordon Press, 1975 [1902]). Historians of the British empire had used "informal empire" earlier to suggest its compatibility with "formal empire" in the nineteenth century. See John Gallagher and Ronald Robinson, "The Imperialism of Free Trade," *Economic History Review* 6, no. 1 (1953): 1–15. For a historiographical review of how imperialism has been theorized and framed in the twentieth century, see Patrick Wolfe, "History and Imperialism: A Century of Theory, from Marx to Postcolonialism," *American Historical Review* 102, no. 2 (April 1997): 388–420.

5. Lisa Lowe, *The Intimacies of Four Continents* (Durham: Duke University Press, 2015); Jodi A. Byrd, *The Transit of Empire: Indigenous Critiques of Colonialism* (Minneapolis: University of Minneapolis Press, 2011).

6. Max Boot, *The Savage Wars of Peace: Small Wars and the Rise of American Power* (New York: Basic Books, 2002), 349; Niall Ferguson, *Empire: The Rise and Demise of the British World Order and the Lessons for Global Power* (New York: Basic Books, 2003).

7. A. G. Hopkins, *American Empire: A Global History* (Princeton: Princeton University Press, 2018), 26; Daniel Immerwahr, *How to Hide an Empire: A History of the Greater United States* (New York: Farrar, Straus and Giroux, 2019).

8. Arundhati Roy, *The End of Imagination* (Chicago: Haymarket Books, 2016), 279–80.

9. Lowe, *The Intimacies of Four Continents,* 175; Roy, *The End of Imagination,* 281–82.

10. *Oxford English Dictionary*, 3rd ed.. In a recent historiographical review, Paul A. Kramer suggested dispensing with the proper noun altogether because it imputes "connotations of unity and coherence" that did not exist. Though useful in revealing the imperial dimensions of US history and in highlighting the process of imperial rule, Kramer's prescription has an odd and ironic effect of sanitizing US imperial history. By making almost everything imperial, the US empire and struggles against it can strangely disappear. See Paul A. Kramer, "Power and Connection: Imperial Histories of the United States in the World," *American Historical Review* 116, no. 5 (December 2011): 1348–91.

11. *Oxford English Dictionary*, 3rd ed.; US Department of the Army, *Counterinsurgency*, Field Manual No. 3–24 (Washington, DC: Headquarters, Department of the Army, and Headquarters, Marine Corps Combat Development Command, Department of the Navy, Headquarters, US Marine Corps, 2006), foreword (no page number), 1.1, 1.3.

12. P. G. Bock and Morton Berkowitz, "The Emerging Field of National Security," *World Politics* 19, no. 1 (October 1966): 122, 134 (emphasis in original); Melvyn P. Leffler, "National Security," in *Explaining the History of American Foreign Relations*, 2nd ed., edited by Michael J. Hogan and Thomas G. Paterson (Cambridge: Cambridge University Press, 2004), 123–36; Andrew Preston, "Monsters Everywhere: A Genealogy of National Security," *Diplomatic History* 83, no. 3 (June 2014): 477–500; Michael J. Hogan, *A Cross of Iron: Harry S. Truman and the Origins of the National Security State* (Cambridge: Cambridge University Press, 1998). On the racial and colonial origins of the field of "international relations," see Robert Vitalis, *White World Order, Black Power Politics: The Birth of American International Relations* (Ithaca: Cornell University Press, 2015).

13. Karen Umemoto, "'On Strike!' San Francisco State College Strike, 1968–69: The Role of Asian American Students," *Amerasia Journal* 15, no. 1 (1989): 15; Daryl J. Maeda, *Chains of Babylon: The Rise of Asian America* (Minneapolis: University of Minnesota Press, 2009).

14. Some of the most influential studies were: Mary Roberts Coolidge, *Chinese Immigration* (New York: Henry Holt, 1909); Elmer Clarence Sandmeyer, *The Anti-Chinese Movement in California* (Urbana: University of Illinois Press, 1991 [1939]); Robert Ezra Park, *Race and Culture* (Glencoe, IL: Free Press, 1950). On Park and the Chicago School of Sociology, see Henry Yu, *Thinking Orientals: Migration, Contact, and Exoticism in Modern America* (New York: Oxford University Press, 2001).

15. Key examples in that vein include Ronald Takaki, *Strangers from a Different Shore: A History of Asian Americans* (Boston: Little, Brown, 1989); Erika Lee, *The Making of Asian America: A History* (New York: Simon and Schuster, 2015).

16. I am indebted to Cedric J. Robinson's framing of racial capitalism and the Black Radical Tradition in *Black Marxism: The Making of the Black Radical Tradition* (Chapel Hill: University of North Carolina Press, 2000). Robinson stressed that racial capitalism was and is capitalism, compelling us to rethink the revolutionary subject of history beyond the European proletariat.

17. T. Fujitani, *Race for Empire: Koreans as Japanese and Japanese as Americans during World War II* (Berkeley: University of California Press, 2011); Simeon Man, *Soldiering through Empire: Race and the Making of the Decolonizing Pacific* (Oakland: University of California Press, 2018).

18. On the "yellow peril" idea, and its gendered connections to the "model minority," see Gary Y. Okihiro, *Margins and Mainstreams: Asians in American History and Culture* (Seattle: University of Washington Press, 1994), 118–47.

19. Alfred W. McCoy, *Policing America's Empire: The United States, the Philippines, and the Rise of the Surveillance State* (Madison: University of Wisconsin Press, 2009).

20. "Message of the President," in *Papers Relating to the Foreign Relations of the United States, with the Annual Message of the President Transmitted to Congress December 5, 1905* (Washington, DC: Government Printing Office, 1906), xxxii. For an overview of categories projected onto Filipino migrants, see Mae M. Ngai, *Impossible Subjects: Illegal Aliens and the Making of Modern America* (Princeton: Princeton University Press, 2004), 96–126.

21. For broad overviews from different perspectives, see, for example: Michael Paul Rogin, *Ronald Reagan, the Movie: And Other Episodes in Political Demonology* (Berkeley: University of California Press, 1987); Joan M. Jensen, *Army Surveillance in America, 1775–1980* (New Haven: Yale University Press, 1991); Simone Browne, *Dark Matters: On the Surveillance of Blackness* (Durham: Duke University Press, 2015); Kelly Lytle Hernández, *City of Inmates: Conquest, Rebellion, and the Rise of Human Caging in Los Angeles, 1771–1965* (Chapel Hill: University of North Carolina Press, 2017).

22. Du Bois, *Darkwater*, 30. On the global impact of Japan's defeat of Russia in 1905 in the making of "modern Asia," including appeals to pan-Asian and pan-Islamic solidarities, see Cemil Aydin, *The Politics of Anti-Westernism in Asia: Visions of World Order in Pan-Islamic and Pan-Asian Thought* (New York: Columbia University Press, 2007); Pankaj Mishra, *From the Ruins of Empire: The Revolt Against the West and the Remaking of Asia* (New York: Picador, 2012).

23. Du Bois, *Darkwater*, 31; Ruth Wilson Gilmore, *Golden Gulag: Prisons, Surplus, Crisis, and Opposition in Globalizing California* (Berkeley: University of California Press, 2007), 28.

24. Moon-Kie Jung, *Beneath the Surface of White Supremacy: Denaturalizing U.S. Racisms Past and Present* (Stanford: Stanford University Press, 2015), 55–81; Alyosha Goldstein, "Toward a Genealogy of the U.S. Colonial Present," in *Formations of United States Colonialism*, edited by Alyosha Goldstein (Durham: Duke University Press, 2014), 1–21.

25. Rogin, *Ronald Reagan, the Movie*, xiii; Peter Linebaugh and Marcus Rediker, *The Many-Headed Hydra: Sailors, Slaves, Commoners, and the Hidden History of the Revolutionary Atlantic* (Boston: Beacon Press, 2000); Esther Lezra, *The Colonial Art of Demonizing Others: A Global Perspective* (London: Routledge, 2014).

26. Ann Laura Stoler, *Along the Archival Grain: Epistemic Anxieties and Colonial Common Sense* (Princeton: Princeton University Press, 2009), 4.

27. Eiichiro Azuma, *In Search of Our Frontier: Japanese America and Settler Colonialism in the Construction of Japan's Borderless Empire* (Oakland: University of California Press, 2019).

28. Byrd, *The Transit of Empire*, xiii, xvii. I also do not mean to essentialize or simplify indigeneity as something that can be measured and quantified. Byrd suggests that it represents a "radical alterity" that recalls "remembrance as a means through which to read counter to the stories empire tells itself" (xiii).

CHAPTER 1. SUPPRESSING ANARCHY AND SEDITION

Epigraph: Jack Daly, "The Gentle Filipinos," *Washington Times*, August 19, 1902, in Box 281, File 2490; Records of the Bureau of Insular Affairs, General Records, 1898–1945 (BIA); Record Group 350 (RG 350); National Archives, Washington, DC (NA).

1. William Henry Scott, *The Union Obrera Democratica: First Filipino Labor Union* (Quezon City: New Day Publishers, 1992), 5–11, 19–41, 44 (newspaper quote).

2. Scott, *The Union Obrera Democratica*, 13–20 (quotes from 15 and 20); Benedict Anderson, *Under Three Flags: Anarchism and the Anti-Colonial Imagination* (London: Verso, 2005), 197–201, 223–29.

3. Scott, *The Union Obrera Democratica*, 19, 43–50 (quotes from 49 and 50).

4. Vicente L. Rafael, *White Love and Other Events in Filipino History* (Durham: Duke University Press, 2000), 39–51 (quote from 43); Scott, *The Union Obrera Democratica*, 57–70 (Taft quote from 69).

5. On the "queerness" of the Philippines and the racial-sexual roots of US colonial governance, see Victor Román Mendoza, *Metroimperial Intimacies: Fantasy, Racial-Sexual Governance, and the Philippines in U.S. Imperialism, 1899–1913* (Durham: Duke University Press, 2015).

6. Brian McAllister Linn, *The Philippine War, 1899–1902* (Lawrence: University Press of Kansas, 2000), 8–25; Paul A. Kramer, *The Blood of Government: Race, Empire, the United States, and the Philippines* (Chapel Hill: University of North Carolina Press, 2006), 94–97; Alfred W. McCoy, "Policing the Imperial Periphery: Philippine Pacification and the Rise of the U.S. National Security State," in *Colonial Crucible: Empire in the Making of the Modern American State*, edited by Alfred W. McCoy and Francisco A. Scarano (Madison: University of Wisconsin Press, 2009), 106.

7. Kramer, *The Blood of Government*, 89–111 (McKinley quote, 110).

8. Willard B. Gatewood Jr., *"Smoked Yankees" and the Struggle for Empire: Letters from Negro Soldiers, 1898–1902* (Fayetteville: University of Arkansas Press, 1987), 257, 280; *New York Times*, September 24, 1899.

9. *New York Times*, April 11, 1899; Kramer, *The Blood of Government*, 122–29; David R. Roediger, *Towards the Abolition of Whiteness: Essays on Race, Politics, and Working Class History* (London: Verso, 1994), 117–20.

10. Kramer, *The Blood of Government*, 130–37 (veterans' quotes, 134); *New York Times*, November 3, 1899; Gatewood, *"Smoked Yankees,"* 305.

11. W. H. Taft to Secretary of War, July 14, 1900 (extract), Box 281, File 2490, BIA, RG 350, NA; Stuart Creighton Miller, *"The Benevolent Assimilation": The American Conquest of the Philippines, 1899–1903* (New Haven: Yale University Press, 1982), 133–34.

12. Linn, *The Philippine War*, 213–15; Kramer, *The Blood of Government*, 152–54; Anderson, *Under Three Flags*, 146; John Lawrence Tone, *War and Genocide in Cuba, 1895–1898* (Chapel Hill: University of North Carolina Press, 2006), 193–224.

13. Linn, *The Philippine War*, 313; *New York Times*, November 3, September 26, 1899.

14. Peter Marshall, *Demanding the Impossible: A History of Anarchism* (Oakland: PM Press, 2008), 239, 282, 295.

15. Marshall, *Demanding the Impossible*, 299–306; George Richard Esenwein, *Anarchist Ideology and the Working-Class Movement in Spain, 1868–1898* (Berkeley: University of California Press, 1989), esp. 11–21, 35–77, 166–99; Tone, *War and Genocide in Cuba*, 225–33 (Angiolillo quote from 233).

16. Marshall, *Demanding the Impossible*, 256–57; George Woodcock, *Anarchism: A History of Libertarian Ideas and Movements* (New York: World Publishing Company, 1962), 369–70; Tone, *War and Genocide in Cuba*, 153–59, 226–31 (Weyler quote from 158).

17. Anderson, *Under Three Flags*, 197–201 (Urales quote from 199–200); Scott, *The Union Obrera Democratica*, 13–14. Urales's Catalán name was Joán Monseny. For an overview of anarchism in Cuba, particularly on tensions and differences between anarchists and nationalists, see Frank Fernández, *Cuban Anarchism: The History of a Movement* (Tucson: See Sharp Press, 2001).

18. Resil B. Mojares, *Brains of the Nation: Pedro Paterno, T. H. Pardo de Tavera, Isabelo de los Reyes and the Production of Modern Knowledge* (Manila: Ateneo de Manila University Press, 2006), 275; *Annual Reports of the War Department for the Fiscal Year Ended June 30, 1902*, vol. 11, *Acts of the Philippine Commission*, 57th Congress, 2nd Session, House of Representatives Document No. 2 (Washington, DC: Government Printing Office, 1902), 51–54.

19. Daniel Kanstroom, *Deportation Nation: Outsiders in American History* (Cambridge: Harvard University Press, 2007), 46–63; *New York Times*, September 24, 1899.

20. Joan M. Jensen, *Army Surveillance in America, 1775–1980* (New Haven: Yale University Press, 1991), 92, 101–3; McCoy, "Policing the Imperial Periphery," 108; Alfred W. McCoy, *Policing America's Empire: The United States, the Philippines, and the Rise of the Surveillance State* (Madison: University of Wisconsin Press, 2009), 61–62; Miller, *"The Benevolent Assimilation,"* 213; Paul Kramer, "The Water Cure," *New Yorker*, February 25, 2008, 38–43. I discuss earlier US military interventions across the Pacific in Moon-Ho Jung, "Seditious Subjects: Race, State Violence, and the US Empire," *Journal of Asian American Studies* 14, no. 2 (June 2011): 225–31.

21. McCoy, *Policing America's Empire*, 60–63, 82–90; J. G. Harbord, "The Constabulary, 1901–1911," Box 8, Harry H. Bandholtz Papers (Bandholtz Papers), Bentley Historical Library, University of Michigan (UM). On the long history of uneven relations between Filipino soldiers and sailors and the US mili-

tary, see Christopher Capozzola, *Bound by War: How the United States and the Philippines Built America's First Pacific Century* (New York: Basic Books, 2020).

22. H.H. Bandholtz to Executive Secretary, January 15, 1903, Roll 1, Bandholtz Papers, UM.

23. A.U. Betts to Wm. H. Taft, January 19, 1903; Report on Second District, n.d. [1903], Roll 1; Bandholtz Papers, UM.

24. Report on Second District, n.d. [1903], Roll 1; H.H. Bandholtz to J.C. Burrows, April 15, 1904; Bandholtz Papers, UM.

25. "Examination of Cenon Nigdao," January 5, 1902, with endorsement by Wm. H. Taft, January 8, 1903, Box 387, File 4587; C.M. Cotterman, General Order No. 24, September 26, 1903, Box 274, File 2358; BIA, RG 350, NA.

26. Scott, *The Union Obrera Democratica*, 52–65 (quote from 61); Mojares, *Brains of the Nation*, 271.

27. [Report on First District?], n.d. [1903], Roll 1, Bandholtz Papers, UM; Scott, *The Union Obrera Democratica*, 70–73; Jim Richardson, *Komunista: The Genesis of the Philippine Communist Party, 1902–1935* (Manila: Ateneo de Manila University Press, 2011), 20–21.

28. Richardson, *Komunista*, 18; Mojares, *Brains of the Nation*, 279; Scott, *The Union Obrera Democratica*, 68 (Gomez quote).

29. H.H. Bandholtz to H.T. Allen, November 14, 1905; H.H. Bandholtz to J.G. Harbord, December 25, 1905, and February 7, 1906; H.H. Bandholtz to H.S. Howland, September 12, 1906; H.H. Bandholtz to Potenciano Lesaca, January 11, 1906; Roll 1, Bandholtz Papers, UM; McCoy, *Policing America's Empire*, 133–36.

30. H.H. Bandholtz to J.G. Harbord, July 28, 1906 and September 27, 1906, Roll 1; H.H. Bandholtz to Luke E. Wright, August 17, 1906, Box 8; Bandholtz Papers, UM; McCoy, *Policing America's Empire*, 137; Renato Constantino, *The Philippines: A Past Revisited* (Quezon City: Tala Publishing Services, 1975), 261 (Sakay quote). *Cacique*, translated roughly as a local boss, was a term US officials used to refer to political corruption under Spanish rule (Kramer, *The Blood of Government*, 196).

31. H.H. Bandholtz to J.G. Harbord, September 1, 1906, Roll 1; H.H. Bandholtz to John H. Bruce, February, 16, 1907, Roll 1; H.H. Bandholtz to A.C. Carson, April 18, 1907, Roll 2; Bandholtz Papers, UM.

32. H.H. Bandholtz to C.R. Edwards, March 2, 1909; H.H. Bandholtz to Leonard Wood, March 22, 1909; Roll 2, Bandholtz Papers, UM.

33. *New York Times,* September 5, 6, 1901.

34. *New York Times,* September 7, 1901; Eric Rauchway, *Murdering McKinley: The Making of Theodore Roosevelt's America* (New York: Hill and Wang, 2003), 3, 15–20, 76–77 (confession on 19).

35. *New York Times,* December 4, 1901.

36. Scott Miller, *The President and the Assassin: McKinley, Terror, and Empire at the Dawn of the Twentieth Century* (New York: Random House, 2011), 39, 55–60, 75–77, 273–75, 285–86; Rauchway, *Murdering McKinley*, 102–5, 170.

37. *New York Times,* December 4, 1901.

38. *New York Times,* December 4, 1901; Rauchway, *Murdering McKinley*, 60.

39. *Report of the Committee on Immigration,* 57th Congress, 2nd Session, Senate Document No. 62 (Washington, DC: Government Printing Office, 1902), iv–vi.

40. *Report of the Committee on Immigration,* 4, 6, 17, 20–21.

41. *Report of the Committee on Immigration,* 13, 281–86.

42. *Report of the Committee on Immigration,* 452–53, 472–76.

43. *The Statutes at Large of the United States of America, from December, 1901, to March, 1903,* vol. 32, part 1 (Washington, DC: Government Printing Office, 1903), 1214–15, 1221; Amy Dru Stanley, *From Bondage to Contract: Wage Labor, Marriage, and the Market in the Age of Slave Emancipation* (Cambridge: Cambridge University Press, 1998); Moon-Ho Jung, *Coolies and Cane: Race, Labor, and Sugar in the Age of Emancipation* (Baltimore: Johns Hopkins University Press, 2006); Lucy E. Salyer, *Laws Harsh as Tigers: Chinese Immigrants and the Shaping of Modern Immigration Law* (Chapel Hill: University of North Carolina Press, 1995); Nayan Shah, *Contagious Divides: Epidemics and Race in San Francisco's Chinatown* (Berkeley: University of California Press, 2001); Erika Lee, *At America's Gates: Chinese Immigration during the Exclusion Era, 1882–1943* (Chapel Hill: University of North Carolina Press, 2003).

44. *New York Times,* December 4, 1901; *The Statutes at Large . . . from December, 1901, to March, 1903,* vol. 32, part 1, 1221–22.

45. *The Statutes at Large . . . from December, 1901, to March, 1903,* vol. 32, part 1, 1219–20.

46. Kanstroom, *Deportation Nation,* 91–130; *Chae Chan Ping v. United States,* 130 US 581 (1889); *Fong Yue Ting v. United States, Wong Quan v. United States, Lee Joe v. United States,* 149 US 698 (1893). *Chae Chan Ping* is often referred to as the *Chinese Exclusion Case.*

47. *Chae Chan Ping v. United States,* 130 US 581 (1889).

48. Manuel Perez y Burger [sic] to Theodore Roosevelt, September 22, 1901, Box 373, File 4098, BIA, RG 350, NA. His last name also appeared as Xeres Burgos on some documents.

49. Manuel Xerez Burgos, *With Cross and Sword: A Philippine Episode* (Manila: n.p., 1901), 4–5, 7–8, in Box 373, File 4098, BIA, RG 350, NA; A.G. Robinson, "Free Speech in the Philippines," *Church Eclectic* 28, no. 2 (May 1900): 155.

50. Xerez Burgos, *With Cross and Sword,* 8–12.

51. Xerez Burgos, *With Cross and Sword,* 11, 15, and 18.

52. Xerez Burgos, *With Cross and Sword,* 21–22. On the historical origins of Guardia Civil, see McCoy, *Policing America's Empire,* 30–33.

53. Xerez Burgos, *With Cross and Sword,* 23–25.

54. Xerez Burgos, *With Cross and Sword,* 26–27, 39.

55. Leon M. Guerrero, *The First Filipino: A Biography of José Rizal* (Manila: National Historical Institute, 1979), 46; Teodoro A. Agoncillo, *Malolos: The Crisis of the Republic* (Quezon City: University of the Philippines, 1960), 284, 786, 789; Dean C. Worcester, *The Philippines, Past and Present* (New York: Macmillan, 1921), 758–63. On Burgos, see, for example, *Father José Burgos: A Documentary History* (Quezon City: Ateneo de Manila University Press, 1999).

56. *Report of the Philippine Commission to the President*, vol. 2 (Washington, DC: Government Printing Office, 1900), 403–5, 409, 412.

57. Daly's poem cited in chapter's epigraph; "An Incendiary Play in Manila," *City and State* 8, no. 13 (March 29, 1900): 195; Chief of Division to A. W. Ferguson, December 7, 1901, Box 373, File 4098, BIA, RG 350, NA.

CHAPTER 2. CONFLATING RACE AND REVOLUTION

1. Artemio Ricarte, *Memoirs of General Artemio Ricarte*, with an introduction by Armando J. Malay (Manila: National Historical Institute, 1992), xvi–xviii, 4; Teodoro A. Agoncillo, *Malolos: The Crisis of the Republic* (Quezon City: University of the Philippines, 1960), 179.

2. Ricarte, *Memoirs of General Artemio Ricarte*, xviii–xx, 105, 110–14, 126.

3. Ricarte, *Memoirs of General Artemio Ricarte*, 122–36; "Memorandum for the Director," February 28, 1911, Roll 6, Harry H. Bandholtz Papers (Bandholtz Papers), Bentley Historical Library, University of Michigan (UM).

4. Ricarte, *Memoirs of General Artemio Ricarte*, xx–xxi, 91; "Memorandum for the Director," February 28, 1911, Roll 6, Bandholtz Papers, UM.

5. "Memorandum for the Director," February 28, 1911; M. Nicolas, "Confidential Report," June 29, 1910; Artemio Ricarte to Sixto Lopez, August 6, 1910; Roll 6, Bandholtz Papers, UM. Ricarte cited anthropologist Ferdinand Blumentritt to explain the political situation in the Philippines.

6. Reynaldo C. Ileto, *Filipinos and Their Revolution: Event, Discourse, and Historiography* (Manila: Ateneo de Manila University Press, 1998), 151–61; "Confidential Report," July 11, 1910, Roll 6, Bandholtz Papers, UM.

7. J. E. Jacob [?], Office of Philippine Affairs, Department of State, to Colonel R. S. Bratton, War Department, June 6, 1940, with Spanish (original) and English (translated) copies of the "Flag Act," Military Intelligence Division Correspondence, 1917–1941 (MID), Record Group (RG) 165, National Archives, Washington, DC (NA).

8. R. Crame to Director of Constabulary, August 29, 1907, Roll 6, Bandholtz Papers, UM.

9. Father Martin de la Acencion to Doctor Morga, Lieutenant Governor of Manila, originally published April 1, 1609; unsigned, unaddressed letter, September 10, 1900; Report of Davila, Captain of the General Staff of the Insurgent Army, October 11, 1900; Roll 6, Bandholtz Papers, UM. The latter two letters were included in a twenty-four-page compilation titled "Communications Showing Relations of Japanese and Filipinos in the Philippine Islands."

10. Walter LaFeber, *The Clash: A History of U.S.-Japan Relations* (New York: W. W. Norton, 1997), 34–52; James K. Eyre Jr., "Japan and the American Annexation of the Philippines," *Pacific Historical Review* 11, no. 1 (March 1942): 55–71 (Japanese delegation quote from 64).

11. LaFeber, *The Clash*, 68–78 (quotes from 70 and 73).

12. Peter Duus, *The Abacus and the Sword: The Japanese Penetration of Korea, 1895–1910* (Berkeley: University of California Press, 1995), 177–95; Protocol, February 23, 1904, in 64th Congress, 1st Session, Senate Document 342 (Serial Set vol. 6952), 12.

13. "Treaty Between the United States of America and the Kingdom of Chosen"; Horace N. Allen to Secretary of State, April 14, 1904; Secretary of State [John] Hay to Horace N. Allen, February 23, 1904; K. Takahira to Secretary of State, November 23, 1904; Secretary of State Elihu Root to Korean Chargé, November 24, 1904; in 64th Congress, 1st Session, Senate Document 342, 3, 11–13, 16–18; Secretary of State Elihu Root to Diplomatic Officers of the United States, November 25, 1905, in *Papers Relating to the Foreign Relations of the United States, with the Annual Message of the President Transmitted to Congress December 5, 1905* (Washington, DC: Government Printing Office, 1906), 26; Duus, *The Abacus and the Sword*, 189 (long Allen quote).

14. "Taft's Telegram to Root, July 29, 1905," edited by John Gilbert Reid, *Pacific Historical Review* 9, no. 1 (March 1940): 69–70. See also Raymond A. Esthus, "The Taft-Katsura Agreement—Reality or Myth?" *Journal of Modern History* 31, no. 1 (March 1959): 46–51.

15. "Taft's Telegram to Root, July 29, 1905," 69–70.

16. LaFeber, *The Clash*, 78–84; "Message of the President," in *Papers Relating to the Foreign Relations . . . Transmitted to Congress December 5, 1905*, xxix–xxxii.

17. *New York Times*, August 4 and 5, 1905; John Edward Wilz, "Did the United States Betray Korea in 1905?" *Pacific Historical Review* 54, no. 3 (August 1985): 251–53.

18. Wilz, "Did the United States Betray Korea in 1905?" 251; Gail Bederman, *Manliness and Civilization: A Cultural History of Gender and Race in the United States, 1880–1917* (Chicago: University of Chicago Press, 1995), 188–200 (quotes from 193 and 198); LaFeber, *The Clash*, 84 (last Roosevelt quote).

19. *Los Angeles Times*, November 28, 1905.

20. *New York Times*, September 5, 1905; David Levering Lewis, *W. E. B. Du Bois: The Fight for Equality and the American Century, 1919–1963* (New York: Henry Holt, 2000), 391; Marc Gallicchio, *The African American Encounter with Japan and China: Black Internationalism in Asia, 1895–1945* (Chapel Hill: University of North Carolina Press, 2000), 7–8, 14; T. Lothrop Stoddard, *The Rising Tide of Color Against White World-Supremacy* (Honolulu: University Press of the Pacific, 2003 [1920]), 12.

21. Cemil Aydin, *The Politics of Anti-Westernism in Asia: Visions of World Order in Pan-Islamic and Pan-Asian Thought* (New York: Columbia University Press, 2007), 72–92 (Ajia Gi Kai quote from 88).

22. Akira Iriye, *Pacific Estrangement: Japanese and American Expansion, 1897–1911* (Cambridge: Harvard University Press, 1972), 133–41 (Kayahara quote from 140); "Message of the President," *Papers Relating to the Foreign Relations of the United States, with the Annual Message of the President Transmitted to Congress December 3, 1906*, part 1 (Washington, DC: Government Printing Office, 1909), xlii–xliii; Yuji Ichioka, *The Issei: The World of the First Generation Japanese Immigrants* (New York: Free Press, 1988), 212–13.

23. Iriye, *Pacific Estrangement*, 126–168 (Roosevelt quote from 151); Eiichiro Azuma, *Between Two Empires: Race, History, and Transnationalism in Japanese America* (New York: Oxford University Press, 2005), 17–60; Edward S. Miller, *War Plan Orange: The U.S. Strategy to Defeat Japan, 1897–*

1945 (Annapolis: Naval Institute Press, 1991), 21–25; LaFeber, *The Clash,* 89–92; Thomas A. Bailey, "The Root-Takahira Agreement of 1908," *Pacific Historical Review* 9, no. 1 (March 1940): 19–35.

24. Ronald Hayashida and David Kittelson, "The Odyssey of Nicholas Russel," *Hawaiian Journal of History* 11 (1977): 110–12 (quotes from 111 and 112).

25. Hayashida and Kittelson, "The Odyssey of Nicholas Russel," 114–20 (quotes from 116).

26. Hayashida and Kittelson, "The Odyssey of Nicholas Russel," 120–22; *New York Times,* November 12, 1905.

27. M. Rosario, Report No. 4 (Extract), March 5, 1906, Roll 6; R.M. Crame, "Part Two," December 1906, Roll 6; Harry H. Bandholtz to Luke E. Wright, February 16, 1907, Box 8; Bandholtz Papers, UM.

28. Rafael Crame, "Memoir of Remors [*sic*] of Japanese Intervention in the Philippines: Part One," January 15, 1907; R.M. Crame, "Part Two," December 1906; Roll 6, Bandholtz Papers, UM. Ishikawa was also spelled Ysikawa.

29. Justo Sagasa to Rafael Crame, September 24, 1907, Roll 6; R. Crame to Director, October 10, 1907, Roll 6; Harry Bandholtz to J.G. Harbord, July 12, 1907 and August 19, 1907, Roll 2; Bandholtz Papers, UM.

30. Mariano Nicolas, Report, October 12, 1907, Roll 6; Harry Bandholtz to A.C. Carson, April 18, 1907, Roll 2; Bandholtz Papers, UM.

31. Alfred W. McCoy, *Policing America's Empire: The United States, the Philippines, and the Rise of the Surveillance State* (Madison: University of Wisconsin Press, 2009), 76–82; Harry Bandholtz to Ralph H. Van Deman, August 21, 1907, Roll 2, Bandholtz Papers, UM.

32. R.H. Van Deman to Harry Bandholtz, October 7, 1907; Harry Bandholtz to R.H. Van Deman, November 13, 1907; Roll 2, Bandholtz Papers, UM.

33. Harry Bandholtz to Milton F. Davis September 5, 1907; Harry Bandholtz to Henry T. Allen, September 1, 1907; Roll 2, Bandholtz Papers, UM; unsigned letter to "My dear———," June 11, 1907, Box 530, MID, RG 165, NA. Emphases in original.

34. T.W. Jones, "A Report Compiled from Reports and Other Data Showing the Activities of Japanese and Japanese Officials in Relation to the United States and Her Possessions," November 6, 1907, i, l; Box 530, MID, RG 165, NA.

35. Jones, "A Report Compiled from Reports and Other Data," ii–x.

36. Jones, "A Report Compiled from Reports and Other Data," xxiv, xxxii, xxxiii, xxxvi, xliii.

37. Jones, "A Report Compiled from Reports and Other Data," xlviii, lvii.

38. McCoy, *Policing America's Empire,* 138–42; Harry Bandholtz to Henry T. Allen, September 11, 1907, Roll 2; Excerpts from *El Renacimiento,* Roll 6; Bandholtz Papers, UM. The quoted editorials were dated January 19, January 20, March 10, and June 24, 1909.

39. Excerpts from *El Renacimiento,* Roll 6, Bandholtz Papers, UM. The quoted editorials were dated March 5, December 3, 1908; March 2, April 23, July 8, and July 18, 1909.

40. Harry Bandholtz to Cornelius De W. Wilcox, March 24, 1909, Roll 2; Harry Bandholtz to Harry F. Nethers, July 28, 1909, Roll 3; Harry Bandholtz to Leonard Wood, July 22, 1909, Roll 3; Harry Bandholtz to C.R. Edwards,

October 25, 1909, Roll 3; R. Crame to Director [Bandholtz], January 11, 1908, Roll 6; Bandholtz Papers, UM; Ikehata Setsuho, "Japan and the Philippines, 1885–1905: Mutual Images and Interests," in *Philippines-Japan Relations*, edited by Ikehata Setsuho and Lydia N. Yu Jose (Manila: Ateneo de Manila University Press, 2003), 35–36.

41. McCoy, *Policing America's Empire*, 189–90; Harry Bandholtz to Luke E. Wright, February 8, March 9,1909, Box 8; J.R. White to Harry Bandholtz, March 25, 1909, Roll 2; Harry Bandholtz to Henry T. Allen, May 6, 1909, Roll 2; Bandholtz Papers, UM.

42. McCoy, *Policing America's Empire*, 130–32; Harry Bandholtz to J.G. Harbord, July 28, 1906, Roll 1; Harry Bandholtz to Henry C. Ide, July 8, 1907, Roll 2; Harry Bandholtz to George Curry, March 8, 1909, Roll 2; John R. White to Harry Bandholtz, March 28, April 13, 1909, Roll 2; Denis E. Nolan to Harry Bandholtz, October 14, 1909, Roll 3; Bandholtz Papers UM.

43. Harry Bandholtz to Harbord and Rivers, May 26, 1909, Roll 3; Harry Bandholtz to J.G. Harbord, July 5, 1909, Roll 3; "Rest Jikiri," *El Renacimiento*, July 7, 1909 (translated excerpt), Roll 6; Bandholtz Papers, UM; *New York Times*, July 6, 1909.

44. Macario D. Tiu, *Davao 1890–1910: Conquest and Resistance in the Garden of the Gods* (Quezon City: Center for Integrative and Development Studies, University of the Philippines, 2003), 85–116; Harry Bandholtz to Luke E. Wright, July 25, 1909, Box 8; Harry Bandholtz to W.C. Rivers, June 29, 1909; Harry Bandholtz to Mark L. Hersey, July 2, 1909; Harry Bandholtz to John R. White, July 2, 1909; Harry Bandholtz to Newton W. Gilbert, July 3, 1909; Harry Bandholtz to Martin Egan, July 3, 4, 1909; Harry Bandholtz to Herman Hall, July 5, 1909; Harry Bandholtz to J.G. Harbord, July 5, 1909; Harry Bandholtz to Harry F. Nethers, July 28, 1909; Harry Bandholtz to Leonard Wood, July 22, 1909; Harry Bandholtz to Fred W. Carpenter, July 24, 1909; Roll 3, Bandholtz Papers, UM.

45. Herman Hall to H.H. Bandholtz, August 19, 1909, Roll 3; Report, December 23, 1909, Roll 6; Report, January 3, 1910, Roll 6; Bandholtz Papers, UM.

46. Eleven, Report, January 10, 1910; Report, January 14, 1910; Report, January 24, 1910; Roll 6, Bandholtz Papers, UM.

47. Harry Bandholtz to Fred W. Carpenter, October 7, November 12, 27, 1909; Harry Bandholtz to J.G. Harbord, October 13, 1909; Harry Bandholtz to C.R. Edwards, October 25, 1909; Harry Bandholtz to Geo. Wray, December 19, 1909; Roll 3, Bandholtz Papers, UM.

48. W. Cameron Forbes to Jacob M. Dickinson, October 11, 1909, Confidential Letter Book (outgoing), vol. 1 (MS Am 1366.1), W. Cameron Forbes Papers, Houghton Library, Harvard University. I thank Ben Weber for sharing this letter with me.

49. Harry Bandholtz to Fred W. Carpenter, November 12, 27, 1909, Roll 3, Bandholtz Papers, UM.

50. Paul A. Kramer, *The Blood of Government: Race, Empire, the United States, and the Philippines* (Chapel Hill: University of North Carolina Press, 2006), 342; Harry Bandholtz to Henry T. Allen, February 26, 1909, Roll 2;

Report, January 21, 1910, Roll 6; Bandholtz Papers, UM. On Hirobumi Ito's tenure in Korea, see Duus, *The Abacus and the Sword*, 197–239.

51. Ileto, *Filipinos and Their Revolution*, 151–52; Report, November 27, 1909, Roll 6; Harry Bandholtz to Henry T. Allen, March 8, 1910, Roll 3; Harry Bandholtz to Leonard Wood, March 11, 1910, Roll 3; Harry Bandholtz to Manuel L. Quezon, April 26, 1910, Roll 3; Bandholtz Papers, UM; Confidential Report, Manila, April 30, 1910, appended to Lea Febiger to Adjutant General of the Army, June 14, 1910, Box 530, MID, RG 165, NA.

52. Report, November 28, 1909; Report, January 12, 1910; Roll 6, Bandholtz Papers, UM.

53. Sixteen, Report, November 18, 1909, Roll 6; Report, January 14, 1910, Roll 6; Pedro Mercado, Confidential Report, December 2, 1910, Roll 6; Harry Bandholtz to Fred W. Carpenter, November 27, 1909, Roll 3; Bandholtz Papers, UM.

54. Report, January 12, 1910; Twenty-two, Confidential Report, May 11, 1910; Roll 6, Bandholtz Papers, UM. A copy of the latter report was forwarded to the MID as Twenty-one, Confidential Report, May 11, 1910, appended to Lea Febiger to Adjutant General of the Army, June 14, 1910, Box 530, MID, RG 165, NA.

55. "The Voyage of the Secretary of War," *El Ideal*, August 16, 1910 (translated copy) and "Last Lines," *El Mercantil*, August 20, 1910; Eleven, Confidential Report, October 4, 1910, appended to Wm. P. Duvall to Adjutant General of the Army, November 11, 1910; Box 530, MID, RG 165, NA. Eleven's report originated from the Philippine Constabulary (Roll 6, Bandholtz Papers, UM).

56. [Harry Bandholtz], "Memorandum Covering Trip to Japan to Meet the Secretary of War," [July 1910]; Harry Bandholtz to Leonard Wood, September 6, 13, 1910; Roll 3, Bandholtz Papers, UM.

57. Confidential Report (translation), April 11, 1910, appended to Lea Febiger to Adjutant General of the Army, June 14, 1910, Box 530, MID, RG 165, NA; Confidential Report, March 4, 1910; Confidential Report, April 29, 1910; Sixteen, Confidential Report, July 27, 1910; Agent 26, Confidential Report, August 1, 1910; Roll 6, Bandholtz Papers, UM.

58. M. Nicolas, Confidential Report, September 15, 1910; Confidential Report, October 10, 1910; Roll 6, Bandholtz Papers, UM.

59. Agent 26, Confidential Report, August 13, September 23, 1910; Superintendent [Rafael Crame] to Director [Harry Bandholtz], August 25, 1910; Eleven, Confidential Report, September 9, 1910; Roll 6, Bandholtz Papers, UM; José de los Reyes, *Biography of Senator Isabelo de los Reyes: Father of Labor and Proclaimer of the Philippine Independent Church* (Manila: Nueva Era Press, 1947), 22–23. According to the biography, Isabelo de los Reyes went to Japan in 1910 to seek medical care for his sick Spanish wife and to publish an Ilocano translation of the Bible (25).

60. Artemio Ricarte to [redacted name] Municipal President, February 13, 1911; Superintendent, "Memorandum for the Director," December 14, 1910; Agent 26, Confidential Report, June 2, 1911; Roll 6, Bandholtz Papers, UM.

61. Agent 26, Confidential Report, March 13, 14, June 2, 17, July 7, 22, 31, 1911; Roll 6, Bandholtz Papers, UM.

62. Agent 26, Confidential Report, March 13, 17, 19, 22, 30, April 5, June 19, 24, July 10, 1911; 35, Confidential Report, May 6, 1911; R.M. Crame, "Memorandum for the Director," May 22, 1911; M. Nicolas, Confidential Report, May 29, 1911; Roll 6, Bandholtz Papers, UM.

63. Eleven, Confidential Report, January 19, 26, 1911; M. Nicolas, Confidential Report, January 5, 1911; Superintendent [Rafael Crame], "Memorandum for the Director," January 5, 1911; n.a. to General of the Constabulary, January 30, 1911; Roll 6, Bandholtz Papers, UM.

64. Superintendent [Rafael Crame], "Memorandum for the Director," January 30, 1911; n.a., Confidential Report, January 31, February 13, 1911; Eleven, Confidential Report, February 2, 1911; Roll 6, Bandholtz Papers, UM. US officials and American business leaders conceived the Manila Carnival in 1907 as a means to attract capital investment and to promote friendly relations between Americans and Filipinos (Genevieve Clutario, "Pageant Politics: Tensions of Power, Empire, and Nationalism in Manila Carnival Queen Contests," in *Gendering the Trans-Pacific World: Diaspora, Empire, and Race*, edited by Catherine Ceniza Choy and Judy Tzu-Chun Wu [Leiden: Brill, 2017], 260–61).

65. N.a., Confidential Report, February 15, 1911; M. Nicolas, Confidential Report, February 22, 23, 25, 27, 1911; Superintendent [Rafael Crame], "Memorandum for the Director," February 8, 1911; Roll 6, Bandholtz Papers, UM.

66. "Filipino Women Appeal for Mercy to Prisoners," *Public Opinion* 30, no. 18 (May 2, 1901): 553; Lilia Quindoza Santiago, "Rebirthing *Babaye*: The Women's Movement in the Philippines," in *The Challenge of Local Feminisms: Women's Movements in Global Perspective*, edited by Amrita Basu (Boulder: Westview Press, 1995), 118; Cynthia Luz P. Rivera, "Filipino Women's Magazines, 1909–1940: Resistance, Cultural Subversion, and Compromise," *Plaridel* 1, no. 2 (August 2004): 2–12; n.a., Confidential Report, February 13, 1911, Roll 6, Bandholtz Papers, UM.

67. Ricarte, *Memoirs of General Artemio Ricarte*, xxii, 137–55; McCoy, *Policing America's Empire*, 194–95. A later profile, published in the Philippines under Japanese occupation during World War II, claimed that the British expelled Ricarte "on suspicion that he was in connivance with some Indians who were planning a movement to obtain independence for India" (E. del Rosario, "General Artemio Ricarte," *Philippine Review* 2, no. 4 [June 1944]: 55).

68. Ricarte, *Memoirs of General Artemio Ricarte*, xxii; Isagani R. Medina, "Agueda Esteban y de la Cruz," in *Women in the Philippine Revolution*, edited by Rafaelita Hilario Soriano (Quezon City: Printon Press, 1995), 40–44; McCoy, *Policing America's Empire*, 195–96.

CHAPTER 3. FIGHTING JOHN BULL AND UNCLE SAM

Epigraph: Translated excerpt from Box 1, Neutrality Case Files, Records of the US District Attorney, Record Group (RG) 118, National Archives, San Bruno, California (NASB).

1. Emily C. Brown, *Har Dayal: Hindu Revolutionary and Rationalist* (Tucson: University of Arizona Press, 1975), 9–81 (quotes from 18 and 57, emphasis in original).

2. Brown, *Har Dayal,* 81–126 (quote from 86); P. A. Baker to Commissioner-General of Immigration, April 3, 1914; W. A. Clark, Academic Secretary, Stanford University, to A. Caminetti, April 21, 1914, File 53572/92–92A, Records of the Immigration and Naturalization Service (INS), RG 85, National Archives, Washington, DC (NA).

3. Brown, *Har Dayal,* 111–12, 131–33 (Hopkinson quote from 133); Joan M. Jensen, *Passage from India: Asian Indian Immigrants in North America* (New Haven: Yale University Press, 1988), 163–64.

4. Brown, *Har Dayal,* 140–44; Jensen, *Passage from India,* 180–83; F. C. Isemonger and J. Slattery, *An Account of the Ghadr Conspiracy (1913–1915)* (Berkeley: Folklore Institute, 1998 [1919]), 14; Har Dayal's translation of *Ghadar,* November 1, 1913, File 53572/92–92A, INS, RG 85, NA. Ghadar was also spelled *Gadar* and *Ghadr.*

5. "Extracts from a Speech Delivered by Ha[r] Dayal in Jefferson Square Hall, San Francisco, California, Friday Evening, October 31, 1913," File 53572/92–92A, INS, RG 85, NA. Of the transcript, Dayal said: "This is a very good report and pleases me very much" (Hearing on Har Dayal by F. H. Ainsworth on Angel Island, March 26, 1914, File 53572/92–92A, INS, RG 85, NA).

6. A. Caminetti to Immigration Service, Seattle and Portland, June 12, 1913 (telegram); Wm. C. Hopkinson to John L. Zurbrick, August 2, 1913; Samuel W. Backus to Commissioner-General of Immigration, January 30, 1914; J. B. Densmore, Acting Secretary of Labor, to Samuel W. Backus, February 10, 1914; File 53572/92–92A, INS, RG 85, NA.

7. Har Dayal to A. Caminetti, March 29, 1914 (telegram); Charles Sferlazzo, Attorney for Har Dayal, "Defendant's Brief, In the Matter of the arrest of Har Dayal, alleged anarchist arrested under the authority of Departmental Warrant dated February 10th, 1914," n.d.; Samuel Backus to Commissioner-General of Immigration, April 24, 1914; Hearing on Har Dayal by F. H. Ainsworth on Angel Island, March 26, 1914; File 53572/92–92A, INS, RG 85, NA; *San Francisco Chronicle,* March 27, 1914.

8. Moon-Ho Jung, *Coolies and Cane: Race, Sugar, and Labor in the Age of Emancipation* (Baltimore: Johns Hopkins University Press, 2006), 14–16.

9. Sucheta Mazumdar, "Colonial Impact and Punjabi Emigration to the United States," in *Labor Immigration under Capitalism: Asian Workers in the United States before World War II,* edited by Lucie Cheng and Edna Bonacich (Berkeley: University of California Press, 1984), 316–36; Jensen, *Passage from India,* 6–9, 24–41.

10. Marilyn Lake and Henry Reynolds, *Drawing the Global Colour Line: White Men's Countries and the International Challenge of Racial Equality* (Cambridge: Cambridge University Press, 2008), 121–33 (Colonial Office quote from 128).

11. Jensen, *Passage from India,* 57–82.

12. W. L. MacKenzie King, *Report by W. L. MacKenzie King on Mission to England to Confer with the British Authorities on the Subject of Immigration to Canada from the Orient and Immigration from India in Particular* (Ottawa: S. E. Dawson, 1908), 7–8, in File 51388, INS, RG 85, NA; Jensen, *Passage from India,* 79.

13. Jensen, *Passage from India*, 42–59; *Seattle Post-Intelligencer,* September 9, 1907; Lake and Reynolds, *Drawing the Global Colour Line,* 184–86 (quote from 185); Seema Sohi, *Echoes of Mutiny: Race, Surveillance, and Indian Anticolonialism in North America* (New York: Oxford University Press, 2014), 25–26.

14. Jensen, *Passage from India,* 99; *The Statutes at Large of the United States of America, from December, 1905, to March, 1907,* vol. 34, part 1 (Washington, DC: Government Printing Office, 1907), 898–99.

15. File 52269/25, INS, RG 85, NA; Paul A. Kramer, *The Blood of Government: Race, Empire, the United States, and the Philippines* (Chapel Hill: University of North Carolina Press, 2006), 211–20; Jensen, *Passage from India,* 111.

16. File 52269/2 and File 52269/26, INS, RG 85, NA; Jensen, *Passage from India,* 107–8, 114.

17. "Memorandum," Office of the Solicitor, Department of Commerce and Labor, February 28, 1908; Oscar S. Straus, Secretary of Commerce and Labor, Department Circular No. 163, March 3, 1908; File 51924, INS, RG 85, NA.

18. William Preston Jr., *Aliens and Dissenters: Federal Suppression of Radicals, 1903–1933,* 2nd ed. (Urbana: University of Illinois Press, 1994), 39–43; W. P. Lawson, Otto Bobsien, H. Arnold, J. Bernstein, G. der Hertag, Abe Beyer to John H. Sargent, March 18, 1908; John H. Sargent to Commissioner General of Immigration, May 20, 1908; File 51924, INS, RG 85, NA.

19. Wilhelm Lutz to Graham L. Rice, May 28, 1908, File 51924, INS, RG 85, NA.

20. Bong-youn Choy, *Koreans in America* (Chicago: Nelson-Hall, 1979), 146–48; John Koster, "Death of an 'American Dictator," *American History* (October 2007): 54–58; *New York Times,* March 24, 27, 1908.

21. Raymond Miller [?] to Commissioner-General of Immigration, June 8, 1908; H. H. North to Commissioner-General of Immigration, May 22, 1908; File 51924, INS, RG 85, NA.

22. T. R. Sareen, "India and the War," in *The Impact of the Russo-Japanese War,* edited by Rotem Kowner (London: Routledge, 2007), 241–46 (newspaper quote from 241); Jensen, *Passage from India,* 4–6; Sohi, *Echoes of Mutiny,* 18–21.

23. *The Statutes at Large . . . from December, 1905, to March, 1907,* vol. 34, part 1, 899; File 52269/21, INS, RG 85, NA.

24. File 52269/50 and File 52269/51, INS, RG 85, NA. Guljara was also spelled *Goolzarrah.* On anti-Chinese violence, see Beth Lew-Williams, *The Chinese Must Go: Violence, Exclusion, and the Making of the Alien in America* (Cambridge, MA: Harvard University Press, 2018).

25. Jensen, *Passage from India,* 103–17; Daniel J. Keefe to Commissioner of Immigration [H. H. North], April 27, 1910, File 52785/18–22, INS, RG 85, NA. North was suspended six months later.

26. Gail Bederman, *Manliness and Civilization: A Cultural History of Gender and Race in the United States, 1880–1917* (Chicago: University of Chicago Press, 1995), 1–4; "Heart-to-Heart Talk with the Candidates," *The White Man* 1, no. 2 (August 1910): 5; Wm. R. Wheeler to Chas. P. Neill, August 11, 1910; Wm. H. Michael, Consul-General, Calcutta, to Assistant Secretary of State,

August 11, 1910; File 52903/110, INS, RG 85, NA. On Jack Johnson's global significance, see Theresa Runstedtler, *Rebel Sojourner: Boxing in the Shadow of the Global Color Line* (Berkeley: University of California Press, 2012).

27. Jensen, *Passage from India*, 118; Rajani Kanta Das, *Hindustani Workers on the Pacific Coast* (Berlin: Walter de Gruyter, 1923), 17; Sohi, *Echoes of Mutiny*, 45–46; D. Chenchiah, "History of Freedom Movement in India: The Ghadar Movement, 1913–1918" (unpublished manuscript, 1956), 1–2, South Asians in North America Collection (SANA), Bancroft Library, University of California, Berkeley. The 1910 census figure does not include Hawai'i. Dayal was also excited by the news of the attempted assassination of Viceroy Lord Hardinge in Delhi in December 1912 (Harish K. Puri, *Ghadar Movement: Ideology, Organisation, and Strategy* [Amritsar: Guru Nanak Dev University Press, 1983], 57–58).

28. Chenchiah, "History of Freedom Movement in India," 3–6. I have corrected some of Chenchiah's typos in Dayal's quote.

29. Tapan K. Mukherjee, *Taraknath Das: Life and Letters of a Revolutionary in Exile* (Calcutta: National Council of Education, Jadavpur University, 1998), 1–9; Jensen, *Passage from India*, 165.

30. *Seattle Post-Intelligencer,* September 9, 10, 11, 12, 13, 1907. I thank Trevor Griffey for calling my attention to these articles.

31. Mukherjee, *Taraknath Das,* 11–16.

32. Jensen, *Passage from India*, 165–69; Mukherjee, *Taraknath Das,* 16–23, 33–34.

33. Ellis DeBruler to Commissioner-General of Immigration, January 11, 1911; Herbert W. Meyers, "Aliens' Brief," in the Matter of the Arrest of Arjan Singh et al., February 28, 1911; File 53154/2–2A, INS, RG 85, NA.

34. Ellis DeBruler to Commissioner-General of Immigration, January 11, 1911; Daniel J. Keefe, "Memorandum for the Acting Secretary," January 27, 1911; File 53154/2–2A, INS, RG 85, NA.

35. Charles Nagel, "Memorandum," March 7, 1911, File 53154/2–2A, INS, RG 85, NA; Agent 30 to Colonel, June 27, 1911, Harry H. Bandholtz Papers, Bentley Historical Library, University of Michigan.

36. Jensen, *Passage from India*, 163–74; Mukherjee, *Taraknath Das,* 9, 34; Sohi, *Echoes of Mutiny,* 84–91; John H. Clark to Commissioner-General of Immigration, June 10, 1913 [including Hopkinson's telegram]; A. Caminetti to Immigration Service, Seattle and Portland, June 12, 1913; File 53572/92–92A, INS, RG 85, NA.

37. Sohi, *Echoes of Mutiny,* 54–56; *Astoria Daily Budget,* June 2, 1913, in File 53572/92–92A, INS, RG 85, NA; Isemonger and Slattery, *An Account of the Ghadr Conspiracy,* 13–16 [Dayal's speeches]. For a slightly different account of Ghadar's origins, see Puri, *Ghadar Movement,* 58–67.

38. Sohi, *Echoes of Mutiny,* 52–56, 90–91, 126; Wm. C. Hopkinson to John L. Zurbrick, August 2, 1913; John H. Clark to Commissioner-General of Immigration, August 11, 1913; A. Caminetti, note on copies furnished to commissioners and inspectors in Boston, Ellis Island, Philadelphia, Baltimore, New Orleans, Norfolk, Jacksonville, and Galveston, August 16, 1913; Wm. C. Hopkinson to John H. Clark, September 9, 1913; G. D. Kumar to "My dear Dass,"

July 8, 1913 (copy); Tarak[nath Das] to "My dear Harnam," August 13, 1913 (copy); File 53572/92–92A, INS, RG 85, NA.

39. Sohi, *Echoes of Mutiny,* 124–26; Amy Kaplan, *The Anarchy of Empire in the Making of U.S. Culture* (Cambridge: Harvard University Press, 2002), 2.

40. Sohi, *Echoes of Mutiny,* 124–25; "Report of Proceedings at Meeting of Hindus, Held in O'Brien Hall, Vancouver, B.C., on September 29, 1913. With Reference to 73 Hindus, held by United States Immigration Authorities at Seattle, Wash.," File 52903/110-C, INS, RG 85, NA. Seven of the two hundred were rejected ostensibly for medical reasons (hookworm), while seventy-three were ordered deported for "likely to become a public charge."

41. Translations of *Ghadar* by Har Dayal in his immigration file, File 53572/92–92A, INS, RG 85, NA; Isemonger and Slattery, *An Account of the Ghadr Conspiracy,* 20. The issues, not all of which were dated, are from March 3, 1914, and December 9 and 23, 1913.

42. Samuel W. Backus to Commissioner-General of Immigration, January 23, 1914, File 52903/110-D, INS, RG 85, NA.

43. Charles H. Reily to Acting Inspector in Charge, Portland, Oregon, January 14, 1914, File 53572/92–92A, INS, RG 85, NA.

44. Samuel W. Backus to Commissioner-General of Immigration, January 30, 1914; *Washington Post,* February 10, 1914; A. Caminetti to John L. Burnett, February 7, 1914; File 53572/92–92A, INS, RG 85, NA; Brown, *Har Dayal,* 154; 63rd Congress, 2nd Session, *Hearings before the Committee on Immigration . . . Relative to Restriction of Immigration of Hindu Laborers,* Part 2 (Washington, DC: Government Printing Office, 1914), 85–86.

45. 63rd Congress, 2nd Session, *Hearings before the Committee on Immigration . . . Relative to Restriction of Immigration of Hindu Laborers,* Part 1 (Washington, DC: Government Printing Office, 1914), 45–46, 48, 50; 63rd Congress, 2nd Session, *Hearings before the Committee on Immigration . . . Relative to Restriction of Immigration of Hindu Laborers,* Part 4 (Washington, DC: Government Printing Office, 1914), 141.

46. 63rd Congress, 2nd Session, *Hearings before the Committee on Immigration,* Part 2, 75, 82; 63rd Congress, 2nd Session, *Hearings before the Committee on Immigration . . . Relative to Restriction of Immigration of Hindu Laborers,* Part 5 (Washington, DC: Government Printing Office, 1914), 167–72. Bhutia's full name was listed as 'T'Ishi Bhutia Kyawgh Hla'. On South Asian migrants and sodomy laws, see Nayan Shah, *Stranger Intimacy: Contesting Race, Sexuality, and the Law in the North American West* (Berkeley: University of California Press, 2011).

47. J. B. Densmore, Acting Secretary of Labor, to Samuel W. Backus, February 10, 1914; *San Francisco Chronicle,* March 29, 1914; *San Francisco Bulletin,* March 27, 1914; *San Francisco Examiner,* March 28, 1914; File 53572/92–92A, INS, RG 85, NA; "Har Dayal on his arrest," *Ghadar,* March 31, 1914 (translated copy in Box 1, Neutrality Case Files, RG 118, NASB).

48. A. Caminetti, Memorandum, April 4, 1914; Charles Sferlazzo, Attorney for Har Dayal, "Defendant's Brief, In the Matter of the arrest of Har Dayal, alleged anarchist arrested under the authority of Departmental Warrant dated February 10th, 1914," n.d.; Har Dayal to A. Caminetti, March 29, 1914 (tele-

gram); Acting Commissioner, Ellis Island, to Commissioner of Immigration, Angel Island Station, Certificate of Admission of Alien, March 27, 1914; Acting Commissioner P. A. Baker to Commissioner-General of Immigration, April 3, 1914; File 53572/92–92A, INS, RG 85, NA.

49. Sohi, *Echoes of Mutiny*, 134–44; Mukherjee, *Taraknath Das*, 57. For a fuller account, see Hugh Johnston, *The Voyage of the Komagata Maru: The Sikh Challenge to Canada's Colour Bar* (Delhi: Oxford University Press, 1979); Renisa Mawani, *Across Oceans of Law: The Komagata Maru and Indian Migration in the Time of Empire* (Durham: Duke University Press, 2018).

50. Robert Lansing, Counselor, Department of State, to Secretary of Labor, April 7, 1914 (quoting Dayal's telegram dated April 4, 1914); Backus to Immigration Bureau, Washington, DC, April 1, 1914 (telegram); Samuel W. Backus to United Sates Fidelity & Guaranty Co., April 28, May 6, 1914; Charles Sferlazzo to Samuel W. Backus, May 2, 1914; Borland & Johns to Samuel W. Backus, May 4, 1914; Samuel W. Backus to Commissioner-General of Immigration, May 11, June 20, 1914; W. J. P., Department of Labor, "Memo. For Mr. Larned," May 26, 1914; Acting Secretary to Commissioner of Immigration, Angel Island Station, June 13, 1914; Commissioner-General to Commissioner of Immigration, San Francisco, June 29, 1914; File 53572/92–92A, INS, RG 85, NA.

51. *The Times of India*, May 27, 1914; Henry D. Baker to Secretary of State, May 27, 1914; Har Dayal to "Sir," July 13, 1914; File 53572/92–92A, INS, RG 85, NA; *Sedition Committee Report 1918* (Calcutta: New Age Publishers Private Limited, 1973 [1918]), 143–46.

52. W. E. Burghardt Du Bois, "The African Roots of War," *Atlantic Monthly* 115 (May 1915): 707–14.

53. "The Trumpet of War," *Ghadar*, August 4, 1918; "Indians, Go and Mutiny," *Ghadar*, August 18, 1914; "Indian Troops Are Coming to Fight the Germans," *Ghadar*, September 1, 1914; translation of a Hindi pamphlet, *Indian Soldiers! Do Not Fight with Germany* [n.d.], emphasis in original; all in Box 1, Neutrality Case Files, RG 118, NASB.

54. Sohi, *Echoes of Mutiny*, 152–56; Arun Coomer Bose, *Indian Revolutionaries Abroad, 1905–1922: In the Background of International Developments* (Patna: Bharati Bhawan, 1971), 121–23 (Chandra quote from 121); *Sedition Committee Report 1918*, 149.

55. *Sedition Committee Report 1918*, 148–50; Isemonger and Slattery, *An Account of the Ghadr Conspiracy*, 59–64; Sohi, *Echoes of Mutiny*, 144–46, 156–57.

56. Isemonger and Slattery, *An Account of the Ghadr Conspiracy*, 59, 72–73; Sohi, *Echoes of Mutiny*, 154–65.

57. Sohi, *Echoes of Mutiny*, 45, 178–82.

58. Charles Warren, Assistant Attorney General, to John W. Preston, US Attorney, San Francisco, May 13, 1916; "Memorandum for Mr. Warren," April 12, 1916; [Appendix titled] "'The Ghadr' and 'The Ghadr Hindustan'"; Box 7, Neutrality Case Files, RG 118, NASB.

59. Charles Warren, Assistant Attorney General, to John W. Preston, US Attorney, San Francisco, May 13, 1916; "Memorandum for Mr. Warren,"

April 12, 1916; "Memorandum on the Indian Revolutionary Movement in the United States," n.d.; Box 7, Neutrality Case Files, RG 118, NASB.

60. Charles Warren, Assistant Attorney General, to John W. Preston, US Attorney, San Francisco, May 13, 1916, Box 7, Neutrality Case Files, RG 118, NASB. I borrow the phrase "possessive investment" from George Lipsitz, *The Possessive Investment in Whiteness: How White People Profit from Identity Politics* (Philadelphia: Temple University Press, 1998).

61. Charles Warren to John W. Preston, February 7. 1917, Box 4; Special Assistant to the Attorney General for War Work [John W. Preston] to Attorney General T. W. Gregory, August 6, 1918, Box 3; Neutrality Case Files, RG 118, NASB.

62. C. McI. Messer, Captain, Superintendent of Police, May 17, 1915; British Embassy, Tokyo, "Bhagwan Singh's Antecedents" (confidential), June 11, 1915; Box 10, Neutrality Case Files, RG 118, NASB.

63. Cemil Aydin, *The Politics of Anti-Westernism in Asia: Visions of World Order in Pan-Islamic and Pan-Asian Thought* (New York: Columbia University Press, 2007), 113–15; Sohi, *Echoes of Mutiny*, 50; "Bhagwan Singh" [no author and no date, but most likely written by British agents for Preston]; John W. Green, Chief, Secret Service Bureau, Department of Police, City of Manila, to F. N. Berry, Acting Secretary to the Governor-General, May 4, 1917; Box 10, Neutrality Case Files, RG 118, NASB. Muhammad was also spelled *Mohamed*.

64. John W. Green to F. N. Berry, May 4, 1917, Box 10; Mr. Blanford, "Documents from Manila," August 2, 1917 (including full copies of Singh's statement, as reported by the Customs Secret Service Agent, Zamboanga, February 13, 1915, and the agent's report, March 1, 1915), Box 7; J. S. Robertson, Custom Secret Service Agent and Philippine Constabulary Agent, Zamboanga, to Chief Custom Secret Service, "Narrative Report, for February 1915," March 1, 1915, Box 2; Perry L. Machlan, Customs Secret Service Agent, Jolo, to Chief, Customs Secret Service, February 13, 1915, Box 2; Neutrality Case Files, RG 118, NASB.

65. F. W. Carpenter, Governor of Mindanao and Sulu, to Executive Secretary, March 25, 1915; John W. Green to F. N. Berry, May 4, 1917; George E. Anderson to Executive Secretary, May 24, 1915; S. Ferguson, Acting Executive Secretary, to George E. Anderson, August 9, 1915; Herman Hall, Chief of Constabulary, to Executive Secretary, June 3, 1915; Box 10, Neutrality Case Files, RG 118, NASB.

66. Notes on defendants, n.d., 30–33, Box 4; Wm. Jennings Price, American Minister, to Secretary of State (confidential), October 30, 1917, Box 1 (and Box 12); American Legation, Panama, "Confidential Memorandum No. 124," to Colonel Commanding, Panama Canal Department, November 12, 1917, Box 12; Neutrality Case Files, RG 118, NASB.

67. Captain, C.A.C., Intelligence Officer, Panama Canal Department, to Chief, Military Intelligence Branch, Washington, DC, March 19, 1918, Box 2; Gregory to US Attorney, San Francisco, April 6, 1917, Box 2; Neutrality Case Files, RG 118, NASB; Sohi, *Echoes of Mutiny*, 171.

68. A. A. Hopkins, "In Re: Bhagwan Singh (Hindu) Fugitive," Warren, Arizona, April 22, 1917, Box 7, Neutrality Case Files, RG 118, NASB.

69. "Extract from Yugantar of Bhagwan Singh," July 1917, Box 4, Neutrality Case Files, RG 118, NASB.

CHAPTER 4. RADICALIZING HAWAI'I

1. Jeffrey B. Perry, *Hubert Harrison: The Voice of Harlem Radicalism, 1883–1918* (New York: Columbia University Press, 2009), 4, 231; Jeffrey B. Perry, ed., *A Hubert Harrison Reader* (Middletown: Wesleyan University Press, 2001), 226; V.I. Lenin, *Imperialism: The Highest Stage of Capitalism* (New York: International Publishers, 1939 [1917]), 88; Mark Ellis, *Race, War, and Surveillance: African Americans and the United States Government during World War I* (Bloomington: Indiana University Press, 2001), 121–25; Theodore Kornweibel Jr., *"Seeing Red": Federal Campaigns against Black Militancy, 1919–1925* (Bloomington: Indiana University Press, 1998), 140–43.

2. George M. Brooke, "Situation Survey for period ending January 31, 1920" and "Situation Survey for week ending 13 March 1920," Military Intelligence Division Correspondence, 1917–1941 (MID), Record Group (RG) 165, National Archives, Washington, DC (NA).

3. George M. Brooke, "Situation Survey for period ending January 31, 1920," "Situation Survey for week ending 31 January 1920," and "Situation Survey for week ending 6 March 1920," MID, RG 165, NA.

4. Michel Foucault, *Security, Territory, Population: Lectures at the Collège de France, 1977–78*, edited by Michel Senellart (New York: Palgrave Macmillan, 2007), 204, 355–57.

5. Tapan K. Mukherjee, *Taraknath Das: Life and Letters of a Revolutionary in Exile* (Calcutta: National Council of Education, Jadavpur University, 1998), 56, 69–88; Notes on defendants, n.d., 51–62, Box 4, Neutrality Case Files, Records of the US District Attorney, RG 118, National Archives, San Bruno, California (NASB). In July 1916, Das applied for a US passport to travel to Japan, China, Java, and Siam (Special Assistant to the Attorney General to John W. Preston, October 15, 1917, Box 2, Neutrality Case Files, RG 118, NASB).

6. Statement by Shir Dayal Kapur Khatri, n.d., Box 9; "Shiv Dyal Kapur," Index to Records and Summary of Prosecution Witnesses, Box 12; Neutrality Case Files, RG 118, NASB. Kapur was later arrested in Bangkok and agreed to testify in the "Hindu Conspiracy" trial.

7. Mukherjee, *Taraknath Das*, 91–94.

8. Mukherjee, *Taraknath Das*, 93–103; [Chandra K. Chakravarty], in letters compiled as "America to Germany," September 27 [in which Chen is referred to as KINGSUCHEN], December 21, 1916; Agent Wright, "In re: Hindusthan Club or Association," Seattle, Washington, May 3, 1917 (quoting the *University of Washington Daily*, April 30, 1917); J.S. H[ale] to [John W.] Preston, September 6, 1917; Box 7, Neutrality Case Files, RG 118, NASB.

9. Taraknath Das, *Is Japan a Menace to Asia?* (Shanghai: n.p., 1917), dedication page, iii.

10. Das, *Is Japan a Menace to Asia?*, 28, 31, 33, 35, 49–51.

11. Das, *Is Japan a Menace to Asia?*, 55, 78–79. Emphases in original.

12. An Asian Statesman, *Isolation of Japan in World Politics* (Tokyo: Asiatic Association of Japan, 1918), preface, v. The English version was published in January 1918. Masayoshi Oshikawa's foreword was titled "Introduction."

13. An Asian Statesman, *Isolation of Japan in World Politics*, 4, 14, 16, 17, 25.

14. An Asian Statesman, *Isolation of Japan in World Politics*, 32, 36, 47–50.

15. An Asian Statesman, *Isolation of Japan in World Politics*, 53, 63 (emphasis in original), 64. Das elaborated on the promise of Japan's "Asiatic Monroe Doctrine" in the last appendix (76–84).

16. Thomas F. Gossett, *Race: The History of an Idea in America* (Dallas: Southern Methodist University Press, 1963), 390–95; Lothrop Stoddard, *The Rising Tide of Color against White World-Supremacy* (New York: Charles Scribner's Sons, 1920), vi–vii, 11, 179, 12.

17. Stoddard, *The Rising Tide of Color*, 229, 231, 247, 232, 289, 308, 305.

18. Stoddard, *The Rising Tide of Color*, 233, 218–21.

19. Stoddard, *The Rising Tide of Color*, 279, 281.

20. "Supplemental Statement of C. Chakraberty," March 8, 1917; Chief to William M. Offley, March 10, 1917; R. Napier to Mr. Storey, April 1, 1917; Chief to Don S. Rathbun, April 3, 1917; Old German (OG) File 1396, Investigative Case Files of the Bureau of Investigation, 1908–1922, Records of the Federal Bureau of Investigation (FBI), RG 65, NA; Mukherjee, *Taraknath Das*, 101.

21. Mukherjee, *Taraknath Das*, 103–5, 107–11; *Japan Advertiser*, July 12, August 7, 1917, in Box 12, Neutrality Case Files, RG 118, NASB. Some Japanese intellectuals, unlike the Japanese state, championed Indian independence and pan-Asian solidarity during World War I and collaborated with Das and others in Japan. See Cemil Aydin, *The Politics of Anti-Westernism in Asia: Visions of World Order in Pan-Islamic and Pan-Asian Thought* (New York: Columbia University Press, 2007), 111–24.

22. S. C. Huber to John W. Preston, June 18 and 22, 1917, Box 2; [John W. Preston] to S. C. Huber, June 8, July 3, 1917, Box 2; A. Carnegie Ross to John Preston, May 21, 1917, Box 2; Sworn deposition by William Todd, Aide for Information, Naval Reserve Force, Territory of Hawaii, interviewing Taraknath Das aboard *Siberia Maru* on August 17, 1917, Box 5; Neutrality Case Files, RG 118, NASB. A year later, Hauswirth demanded the return of her papers used in the "Hindu Prosecution" (Frieda Hauswirth Das to [Je]anette Adams, Assistant District Attorney, June 11, 1918, Box 3, Neutrality Case Files, RG 118, NASB).

23. Seema Sohi, *Echoes of Mutiny: Race, Surveillance, and Indian Anticolonialism in North America* (New York: Oxford University Press, 2014), 167; Moon-Kie Jung, *Reworking Race: The Making of Hawaii's Interracial Labor Movement* (New York: Columbia University Press, 2006), 17–19; United States Attorney [Preston] to S. C. Huber, July 26, 1917, Box 4; S. C. Huber to John W. Preston, June 18, 1917, Box 2; Neutrality Case Files, RG 118, NASB.

24. Gary Y. Okihiro, *Cane Fires: The Anti-Japanese Movement in Hawaii, 1865–1945* (Philadelphia: Temple University Press, 1991), 7–18, 59; Jung, *Reworking Race*, 11–21.

25. Okihiro, *Cane Fires*, 41–57 (sheriff quote, 53); Jung, *Reworking Race*, 21–33.

26. George Davies to Geo. McCubbin, July 13, 1909; F. M. Swanzy to Geo. McCubbin, August 16, 1909; Laupahoehoe Sugar Company (LSC), Hawaiian Sugar Planters' Association Plantation Archives (HSPA), Hawaiian Collection, University of Hawai'i at Mānoa Library (UH).

27. 62nd Congress, 2nd Session, *Hearings Relative to the Excepting of Hawaii from the Educational Test for Immigrants before the Committee on Immigration and Naturalization, Part 7* (Washington, DC: Government Printing Office, 1912), 3–7, 24, 31–32.

28. Wm. Haywood to Secretary of War, June 19, 1901; Philippine Commission, Executive Session, Minutes of Proceedings, July 23, 1906; Wm. Matson to W.I. Brobeck, September 16, 1914; Records of the Bureau of Insular Affairs, General Records, 1898–1945 (BIA), File 3037; RG 350, NA; Okihiro, *Cane Fires,* 55, 59; Jung, *Reworking Race,* 34, 42–44.

29. Okihiro, *Cane Fires,* 65; Jung, *Reworking Race,* 33; Edward D. Beechert, *Working in Hawaii: A Labor History* (Honolulu: University of Hawai'i Press, 1985), 196–97; R. D. Mead to Manager, Pepeekeo Sugar Company, July 30, 1917; S. O. Halls to Messrs. C. Brewer & Company, July 18, 1917 (quoting Henry St. Goar to E. F. Bishop); Hilo Coast Processing Company (HCP), HSPA, UH.

30. Michael Lewis, *Rioters and Citizens: Mass Protest in Imperial Japan* (Berkeley: University of California Press, 1990); Masayo Umezawa Duus, *The Japanese Conspiracy: The Oahu Sugar Strike of 1920* (Berkeley: University of California Press, 1999), 45–47; Beechert, *Working in Hawaii,* 197–99; translated copy of *Hawaii Hochi* in George M. Brooke, "Oriental labor question in Hawaii," August 29, 1919, MID, RG 165, NA

31. Melinda Tria Kerkvliet, *Unbending Cane: Pablo Manlapit, A Filipino Labor Leader in Hawai'i* (Honolulu: Office of Multicultural Student Services, University of Hawai'i at Mānoa, 2002), 5–21; R. A. Cooke to James Webster, August 1, 1919; R. D. Mead to E. D. Tenney, July 29, 1919, HCP, HSPA, UH; Beechert, *Working in Hawaii,* 158, 197–201; Jung, *Reworking Race,* 34–35.

32. Beechert, *Working in Hawaii,* 201–3; Okihiro, *Cane Fires,* 69–71.

33. J. N. S. Williams to R. A. Hutchison, January 24, 1920, LSC; E. H. Wodehouse to R. A. Hutchison, January 30, 1920, LSC; "Strike Memoranda," February 3, 4, 1920, HCP; HSPA, UH.

34. Brooke to Milstaff, January 22 and 24, 1920; George M. Brooke, "Situation Survey for week ending 31 January 1920"; MID, RG 165, NA.

35. "What the Japanese Agitators Want," *Honolulu Star-Bulletin,* February 13, 1920, appended to George M. Brooke, "Situation Survey for week ending 6 March 1920"; John Waterhouse, President of HSPA, to Messrs. Albert W. Palmer et al., February 27, 1920, and "Opening Address by Department Commander Leonard Withington before the Convention of American Legion Department of Hawaii at Honolulu," February 23, 1920, both appended to George M. Brooke, "Situation Survey for period ending 29 February 1920," MID, RG 165, NA.

36. Okihiro, *Cane Fires,* 69, 71; I. Goto, Secretary, "Instructions to Members of Federation of Japanese Labor in Hawaii," January 17, 1920, appended to George M. Brooke, "Situation Survey for period ending 31 January 1920," MID, RG 165, NA.

37. "The Voice of Labor in Hawaii," appended to George M. Brooke, "Situation Survey for period ending 29 February 1920," MID, RG 165, NA.

38. N.a. to "Dear Sir," February 5, 1920, LSC; Allen W.T. Bottomley to A.W. Collins, February 11, 1920, Pioneer Mill Company Records (PMC); HSPA, UH.

39. Albert W. Palmer et al. to the Hawaiian Sugar Planters' Association, February 27, 1920 [the wrong date is listed on the MID copy; it should be dated February 14, 1920]; Federation of Japanese Labor in Hawaii to Curtis P. Iaukea, Acting Governor of Hawaii, February 25, 1920; both appended to George M. Brooke, "Situation Survey for period ending 29 February 1920," MID, RG 165, NA.

40. "Sermon Delivered February 22, 1920," appended to George M. Brooke, "Situation Survey for period ending 29 February 1920," MID, RG 165, NA.

41. Okihiro, Cane Fires, 73; Duus, The Japanese Conspiracy, 73–75, 90–93; John Waterhouse, President of HSPA, to Messrs. Albert W. Palmer et al., February 27, 1920, and "Iaukea Calls on Planters to Back Conspiracy Claim," both appended to George M. Brooke, "Situation Survey for period ending 29 February 1920," MID, RG 165, NA.

42. "Iaukea Calls on Planters to Back Conspiracy Claim"; "Mr. Palmer's Reply"; "Opinion of Jonah Kumalae, City and County Supervisor, of Japanese Language Schools, As Expressed in an Interview for the Nippu Jiji, January 8th"; all appended to George M. Brooke, "Situation Survey for period ending 29 February 1920," MID, RG 165, NA.

43. Beechert, Working in Hawaii, 203–4; "Filipinos Threatened with Death by Board of Health, Is Charged by Japanese Paper" and "Pablo Manlapit today Signed the Following Statement," February 9, 1920, appended to George M. Brooke, "Situation Survey for period ending 29 February 1920," MID, RG 165, NA.

44. "Strike Memoranda," March 5, 6, 9, 1920, LCS, HSPA, UH; George M. Brooke, "Situation Survey for week ending 10 April 1920," MID, RG 165, NA; Okihiro, Cane Fires, 73–74; Duus, The Japanese Conspiracy, 108–9.

45. Duus, The Japanese Conspiracy, 110–11; Okihiro, Cane Fires, 72, 74; Jung, Reworking Race, 38; "Amended Constitution of the Hawaiian Federation of Labor," April 17, 1920, appended to George M. Brooke, "Strategic Situation Survey #18 for week ending 22 May 1920," MID, RG 165, NA; "Something for the Japanese Laborers to Think Over," n.d. [April 1920, most likely], LSC, HSPA, UH.

46. "Plantation Conditions," n.d. [placed between reports dated May 3 and May 4, 1920], LSC, HSPA, UH; Brooke, "Strategic Situation Survey #18 for week ending 22 May 1920," MID, RG 165, NA; Allen W.T. Bottomley to A.W. Collins, May 15, June 1, 1920; S. Kanda to F.F. Baldwin, May 26, 1920; [A.W. Collins] to John Waterhouse, May 28, 1920; F.F. Baldwin to A.W. Collins, May 28, 1920; PMC, HSPA, UH.

47. [A.W. Collins] to A.W.T. Bottomley, February 4, May 17, 21, 22, June 2, 1920; Allen W.T. Bottomley to A.W. Collins, May 15, 1920; PMC, HSPA, UH.

48. "Minutes of a Meeting of a Certain Group of Japanese Laborers Called by Mr. Isobe to meet with Mr. John Waterhouse, President of the HSPA, at the Alexander Young Hotel on July 1, 1920 at 10 A.M.," LSC, HPSA, UH; Okihiro, Cane Fires, 75–76; The Japanese Conspiracy, 119–22.

49. Allen W. T. Bottomley to A. W. Collins, July 1, 3, 14 1920, PMC, HSPA, UH; "Notice," n.d., attached to E. H. Wodehouse to R. A. Hutchison, July 7, 1920, LSC, HSPA, UH.

50. J. Kēhaulani Kauanui, *Hawaiian Blood: Colonialism and the Politics of Sovereignty and Indigeneity* (Durham: Duke University Press, 2008), 68–69, 83, 104, 109.

51. Kauanui, *Hawaiian Blood*, 121–70; Alan Murakami, "The Hawaiian Homes Commission Act," in *Native Hawaiian Rights Handbook*, edited by Melody Kapilialoha MacKenzie (Honolulu: Native Hawaiian Legal Corporation and Office of Hawaiian Affairs, 1991), 43–48.

52. George M. Brooke, "Estimate of the Japanese Situation as It Affects the Territory of Hawaii, from the Military Point of View," October 11, 1920, MID, RG 165, NA.

53. George M. Brooke, "Estimate of the Japanese Situation as It Affects the Territory of Hawaii, from the Military Point of View," October 11, 1920, MID, RG 165, NA.

54. Quoted in Okihiro, *Cane Fires*, 103–5.

55. George M. Brooke to [A.] W. Collins, May 7, September 3, 1920; H. R. Preston [pseudonym for Brooke] to A. W. Collins, October 12, 1920, March 25, 1921; PMC, HSPA, UH; A. A. Hopkins, "Confidential Survey Territory of Hawaii: Japanese Activities," January 31, 1921, MID, RG 165, NA. The number of BI agents increased from three hundred to 1,500 during World War I (Kornweibel, *"Seeing Red,"* 7).

56. A. A. Hopkins, "Confidential Survey Territory of Hawaii: Japanese Activities," January 31, 1921, MID, RG 165, NA; Beechert, *Working in Hawaii*, 214–15; Duus, *The Japanese Conspiracy*, 138–229.

57. L. McNamee and R. E. Ingersoll, ONI, to State (Mr. Hurley), Military Intelligence Division, Justice (Mr. Burns), General Board, Operations (Plans), Naval War College, "Labor Conditions in the Hawaiian Islands," June 26, 1922; Stephen O. Fuqua, "Statistical data on the Japanese situation in the Hawaiian Islands," December 26, 1922, attaching [Charles P. Summerall], "Summary of Data on Factors Bearing on the Japanese Situation in Relation to Our Military Problem"; MID, RG 165, NA. On the HELC, see John E. Reinecke, *Feigned Necessity: Hawaii's Attempt to Obtain Chinese Contract Labor, 1921–1923* (San Francisco: Chinese Materials Center, 1979).

58. [Summerall], "Summary of Data on Factors Bearing on the Japanese Situation in Relation to Our Military Problem," MID, RG 165, NA.

59. Armin W. Riley, Philippine Department Intelligence Officer, to Director of Military Intelligence, Washington, DC, March 11, 1919, MID, RG 165, NA.

60. Armin W. Riley, Philippine Department Intelligence Officer, to Director of Military Intelligence, Washington, DC, March 11, 1919; Hugh Straughn, Philippine Scouts, Acting Department Intelligence Officer, to Director of Military Intelligence, Washington, DC, May 14, 1919; MID, RG 165, NA.

61. Joan M. Jensen, *Army Surveillance in America, 1775–1980* (New Haven: Yale University Press, 1991), 111–36, 160–77; Alfred W. McCoy, *Policing America's Empire: The United States, the Philippines, and the Rise of the Surveillance State* (Madison: University of Wisconsin Press, 2009), 296–319;

[Ralph H.] Van Deman to [Dennis E.] Nolan, November 20, 1920, MID, RG 165, NA.

62. [Ralph H.] Van [Deman], to [Dennis E.] Nolan, May 24, 1921, MID, RG 165, NA.

63. [Ralph H.] Van [Deman], to [Dennis E.] Nolan, May 24, 1921; Mathew C. Smith (for the Director, Military Intelligence Division) to J. E. Hoover, July 15, 1921; James L. Collins (for the Director, Military Intelligence Division), July 15, 1921; MID, RG 165, NA. Van Deman's private letter was received by MID headquarters in Washington, DC, on July 7, 1921.

64. Adrian L. Potter, Weekly Confidential Report, March 29-April 4, 1921, April 5–11, 1921, April 12–18, 1921, April 26-May 2, 1921, May 3–9, 1921, May 10–16, 1921, May 17–23, 1921, May 24–30, 1921, Bureau Section (BS) File 202600–22; Adrian L. Potter, Weekly Confidential Report, June 7–13, 1921, June 14–20, 1921, September 6–12, 1921, September 13–19, 1921, September 20–26, 1921, BS File 202600–1804; FBI, RG 65, NA.

65. P-138, "In re: Negro Activities," July 30, 1921, BS File 202600–667, FBI, RG 65, NA.

CHAPTER 5. RED AND YELLOW MAKE ORANGE

1. Alfred W. McCoy, *Policing America's Empire: The United States, the Philippines, and the Rise of the Surveillance State* (Madison: University of Wisconsin Press, 2009), 296; "Communist Convention and Communist Labor Party Convention," Chicago, August 28 to September 5, 1919, Old German (OG) File 229372, Investigative Case Files of the Bureau of Investigation, 1908–1922, Records of the Federal Bureau of Investigation (FBI), Record Group (RG) 65, National Archives, Washington, DC (NA).

2. Hyman Kublin, *Asian Revolutionary: The Life of Sen Katayama* (Princeton: Princeton University Press, 1964), 47–215; Sen Katayama, *The Labor Movement in Japan* (Chicago: Charles H. Kerr, 1918), 134–35; Sen Katayama to H. Hyndman, December 12, 1914, published in H. M. Hyndman, *The Awakening of Asia* (London: Cassell, 1919), 190. On Shūsui's anticolonial politics, see Robert Thomas Tierney, *Monster of the Twentieth Century: Kōtoku Shūsui and Japan's First Anti-Imperialist Movement* (Oakland: University of California Press, 2015).

3. Kublin, *Asian Revolutionary,* 235–78; *The Heimin,* no. 3 (July 1916), no. 15 (April 1918), no. 21 (July 1919), Yuji Ichioka Papers, Department of Special Collections, Charles E. Young Research Library, University of California, Los Angeles (UCLA); W. J. Flynn to "All Special Agents and Employees," August 12, 1919, 66th Congress, 1st Session, Senate Document No. 153 (Washington, DC: Government Printing Office, 1919), 30; Daniel Kanstroom, *Deportation Nation: Outsiders in American History* (Cambridge: Harvard University Press, 2007), 146–55.

4. Kublin, *Asian Revolutionary,* 276–86; "No. 2347," Mexico City, May 12, 1921, Bureau Section (BS) File 202600–58–11, FBI, RG 65, NA.

5. Kublin, *Asian Revolutionary,* 286–336 (quotes from 292 and 329).

6. *The Heimin,* no. 21 (July 1919), Yuji Ichioka Papers, UCLA.

7. Commandant, Twelfth Naval District, to Director of Naval Intelligence, "Weekly Report of Japanese Activities, Week ending 31 December 1921," Janu-

ary 3, 1922; A.A. Hopkins, "Japanese Situation: Los Angeles District, Week ending January 14, 1922," January 14, 1922; Box 30, File 20964–2194, Records of the Office of the Chief of Naval Operations, Office of Naval Intelligence (ONI), RG 38, NA.

8. *New York Times,* January 24, 1920; A.A. Hopkins, "Communist Labor Party and Communist Party of America, Los Angeles," January 28, 1920, OG File 379625; W.P. Hall, "Y. Nakadate (or Nakadata) and S. Nonaka, Communist Party," January 19, 1920, and A. Caminetti to J.E. Hoover, March 23, 1920, OG 388451; A.A. Hopkins, "Communist Labor Party and Communist Party of America, Los Angeles, Cal., Radical Activities," February 7, 1920 (including a transcript of S.A. Connnell, Special Agent in Charge, to A.E. Burnett, Inspector in Charge, February 2, 1920), OG File 55 and OG File 386165; FBI, RG 65, NA; "Nakadate Arrested on the Charge of Alleged I.W.W.ism," *Nippu Jiji,* February 5, 1920, in Military Intelligence Division Correspondence, 1917–1941 (MID), RG 165, NA; Acting Secretary of State to Attorney General, December 28, 1920, BS File 213463–1, FBI, RG 65, NA.

9. A.H. Loula, "In re: Alleged Japanese I.W.W. Propagandists, I.W.W. Matter," August 11, 1919, OG 55, FBI, RG 65, NA; Frank McIntyre to Francis Burton Harrison, Governor General of the Philippine Islands, June 21, 1920; U. Tokinaga to Frank McIntyre, [no month] 25, 1920; Records of the Bureau of Insular Affairs, General Records, 1898–1945 (BIA), File 16692, RG 350, NA. On the origins of the Bureau of Insular Affairs, see Paul A. Kramer, *The Blood of Government: Race, Empire, the United States, and the Philippines* (Chapel Hill: University of North Carolina Press, 2006), 164–65.

10. Walter LaFeber, *The Clash: A History of U.S.-Japan Relations* (New York: W.W. Norton, 1997), 99–127; Frederick R. Dickinson, *War and National Reinvention: Japan in the Great War, 1914–1919* (Cambridge: Harvard University Asia Center, 1999), 154–203; Brigadier General M. Churchill, General Staff, Office of the Chief of Staff, War Department, to Rear Admiral Roger Wells [*sic*], Director of Naval Intelligence, September 9, 1918; Roger Welles to Officer-in-Charge, Branch Office of Naval Intelligence, San Francisco, September 18, 1918; Officer in Charge, San Francisco, to Director of Naval Intelligence, October 2, 1918; Naval Attaché, Peking, to Director of Naval Intelligence, February 17, 1919; Confidential General Correspondence, 1913–1924 (Entry 78), Box 47, File 20978–240, ONI, RG 38, NA.

11. V.I. Lenin, *Imperialism: The Highest Stage of Capitalism* (New York: International Publishers, 1939 [1917]), 88–89; Erez Manela, *The Wilsonian Moment: Self-Determination and the International Origins of Anticolonial Nationalism* (New York: Oxford University Press, 2007), 36–45 (quotes from 36, 37, 41); Naoko Shimazu, *Japan, Race and Equality: The Racial Equality Proposal of 1919* (London: Routledge, 1998); Dickinson, *War and National Reinvention,* 204–37. For historical and historiographical insights on the Bolshevik Revolution and its legacies, see Walter Rodney, *The Russian Revolution: A View from the Third World,* edited by Robin D.G. Kelley and Jesse J. Benjamin (London: Verso, 2018); C.L.R. James, *World Revolution, 1917–1936: The Rise and Fall of the Communist International,* edited and introduced by Christian Høgsbjerg (Durham: Duke University Press, 2017 [1937]).

12. Commandant, Twelfth Naval District, to Director of Naval Intelligence, "Weekly Report of Japanese Activities, Week ending 26 November 1921," November 26, 1921; Box 30, File 20964–2194, ONI, RG 38, NA.

13. Commandant, Twelfth Naval District, to Director of Naval Intelligence, "Weekly Report of Japanese Activities, Week ending 7 January 1922," January 9, 1922; Box 30, File 20964–2194, ONI, RG 38, NA.

14. Commandant, Twelfth Naval District, to Director of Naval Intelligence, "Weekly Report of Japanese Activities, Week ending 7 January 1922," January 9, 1922; Box 30, File 20964–2194, ONI, RG 38, NA.

15. War Department, Office of the Chief of Staff, MID, to Frank Burke, Assistant Director and Chief, Bureau of Investigation and "Attention-Mr. J. E. Hoover," March 17, 1920; Assistant Director and Chief to E. M. Blanford, May 21, 1920; W. W. Spain, "Cosmopolitan Club," June 4 and 10, 1920; E. M. Blanford, "Cosmopolitan Club of University of California," June 24, 1920; C. D. Roche, "Cosmopolitan Club, Oberlin College, Oberlin, Ohio, Radical Activities," May 27, 1920; OG File 383391, FBI, RG 65, NA.

16. Adrian L. Potter, "Wang Shih Ching alias S. C. Wang also Wang Hem Lin alias W. L. Wang, . . . Alleged Bolshevists and alien enemies," April 24, 1920, OG 386128, FBI, RG 65, NA.

17. Adriane Lentz-Smith, *Freedom Struggles: African Americans and World War I* (Cambridge: Harvard University Press, 2009). Johnson's experience on the steamer appears on p. 210.

18. Yuichiro Onishi, *Transpacific Antiracism: Afro-Asian Solidarity in Twentieth-Century Black America, Japan, and Okinawa* (New York: New York University Press, 2013), 19–53 (quotes from 38, 32, and 47). The BI noted and quoted extensively from Briggs's piece (J. G. Tucker, "Special Weekly Report, Radical Activities," December 11, 1920, BS File 202600–33, FBI, RG 65, NA).

19. Geo. T. Holman, "In re TOM BRADY (Negro) Japanese Activities," October 28, 1919, OG File 375308, FBI, RG 65, NA.

20. General Intelligence Bulletin, Boston, Massachusetts, December 18, 1920, BS File 202600–22, FBI, RG 65, NA.

21. P-138, "In re: Negro Activities," October 10, 1920, March 2, 1921, April 4, 1921, June 8, 1921, July 30, 1921, BS File 202600–667, FBI, RG 65, NA.

22. Commandant, Twelfth Naval District, to Director of Naval Intelligence, "Weekly Report of Japanese Activities, Week ending 3 December 1921," December 6, 1921; Box 30, File 20964–2194, ONI, RG 38, NA; Karl Evanzz, *The Messenger: The Rise and Fall of Elijah Muhammad* (New York: Pantheon Books, 1999), 402–5; Vijay Prashad, *Everybody Was Kung Fu Fighting: Afro-Asian Connections and the Myth of Cultural Purity* (Boston: Beacon Press, 2001), 107–11; Michael A. Gomez, *Black Crescent: The Experience and Legacy of African Muslims in the Americas* (New York: Cambridge University Press, 2005), 276–79.

23. Commandant, Twelfth Naval District, to Director of Naval Intelligence, "Weekly Report of Japanese Activities, Week ending 3 December 1921," December 6, 1921; same, "Weekly Report of Japanese Activities, Week ending 24 December 1921," December 27, 1921; same, "Weekly Report of Japanese Activities, Week ending 7 January 1922," January 9, 1922; Box 30, File 20964–2194, ONI, RG 38, NA.

24. Officer-in-Charge, Branch Office of Naval Intelligence, San Francisco, to Director of Naval Intelligence, March 18 1918, Box 19, File 20957–218, ONI, RG 38, NA; A.A. Hopkins, "Communist Labor Party and Communist Party of America, Los Angeles, Cal., Radical Activities," February 7, 1920, OG File 55; A.A. Hopkins, "Communist Labor Party and Communist Party of America," February 14, 1920, OG File 379625; A.A. Hopkins, "Jothat [*sic*] Nishida, alias Abdul Ali," April 9, 1921, BS File 215365; FBI, RG 65, NA; Woodrow C. Whitten, "Criminal Syndicalism and the Law in California, 1919–1927," *Transactions of the American Philosophical Society* 59, no. 2 (1969): 65.

25. Leon E. Howe, "Jothar W. Nishida-Hawaii-'International Socialist' and Negro Agitator," April 5, 1921, BS File 215365; FBI, RG 65, NA. On Miami's UNIA chapter, see N.D.B. Connolly, *A World More Concrete: Real Estate and the Remaking of Jim Crow South Florida* (Chicago: University of Chicago Press, 2014), 60–61.

26. "Lecture, by Mr. Nishida," attached to A.A. Hopkins, "Jothat [*sic*] Nishida, alias Abdul Ali," April 9, 1921, BS File 215365; FBI, RG 65, NA.

27. A.A. Hopkins, "Jothat [*sic*] Nishida, alias Abdul Ali," April 9, 1921; A.C. Sullivan, Johtar [*sic*] (Jonhart) W. Nishida: Los Angeles, California: Radical," April 8, 1921; Louis DeNette, "Jonhar Nishida, Probably in Mexico, Radical," April 25, 1921; BS File 215365; FBI, RG 65, NA.

28. Louis DeNette, "Jonhar Nishida, Probably in Mexico, Radical," April 25, 1921; A.A. Hopkins, "Jothat [*sic*] Nishida, alias Abdul Ali," April 9, 1921; Leon E. Howe, "Jothar W. Nishida-Hawaii-'International Socialist' and Negro Agitator," April 5, 1921; Leon E. Howe, "Jothar W. Nishida, Los Angeles Cal, Radical Socialist and Inciting Negroes," April 6, 1921; BS File 215365; FBI, RG 65, NA. Fears of an alliance between African Americans and Japan would persist through World War II. See T. Fujitani, *Race for Empire: Koreans as Japanese and Japanese as Americans during World War II* (Berkeley: University of California Press, 2011), 90–96; Gerald Horne, *Facing the Rising Sun: African Americans, Japan, and the Rise of Afro-Asian Solidarity* (New York: New York University Press, 2018).

29. M.N. Roy, *Memoirs* (Bombay: Allied Publishers, 1964), 3–14; Kris Manjapra, *M.N. Roy: Marxism and Colonial Cosmopolitanism* (London: Routledge, 2010), 1–23.

30. Roy, *Memoirs*, 14–37; Charles Warren, Assistant Attorney General (for the Attorney General), to John W. Preston, April 11, 1917, May 19, 1917, Box 4, Neutrality Case Files, Records of the US District Attorney, RG 118, National Archives, San Bruno, California (NASB); Janice R. MacKinnon and Stephen R. MacKinnon, *Agnes Smedley: The Life and Times of an American Radical* (Berkeley: University of California Press, 1988), 38–39.

31. Roy, *Memoirs*, 217, 38–44, 76, 79. On how anti-Chinese politics legitimized a mestizo national identity and the revolutionary state in Mexico, see Jason Oliver Chang, *Chino: Anti-Chinese Racism in Mexico, 1880–1940* (Urbana: University of Illinois Press, 2017).

32. Roy, *Memoirs*, 80, 119, 131, 135–147, 211, 217; John Mason Hart, *Revolutionary Mexico: The Coming and Process of the Mexican Revolution* (Berkeley: University of California Press, 1987), 330–31.

33. *Workers of the World and Oppressed Peoples, Unite! Proceedings and Documents of the Second Congress, 1920*, vol. 1, edited by John Riddell (New York: Pathfinder Press, 1991), 118, 124, 219, 290; Roy, *Memoirs*, 379–82; Minkah Makalani, *In the Cause of Freedom: Radical Black Internationalism from Harlem to London, 1917–1939* (Chapel Hill: University of North Carolina Press, 2011), 76–81. The final draft, however, redacted some of Roy's critical insights (Makalani, 81).

34. "Theses on the National and Colonial Question Adopted by the Second Comintern Congress," in *The Communist International, 1919–1943: Documents, Vol. 1, 1919–1922*, edited by Jane Degras (London: Oxford University Press, 1956), 138–44; *Workers of the World and Oppressed Peoples, Unite!*, 245. The Third International followed quickly with the First Congress of the Peoples of the East in Baku, Azerbaijan, in September 1920 that focused on the Middle East and Central Asia. See *To See the Dawn: Baku, 1920—First Congress of the Peoples of the East*, edited by John Riddell (New York: Pathfinder Press, 1993).

35. "Theses on the National and Colonial Question," 138–44. For penetrating critiques of Marxist theory and Marxist historiography in recognizing race in capitalist development and anticapitalist struggles, see Cedric J. Robinson, *Black Marxism: The Making of the Black Radical Tradition* (Chapel Hill: University of North Carolina Press, 2000), esp. 45–68; Lisa Lowe, *The Intimacies of Four Continents* (Durham: Duke University Press, 2015), 135–75.

36. *Workers of the World and Oppressed Peoples, Unite!*, 224–28.

37. Makalani, *In the Cause of Freedom*, 82–83; "The Path Which Led Me to Leninism," *Ho Chi Minh on Revolution: Selected Writings, 1920–1966*, edited by Bernard B. Fall (New York: New American Library, 1967), 24 (first quote); Pierre Brocheux, *Ho Chi Minh: A Biography*, translated by Claire Duiker (Cambridge: Cambridge University Press, 2007), 1–29 (second quote from 24).

38. Harry Haywood, *Black Bolshevik: Autobiography of an Afro-American Communist* (Chicago: Liberator Press, 1978), 33, 42, 55, 72, 82.

39. Haywood, *Black Bolshevik*, 92, 110, 112, 119, 121–54.

40. Haywood, *Black Bolshevik*, 156, 164; Dada Amir Haider Khan, *Chains to Lose: Life and Struggles of a Revolutionary: Memoirs of Dada Amir Haider Khan*, edited by Hasan N. Gardezi (Karachi: Pakistan Study Centre, University of Karachi, 2007), 582–84; Ani Mukherji, "The Anticolonial Imagination: The Exile Productions of American Radicalism in Interwar Moscow" (PhD diss., Brown University, 2011), 50–75. I thank Ani for sharing his unpublished work. I discuss Khan's personal history in the prologue.

41. Makalani, *In the Cause of Freedom*, 90–97 (McKay quote from 95); "Theses of the Fourth Comintern Congress on the Negro Question," in *The Communist International*, 1:398–401.

42. "Theses of the Fourth Comintern Congress on the Negro Question," in *The Communist International*, 1:400–401.

43. "Theses on the Eastern Question Adopted by the Fourth Comintern Congress," in *The Communist International*, 1:382–93.

44. Haywood, *Black Bolshevik*, 198, 218–35.

45. Haywood, *Black Bolshevik*, 245–69; "Extracts from an ECCI Resolution on the Negro Question," in *The Communist International, 1919–1943:*

Documents, Vol. 2, 1923–1928, edited by Jane Degras (London: Oxford University Press, 1960), 552–57.

46. "Lenin and the Colonial Peoples," "Indochina and the Pacific," "The U.S.S.R. and the Colonial Peoples," "Lynching," "The Ku Klux Klan," in *Ho Chi Minh on Revolution*, 39–46, 51–58.

47. Benjamin Heber Johnson, *Revolution in Texas: How a Forgotten Rebellion and Its Bloody Suppression Turned Mexicans into Americans* (New Haven: Yale University Press, 2003), 72–81; James A. Sandos, *Rebellion in the Borderlands: Anarchism and the Plan of San Diego, 1904–1923* (Norman: University of Oklahoma Press, 1992), 79–85. Charles H. Harris III and Louis R. Sadler, *The Plan de San Diego: Tejano Rebellion, Mexican Intrigue* (Lincoln: University of Nebraska Press, 2013), which stresses the role played by Carranza's government in aiding and suppressing the rebellion, provides a complete translation of the original plan (1–4).

48. Sandos, *Rebellion in the Borderlands*, 87–153 (quote from 107); Johnson, *Revolution in Texas*, 85–143.

49. Sandos, *Rebellion in the Borderlands*, 143–44, 166; Daniel Trasivuk, "In re S. Takao, Japanese Suspect," October 9, 1917, OG File 72519, FBI, RG 65, NA. For a discussion of Japan and the Japanese in the Mexican Revolution and US-Mexico relations, see Jerry García, *Looking like the Enemy: Japanese Mexicans, the Mexican State, and US Hegemony, 1897–1945* (Tucson: University of Arizona Press, 2014), 42–73.

50. Mark Ellis, *Race, War, and Surveillance: African Americans and the United States Government during World War I* (Bloomington: Indiana University Press, 2001), 44–45, 48, 110–12.

51. Seema Sohi, *Echoes of Mutiny: Race, Surveillance, and Indian Anticolonialism in North America* (New York: Oxford University Press, 2014), 178–89; United States Attorney [John W. Preston] to Attorney General, November 17, 1917, Box 2, Neutrality Case Files, RG 118, NASB.

52. A. Carnegie Ross to J. W. Preston, June 21, 1917, Box 2; Dave Gershon, "In Re: Conspiracy to Set on Foot Military Expedition against India," July 26, 1917, Box 7; George Hartz's Testimony "Re: Harry [*sic*] Singh," n.d., Box 10; Assistant Attorney General to John W. Preston, April 2, 1918, Box 2; Telegram, Zimmermann, Berlin to Washington, January 4, 1917, Box 2 (and Box 9); Certificate of Admission of Alien, Hideo Nakao, Ellis Island, New York, November 21 1917 (listing April 29, 1917 as the date of arrival), and Coupon for Nideo [*sic*] Nakao, Alien Passenger on *S.S. Monterey*, May 19, 1917, Box 8; Neutrality Case Files, RG 118, NASB.

53. Sohi, *Echoes of Mutiny*, 192–93; "Opening Statement by George McGowan, Esq.," 4029–34, Box 8, Neutrality Case Files, RG 118, NASB.

54. "Opening Statement by George McGowan, Esq.," 4035–48, Box 8, Neutrality Case Files, RG 118, NASB.

55. Sohi, *Echoes of Mutiny*, 194–95; United States Attorney [Preston] to Paul C. Mori, May 3, 1918; United States Attorney [Preston] to Wm. Penn Humphreys, May 3, 1918; Box 3, Neutrality Case Files, RG 118, NASB.

56. Special Attorney to the Attorney General for War Work [Preston] to Attorney General T. W. Gregory, August 6, 1918, Box 3; C-351, Intelligence

Office, US Army, Western Department, "Hindu Conspiracy," May 14, 1918, Box 8; US Attorney [Preston] to Geo. McGowan, May 16, 1918, Box 3; H. B Nicholas to John W. Preston, September 14, 1918; Special Attorney to the Attorney General for War Work [Preston] to H. B. Nicholas, September 24, 1918, Box 3; Neutrality Case Files, RG 118, NASB; Sohi, *Echoes of Mutiny*, 194–95.

57. Acting Commissioner John H. Sargent to United States Attorney [Preston], San Francisco, May 27, 1918; [Preston] to Attorney General, June 3 and July 18, 1918; Robert Lansing, Department of State, to Attorney General, July 8, 1918; Box 3, Neutrality Case Files, RG 118, NASB.

58. United States Attorney [Preston] to Attorney General, July 28, 1917, Box 4; K. Fuyu, Acting Consul General of Japan, to John W. Preston, April 30, 1918, Box 3; United States Attorney [Preston] to M. Hanihara, April 29, 1918, Box 3; Louis F. Post, Assistant Secretary of Labor, to Attorney General, July 12, 1918, Box 3; n.a. to the Commissioner of Immigration, "Memorandum Regarding Hindus Convicted in the German-Hindu Conspiracy Case," n.d., Box 4; Neutrality Case Files, RG 118, NASB. Taraknath Das's departure from Japan is discussed in chap. 4.

59. R. H. Van Deman, Chief, Military Intelligence Branch, Executive Division, to Labor Department, Attention Mr. Parker, May 6, 1918 (received date), and accompanying report, File 53854, Records of the Immigration and Naturalization Service (INS), RG 85, NA. Some of the quoted text were in capital letters in the original.

60. C-351, Intelligence Office, US Army, Western Department, "Circulation of Hindu Literature," July 31, 1918; C-351, Intelligence Office, US Army, Western Department, "Hindu Situation," August 9, 1918; Hindustan Gadar Party to the Friends of India, n.d. [1919]; Box 8, Neutrality Case Files, RG 118, NASB.

61. Editor, Hindustan Ghadr, per Nidhan Singh, to Indar Singh, January 28, 1919, Box 4, Neutrality Case Files, RG 118, NASB; "Our Aims," *Independent Hindustan* 1, no. 1 (September 1920): 1; Taraknath Das, "Sino-Japanese Relations and Asian Independence," *Independent Hindustan* 1, no. 1 (September 1920): 9; Taraknath Das, "International Aspects of the Indian Question," *Independent Hindustan* 1, no. 5 (January 1921): 111.

62. Sohan Singh Josh, *Hindustan Gadar Party: A Short History, vol. 2, Towards Scientific Socialism* (New Delhi: People's Publishing House, 1978), 120–24, 195–223, 272–96 (Barakatullah quote from 280); Das, "International Aspects of the Indian Question," 110; David Petrie, *Communism in India, 1924–1927*, edited with an introduction by Mahadevaprasad Saha (Calcutta: Editions Indian, 1972), 140–41; Maia Ramnath, *Haj to Utopia: How the Ghadar Movement Charted Global Radicalism and Attempted to Overthrow the British Empire* (Berkeley: University of California Press, 2011), 136–51.

63. "Every Day in Every Way Is India Becoming More and More United and Democratic" and "The United States of India," *United States of India* 1, no. 1 (July 1923): 3; "Soviet Russia's Manly Reply to England's Ultimatum," *United States of India* 1, no. 2 (August 1923): 3. Rather than the Hindustan Gadar Party, the publisher was now listed as the Pacific Coast Hindustani Association.

64. MacKinnon and MacKinnon, *Agnes Smedley*, 29–68; Ramnath, *Haj to Utopia*, 128–35; Herman Defrem and Sailendranath Ghose on behalf of the

Friends of Freedom for India to Samuel Gompers, "Brief on the Threatened Deportation of Hindu Political Prisoners and Refugees," and Samuel Gompers to William B. Wilson, Secretary of Labor, July 3, 1919 (alongside many other letters and resolutions), File 53854, INS, RG 85, NA; N.H. Castle, "In re: Ed. J.J. Gammons-I.W.W. and Radical, July 31, 1919 (includes Agnes Smedley to "Dear Comrade," July 23, 1919), OG File 337716, FBI, RG 65, NA; R.W. Finch, "In Re: Soldiers, Sailors and Marines Protective Association Agnes Smedley (includes a circular by Smedley to "Comrades!"), April 15, 1919, OG File 335270, FBI, RG 65, NA.

65. MacKinnon and MacKinnon, *Agnes Smedley*, 46; Kanstroom, *Deportation Nation*, 133–34, 140; US Department of Labor, Bureau of Immigration, *Immigration Laws (Act of February 5, 1917)* (Washington, DC: Government Printing Office, 1917), 5–6, 20–21.

66. Joan M. Jensen, *Passage from India: Asian Indian Immigrants in North America* (New Haven: Yale University Press, 1988), 242, 246–64; *The Statutes at Large of the United States of America from December, 1923, to March, 1925, vol. 43, part 1* (Washington, DC: Government Printing Office, 1925), 162; Kanstroom, *Deportation Nation*, 134–35; "Here's Letter to the World from Suicide," *San Francisco Examiner*, March 17, 1928, in South Asians in North America Collection (SANA), Bancroft Library, University of California, Berkeley (Berkeley). On the Immigration Act of 1924, see Mae M. Ngai, *Impossible Subjects: Illegal Aliens and the Making of Modern America* (Princeton: Princeton University Press, 2004), 21–55.

67. Ramnath, *Haj to Utopia*, 146–57; Josh, *Hindustan Gadar Party*, 256–71; Makalani, *In the Cause of Freedom*, 137–45; Gail Omvedt, "Armed Struggle in India: The Ghadar Party—III," *Frontier* 7, no. 31 (November 23, 1974): 9–11; *Resolutions of the League against Imperialism for India* (San Francisco: Hindustan Gadar Party, n.d.), in SANA, Berkeley. After World War I, Har Dayal championed the British empire as a means to liberal progress in India and Africa. See, e.g., Har Dayal, "The Future of the British Empire in Asia—II," *New Statesman* 12, no. 312 (March 29, 1919): 573–75.

68. E.R. Wilson, Department Intelligence Officer, Manila, to Director of Military Intelligence, Washington, DC, November 10, 1919; "Japanese Activities in the Philippine Islands," November 18, 1919; F.H. French, Brigadier General, Commanding, to Adjutant General of the Army, November 14, 1919; Box 552; MID, RG 165, NA.

69. A.A.—, "Ghadr party and Japanese," October 3, 1919, Box 552; ; John C.H. Lee, Assistant Chief of Staff, Intelligence Office, Headquarters Philippine Department, "Situation Survey for the Week Ending September 10, 1921," Box 1918; "Japan's Freedom Threatened by Philippine Anti-Alien Land Law" (translated from *North American Times*, March 5, 1920), Box 552; MID, RG 165, NA.

70. George M. Brooke, "The Economic Situation in Hawaii as Relating to Japanese Activity," February 10, 1921; S.A. Wood Jr., "The Japanese Situation in Hawaii," July 27, 1921; Box 552, MID, RG 165, NA; Gary Y. Okihiro, *Cane Fires: The Anti-Japanese Movement in Hawaii, 1865–1945* (Philadelphia: Temple University Press, 1991), 123–26; Edward S. Miller, *War Plan Orange: The U.S. Strategy to Defeat Japan, 1897–1945* (Annapolis: Naval Institute Press, 1991).

CHAPTER 6. COLLABORATION AND REVOLUTION

Epigraph: Quoted in Joseph R. Hayden to [Jesse Reeves], October 7, 1935, Box 41, Joseph Ralston Hayden Papers (Hayden Papers), Bentley Historical Library, University of Michigan (UM).

1. Headquarters, United States Army Forces in the Far East, Office of the A[ssistant] C[hief] of S[taff], G-2, "The Hukbalahap," March 3, 1945, Box 42, Hayden Papers, UM.

2. Luis M. Taruc, "Memorandum for Gen. MacArthur and Pres. Osmena," February 13, 1945, Box 42, Hayden Papers, UM. On the Huk rebellion, see Benedict J. Tria Kerkvliet, *The Huk Rebellion: A Study of Peasant Revolt in the Philippines* (Quezon City: Ateneo de Manila University Press, 2014 [1977]); Vina A. Lanzona, *Amazons of the Huk Rebellion: Gender, Sex, and Revolution in the Philippines* (Madison: University of Wisconsin Press, 2009).

3. Luis Taruc, *Born of the People* (New York: International Publishers, 1953), 13–52; Motoe Terami-Wada, *Sakdalistas' Struggle for Philippine Independence, 1930–1945* (Manila: Ateneo de Manila University Press, 2014), 204.

4. Jose P. Laurel to Manuel L. Quezon (confidential), May 31, 1941, Box 26 (Communism), Manuel L. Quezon Papers (Quezon Papers), Rare Books and Manuscripts Section, Filipiniana Division, National Library of the Philippines, Manila, Philippines (NLP).

5. "Inaugural Address of His Excellency José P. Laurel, President of the Republic of the Philippines," October 14, 1943, Box 21, Hayden Papers, UM.

6. Jodi A. Byrd, *The Transit of Empire: Indigenous Critiques of Colonialism* (Minneapolis: University of Minnesota Press, 2011), xvii; Cemil Aydin, *The Politics of Anti-Westernism in Asia: Visions of World Order in Pan-Islamic and Pan-Asian Thought* (New York: Columbia University Press, 2007), 161–89. Byrd's analysis focuses on the more recent period of multiculturalism. On US and Japanese states' efforts to remake racialized and colonized subjects into "loyal," liberal subjects of the nation and empire during World War II, see T. Fujitani, *Race for Empire: Koreans as Japanese and Japanese as Americans during World War II* (Berkeley: University of California Press, 2011). On Filipino collaboration with Japanese occupation during World War II, see, for example, Augusto V. de Viana, *Kulaboretor!: The Issue of Political Collaboration during World War II*, rev. ed. (Manila: University of Santo Tomas Publishing House, 2016).

7. Paul A. Kramer, *The Blood of Government: Race, Empire, the United States, and the Philippines* (Chapel Hill: University of North Carolina Press, 2006), 344–46, 352–63, 388–92; Frank Hindman Golay, *Face of Empire: United States-Philippine Relations, 1898–1946* (Madison: Center for Southeast Asian Studies, University of Wisconsin, Madison, 1998), 172–269; Lieutenant-Colonel M. E. Locke, General Staff, G-2, Military Intelligence Division, War Department, to Chief, Bureau of Insular Affairs, May 7, 1924, enclosing "extract copy" of the "confidential" report, May 3, 1924, Box 1067, File 26388, Records of the Bureau of Insular Affairs, General Records, 1898–1945 (BIA), Record Group 350 (RG 350); National Archives, Washington, DC (NA).

8. David R. Sturtevant, *Popular Uprisings in the Philippines, 1840–1940* (Ithaca: Cornell University Press, 1976), 141–57; Christopher Capozzola, "The Secret Soldiers' Union: Labor and Soldier Politics in the Philippine Scout Mutiny

of 1924," in *Making the Empire Work: Labor and United States Imperialism,* edited by Daniel E. Bender and Jana K. Lipman (New York: New York University Press, 2015), 85–103 (US Army quote from 94); Carol Morris Petillo, *Douglas MacArthur: The Philippine Years* (Bloomington: Indiana University Press, 1981), 129–35.

9. John E. Reinecke, *The Filipino Piecemeal Sugar Strike of 1924–1925* (Honolulu: Social Science Research Institute, University of Hawai'i, 1996); Moon-Kie Jung, *Reworking Race: The Making of Hawaii's Interracial Labor Movement* (New York: Columbia University Press, 2006), 39–42; Edward D. Beechert, *Working in Hawaii: A Labor History* (Honolulu: University of Hawai'i Press, 1985), 217–23; J. K. Butler to Plantation Managers on Hawaii and Maui, June 6, 1924; Theo. H. Davies and Co. to John T. Moir, June 26, 1924; H. A. Walker to John T. Moir, June 27, 1924; S. O. Halls to Onomea Sugar Company, September 16, 1924; J. K. Butler to All Managers on Hawaii, July 25, 1924; "Memo for Mr. Butler: Speeches at Mooheau Park, Sunday June the 15th, at 9:30 A.M."; C. Ligot to "Fellow Countrymen," September 15, 1924, attached to J. K. Butler to Plantation Managers and Agencies, September 24, 1924; Register of the Mauna Kea Sugar Company (MKSC), Hawaiian Sugar Planters' Association Plantation Archives (HSPA), Hawaiian Collection, University of Hawai'i at Mānoa Library (UH).

10. Quotes from Reinecke, *The Filipino Piecemeal Sugar Strike,* 81–82, 86. Filipino workers continued to organize in Hawai'i, underground years later as "Vibora Luviminda," named after Artemio Ricarte's nickname (Jung, *Reworking Race,* 104).

11. A. Lozovsky, *The Pan-Pacific Trade Union Conference, Hankow, May 20–26, 1927* (Moscow: RILU, 1927), 3, 21, 27–29, 36–42.

12. Jim Richardson, *Komunista: The Genesis of the Philippine Communist Party, 1902–1935* (Manila: Ateneo de Manila University Press, 2011), 25–41, 66–93 (quote from 90); Alfredo B. Saulo, *Communism in the Philippines: An Introduction* (Manila: Ateneo de Manila University Press, 1990), 7–9.

13. Lozovsky, *The Pan-Pacific Trade Union Conference,* 48 (quote); Richardson, *Komunista,* 102–5.

14. Melinda Tria Kerkvliet, *Manila Workers' Unions, 1900–1950* (Quezon City: New Day Publishers, 1992), 76–77; Richardson, *Komunista,* 103–58 (last quote from 158).

15. C. H. Bowers to Chief of Constabulary, September 12, 1928, Box 1295, File 28342, BIA, RG 350, NA.

16. Richardson, *Komunista,* 116–18, 131–32; "Joint Manifesto of the Philippine Labor Congress (COF) and the Philippine Chinese Laborers' Association," *Pan-Pacific Monthly,* no. 28 (July 1929): 26–28; C. H. Bowers to Chief of the Constabulary, "Communistic Activities in the PI," August 22, 1929, Box 1295, File 28342, BIA, RG 350, NA.

17. C. H. Bowers to Chief of Constabulary, September 12, 1928, Box 1295, File 28342, BIA, RG 350, NA; Domingo Ponce, "Memorandum Para El Hon. Manuel L. Quezon: Materia: Las actividades 'rojas' en Filipinas," January 21, 1929, Box 26, Quezon Papers, NLP; Richardson, *Komunista,* 72–73, 79–80, 126–30. Translations from the Spanish are my own.

18. Richardson *Komunista*, 159–60 (quotes from 160), 184–87; Sturtevant, *Popular Uprisings in the Philippines*, 183–92; Philippine Constabulary reports (hand-written) on "Tayug" and "Colorums," January 14 and 15, 1931, Box 25, Hayden Papers, UM; "Red Leader's Funeral in Manila Is Orderly," *New York Times*, January 26, 1931; Dwight F. Davis, Governor-General, to Francis LeJ. Parker, Chief, Bureau of Insular Affairs, Washington, DC, February 6, 1931; Davis to Parker (cablegram), February 6, 1931; Box 1295, File 28342, BIA, RG 350, NA.

19. *Records of the Bureau of Insular Affairs, Transcript of Record Crisanto Evangelista, et al., Guillermo Capadocia, et al., Petitioners, versus the People of the Philippine Islands, Respondents. Supreme Court of the Philippine Islands* (Washington, DC: National Archives of the United States, 1949), 6–11. The first report was filed on or about February 4, 1931. Hereafter, *Crisanto Evangelista et al.*

20. War Department, *Annual Reports, 1907: Volume X: Acts of the Philippine Commission, Public Resolutions, Etc.* (Washington, DC: Government Printing Office, 1907), 298; *Crisanto Evangelista et al.*, 16, 78.

21. [Secretary of State] to Secretary of War, March 9, 1931 (including "Manila Reports Plot of 4,000 Reds to Rebel; Says They Planned to Get Arms from Japan," *New York Times*, March 4, 1931); Patrick J. Hurley, Secretary of War, to Secretary of State, March 11, 1931; Parker to "Butte" (cablegram), March 11, 1931; "Butte" to Secretary of War and Parker, March 23, 1931 (cablegram); Dwight F. Davis to Patrick J. Hurley, March 19, 1931; Box 1295, File 28342, BIA, RG 350, NA.

22. C.H. Bowers to Chief of Constabulary, September 12, 1928, Box 1295, File 28342, BIA, RG 350, NA; Agnes Smedley, "Philippine Sketches," *New Masses* 7, no. 1 (June 1931): 14.

23. Modesto Castillo, Chief, Executive Bureau, and approved by Honorio Ventura, Secretary of the Interior, to "all Provincial Governors, Municipal presidents and members of the Police Forces in the provinces and municipalities under the jurisdiction of the Executive Bureau," on "The so-called Communist Party and members thereof, opinion regarding the gathering or meeting of," April 30, 1931; H.L. Stimson to Patrick J. Hurley, February 13, 1931; W.R. Castle Jr., to Patrick J. Hurley, July 20, 1931; Box 1295, File 28342, BIA, RG 350, NA.

24. *Crisanto Evangelista et al.*, 57–98. Evangelista faced two charges of sedition, for which he was sentenced to one year and six months.

25. *Crisanto Evangelista et al.*, 99–191 (quotes from 136, 137, 156, 169, 162–63). Evangelista also appealed his lawsuit against the mayor of Manila for denying the PKP permits to hold meetings. The Philippine Supreme Court ruled against Evangelista in September 1932 (*Crisanto Evangelista vs. Tomas Earnshaw*, in C.H. Bowers, Philippine Constabulary Bulletin No. 39, October 7, 1932, Box 1295, File 28342, BIA, RG 350, NA).

26. *Crisanto Evangelista et al.*, 150–52; Richardson, *Komunista*, 160–61.

27. *Crisanto Evangelista et al.*, 160, 174, 176, 177.

28. *Crisanto Evangelista et al.*, 178, 181; Richardson, *Komunista*, 163, 208–14; Roger N. Baldwin to [U.] Grant-Smith, November 16, 1931; F. LeJ. Parker

to U. Grant-Smith, December 3, 1931; BIA to the Governor-General of the Philippine Islands (radiogram extract), December 3, 1931; Governor-General, PI [to BIA], December 7, 1931 (radiogram); Box 1295, File 28342, BIA, RG 350, NA.

29. Crisanto Evangelista, "Why Should the Workers Between Philippines and China Secure Their Mutual Understanding?" (attached to unnamed agent to C.H. Bowers, October 11, 1928), Box 1295, File 28342, BIA, RG 350, NA.

30. Rick Baldoz, *The Third Asiatic Invasion: Empire and Migration in Filipino America, 1898–1946* (New York: New York University Press, 2011), 59–66; Melinda Tria Kerkvliet, *Unbending Cane: Pablo Manlapit, A Filipino Labor Leader in Hawai'i* (Honolulu: Office of Multicultural Student Services, University of Hawai'i at Mānoa, 2002), 41–65; James I. Muir, General Staff Corps, Hawaiian Department, Office of the Assistant Chief of Staff for Military Intelligence, Memorandum for General Creed F. Cox, May 22, 1933, Box 459, File 3037, BIA, RG 350, NA. On the Immigration Act of 1924, or the Johnson-Reed Act, see Mae M. Ngai, *Impossible Subjects: Illegal Aliens and the Making of Modern America* (Princeton: Princeton University Press, 2004), 21–55.

31. US Immigration Service, "Statement Taken from Sadaichi Kenmotsu, to determine status," December 16, 1929, Case File 12020/16533, Case Files of Investigations Resulting in Warrant Proceedings, 1912–1950, Records of the Immigration and Naturalization Service (INS), RG 85, National Archives-Pacific Region, San Bruno, California (NASB); Josephine Fowler, *Japanese and Chinese Immigrant Activists: Organizing in American and International Communist Movements, 1919–1933* (New Brunswick: Rutgers University Press, 2007), 45–47; Karl G. Yoneda, *Ganbatte: Sixty-Year Struggle of a Kibei Worker* (Los Angeles: Asian American Studies Center, UCLA, 1983), 16–17.

32. Yuji Ichioka, *The Issei: The World of the First Generation Japanese Immigrants, 1885–1924* (New York: The Free Press, 1988), 102–13; Eiichiro Azuma, *Between Two Empires: Race, History, and Transnationalism in Japanese America* (New York: Oxford University Press, 2005), 44–46.

33. Yoneda, *Ganbatte,* 3–24 (quotes from 10 and 17).

34. Paul Scharrenberg's Speech before the Commonwealth Club of California, June 7, 1928, summarized and excerpted by Aaron M. Sargent, included in C.W. Franks, "The Filipino Labor Situation in the United States," December 13, 1928; "Resolution Unanimously Approved by the 'Kapatirang Magsasaka,' a Labor Union in the Philippine Islands Requesting His Excellency, the President of the United States . . . to Remedy the Situation of the Filipino Laborers as Consequence of the Unhappy Incident Which Took Place between the American Laborers and the Filipino Laborers in Yakima Valley, Washington, United States, America," attached to Teodoro Sandiko to President John Calvin Coolidge, November 30, 1927; Box 1103, File 26671, BIA, RG 350, NA; Baldoz, *The Third Asiatic Invasion,* 136, 150, 160–61; Terami-Wada, *Sakdalistas' Struggle,* 9–10.

35. Yoneda, *Ganbatte,* 25–27 (quote from 26), 32; Fowler, *Japanese and Chinese Immigrant Activists,* 177–81 (Kenmotsu quote from 179–80).

36. Fowler, *Japanese and Chinese Immigrant Activists,* 182–87 (Kenmotsu quotes from 182–83); Yoneda, *Ganbatte,* 27–32. On the US military occupation

of Haiti, see Mary A. Renda, *Taking Haiti: Military Occupation and the Culture of U.S. Imperialism, 1915–1940* (Chapel Hill: University of North Carolina Press, 2001).

37. Frank Donner, *Protectors of Privilege: Red Squads and Police Repression in Urban America* (Berkeley: University of California Press, 1990), 42–43, 59–62; Yoneda, *Ganbatte*, 30; T. V. Donoghue, Immigrant Inspector, "Memorandum," April 20, 1931, Case File 12020/16533, INS, RG 85, NASB; Fowler, *Japanese and Chinese Immigrant Activists*, 190.

38. "An Act to exclude and expel from the United States aliens who are members of the anarchistic and similar classes," *The Statutes at Large of the United States of America, from April, 1917, to March, 1919 . . . Vol. 40* (Washington, DC: Government Printing Office, 1919), 1012–13; US Immigration Service, "Statement Taken from Sadaichi Kenmotsu, to determine status," December 16, 1929, Case File 12020/16533, INS, RG 85, NASB.

39. US Immigration Service, "Statement Taken from Sadaichi Kenmotsu, to determine status," December 16, 1929, Case File 12020/16533, INS, RG 85, NASB.

40. US Immigration Service, "Statement Taken from Sadaichi Kenmotsu, to determine status," December 16, 1929; US Department of Labor, Immigration Service, "Supplementary statement of: Sadaichi Kenmotsu to determine status," December 16, 1929; Austin Lewis, Attorney for Alien, "In the Matter of the right of Sadaichi Kenmotsu . . . to be and remain in the United States," n.d.; Commissioner of Immigration, Angel Island Station, to Commissioner General of Immigration, June 28, 1930, and July 25, 1930; Sadaichi Kenmotsu and Austin Lewis to Commissioner of Immigration, Angel Island Station, December 23, 1930; Case File 12020/16533, INS, RG 85, NASB. In 1928 and later, the Japanese government waged a violent wave of anticommunist raids and arrests (George M. Beckmann and Okubo Genji, *The Japanese Communist Party, 1922–1945* [Stanford: Stanford University Press, 1969], 138–63).

41. Sadaichi Kenmotsu and Austin Lewis to Commissioner of Immigration, Angel Island Station, December 23, 1930; Toyoji Kaneko, Vice Consul, Consulate General of Japan, to John D. Nagle, Commissioner of Immigration, San Francisco District, December 23, 1930, March 27, 1931; James P. Lawler, Immigrant Inspector, to Commissioner of Immigration, January 6, 1931; Harry E. Hull, Commissioner General, to George C. Vournas, January 10, 1931; George J. Harris, Assistant Commissioner General, to Commissioner of Immigration, Angel Island Station, January 19, 1931; Arthur J. Phelan, Law Officer, "Memo for Commissioner," April 2, 1931; Harry E. Hull to Isaac Shorr, April 8, 1931; Edw. L. Haff, Acting Commissioner of Immigration, San Francisco District, to Commissioner General of Immigration, April 21, 1931, October 13, 1931, January 21, 1932; Judge A. F. St. Sure, "In the Matter of the Application of Sadaichi Kenmotsu for a Writ of Habeas Corpus," April 8, 1931; Edw. L. Haff to Austin Lewis, November 18, 1931; Commissioner of Immigration, San Francisco District, to Consul General of Japan, November 23, 1931; W. E. W[alsh], Hand-Written Note, Department of Labor, November 25, 1931; Austin Lewis to Commissioner of Immigration, November 25, 1931; Edward J. Shaughnessy, Acting Commissioner General of Immigration, to Commissioner

of Immigration, Angel Island Station, November 11, 1931, January 6, 1932; W. E. Walsh, Hand-Written Bill for "Sadaichi Kenmotsu Days in detention from Nov., 19, 1931 to Dec[.] 15, 1931"; Walsh to Immigration Bureau, Washington, December 14, 1931 (telegram); W. E. Walsh, Acting Commissioner of Immigration, "Description of Person Deported," December 16, 1931; Kogyo Yonegaki, Vice Consul of Japan, to John D. Nagle, January 6, 1932; Case File 12020/16533, INS, RG 85, NASB.

42. District Thirteen Communist Party Organizational Conference to Denmotsu [sic], November 30, 1931, Case File 12020/16533, INS, RG 85, NASB; Sadaichi Kenmotsu to Frank Spector, December 16, 1931, Karl G. Yoneda Papers (Yoneda Papers), Department of Special Collections, Charles E. Young Research Library, University of California, Los Angeles (UCLA). On CP activities among Black workers in Alabama, including the defense of the "Scottsboro Boys," see Robin D. G. Kelley, *Hammer and Hoe: Alabama Communists during the Great Depression* (Chapel Hill: University of North Carolina Press, 1990).

43. Baldoz, *The Third Asiatic Invasion*, 137–41; "Philippino Community" to Philippine Resident Commissioner, January 23, 1930 (telegram); "Detagle Secretary Salinas Community League" to Philippine Commissioners, January 23, 1930 (telegram); D. L. Marcuelo, Editor, *Three Stars*, to "Commissioner Guevara and Osias," January 24, 1930 (telegram); B. G. Sanchez to Philippine Commissioners, January 24, 1930 (telegram); Pablo Manlapit to Bureau of Insular Affairs, January 28, 1930, enclosing the resolution adopted by "Filipino residents of the City and County of Los Angeles," January 26, 1930; Box 1104, File 26671, BIA, RG 350, NA.

44. Communist Party, Young Communist League, District 13, to "All Agricultural Workers in the Palaro Valley," n.d., [January 1930], Box 1104, File 26671, BIA, RG 350, NA; Baldoz, *The Third Asiatic Invasion*, 146. In receiving the circular, Secretary of War Patrick J. Hurley expressed gratitude for "this information" (Patrick J. Hurley to Leland T. Harder, February 4, 1930, Box 1104, File 26671, BIA, RG 350).

45. Fowler, *Japanese and Chinese Immigrant Activists*, 184–99; Yoneda, *Ganbatte*, 37–64. Kenmotsu and other Japanese in the Soviet Union continued to face state violence, falling victim to Stalin's reign of terror (Fowler, *Japanese and Chinese Immigrant Activists*, 3).

46. "The Veterans of the Revolution, Department of Silay, Northern Zone, on the 7th of February [1930], Assembled in their General Headquarter[s] in Silay, Occidental Negros, Philippine Islands as a result of the recent insults inflicted upon Filipinos in California"; Chamber of Commerce of the Philippine Islands, "Resolution Protesting against the Acts of Violence Committed on the Person and Properties of Filipinos Residing at California," January 28, 1930; Box 1104, File 26671, BIA, RG 350, NA; Terami-Wada, *Sakdalistas' Struggle*, 12–15.

47. Terami-Wada, *Sakdalistas' Struggle*, 15–35. On the politics behind the Hare-Hawes-Cutting Act, including its rejection by the Philippine Legislature, see Golay, *Face of Empire*, 303–22.

48. Terami-Wada, *Sakdalistas' Struggle*, 38–46; Golay, *Face of Empire*, 322–27; Kramer, *The Blood of Government*, 424–27.

49. Golay, *Face of Empire*, 333; Luther B. Bewley, Director of Education, to Governor-General of the Philippine Islands, June 2, 1934, with excerpt from the annual report of the Division Superintendent of Schools for Bulacan, Box 25, Hayden Papers, UM; Terami-Wada, *Sakdalistas' Struggle*, 46–52.

50. BUTTE to SECWAR and Parker, January 7, 1932 (radiogram); F. LeJ. Parker to American Civil Liberties Union, December 31, 1931; Box 41, File 2358, BIA, RG 350, NA; Terami-Wada, *Sakdalistas' Struggle*, 28–29, 55–56 (Ramos quote from 55).

51. Terami-Wada, *Sakdalistas' Struggle*, 29, 59, 68–70; *Free Filipinos*, April 1, 1935, Box 25, Hayden Papers, UM. *Free Filipinos* carried sections in English, Spanish, Tagalog, and Japanese.

52. *Free Filipinos*, April 1, 1935, Box 25, Hayden Papers, UM.

53. Eulogio Rodriguez to J. R. Hayden, April 2, 1935; Basilio J. Valdes to Colonel F. W. Manley, May 2, 1935, forwarding a confidential memorandum dated May 2, 1935; Box 25, Hayden Papers, UM. Secretary Rodriguez subsequently issued a general order to employees in his department "to conduct an intensive campaign of enlightenment and information among the people in their respective localities" (General Circular No. 11, "Subject: Sakdalista Propaganda," April 12, 1935, Box 25, Hayden Papers, UM).

54. Terami-Wada, *Sakdalistas' Struggle*, 1–5; "Memo for the Gov. Gen. Partial Report from Col. Van Schaick on the Sakdal Investigation Requested by Gov. Gen. Hayden This Morning," May 7, 1935, 4; "Memo for the Gov. Gen. Summary No. 3 Sakdal Uprising," May 9, 1935, 7; Box 25, Hayden Papers, UM.

55. "Memo for the Gov. Gen. Partial Report from Col. Van Schaick on the Sakdal Investigation Requested by Gov. Gen. Hayden This Morning," May 7, 1935, 7, 9; "Memo for the Gov. Gen. Trend of Sakdal Investigation," May 8, 1935, 2–3; "Sakdal Uprising Crushed," *Graphic*, May 9, 1935; Box 25, Hayden Papers, UM.

56. "Sakdal Uprising Crushed," *Graphic*, May 9, 1935; "Memo for the Gov. Gen. Partial Report from Col. Van Schaick on the Sakdal Investigation Requested by Gov. Gen. Hayden This Morning," May 7, 1935, 4–5; C. Dunham, Louis J. Van Schaick, F. W. Manley, E. G. Chapman, "Report of the Committee Appointed by Acting Governor-General J. R. Hayden to Investigate the Uprisings of May 2 and 3, 1935," May 18, 1935, 6; Box 25, Hayden Papers, UM; Terami-Wada, *Sakdalistas' Struggle*, 2–4. In Cabuyao, four Constabulary soldiers sustained wounds. Overall, the Sakdalista uprising and its repression resulted in sixty-three deaths (fifty-nine Sakdalista, four Constabulary).

57. G. C. Dunham, Louis J. Van Schaick, F. W. Manley, E. G. Chapman, "Report of the Committee Appointed by Acting Governor-General J. R. Hayden to Investigate the Uprisings of May 2 and 3, 1935," May 18, 1935, 3, 7, 8; G. C. Dunham, "Action by Constabulary in Suppressing the Uprising at Cabuyao, Laguna: Minority Report," 3; Box 25, Hayden Papers, UM; Edward G. Kemp to Governor-General Murphy, "Further Observations on the Sakdalistic Revolt," May 6, 1935, Roll 100, Frank Murphy Papers (Murphy Papers), UM. On Kemp's very close, lifelong relationship with Murphy, see Sidney Fine, *Frank Murphy: The Detroit Years* (Ann Arbor: University of Michigan Press, 1975), 28, 74.

58. Louis J. Van Schaick, "Political, Economic and Social Background of the Filipino People," May 21, 1935, 1–4, Box 25, Hayden Papers, UM.

59. G. C. Dunham, Louis J. Van Schaick, F. W. Manley, E. G. Chapman, "Report of the Committee Appointed by Acting Governor-General J. R. Hayden to Investigate the Uprisings of May 2 and 3, 1935," May 18, 1935, 8; Hayden to Secwar, May 9, 1935, quoting G. B. Francisco for Chief of Constabulary, May 7, 1935; Box 25, Hayden Papers, UM; Miguel Nicdao to Adjutant General, P.C., Manila, "Subject: Sakdal Uprising," May 16, 1935, 2–3, Roll 100, Murphy Papers, UM.

60. Your Comrades of Bulacan to "Comrades," "An Open Letter to All Sakdalistas," May 23, 1935 [written by hand on the typed translation], Roll 100, Murphy Papers, UM.

61. Richardson, *Komunista,* 151; "One of the Unfated Uprisings Against American Yoke," *Free Filipinos,* April 1, 1935, Box 25, Hayden Papers, UM; "An Interview with Salud Algabre," from Sturtevant, *Popular Uprisings in the Philippines,* 292, 298. *Free Filipinos* featured two photographs, one of three "officers" leading the revolt and another of corpses of those killed by the Constabulary.

62. "Sakdals Out to Foil Plebiscite Ramos Explains," *Manila Daily Bulletin,* May 7, 1935; "Japan Not to Give Up Ramos," *Manila Daily Bulletin,* May 8, 1935; Jose P. Guido, Captain, PC, Assistant-Superintendent, Intelligence Division, "Memorandum for the Superintendent" (Confidential), May 9, 1935; Juan Dominguez, Chief, "Confidential Memorandum for the Chief of Police," May 23 and 24, 1935; Box 25, Hayden Papers, UM.

63. Terami-Wada, *Sakdalistas' Struggle,* 75, 77 (Cavite quote); Joseph R. Hayden to [Jesse Reeves], September 29 and October 12, 1935, Box 41, Hayden Papers, UM.

64. Joseph R. Hayden to [Jesse Reeves], October 12, 1935, Box 41, Hayden Papers, UM.

65. Terami-Wada, *Sakdalistas' Struggle,* 79–122; Saulo, *Communism in the Philippines,* 26–28; Ken Fuller, *Forcing the Pace: The Partido Komunista ng Pilipinas: From Foundation to Armed Struggle* (Quezon City: University of the Philippines Press, 2007), 102–14. Upon his release, Evangelista left for the Soviet Union to receive medical treatment.

66. James S. Allen, "Report on the Philippines," February 13, 1939, 1, 32; Appendix II on "Independence, Democracy, and Peace," 1, 4; James S. Allen Papers; TAM 142; Box 3, Folder 7; Tamiment Library and Robert F. Wagner Labor Archives, New York University; Manuel L. Quezon, "To my fellow-countrymen," *Free Philippines,* January 1, 1944, Box 41, Hayden Papers, UM. On how state violence against communism and Philippine independence emerged hand in hand, see Colleen Woods, *Freedom Incorporated: Anticommunism and Philippine Independence in the Age of Decolonization* (Ithaca: Cornell University Press, 2020).

CONCLUSION

Epigraph: Hisaye Yamamoto, "Don't Think It Ain't Been Charming," January 5, 1941, Yuji Ichioka Papers, Department of Special Collections, Charles E.

Young Research Library, University of California, Los Angeles (UCLA). Yamamoto began publishing her column as a teenager under a pseudonym in *Kashu Mainichi* (Greg Robinson, *The Great Unknown: Japanese American Sketches* [Boulder: University Press of Colorado, 2016], 87). The Nisei were US-born citizens, children of the Issei, Japanese migrants who were categorized in the United States as "aliens ineligible to citizenship."

1. Carlos Bulosan, *America Is in the Heart: A Personal History* (Seattle: University of Washington Press, 1973 [1946]), 315, 310–11, 313, 316, 323.

2. Karl G. Yoneda, *Ganbatte: Sixty-Year Struggle of a Kibei Worker* (Los Angeles: Asian American Studies Center, UCLA, 1983), 113–23. On how Popular Front Americanism evolved into anticommunist imperialism, see George Lipsitz, *American Studies in a Moment of Danger* (Minneapolis: University of Minnesota Press, 2001), 31–56.

3. FBI Memorandum, April 23, 1941; N. J. L. Pieper, Special Agent in Charge (SAC), FBI, San Francisco, to Director, FBI, July 14, 1941, and January 20, 1942; FBI Report, San Francisco, July 12, 1941; FBI Report, San Francisco, May 21, 1942; Wendell Berge, Assistant Attorney General, to J. Edgar Hoover, December 24, 1941; John Edgar Hoover to SAC, San Francisco, January 9, 1942; Karl G. Yoneda Papers, UCLA; Elaine Black Yoneda, "Statement to the Commission on Wartime Relocation and Internment of Civilians," 2, Elaine Black Yoneda Collection, Labor Archives and Research Center, San Francisco State University.

4. Counter-Subversion Section, Office of Naval Intelligence, "Japanese Tokyo Club Syndicate, with Interlocking Affiliations," Navy Department, Washington, DC, December 24, 1941, attached to a Department of State report (dated February 2, 1942), Yuji Ichioka Papers, UCLA. On the interracial and interethnic formation of the CWFLU, see Chris Friday, *Organizing Asian American Labor: The Pacific Coast Canned-Salmon Industry, 1870–1942* (Philadelphia: Temple University Press, 1994).

5. FBI Report, San Francisco, May 21, 1942; Karl G. Yoneda to E. R. Fryer, Regional Director, WRA, San Francisco, July 11, 1942; Karl G. Yoneda to Dillon Myer, August 13, 1942; Roy Nash, Project Director, WRA, San Francisco, to E. R. Fryer, June 29, 1942; E. R. Fryer to Karl R. Bendetsen, June 29, 1942; Karl R. Bendetsen, Assistant Chief of Staff, Civil Affairs Division, to E. R. Fryer, June 13, 1942; D. S. Myer, Director, WRA, to J. Edgar Hoover, September 2, 1942; John Edgar Hoover to D. S. Myer, September 23, 1942; Karl G. Yoneda Papers, UCLA; Yoneda, *Ganbatte*, 136. On the politics of collaboration and resistance among Japanese Americans, see Richard Drinnon, *Keeper of Concentration Camps: Dillon S. Myer and American Racism* (Berkeley: University of California Press, 1987).

6. Artemio Ricarte, *Memoirs of General Artemio Ricarte*, with an introduction by Armando J. Malay (Manila: National Historical Institute, 1992), xxii–xxv; E. del Rosario, "General Artemio Ricarte," *Philippine Review* 2, no. 4 (June 1944): 56.

7. Bulosan, *America Is in the Heart*, 324, 326–27.

8. SAC, Seattle, to Director, FBI, October 30, 1950 (FBI Document 100–32735–16), FBI File on Carlos Bulosan (Bulosan FBI File). I am very grateful to

Trevor Griffey for sharing various FBI files with me, especially Bulosan's, that he obtained through the Freedom of Information/Privacy Acts. Griffey has made Bulosan's file available online at https://archive.org/details/FBI-Carlos-Bulosan/page/n12/mode/2up.

9. SAC, San Francisco, to SAC, Los Angeles, July 25, 1950 (100–32735–11); H. Edward White, FBI Report, Los Angeles, January 30, 1951 (105–2457–1); Interview with Ray Alvine Cabanilla, 1950, appended to Special Agent (SA) [redacted], to SAC, San Francisco, "Ray Cabanilla," January 27, 1953 (105–1530–2); Bulosan FBI File; Michael Denning, *The Cultural Front: The Laboring of American Culture in the Twentieth Century* (London: Verso, 1997), 223–24.

10. SAC, Seattle, to Director, FBI, July 31, 1950 (100–32735–1); SAC, Portland, to SAC, Los Angeles, December 12, 1950 (100–32735–25); SAC, Los Angeles, to Director, FBI, May 18, 1951 (100–32735–39); SA H. Edward White to SAC, June 5, 1951(100–32735–44), and August 3, 1951 (100–32735–46); James T. Moreland, FBI Report, Anchorage, Alaska (100–32735–45); Bulosan FBI File; Melinda Tria Kerkvliet, *Manila Workers' Unions, 1900–1950* (Quezon City: New Day Publishers, 1992), 92–103.

11. "For a Democratic Peace for All in the Philippines" (pamphlet), including Amado V. Hernandez to Luis M. Taruc, June 28, 1948, enclosed in SA William F. Doyle to SAC, "Communist Infiltration of Congress of Labor Organizations, Philippine Islands," May 13, 1949 (100–5147–1); "Report to the Convention (prepared by the CLO Executive Committee)," enclosed in S.L. Platt, Secretary, Industrial Relations Committee, Hawaiian Sugar Planters' Association, to Industrial Relations Committee, September 14, 1949 (100–5147–2), FBI File on Congress of Labor Organizations (CLO FBI File).

12. N.J.L. Pieper, SAC, San Francisco, to Director, FBI, January 10, 1945, enclosed in [Director] to James Cummings, Commissioner of Police for New Zealand, January 30, 1945 (64–200–239–10); [Director] to Brigadier W.B. Simpson, Director General, Security Services, Canberra, January 30, 1945 (64–200–239–11); N.J. Alaga to Director, FBI, November 16, 1945 (64–200–239–49); FBI File on the Communist Party of the Philippines. Hoover had become interested in the communist movement in the Philippines in November 1944 (John Edgar Hoover to SAC, New York, "Communism in the Philippine Islands, Internal Security-R," November 28, 1944 [64–200–239–9]).

13. SA William F. Doyle to SAC, "Communist Infiltration of Congress of Labor Organizations, Philippine Islands, Internal Security-C," May 13, 1949 (100–5147–1); S.L. Platt, Secretary, Industrial Relations Committee, Hawaiian Sugar Planters' Association, to Industrial Relations Committee, September 14, 1949, enclosing "Report to the Convention (prepared by the CLO Executive Committee)" (100–5147–2), CLO FBI File.

14. Committee on Un-Filipino Activities (CUFA), House of Representatives, Republic of the Philippines, *General Report on Communism and the Communist Party* (Manila: Bureau of Printing, 1949); H. Edward White, Los Angeles, FBI Report on "Carlos Bulosan," October 31, 1951 (105–2457–6), Bulosan FBI File. White transcribed both letters on pp. 8–13. On the persecution of CWFLU officials, see Arleen de Vera, "Without Parallel: The Local 7 Deportation Cases, 1949–1955," *Amerasia Journal* 20, no. 2 (1994): 1–25. On anticommunist

attacks against the ILWU in Hawai'i, see Edward D. Beechert, *Working in Hawaii: A Labor History* (Honolulu: University of Hawai'i Press, 1985), 305–10. Bulosan edited the *1952 Yearbook, Local 37*, a testament to the local's radical politics and legal struggles (available online at http://depts.washington.edu/civilr3/pdf/local37yearbook-op.pdf).

15. H. Edward White, Los Angeles, FBI Report on "Carlos Bulosan," October 31, 1951 (105–2457–6), Bulosan FBI File. Bulosan's fictional account would be published years later as *The Cry and the Dedication,* edited by E. San Juan Jr. (Philadelphia: Temple University Press, 1995).

16. SA Robert H. Wick to SAC, Seattle, August 24, 1954 (100–20689–96); Director, FBI, to SAC, San Francisco, April 29, 1954 (100–370827–18); Director, FBI, to Assistant Attorney General William F. Tompkins, September 17, 1954 (100–370827–52); SAC, Seattle, to Director, FBI, May 11, 1955 (100–370827–53) and June 2, 1955 (100–370827–54); Bulosan FBI File.

17. Ferdinand M. De Leon, "Revisiting the Life and Legacy of a Pioneering Filipino Author," *Seattle Times,* August 8, 1999; SAC, Seattle, to Director, FBI, October 17, 1956 (100–370827–55); Federal Bureau of Investigation, New York City, "Re: Alleged Communist Influence in Labor Movement—Philippine Islands," November 9, 1959 (100–20689–128); Bulosan FBI File.

18. George W. Bush, "Remarks by the President to the Philippine Congress," October 18, 2003, US Department of State Archive, accessed March 3, 2021, https://2001-2009.state.gov/p/eap/rls/rm/2003/25455.htm.

19. Bush, "Remarks by the President."

20. David Campbell, *Writing Security: United State Foreign Policy and the Politics of Identity,* revised edition (Minneapolis: University of Minnesota Press, 1998), 12.

21. Cemil Aydin, *The Politics of Anti-Westernism in Asia: Visions of World Order in Pan-Islamic and Pan-Asian Thought* (New York: Columbia University Press, 2007), 161–89; Prasenjit Duara, *Sovereignty and Authenticity: Manchukuo and the East Asian Modern* (Lanham: Rowman and Littlefield, 2003).

22. David E. Sanger, "Bush Cites Philippines as Model in Rebuilding Iraq," *New York Times,* October 19, 2003.

Index

AMERICAN CROSSROADS

Edited by Earl Lewis, George Lipsitz, George Sánchez, Dana Takagi, Laura Briggs, and Nikhil Pal Singh

Founded in 1893,
UNIVERSITY OF CALIFORNIA PRESS
publishes bold, progressive books and journals
on topics in the arts, humanities, social sciences,
and natural sciences—with a focus on social
justice issues—that inspire thought and action
among readers worldwide.

The UC PRESS FOUNDATION
raises funds to uphold the press's vital role
as an independent, nonprofit publisher, and
receives philanthropic support from a wide
range of individuals and institutions—and from
committed readers like you. To learn more, visit
ucpress.edu/supportus.